SWEET HOME

Sweet Home

Invisible Cities in
the Afro-American Novel

CHARLES SCRUGGS

The Johns Hopkins University Press
Baltimore and London

For my father

© 1993 The Johns Hopkins University Press
All rights reserved
Printed in the United States of America on acid-free paper

The Johns Hopkins University Press
2715 North Charles Street
Baltimore, Maryland 21218-4319
The Johns Hopkins Press Ltd., London

Library of Congress Cataloging-in-Publication Data
Scruggs, Charles.
    Sweet home : invisible cities in the Afro-American novel / Charles Scruggs.
        p.   cm.
    Includes bibliographical references and index.
    ISBN 0-8018-4502-5 (acid-free paper)
        1. American fiction—Afro-American authors—History and criticism.   2. City
and town life in literature.   3. Cities and towns in literature.   4. Afro-
Americans in literature.   5. Home in literature.   I. Title.
PS374.N4S37   1993
813'.509321732—dc20   92-30830

A catalog record for this book is available from the British Library.

Contents

Preface

This is a book that did not write itself. What book does? Yet it is also true that some books are easier to write than others. In trying to define the perimeters of my subject, I had to face the fact that the Afro-American city novel is a rich, complicated, and diffuse subject. First, there was the difficulty of deciding what to leave out; the theme of the city in the literature of Harlem Renaissance alone is worth a book, perhaps two. What I wanted to avoid was the shotgun approach—half a page for this novel, half a page for that one. The solution I came up with was to discuss in detail three city novels by three Afro-American male novelists and then focus upon a fourth, written by a black woman, that continued a tradition albeit in a new way. A second problem occurred when I found myself as a scholar being torn between my interest in literature as art and literature as sociology. As I read and studied these novelists, however, I discovered that my problem had been theirs; they too wanted to write as well as they could without ignoring things as they are—specifically the exigencies of black life in these United States. They, of course, had attempted to solve the conflict between art and life in their own unique ways, while I still had to solve my problem. The critical course I chose is one that I think should always be basic to literary studies: a discussion of the works' meanings informed by all the information—historical, political, sociological, psychological, philosophical—that the scholar can bring to bear on the texts. The general historical narrative I have organized my discussion around may be familiar; I hope what I have to say about it is new and less familiar.

The notes to my main text are meant to extend my narrative in directions that I could not follow very far if my narrative was to have coherence and continuity. They constitute a considered and intentional subtext, as well as offering background and substantiation for my arguments. In spite of the length of my manuscript and the extensiveness of my notes, I feel now that so much more could have been said on the subject of the Afro-American city novel. One regret I have is that Toni Morrison's *Jazz* (1992) was published too late for inclusion in this study. While her novel might have complicated or enlarged my thesis, it doesn't contradict anything I have said. Indeed, it confirms the emphasis I have placed on mass culture and the impact this has had upon the contemporary black novelist of the city.

I wish to thank the National Endowment for the Humanities for a year-long grant that allowed me to work on this project; I apologize to that invaluable institution for taking so long to complete it. Thanks as well to *American Literature, Arizona Quarterly,* and *Ariel: A Review of International English Literature* for permitting me to publish earlier versions of chapters in this book. I am especially grateful to Miriam Kleiger for her rigorous copyediting of the original manuscript. As I worked on this project, my wife, Teresa, saw me through some pretty rough times, especially the period of my recovery from a serious bicycle accident. I am also indebted as well to Walter Rideout and Ben Schneider, distinguished scholars both, for their stimulating conversation and insights; indirectly they are both present in this book, though I would not want to burden either one with the responsibility of answering for its content. Last, I wish to acknowledge my indebtedness to Lee Van Demarr—scholar, poet, editor, man of all seasons. Mr. Van Demarr's "fingerprints" (to echo Amiri Bakara) are all over this book. He was my intellectual companion during its writing and my good friend and counselor when I most needed emotional support. In many ways I feel it is as much his book as mine.

Utopia and Dystopia

> Oh baby, don't you want to go
> Back to the land of California
> To my sweet home Chicago.
> > —Robert Johnson, "Sweet Home Chicago"

Robert Johnson's famous lyrics were originally recorded in a San Antonio hotel room in 1936. Johnson was recasting a Kokomo Arnold song, drawing from the tradition of a collective blues text worked and reworked by musicians who had been singing their songs long before they were put on records. A powerful innovator within that tradition, Johnson, who was from the Mississippi Delta country, called his version "Sweet Home Chicago." If taken literally, the singer sounds lost, since he expects to find Chicago in California. Johnson might have confused the west and the north; or he may have had a cousin living in the small town of Port Chicago, California, outside Los Angeles, as a recent researcher has suggested.[1] But listening to the whole of his work, the forty-one surviving recordings, it is also clear that Johnson could have been speaking in metaphor, creating his own elliptical shorthand for the myth of the Exodus. His songs are a kind of modernist poetry, describing in brilliant fragments his world and his cultural milieu, including what had become for black Americans the newly vital connection between country and city.

A few years before Johnson recorded his songs, a black intellectual and academic from a very different milieu published a book offering a more detailed but no less mythical vision of an Afro-American urban home. In *The New Negro* (1925), Alain Locke combined, among other things, Frederick Jackson Turner's thesis of the frontier, Josiah Royce's theory of the "province," and Robert Park's recent investigations of city life, in order to create his own image of the Harlem

1

district of New York City as "home" for a New Negro. Drawing from diverse sources to present a synthetic utopian image of the city, Locke's method was modernist;[2] and although he had borrowed the phrase "New Negro,"[3] his application of it to city life was original. Around the same time, of course, T. S. Eliot was practicing in London an eclectic, elliptical art that would become the paradigm of high modernism. He observed things falling apart, and saw the city as dystopia. Perhaps he was still writing, for private circulation, his "King Bolo" poems, scurrilous verses about a black "cannibal king."[4]

This book's concern is the conceptual meeting of utopia and dystopia in twentieth-century Afro-American literature, and specifically in four post–Harlem Renaissance novels: Richard Wright's *Native Son* (1940), Ralph Ellison's *Invisible Man* (1952), James Baldwin's *Go Tell It on the Mountain* (1953), and Toni Morrison's *Beloved* (1987). These novels, of course, aren't random selections. Richard Wright's *Native Son* is a crucial work, a watershed in Afro-American writing; and Wright, Ellison, and Baldwin were friends, rivals, antagonists, and ultimately collaborators in a continuing discussion about the place of Afro-Americans in modern urban life: that discussion is the touchstone for all of their writing. The arguments between them entered their fiction, fixed in an urban context the older question of black relationships to a white society, and to a degree established the parameters of discussion for succeeding generations. Toni Morrison's work entered that argument at a different historical point and with different perspectives; yet she is equally drawn to the same problems and questions as the older writers: all four of these novels describe relations between black people and urban life and mediate, balance, or swing radically between utopian and dystopian vision. They all depict the "social co-ordinates" of black urban space,[5] both public and private, and mark the social configurations of a new city environment, a mass society in which Afro-Americans have been ubiquitous as an influence and negligible as a presence.

Given what we know about the position of black Americans within a racist society, the idea of a black utopian city may seem absurd on the face of it. Yet in the novels of Wright, Baldwin, Ellison, and Morrison, the visionary city is always present within the tangible, and often terrible, conditions of black urban life. The critique of a society or of social conditions—even the realistic depiction of the most wretched horrors—inevitably implies something different and better.

As Morrison recently observed in another context: "We can agree, I think, that invisible things are not necessarily 'not there.'"[6] Often the visionary city lies dormant, asleep; but it contains within its dormant state the potency of dream and the possibility of making the dream manifest, if only temporarily.

The phrase "invisible cities" in the title of this book refers to aspects of urban life which are both "there" and "not there": invisible yet present, as are the black people in Ralph Ellison's novel, their existence denied or diminished by the majority culture. Often migrants, always outsiders by virtue of their race, they may see the city as a labyrinth, a system of false leads, dead-ends, pointless circling. The walls that contain and divide people may be equally transparent, structures of economics and culture which condition and move the lives of human individuals, the sort of structures that Adam Smith long ago characterized as the workings of a "hidden hand."[7] These forms of the invisible city are joined at key points: the invisibility of Afro-Americans in this culture, their reduction to stereotype, is closely related to the phenomena of the mass media and the world of consumer desire, part of an economics of mass consumption. As I will show, all of these matters have been depicted, and dissected, in the Afro-American literature of the city written in this century.

If the invisible cities of the economist or sociologist have described largely negative conditions in black urban life, there has also been an opposing vision of the city as a social ideal, what Josiah Royce in 1913 called the "Beloved Community." Around that key phrase developed an important school of American social thought, including in its first generation Van Wyck Brooks, Randolph Bourne, Lewis Mumford, Waldo Frank, Kenneth Burke, and other critics, poets, and novelists. Among those it influenced were Jean Toomer and Alain Locke, in the 1920s; Richard Wright, in the 1930s; and Martin Luther King, Jr., in the 1950s and 60s. King, referring to the goals of the new Southern Christian Leadership Conference, would write in 1957 that "the ultimate aim of SCLC is to foster and create the 'beloved community' in America."[8] What King came to see as a goal for human society in general had already been presented as a model in Alain Locke's anthology *The New Negro* in 1925. Locke compared two kinds of "bonds," the bond between Negroes in the past, which Locke said had been created by the de jure and de facto condition of bondage, and those created by the new city of Harlem, which was "the laboratory of a great race welding." This new city within a city promised an authentic, spiritual bonding: "hitherto . . . the chief bond between them [Negroes] has been that of a common condition rather than a common consciousness; a problem in common rather than a life in common. In Harlem, Negro life is seizing upon its first chances for group expression and self-determination."[9] In Harlem, an invisible city ("a common consciousness . . . a life in common") would replace a visible "condition."

It might be possible to interpret in a rote way the novels I have chosen to focus on, identifying each with a version of the invisible city: the city of black nonexistence in *Invisible Man*; the Marxist view of the economically determined self in *Native Son*; the presence of the Beloved Community in *Go Tell It on the Mountain* and *Beloved*. But these writers' understanding of their urban milieu is not rote; it is complex and varied, much of it existing between the lines, in Morrison's state of the implied "'not there,'" in a texture of allusion and historical reference that extends from classical literature and the Bible to black folkways and Hollywood "B" movies. Moreover, I will argue that there is a development through these writers, perhaps even one that comes full circle to return, albeit in very different terms, to Alain Locke's conception of the visionary city in the Harlem Renaissance.[10] In Wright, Ellison, and Baldwin, the idea of the visionary city is heavily qualified: in Wright by his protagonist Bigger's implicit exclusion from Max's vision of the Beloved Community, in Ellison by the fact that "the principle" can never be realized in actuality, in Baldwin by the circumscribed nature of the refuge community. All of Toni Morrison's fiction concerns itself with the nature of the Afro-American community, and while it might seem that her earlier books, *Tar Baby* and *Song of Solomon*, are more specifically novels of black urban life, it is *Beloved* that in a sense "caps" her long discussion of the nature and possibilities of that life; less concerned with the *telos* of the visionary city, she delights in describing the living dynamics of its formation and continuation.

My view is that the idea of a visionary city is a durable and ongoing tradition within black urban literature. There may have been at times nostalgia expressed for some pastoral past,[11] but since this century began a major theme of Afro-American writing has been a coming to terms with Afro-Americans' lives in the city. The city as a symbol of community, of civilization, of home—this image lies beneath the city of brute fact in which blacks in the twentieth century have had to live. This kernel has never been lost. It is one of the aspirations expressed in an ongoing dialogue that the Afro-American community has with itself, a dialogue that sets a city of the imagination, the city that one wants, against the empirical reality of the city that one has. This visionary city changes from generation to generation, from writer to writer, and its presence continues to be felt in the Afro-American art of the 1990s. Even those black writers heavily indebted to literary naturalism have this in common with Plato and the Apostle Paul: the belief in the evidence of "things not seen" (2 Cor. 4:18).[12]

The writing of Wright, Ellison, Baldwin, and Morrison comprises an important part of the Afro-American literature of the city; in fact, as I've suggested, these authors are central to understanding the history and concerns of that literature. But black city writing doesn't begin with the 1940 publication of *Native Son*, and my first two chapters survey the background that Wright, and those after him inherited and, to a degree, rejected. That background includes not only urban fiction but also sociological and historical writing, essays, poems, music, biography, and cultural criticism of various kinds—the whole panoply of texts by which Afro-Americans attempted to describe, analyze, and imagine—and express their hopes for—their lives in American cities.

There is an imperative reason, however, for regarding Richard Wright as the pivotal author in this study. He was himself a migrant from the rural south to the northern cities, as well as a writer formed by the experience of the Great Depression; and for Afro-Americans in this century the division between the city as dystopia and the city as utopia has hinged on the decade of the Depression. The first prominent summary histories of modern black literature—Sterling Brown's *Negro in American Fiction* (1937), Hugh Gloster's *Negro Voices in American Fiction* (1948), and Robert Bone's *Negro Novel in America* (1958)—all stressed the break between the literature of the 1920s and that of the 1930s. As Bone puts it in his revised 1965 edition: "An inevitable reaction had set in; the carefree abandon of the Harlem School was soon to be challenged by a grimmer view of Negro life in the 'proletarian' fiction of the 1930s. Meanwhile the Negro Renaissance suffered an unspectacular demise."[13] No one today, of course, would glibly wrap the "Harlem School" in the phrase "carefree abandon," but Bone does make an important point, for the literature *did* change in the 1930s, as did the literary attitudes of the white intelligentsia.[14] The Harlem "vogue" had gone out of fashion, and fashion plays a key part in determining how Afro-American literary art is received.[15] The social reception given black writing by the majority society and its literary institutions—editors, publishers, reviewers, and professors— can help determine both a "renaissance" and a "demise." At certain historical moments, Afro-American literature has also been subject to the policy characterized by Daniel Moynihan's infamous oxymoron "benign neglect"; and for most of its history it has seemed that only a literary action as violent and uncompromising as Walter White's *Fire in the Flint* (1924) or *Native Son* could gain the serious attention of a white public.

It was the Civil Rights movement that effectively began to change the position of Afro-Americans within the culture at large: whatever economic or political failures it ended with, culturally the movement made visible those who had been invisible. The conjunction of Civil Rights activism in the south, rebellion in the northern cities, and technological revolution in the media gave black Americans national attention they had rarely received since the abolitionist agitation one hundred years earlier. By the end of the 1960s there was massive public evidence of crisis, produced in large part by an Afro-American militancy that drew attention to the social conditions of their oppression.

One result of this social transformation was a radical shift in the course of Afro-American literature and its criticism. No writing is outside of history or a social context, no writing is nonideological; however, there are clearly times when history is more consciously present and ideological choices more considered, or at least more subject to general notice. In the 1960s the Black Arts movement asserted a black aesthetic, one based on the particular background, experience, and outlook of Afro-Americans. This was an act of cultural empowerment analogous to the efforts of Martin Luther King, Jr., and the Student Nonviolent Coordinating Committee (SNCC) to achieve de jure civic empowerment for black citizens, or to the attempts of groups such as the Black Panthers or school-monitoring committees to create de facto black authority within their own communities. The institutions of white power responded to these attempts with resistance that was often violent, especially in the case of the Black Panthers.

The Afro-American activism of the 1960s and the new scholarship it inspired also spurred a critical expression in which black urban literature was increasingly characterized by the earlier thesis of Gloster and Bone: the "City of Dreadful Night" replaced the "heavenly city" promoted by Alain Locke during the Harlem Renaissance. In this new criticism the city becomes a "Hell" (Roger Rosenblatt) or a "concentration camp environment" (Addison Gayle, Jr.), tropes that reflect a correct perception of empirical conditions; as David Levering Lewis puts it, "For Afro-American urban dwellers, the more things changed, the more they worsened."[16] This argument was extended in some cases to include literature written before the 1920s. The emancipated slaves may at first have used the Bible to phrase their view of the city as the Promised Land, but almost overnight "the dream turned to ashes." The city as ash heap, then, was seen as a continuing tradition in black literature, and not one limited to a rejection of an urban ideal put forth by the Harlem Renaissance. From Dunbar's *Sport of the Gods* (1902) to the present, there was a consistent pattern denying the urban dream, a rejection that only becomes more absolute as we move into the 1940s and 50s: "By the time we reach Baldwin and Ellison, the idea of comparing Chicago, New York, Detroit . . . with St. John's vision of the holy city is entirely farfetched."[17]

Since the early 1970s, the apogee of the Black Arts movement, Afro-American letters have continued to be important in American writing. This has been so despite a shift in the country's racial politics, as the liberal assumptions and social agendas that had been formulated during the years of the Civil Rights movement have been undercut or abandoned bit by bit, in tandem with a political strategy that has emphasized the exploitation of racial antagonisms to secure electoral power. (This strategy has been discussed more or less publicly and its history has been thoroughly documented by Thomas and Mary Edsall in their book *Chain Reaction* [1991].) The observable results of this shift have been the relegitimization of racism as a public attitude (though it may still be considered necessary to "encode" that attitude in various "neutral" phrasings) and a great increase in the economic, social, and political deprivation of a large segment of the Afro-American population. However, in accordance with the general widening of economic disparities of the 1980s, some black Americans have prospered during this period, aided by the new educational possibilities opened up through Civil Rights rulings and federal funding, and by "equal opportunity" legislation. In fact, the disparities in income distribution have become much greater between wealthy blacks and poor blacks than between comparable classes of whites.[18]

This division of high and low, and its consequences for the Afro-American community, are not only recent sociological phenomena; they are also an important literary subject, one that appears in the earliest writing about the new black city culture—for example, W.E.B. Du Bois's *Philadelphia Negro* (1899)—and then runs continuously through the twentieth century. Rarely is the subject treated directly, as, for instance, in Richard Wright's works, or to a degree in Jean Toomer's. More frequently, as is often the case with matters of class in the United States, it has been displaced into discussions of culture. Thus the divisions within Afro-American literature and criticism that have occurred since the early 1970s at least partially reflect the growing distance between Black Arts advocates committed to a populist, community-oriented, and performative notion of art, and a new class of black literary professionals concerned with fitting the study of black literature into an academic context.[19]

That context in the 1970s and 80s included both a new interest in Afro-American literature and criticism and a large boom in the critical methodologies lumped together as poststructuralism. The attention to black writers and their works obviously has not made up for decades of neglect; in some ways, progress—in opening the canon, in hiring teachers, and especially in getting minority students into universities—has been slight.[20] But relatively speaking, Afro-American literature and its criticism are now given serious and extensive consideration in the academy, and that attention has some ripple effect on the wider culture. Inevitably there has also been a meeting of poststructuralist methodology and Afro-American writing.

Poststructuralist criticism, with its concentration on texts and signs and linguistic definitions of all cultural relations, became virtually a new intellectual climate of opinion in the decade of the 1980s and has been particularly influential in literary studies. This change, it has been frequently pointed out, is not as radical as its proponents sometimes claim.[21] There exists a strong thread of continuity, for example, between the rhetorical methods of the New Criticism of the 1940s and 50s and the Saussurian linguistic methods of the 1970s and 80s; and it could be argued that the change from the unconcern with referentiality in New Criticism to the denial of referentiality in poststructuralism is small change indeed. Further, the assumption that poststructuralism or its most common literary-critical version, deconstruction, is somehow associated with a radical social critique— an assumption frequently made by critics of both the Left and the Right—is hardly justified. As Peter Dews put the matter in his *Logics of Disintegration* (1987): "While there has often been a *de facto* alliance between the intellectual Left and recent French theory, with post-structuralism providing tools of analysis which have been widely applied, there has sometimes been little attempt to think through the ultimate compatibility of progressive political commitments with the dissolution of the subject, or a totalizing suspicion of the concept of truth."[22] Dews speaks in a European context, but his point is one that underlies some present discussion of Afro-American literary criticism.

There was an odd conjunction between the decline of Afro-American political power in the 1970s and 80s and the growing authority of literary theory in the interpretation of Afro-American literature during the same period. The relationship was perhaps not causal, but it might have been complementary, in the way Cornel West suggests: "I would go so far as to postulate that the glacier shift from an Afro-American literature of racial confrontation during the four decades of the forties to the seventies to one of cultural introspection in our time is linked in some complex and mediated way to the existential needs and accommodating values of the black and white literary professional-managerial classes who assess and promote most of this literature."[23]

Literature or criticism at this historical moment, of course, has a very limited potential to effect social change, but the devaluing of the activist potential of language, even unintentionally, in favor of a deferred meaning, an endlessly discussable ambiguity, must always serve the interests of the status quo. The status quo may be comfortable for the middle class, even the black middle class, but its maintenance requires "blindness" of a different sort than Paul de Man spoke of; it requires *not* using language to see down certain streets, or through certain doorways. The sense that literary theory was a practical dead-end has been an important factor in the rise of cultural studies as an approach to the meanings of (among other things) literary texts.[24]

These matters *do* touch directly on the Afro-American vision of the invisible city, in literature as well as life. The Whig view of history as a steady social progress has not applied to Afro-Americans, or if it has, it has applied very intermittently and inequitably, and that fact explains much about conflicting views of the city in black literature and about the conflicting attitudes of Afro-American writers and critics of that literature. Two books nearly one hundred years apart— *The Philadelphia Negro* and *The Promised Land*, the latter Nicholas Lemann's recent study of black urban migration—speak to a crisis situation in urban life for Afro-Americans, and although the historical circumstances of each book are unique, the sense of urgency remains.[25] Similarly, the dialogues and disagreements among black intellectuals tend to repeat themselves, though particularities may differ, because the division between the urban underclass and the "professing" class underlies much black writing from Du Bois to the 1990s; the echo extends back to the ambivalence Du Bois himself expressed when in *The Souls of Black Folk* (1903) he defined the invisible city in terms of "the *trivium* and *quadrivium*" of the college curriculum at Atlanta University.[26]

In 1943 Twentieth Century–Fox released a musical film with an all-black cast: *Stormy Weather*, starring Lena Horne, Bill Robinson, Fats Waller, and Cab Calloway. As the *New York Times* noted before that release, Hollywood was yielding to the wartime requests of the government, which "felt that its program for increased employment of Negro citizens in certain heretofore restricted fields of industry would be helped by a general distribution of important pictures in which Negroes played a major part."[27] Since Afro-American labor was important to the wartime economy, the Roosevelt administration hoped that its "suggestions" would produce mass-cultural images that placated blacks and contributed to easing the tensions caused by blacks' migration into northern urban areas. In 1942 Walter White and negotiators for the National Association for the Advancement of Colored People had met with studio heads in Hollywood and obtained a somewhat ambiguous agreement that the film makers would try both to employ more Afro-Americans and also to depict Afro-Americans more positively in their movies.[28]

Despite these pressures and probable good intentions, when the nearly all-white production staff for *Stormy Weather* had to create scenes to frame the singing, playing, and dancing of their black musical stars, what they came up with was a series of classic stereotypes:

Afro-Americans as cake-walking minstrels, as African "natives," in a northern Harlem nightclub, and in a southern juke-joint. Bill Robinson tap-dances on a riverboat in a scene that could almost illustrate a nineteenth-century plantation novel. The story, a vintage Hollywood rags-to-riches tale, incorporates a vague sense of Afro-American history, opening with black troops returning from World War I and closing with a "blow-out" party to celebrate black troops going overseas for World War II. The successful characters—all stage performers—move from the south (Memphis) to the north (Chicago) or the west (Hollywood), and the final sequence opens with a long file of zoot-suiters and zoot girls dancing in front of a Hollywood "cottage," a remarkable and bizarre image that, despite its confusion, seems to recognize the transformation from country to city occurring in black life.

In historic retrospect that image becomes very ironic, because the same year that *Stormy Weather* was released, the "zoot-suit riots" erupted in several western and northern cities. The style of dress for Afro-American and Mexican-American youth—"a killer-diller coat with a drape-shape, reat-pleats and shoulders padded like a lunatic's cell"—became the focal point for race rioting on a large scale as off-duty white military personnel in Los Angeles attacked anyone wearing a zoot suit. The suits were seen as unpatriotic (they violated War Production Board standards of cloth rationing), but more importantly they were the "uniform" of the nonwhite population that was challenging the status quo within the context of the social disruption of World War II. As Stuart Cosgrove says, "The zoot suit was more than the drape-shape of 1940s fashion, more than a colourful stage-prop hanging from the shoulders of Cab Calloway; it was, in the most direct and obvious ways, an emblem of ethnicity and a way of negotiating an identity. The zoot suit was a refusal: a subcultural gesture that refused to concede to the manners of subservience."[29] Within Afro-American culture, that distinctive style even now has an iconic and metaphoric status. It remains an image of the black jazzman of the 1940s, the beboppers who asserted their music's separateness. In *Invisible Man* Ralph Ellison made it symbolic of the social potential for unpredictable change, an affirmation, perhaps, of history's devious complexity.

But it is the juxtaposition of urban riot and "coats long and hip-tight"—of the action in northern ghettos in the summer of 1943 and the finale of *Stormy Weather*—which makes the film seem peculiarly contemporary.[30] Hollywood's attempt to appropriate black style mis-reads even as it glamorizes, for it deliberately separates that style from its social setting. This misreading results in a film that is simultaneously a record of performative brilliance and of an incorrigibly racist outlook.[31] Located approximately midway between the publication of Wright's *Native Son* and the period in which Ellison and Baldwin began their first novels, *Stormy Weather* provides a useful reference point. Whatever else they intended, these three writers meant to present a different version of Afro-American life in the city, one that could resist and subvert the already hardened clichés proliferating in the mainstream culture. As Ralph Ellison has observed, "Hollywood is not the creator" of these clichés about black life, "but the manipulator." Yet that manipulation encases the clichés in cement: "If the film [*The Birth of a Nation*] became the main manipulator of the American dream, for Negroes that dream contained a strong dose of what nightmares are made of."[32] It should be clear that the differences among Wright, Ellison, and Baldwin, which remain important, are much less significant than their common distance from the mainstream culture's understanding of black life. Similarly, Toni Morrison's novels, culminating in *Beloved*, work toward the same revisionist end, though perhaps because she started from an experience of communal engagement in the 1960s, she can more easily imagine an end that includes in some form an empowered Beloved Community within the city.

CHAPTER ONE

City Bound

I got to keep moving,
I got to keep moving,
Blues falling down like hail.
                    —Robert Johnson, "Hellhound on My Trail"

Colored people will congregate in the large towns and cities
and they will endure any amount of hardship and privation.
                    —Letter from Frederick Douglass to
                    Harriet Beecher Stowe (1853)

In 1918 the Carnegie Endowment for International Peace commissioned a study by the black writer and editor Emmett J. Scott which was published as *Negro Migration during the War* (1920) and included the work of Chicago sociologist Robert Park and his graduate student Charles S. Johnson, who would later contribute to Locke's *New Negro*. Scott's book began, "Within a brief period of three years following the outbreak of the great war in Europe, more than four hundred thousand negroes suddenly moved north."[1] That statistical opening was only the first salvo; it would be followed by seventy years of reiteration and updating, studies mathematical and anecdotal, general surveys, and particular case histories.[2] Some of the most important of these studies have appeared within the last five years, including Nicholas Lemann's widely noted *The Promised Land*, a work in which he attempted to summarize the nature and effects of black migration north. Though Lemann concentrated on a later phase of migration, following World War II, he wrote of it with the same sense of crisis that is detectable in Scott's work; indeed, virtually every commentator who has bothered to look at Afro-American economic and social conditions in the north in this century has referred to that crisis, from the Chicago Commission on Race Relations formed after the

13

riots of 1919 to the Kerner Commission in the 1960s. What recent scholarship has pointed out, however, is the fallacy of reducing an American urban crisis to the "Negro problem," or of tacitly accepting as given or "natural," and therefore causeless, the economic and social context within which blacks have migrated to the northern cities and made homes there.[3] One accomplishment of Afro-American urban novels, particularly those written after 1925, has been to denaturalize that given context by speaking from within it.

Although Emmett J. Scott wrote of a new scale of black migration, the movement of Afro-Americans from south to north had begun before the twentieth century. "Since the end of the Civil War," notes Gilbert Osofsky, "there was a steady but small movement of Negroes northward. It averaged 41,378 persons for each decade between 1870 and 1890. In the following ten years, however, the migration more than doubled as at least 107,796 southern Negroes moved north and west."[4] By 1900, then, there were substantial black communities in many northern cities,[5] and this presence was producing a new black urban literature.

In the nineteenth century, although some blacks had moved to cities and had moved from south to north, there had been a basic stability in their demographic patterns. After 1910—probably, more precisely, after 1915—the rates of migration increased so dramatically as to turn those patterns upside down.[6] The net effects of this movement in the first half of the twentieth century are summarized by Robert Hall: "In 1910 nearly 90 per cent of all U.S. blacks lived in the former Confederate states and 73 percent in rural areas, but by 1960 about 40 per cent lived outside the South and about 65 per cent resided in 212 Standard Metropolitan Statistical Areas."[7] Nicholas Lemann puts it more dramatically: "During the 1940s, the black population of Chicago increased by 77 per cent, from 278,000 to 492,000. In the 1950s, it grew by another 65 per cent, to 813,000; at one point 2,200 black people were moving to Chicago every week."[8]

This was a phenomenon unlike any other migratory movement in American history. It was a displacement of a people on so vast a scale and in so short a time that the mythical westward movement in the nineteenth century seems small by comparison. Inevitably it became the central fact in Afro-American literature after World War I: that migration was the important circumstance behind *The New Negro* and the writing referred to as the Harlem Renaissance. And the migration of the 1920s and 30s also provided the narrative impulse for the novels of Wright, Ellison, and, somewhat less directly, Baldwin. In the most general sense, each of these authors' novels is about the adaptation of southern rural blacks to the milieu of the northern city; so too is Toni Morrison's *Beloved*, though it is set in the nineteenth century, part of it even in the antebellum period. Morrison's novel evokes contemporary situations by historical parallel; its narrative of the nineteenth-century period of the Reconstruction calls up for the reader the events of the second Reconstruction, 1960–1975. Its characters anticipate history just as Ellison's *Invisible Man* recapitulates it.

Ironically, the Afro-American community in *Beloved* is a suburb of Cincinnati, the nineteenth-century pattern a reversal of the late twentieth-century one. For while blacks moved north, R. D. McKenzie observed as early as 1933 a different kind of migration: whites had already begun leaving the northern cities for belts of suburbs that grew up along transit lines and new arterial roads.[9] The final effect of these changes in habitation patterns was becoming noticeable in the late 1940s and became a major social theme in the 1950s—the inner cities filled with Afro-American immigrants, primarily from the south, while white middle and even working classes were suburbanized. In the twentieth century it became blacks and not whites whose orientation was distinctly urban. The Great Migration was not one massive relocation but rather a series of waves that would ebb and flow but never cease, so that by 1970, as Rex R. Campbell and Daniel M. Johnson would observe, "a greater proportion of blacks were urban dwellers than were whites."[10] Or as Theodore Kornweibel, Jr., put it in 1981, with a slightly different emphasis, "As a consequence of these shifts [blacks to cities, both southern and northern] today Negroes are more urbanized than the white population."[11]

This huge social rearrangement has apparently ended at last.[12] Since the early 1970s the growth in the black population of northern cities has been due to natural increase rather than immigration, and the traditional push/pull motivations—the "push" of the Jim Crow laws of the south, the "pull" of the job opportunities in northern urban industries—are no longer working. But the consequences of the Great Migration remain, and remain central to Afro-American life. The effects of what Alain Locke described in 1925 as a flight "from medieval America to modern" have not ceased.[13] Ralph Ellison expressed the psychological trauma of the Great Migration with an acute image in *Invisible Man*: "Yes, I thought, what about those of us who shoot up from the South into the busy city like wild jacks-in-the-box broken loose from our springs—so sudden that our gait becomes like that of deep-sea divers suffering from the bends?"[14] The bends still afflict Afro-American life, perhaps more severely now than ever before. The persistence of the condition has meant that black urban literature, whatever its date, is still relevant; the questions, social and other, which that literature raises are still unanswered.

Trying to fix a precise date when the impact of urban migration began to appear in black literary texts is almost impossible, but it is significant that Du Bois's *Philadelphia Negro* (1899), Dunbar's *Sport of the Gods* (1902), Pauline Hopkins's *Contending Forces* (1900), and Charles Chesnutt's *Wife of His Youth* (1899) appeared at the turn of the century. It is hard to imagine these books being written before migration had created a substantial black presence in northern cities, and their narratives and themes include most of the major elements of later Afro-American urban fiction, particularly the central matters of class and cultural divisions, of individual and communal identity within an alien and usually hostile environment.[15] Already recognizable in their stories are the beginnings of mass culture and the ambiguous state of isolation in the city. While "passing" as a literary theme was not unknown in the nineteenth century, having been used by Frank Webb, for instance, in *The Garies and Their Friends* (1857), James Weldon Johnson's anonymously written *The Autobiography of an Ex-Colored Man* (1912) makes an assumption that even Frank Webb's city-centered *Garies* did not make but that will be taken for granted by the "passing" novels of the 1920s: "passing" is intimately connected to the anonymity of modern city life.[16]

This is not to say, of course, that the city was unimportant in earlier black American literature. Boston, as we know, is significant in the poetry of Phyllis Wheatley as a symbol of both civility and civilization. Nor must we forget that the city is crucial to understanding the slave narratives, especially the north's association with the twin themes of "freedom and literacy."[17] Yet until the publication of Du Bois's *Philadelphia Negro*, there is in this earlier literature little indication of a mass movement that in itself creates a new city within the old American city. Rather, the focus in earlier black literature is almost exclusively upon *typology*, a kind of moral classification indebted to a classical and Christian tradition. Thus in many slave narratives, literary forms that usually rely on an elaborate documentation of the "thingy world,"[18] the author often, paradoxically, leaves out a detailed urban map. Solomon Northup's ironic observation "A slave pen within the very shadow of the Capitol!" focuses primarily on a symbolic geography, as does Linda Brent's cry "So I was *sold* at last! A human being *sold* in the free city of New York!"[19] A literature that simplifies the city in this way does not thereby lessen its own power as satire. Consider Linda Brent's observation on how two groups of people respond to the presence of the Fugitive Slave Law in New York City: "While fashionables were listening to the thrilling voice of Jenny Lind in Metropolitan Hall, the thrilling voices of poor hunted colored people went up in an agony of supplication, to the Lord, in Zion's church."[20]

This framing of the city in reductive moral terms does not disappear in the twentieth century—it is present to a greater or lesser degree in the four novels I discuss—but modern black writers will imply, or make explicit, an empirically verifiable cityscape behind "the city of iniquity" or "the celestial city." In contrast, Olaudah Equiano's London, Frederick Douglass's Baltimore, and Solomon Northup's Washington exist primarily as symbols, just as in the novels of the time that treat the north and/or cities—Harriet Wilson's *Our Nig* (1859), William Wells Brown's *Clotel* (1853, 1860–61, 1864, 1867), and Martin Delany's *Blake* (1861–62)—one has little indication of an urban "reference system" (e.g., street names, districts, boundaries) of the kind that, according to Kevin Lynch, makes up an urban texture or an urban text.[21] Both Wilson and Jacobs expressed an intimate world of interior space (what Toni Morrison has referred to as "a woman's strong sense of being in a room, a place, or . . . a house"),[22] but among most black writers of the nineteenth century, antebellum and after, there is almost an indifference to defining city space as "articulated space."[23] Possibly this indifference resulted from the comparative unimportance of urban "place" set against the ecstatic fact of "arrival." As James Grossman says, "Slaves suffered both restrictions on their freedom of movement and coerced migration within the South, and many blacks came to regard the ability to move as, in writer Howard Thurman's words, 'the most psychologically dramatic of all manifestations of freedom.'"[24] But possibly, too, this focus upon space *not* defined by American urban maps already foreshadows

Morrison's Not Doctor Street and John Edgar Wideman's Homewood, invisible cities formed within the dominant American city.

It was Du Bois who first defined exterior urban space as place in *The Philadelphia Negro*, recognizing that the city was an environment radically different from the small towns and rural plantations of the south, and that these urban immigrants were, as Ellison's pun implies, "broken loose from [their] springs"—from the sources of strength provided by old cultural attachments. This point is, indeed, developed in *The Philadelphia Negro*. What they found in the city was what other alien urban immigrants have always found: poverty, loneliness, disconnection, a confusion of sights and sounds, a new intensity of both economic and social pressure. Wages for city jobs were higher, but so were costs of living, and though many blacks moved north as families or with relatives, or even in whole communities, those bonds were subject to new conditions and extreme tests within the setting of the city.[25]

In the 1960s, LeRoi Jones (Amiri Baraka) published a poem, one section of which speaks about the geography of desire in which the articulated space of the city, in the form of an old street name, acts to alienate the speaker by its evocation of a previous history. Jones assumes that enslaved Africans and present-day black Americans come to a city whose physical and metaphysical space is already defined:

> Each Morning
> I go down
> to Gansevoort St.
> and stand on the docks.
> I stare out
> at the horizon
> until it gets up
> and comes to embrace
> me. I make believe
> it is my father.
> This is known
> as genealogy.[26]

The street, named for a prominent Dutch family, recalls the time when New York was called New Amsterdam; yet as either "New York" or "New Amsterdam," the city's human history, its attempt to recreate the spatial maps of the Old World, has not included Jones within its conception of civilized space: his ancestors were a group of anonymous "negars" aboard a Dutch ship to the New World (1619), and he continues to remain an outsider in a city that still recognizes, through its street name, a link with that past.[27] His true "father" is not the visible city but an invisible "it," a "horizon," open space that the poem itself fails to define or domesticate. Indeed, that failure is the poem's subject.

There is a second irony in Jones's poem. A "horizon" is a definition of sorts, a boundary line separating heaven and earth, representing a ship "at a distance," as Zora Neale Hurston puts it in *Their Eyes Were Watching God*. Since one of the poem's themes is the mystery of origins, the eastern horizon whose embrace Jones awaits also suggests the nightmare of history, a slave ship whose cargo helped build the material city that people like the Gansevoorts mapped. The Gansevoorts were a family of lawyers, and law became the cornerstone of the American polis; yet the system of law that ordered the American polis into existence would enslave, and later segregate, blacks in the urban north as well as the rural south. The relationship of law to the question of black identity in the mapped city also concerns Du Bois in *The Philadelphia Negro*.

As John Stilgoe notes, "William Penn introduced the grid to the English colonies in 1681, when he directed his agents and surveyors to lay out a city in Pennsylvania."[28] Philadelphia was thus an "invented" city, a city built upon the abstract, rational laws of geometry, one laid out in terms of squares and right angles. According to Richard Sennett, the source for Penn's plan was the Roman military camp, a practical design never entirely divorced from its original religious significance.[29] Penn would carry Roman secularization a step further, for although the original plan of Philadelphia called for a central square,[30] the secularized grid created a city without a center, one in which all space appeared to be undifferentiated. The effect of this grid, as in other American cities built on the same plan (New York, Chicago, and Cincinnati), would be to "deny that complexity and difference existed in the environment."[31] Because the grid facilitated trade, in the nineteenth century it helped to make Philadelphia the "nation's leading industrial center, its official population nearly doubling in the thirty years between 1870 and 1900."[32] Thus a conflict between image and reality came to beset the city, its dream of the Beloved Community (the "City of Brotherly Love") running against the hard facts of its economic interests.

None of this history escaped Du Bois, who would write the first book by a black author to deal with Philadelphia as the location of a distinct black community, "a city within a city."[33] In a sense, *The Philadelphia Negro* makes visible the city's history of "difference," which the abstract grid seems to deny. At its simplest level, the book introduces one version of the invisible city—Du Bois wants to make the presence of urban blacks visible to his white readers; his sociological treatise describes a "new" phenomenon to people who continue to place Afro-Americans within a pastoral setting. Yes, Du Bois declares early on, there is such a thing as an urban Negro, and his arrival in the city is hardly recent: "We are studying a group of people the size of the capital of Pennsylvania in 1890, and as large as Philadelphia itself in 1800" (53). Segregated from the white city, blacks in Philadelphia represent a hidden world within the white metropolis, and Du Bois wishes to explain this unknown terrain in detail, recognizing that, as Charles Booth said, "it is in the town and not in the country that 'terra incognita' needs to be written on our social maps."[34] Philadelphia's grid may claim to be "neutral," but Du Bois includes a map of the Seventh Ward that shows the invisible walls. Within these walls, Du Bois claims, there is considerable diversity and difference, enough to dispel another mistaken notion: the belief that the city has created a "homogeneous" black race whose collective poverty illustrates that black people are unfit for urban living (73–74).

In Du Bois's book, the black city within Philadelphia is described with specific reference to a black middle class, many of whom don't live in the Seventh Ward:

> The best class of Philadelphia Negroes, though sometimes forgotten or ignored in discussing the Negro's problems, is nevertheless known to many Philadelphians. Scattered throughout the better parts of the Seventh Ward, and on Twelfth, lower Seventeenth and Nineteenth streets, and here and there in the residence wards of northern, southern, and western sections of the city is a class of caterers, clerks, teachers, professional men, small merchants, etc., who constitute the aristocracy of the Negroes. (7)

What we note about these remarks is not only Du Bois's geographical exactness but also the emphasis he places on social class and economic status; his focus on the middle class will inform a conception of the black city which will continue through the Harlem Renaissance. And his eye for practical observation marks a different emphasis from the "typological" one of the slave narratives.

Du Bois understands communities' need for the structure and centering provided by institutions, and the institutions he writes about will continue to be crucial for black writers: the library for Richard Wright, the university for Ralph Ellison, and the black church for James Baldwin. Toni Morrison will herself be a product of the university, but she—like Ellison—will come to question its relevance to black life.

Du Bois's preferred institutions are the library and the university, and his conception of class relationships within the black city will lead him to that view of self-improvement which strongly influenced Alain Locke's vision of Harlem. Du Bois singles out the rise to "prominence" of the caterers in mid-nineteenth-century black Philadelphia, employing a telling metaphor to describe them as a collective group: "as remarkable a trade guild as ever ruled in a medieval city." During the race riots of the 1840s, it was this guild that "took complete leadership of the bewildered group of [middle-class] Negroes, and led them steadily on to a degree of affluence, culture and respect such as has probably never been surpassed in the history of the Negro in America" (32). Although Du Bois is primarily writing one kind of work, sociology, he is also using his powers as a poet to mythologize the urban scene. If Philadelphia itself lacks a center, both literally and figuratively, this is all the more reason why black Philadelphians should find one; in Du Bois's text the black middle class is to become the "centre" (a ubiquitous word in *The Philadelphia Negro*) of an invisible city that will grow around it, as the city of Chartres grew around its cathedral; and the masses will look to this "aristocracy" for leadership and example.

Du Bois believes that the Talented Tenth in the city, the educated and successful blacks, are the focus of a "higher life," and that spiritual goods should flow from that source to nourish the entire black community. The only justification for being a member of an elite class is to help those lower down: the "better classes have their chief excuse for being in the work they may do for lifting the rabble" (393).

Du Bois here reveals a bias against the masses ("rabble") that belies his true sympathy, for he recognizes that their grim situation is one created by the racial prejudices of the city. Over and over, he points to the exclusionary practices of the city's factories, stores, and trade unions, sometimes barely concealing his anger; if black office boys or porters are denied opportunities offered comparable white workers, "the city has no right to complain that black boys lose interest in work and drift into idleness and crime" (395).[35]

However, it is the tragic failure of members of the elite class to assume leadership that begins to preoccupy Du Bois in *The Philadelphia Negro*, and it is here that we have a glimpse of the future Marxist. Du Bois notes that the once-powerful guilds of Negro caterers have seen their power eroded in Philadelphia by forces from outside the city; the "modern" commercial establishments such as Delmonico's "represent a large investment of capital" and claim to follow the "fashion from New York, London, Paris" (120).[36] Because he observes that a "local" guild cannot compete with huge corporations created by the new mass society, we expect Du Bois to make a more radical social statement about the nature of black urban life, one that would see both the masses and the middle class as equal victims. Yet in *The Philadelphia Negro* he remains loyal to his belief that culture and class represent matters of intrinsic worth independent of the economic system. Hence his criticism of those whites who reduce all blacks to either "chambermaids or bootblacks" is both insightful and nearsighted. For Du Bois, "it is as wrong to make scullions of engineers as it is to make engineers of scullions" (396), because it ignores intrinsic differences that he believes are reflected in class and culture; yet his patrician attitude kept him from fully appreciating the kind of culture that chambermaids and bootblacks actually created. As we shall see, in this attitude he reflects the developing social forms of his time.

Du Bois's attitude toward the middle class reveals a crucial ambivalence. He understands that the economic insecurity of its members makes them cling to an image of respectability because of the suspicion that the color line that binds all will be drawn even more tightly around them. Yet this fear, understandable in itself, is death to the idea of community: "Instead then of social classes held together by strong ties of mutual interest we have in the case of the Negroes, classes who have much to keep them apart, and only community of blood and color prejudice to bind them together" (317). The masses recoil from an aristocracy who should lead them, because of that aristocracy's snobbishness; and the aristocrats reject fraternity, fleeing contact with those who threaten to drag them down into the barrel of crabs. Yet in *The Philadelphia Negro*, Du Bois shows a real fear of falling into that barrel himself, associating its bottom with the streets and not the home, which should be, he argues, "the centre of social life and moral guardianship" (196). What Du Bois did not see in his brilliant study is that street life, alley life, and juke joints made the city bearable for those at the bottom. What he did perceptively see was that blacks' high death rate (especially infant mortality) and high crime rate, and other social ills, were caused by the intolerable conditions of a city that was riddled with race prejudice. And he understood that the industrial Philadelphia of the nineteenth century was entirely different from the colonial city that claimed to be the "City of Brotherly Love." It was a tough, new Philadelphia, one committed to the exclusion of blacks from its economic life.[37]

Hence Du Bois always returned to another major theme in his book: the possible death of the city itself. A system of exclusion, such as exists in Philadelphia, ensures a democracy based on the poverty of an underclass. Such a system, Du Bois warns, threatens the future of Philadelphia:

> How long can a city say to a part of its citizens, "It is useless to work; it is fruitless to serve well of men; education will gain you nothing but disappointment and humiliation?" How long can a city teach its black children that the road to success is to have a white face? How long can a city do this and escape the inevitable penalty? (351)

The conclusion to *The Philadelphia Negro* sarcastically refers to the larger "civilized community" (355, 388) of the commonwealth itself. Because of this injustice in the city—and the classical scholar Du Bois is thinking of Cicero and Plato—there is neither community nor civilization in Philadelphia, and by extension, in America. Du Bois's warning—"How long can a city teach its black children that the road to success is to have a white face?"—will be echoed in Morrison's *Bluest Eye* (1970). His observation that "in the slums of modern society lie the answers to most of our puzzling problems of organization and life" (392) will be repeated in contemporary analyses of the black urban scene made almost a hundred years later.[38] Du Bois's statement in *The Souls of Black Folk* (1903) that the "problem of the Twentieth Century is the problem of the color-line" is justifiably famous, but he should be equally well known for his brilliant book on the first "invented" American city.

In *The Philadelphia Negro* Du Bois employs a carefully modulated, secular language: he is writing a scientific treatise for a primarily white audience, and his reference to an invisible city of communal life appears mainly through his allusions to the "City of Brotherly Love" (the literal meaning, of course, of "Philadelphia"). In his more personal or political writing, however, Du Bois uses a language replete with biblical quotations and allusions, returning to the strongest single tradition of Afro-American culture. From that tradition black writers took images and tropes to describe their common life, including the ideal life of the invisible city. In a 1913 article for the *Crisis*, Du Bois, for instance, links both real and imaginary cities in a single vision:

> Coming out of the West I have some way again and again dreamed a vision of some city set like Seattle on a hill with the roses of Los Angeles and the Golden Gate of San Francisco in the dim distance and the Grand Canyon looming down from heaven. Through that city two great and thick-thronged avenues cross forming four arms—Prince's Street of Edinburgh is one, the Elysian Fields of Paris another. Orange Grove Avenue of Pasadena is a third, and the fourth may be the Kansas City Paseo, or Piccadilly—I am not sure which. Then high in that central square I think would be a fit place for the Throne of God.[39]

The trope reappears at the end of Du Bois's "The Negro Mind Reaches Out" (an essay that concludes Alain Locke's *New Negro* [1925]), where he refers to Liberia as "a little thing set upon a Hill," a beacon light to the pan-African movement.[40]

Of the three primary sources for the images in the Du Bois passage, the most obvious is the trope made famous by John Winthrop aboard the *Arbella* in 1630, the city on a hill from Matthew 5:14–16: "You are the light of the world. A city on a hill cannot be hid. Nor do men light a lamp and put it under a bushel, but on a stand, and it gives light to all in the house. Let your light so shine before men that they may see your good works and give glory to your Father who is in heaven." The city on a hill is associated with light, something intangible, just as Christ in his Sermon on the Mount is suggesting that his few humble followers constitute a city not in terms of size and grandeur but in terms of an invisible entity, a spiritual community. A similar point is made by John of Patmos in the Book of Revelation, a second source for the Du Bois passage. John notes that light is also the essence of the heavenly city; but more importantly, no visible temple is necessary there: "And I saw no temple in the city, for its temple is the Lord God the Almighty and the Lamb" (Rev. 21:22). John himself is alluding to the restored temple in Ezekiel, the outward and visible sign of the restored Jerusalem in the Old Testament; but at the end of the New Testament John is saying that the spiritual presence of God and his Son replaces the need for a visible temple. Again, the emphasis is on the invisibility of the heavenly city.

This is the point also made by Augustine in *The City of God*, another text to which Du Bois alludes. In tracing the historical lineage of the earthly city from the descendants of Cain, and the lineage of the heavenly city from the descendants of Seth, Augustine notes, "Here then the two cities are presented, one existing in actuality, the other existing in hope which rests with God. They come out, we may say, from the same door of mortality."[41] This "door of mortality" is like a "veil," now closed, now open; and those who are most lowly in the world, those who seem to be most "veiled," are often those who see with an inner vision.[42] So, too, Du Bois's famous reference in *The Souls of Black Folk* to the "veil"—between the Negro and the world lies a veil—is double-edged: the Negro is both outside and inside, outside the pale of American society but "gifted with second sight in this American world." Although he is excluded from participation in the earthly city, he is a kind of "seventh son," a condition that, according to folklorists, gives him the "gift" of "clairvoyance . . . by which hidden things are brought to light."[43] Augustine also observes of the word *seven* (with special reference to the child promised to the superannuated Abraham and Sarah) that "the renewal of nature" is invisible: "And what does the eighth day symbolize but Christ, who rose again after the completion of seven days, that is, after the Sabbath. . . . 'Newness' is the note struck in every detail; and the new covenant is presented, in a veiled manner, in the old" (687). Du Bois's allusion to Augustine is a preface to his own version of the city on a hill in chapter 5 of *The Souls of Black Folk*, entitled "Of the Wings of Atalanta."

The early Christian writings are literary sources for Du Bois and other black intellectuals, but the sources themselves also find a ubiquitous expression in popular culture: sermons and black music. The trope that appears most often in black spirituals is not the lost garden but the beckoning city; the image of the traveler going *forward* on the road toward Zion is the dominant one. In James Weldon Johnson's *Book of American Negro Spirituals* (1925) and *Second Book of American Negro Spirituals* (1926), there are repeated images of walking, train rides, crossings (over Jordan); always a figure is moving toward a heavenly city. In the spirituals people confront and overcome hazards along the way—hard times, loneliness, and weariness—in the hopes of building up "Zion's walls"; and conversely, that city offers refuge. Theologically that refuge is in an afterlife, but practically, as the most important black communal institution, the church represented a refuge in this world as well. The blues, as secularized spirituals, frequently make use of biblical references, though these may be used with some irony—for Robert Johnson the "Land of Canaan" becomes the "land of California"—or may even be used in an antithetical sense—Peetie Wheatstraw refers to himself as "the High Sheriff of Hell," and Bessie Smith sings in "Preachin' the Blues": "I ain't here: to try to save your soul / Just want to teach you: how to save your good jellyroll."[44]

Du Bois felt the strong pull of folk wisdom and expression, but it is worth noting that the "Sorrow Songs" he refers to in *The Souls of Black Folk* represent sacred, not secular, music. Even though we know that by 1903 many forms of blues music existed and ragtime was especially popular (along with "coon songs"), Du Bois refused to talk about those forms of music in his excellent book. That is, when he talked about "our spiritual strivings," he put an emphasis on the "spiritual."[45] He was interested in black "souls," and he hesitated to admit that language about the body could be soulful, for it dredged up too many stereotypes from an unusable past.

An advocate of print culture, Du Bois finally backed away from identifying the ideal city either with the black church or with folk art. The real "temple" lay elsewhere, in the city on the hill—Atlanta University—which towered above the earthly city of Atlanta. Here was a secular institution whose long history promoted an ideal vision of the good life: "The riddle of existence is the college curriculum that was laid before the Pharaohs, that was taught in the groves by Plato, that formed the *trivium* and *quadrivium* and is today laid before the freedman's sons by Atlanta University" (69). In Du Bois's juxtaposition of the city of Atlanta and Atlanta University in *The Souls of Black Folk*, he notes the parallel between the goddess who succumbed to the lure of the golden apples and lost the race, and the city that yielded to the myth of northern industrialism and materialism and lost its soul. Behind the classical myth, of course, is a biblical story: Esau who sold his birthright for a mess of pottage. The fate of Atalanta and Atlanta should not become the fate of Atlanta University.

Du Bois's vision is of a university that must mediate between Mammon's city and raw, unadorned nature. Hence he employs two images of enclosed, "civilized" space to describe his perfect world: city and garden. The university both sits upon a hill and is a "green oasis" (69). Du Bois knows his Bible well: not only does the Bible begin with a garden and end with a city,[46] but John's vision of the holy city is that of a garden city: "Then he showed me the river of the water of life, bright as crystal, flowing from the throne of God and of the Lamb through the middle of the street of the city; also on either side of the river, the tree of life with its twelve kinds of fruit" (Rev. 22:1–2).

In iconographical terms, Du Bois's portrait of Atlanta University lifts it above two opposites: the barren city below, given over to empty materialism, and the countryside "out there," given over to Booker T. Washington's uncultivated agrarianism. To "plant deeply" for Du Bois means cultivating the full range of human potential: "The function of the university is not simply to teach bread-winning, or to furnish teachers for the public schools or to be a centre of polite society; it is, above all, to be the organ of that fine adjustment between real life and the growing knowledge of life, an adjustment which forms the secret of civilization" (70).

"What is Civilization?" Du Bois once asked, and he answered, "The cityfying of a people."[47] Du Bois the classical scholar links civilization with the city because "a growing knowledge of life" must include both outside and inside, public and private; and it is the city that shapes the public man. Du Bois the admirer of medieval culture links the university with the cathedral—as, in fact, it often was linked in the Middle Ages—because the cathedral literally defines a place as a city.[48] The "trivium"—rhetoric, logic, and grammar—taught at the university emphasized the divine *logos*, that mediation between flesh and spirit which the cathedral itself symbolized. Thus the true university at the city's heart scorns a reductive definition of knowledge (e.g., vocational training). The university's function is to shape human perception of empirical reality before the latter irrevocably molds the human clay. This secular-spiritual center of the city should be set against Washington's statement in *Up from Slavery* about Tuskegee: "We wanted to be careful not to educate our students out of sympathy with the agricultural life, so that they would be attracted from the country to the cities, and yield to the temptation of trying to live by their wits."[49] Du Bois believed that living by one's wits is the essence of being human, and he also saw that Washington's return to a nation of Jeffersonian yeomen could have little to do with the twentieth century. The city would be the human fate during the foreseeable future, and in his writing and social thinking Du Bois tried to come to terms with that fact.

His university, however, has a crucial ambiguity at its heart, in its function as "the organ of that fine adjustment between real life and the growing knowledge of life." This function could mean, for instance, teaching individuals to think critically about their life, their society, and their work; or it could mean producing functionaries whose "mediation" between middle-class culture and the rest of society is only a form of social control. Uplift somehow assumes making "them" like "us"; the original "Philistines," after all, were defined not by cultural poverty but by their otherness. Writing at the turn of the century, Du Bois did not yet see the narrow uniformity that conventions of middle-class life could produce, or the way in which those conventions could tie the invisible self to a value system determined only by economic and class needs. Indeed, even gender needs: Nella Larsen in *Quicksand* (1928) was to critique the enclosed spaces of city, garden, and university as masculine definitions of space.

Du Bois depicts one shape that the invisible city takes for Afro-American artists, a city of high culture existing as a guide for those who must live in the real city. This elite conception can be found in other writers around the turn of the century—James Weldon Johnson, Pauline Hopkins, and Charles Chesnutt, for example—and it

points both to an understandable insecurity about relations with
white America and to a major social change taking place in American
society, what Lawrence Levine has called "the emergence of cultural
hierarchy." In the last part of the nineteenth century, the pressures of
industrial and commercial expansion, urbanization, and large-scale
immigration created a "sense of anarchic change, of looming chaos,
of fragmentation, which seemed to imperil the very basis of the traditional order" and encouraged the upper classes as well as the rising
middle classes to find ways of separating themselves from the common crowd. One way of separation was a newly emphasized cultural
differentiation—between "highbrow" and "lowbrow," in broad
terms—which was not only class-determined but also related to a
growing body of "race" theory which could, and would, be used to
advocate white, or even more narrowly, "Anglo-Saxon," supremacy.[50]

Levine quotes a magazine essay of the period which summarizes
the lines being drawn:

> In 1894 Hiram M. Stanley defined the "masses" as those whose
> sole delight rested in "eating, drinking, smoking, society of the
> other sex, with dancing, music of a noisy and lively character,
> spectacular shows, and athletic exhibitions." Anyone demonstrat-
> ing "a permanent taste for higher pleasures," Stanley argued, "ceas-
> es, *ipso facto*, to belong to the 'masses.'"[51]

The "higher pleasures" included a newly exclusive grand opera
(preferably German), museum-going, "serious" theater, piano recitals,
symphonic music (also preferably German), and uplifting literature.
The uplifting was, by the Arnoldian ideology of the times, to be
shared with the masses to the extent that was thought possible. As
Levine points out, however, possible sharing was limited because of
the assumed inferiority of the lower orders and because, after all, the
point of establishing cultural difference was to maintain a separation
that assured authority and eminence. "The cloak of culture—ap-
proved, sanctified, conspicuous culture—promised to become a cara-
pace impervious to assault from above or below."[52]

Du Bois, as we've seen, detected within the black middle class in
Philadelphia a hostile attitude toward the mass of the Afro-American
citizenry, and he vigorously denounced that attitude. Similarly, for
most black writers and intellectuals it seemed apparent that the social
status of their race was something all Afro-Americans had in com-

mon, and that this shared status required their acting in common. Indeed, the racist structure of the society made it impossible for most of the black elite to have the sort of cultural and physical separateness that white elites increasingly sought. This meant that efforts to improve social status, at least legally or politically, had to be efforts for the entire race. As long as the goal remained integrationist, this led to an emphasis on uplift, in the hope of narrowing the cultural differences whites perceived between themselves and black Americans.

Given this historical context it is not surprising that prominent Afro-American writers urged the necessity of a higher culture, of institutions that raise or "uplift" the black masses into the middle class. Although each of the turn-of-the-century writers I have mentioned shows appreciation of black folk culture, all would agree in theory with James Weldon Johnson's assessment of ragtime and the cakewalk: they are authentic reflections of the art of the folk but are nonetheless "lower forms of art." Cultural uplift implies progress, and progress assumes that what is replaced is inferior. The great virtue of folk arts is the fact that "they give evidence of a power that will some day be applied to the higher forms."[53] Du Bois truly admired the "Sorrow Songs"; Charles Chesnutt, the conjure tales; Hopkins, folk humor; but each, finally, wanted something "higher" than folk culture.

Ideally, it seems, they wanted to see the whole of black urban culture become like the middle-class—not a middle class composed of money-grubbing philistines, but a middle class aspiring to the "higher life." For Du Bois, Chesnutt, and others, this "higher life" not only is associated with "civilization" (which by implication is "white civilization"), but is also connected with the ideals of an institution: the university. James Weldon Johnson, for instance, will sound very much like Du Bois in his pre-Harlem Renaissance column in the *New York Age*: "The City College [of New York] is situated on the heights which overlook Harlem. It is within six blocks of the center of a Negro population of 100,000; and yet the sight of colored students there is so rare as to excite curiosity. There is no excuse for this."[54] That there was "absolutely no discrimination" at the City College and that "the tuition was practically free" made the trope of the university as the city upon a hill seem even more appropriate. In an earlier article celebrating City College, Johnson also expressed his exasperation that the city on the hill is apparently unseen by the citizenry: "The city College stands overlooking Harlem. A pistol shot fired from its tower would fall in the very midst of one hundred thousand Negroes, yet it is doubtful if fifty per cent of the colored people in Harlem know what those gray buildings on Morningside Heights are, whether they are a university, an armory or a factory."[55] The city on the hill and "Morningside Heights"—the symbolic geography is derived from the actual landscape. And note that Johnson does not use the university as a symbol of the invisible city; it *is* the invisible city: the outward and visible is a sign of the inward and spiritual. Johnson's column was read by the common reader as well as by intellectuals, and he was also interested in institutions other than the university. In one article in the *New York Age*, he argued that the future Young Men's Christian Association building planned for Harlem "should be a light set on a hill to draw men up to it."[56] But while the YMCA was not the university, nonetheless, as Langston Hughes and Du Bois would also note, it was valuable to the extent that it could function as one. Less elitist in principle, it was still seen as a way to bring Culture to the masses, for like the 135th Street library in Harlem, it was to be a center where people would meet to discuss books and ideas.[57] The biblical imagery still points the way to a community "civilized" by high culture.

Both Du Bois and Johnson express their ideal city in terms of imagery borrowed from the Sermon on the Mount, but given the way this city is shaped by the two men, its relationship to the Beloved Community, or even the common community, is dubious. This secularized city on a hill often remained unseen by common black citizens, not because they were indifferent but because it had little to do with the common life—besides, only the privileged could find seats on the trains that ran there. It is precisely this elitist conception of the celestial city that will be rejected by Wright, Ellison, Baldwin, and Morrison. Wright will show that within the conditions of American society you can't metamorphose a Bigger Thomas into a standard member of the middle class; and while Toni Morrison's belief in the possibility of Afro-American community will be very different from Wright's, she is equally skeptical that white culture, mass or high, can win blacks' general acceptance.

The major institution of black life everywhere remained the church, though in Du Bois's view this "centre" of the Negro community in the south was incapable of dealing with urban complexity in the north. As an institution, "the Negro church may be said to have antedated the Negro family on American soil"; it continued to preserve "many functions of tribal organization" from the past—acting as an extended family, and serving as "a newspaper and intelligence bureau"—but too often its puritanical code stultified the "higher life."[58] While James Baldwin will share that last view in *Go Tell It on the Mountain*, his evaluation of the black church will revise Du Bois's criticism of it: the church might be inadequate to deal with the continuing chaos of urban life, but it is the only refuge for Afro-Americans in the city of destruction. This kind of expedient and necessary redefinition will also lead Baldwin, Wright, and Ellison to redefine the idea of "higher life" to include elements of popular and mass culture which Du Bois would have lumped together with the *Police Gazette*, which he ranked only slightly higher than Carl Van Vechten's novel *Nigger Heaven*.

Yet Du Bois in *The Souls of Black Folk* expressed some doubts about his version of the invisible city. These doubts are seen indirectly in his ironic comments on the overwhelming fact of American "progress"; in his tragic portraits of Alexander Crummell and "John," members of the Talented Tenth; and in his sad tale of the hopeful but doomed Josie, the young girl who hungered for knowledge. For existing side by side with the "strivings" of black folk is the oppression of history, an oppression that does not end. The same greed that once enslaved the Africans now drives the citizens of Atlanta to metamorphose their city into "satanic mills," and drives southerners to reenslave blacks by the arrangement of tenant farming. The white south's quest for cotton—modernity's "Golden Fleece"—leads Du Bois to a grim assessment of the possibility of finding a refuge in the city: "Just as centuries ago it was no easy thing for the serf to escape into the freedom of town life, even so to-day there are hindrances laid in the way of country laborers" (123–4). And as Du Bois's tragic stories show, the "hindrances" of racism cast a shadow upon his utopian "oasis" of higher learning set above the strife. Understandably then, in *The Souls of Black Folk* Du Bois posits an alternative "temple," one closer to common humanity. In a chapter devoted to the "Sorrow Songs," he describes the "great temple builded of these songs towering over the pale city [Nashville]. To me Jubilee Hall seemed ever made of the songs themselves, and its bricks were red with the blood of dust and toil" (204–5). Here is a more democratic Chartres, a cathedral built out of the common life, which Du Bois intuitively recognizes as speaking directly to the masses. He seems to imply that this "temple" would remain steadfast even if the more exalted city on a hill failed.

Not only Du Bois but also Hopkins, Chesnutt, and Johnson had serious reservations about sacrificing black culture to the cause of "higher" culture. In several of Chesnutt's stories (e.g., "The Wife of His Youth" and "A Matter of Principle") the individual pays a high price in moving from a village community to a city culture that imitates the white society. And James Weldon Johnson's only venture into novel writing severely qualifies the optimism expressed in his newspaper articles and essays, and his cultural history of New York, *Black Manhattan. The Autobiography of an Ex-Colored Man* (1912) is an extensive and explicit treatment of the cost involved in choosing the inauthentic over the authentic. Johnson's protagonist loses his identity when he chooses to define New York in terms of real estate and not race, becoming an "ex-colored man" without even a name and ending as "an ordinary successful white man who has made a little money" (154). But the story is more complex than this, because the ex-colored man's experience reflects Johnson's own deep ambivalence about the city, and about the place of black art within the culture.

There are two figures of a "dame sans merci" in the novel, the white widow who frequents the "Club" in the black district known as the Tenderloin, where the narrator plays piano, and the "witch," a metaphoric figure Johnson uses to characterize New York City, a

> great witch at the gate of the country, showing her alluring white face and hiding her crooked hands and feet under the folds of her wide garments—constantly enticing thousands. . . . Some she at once crushes beneath her cruel feet; others she condemns to a fate like that of galley slaves; a few she favors and fondles, riding them high on the bubbles of fortune; then with a sudden breath she blows the bubbles out and laughs mockingly as she watches them fall. (65–66)

The white widow is the embodiment of that figure; when she flirts with the narrator and is brutally murdered by her lover, the ex-colored man runs from the scene "like one fleeing in a horrible nightmare" (90). The nightmare is the history of black-white relationships in the United States, a special case of the witch's "crooked hands and feet," the social deformation not only of the city but of the country, as the later burning of the black man in Georgia proves.

The two killings are linked to the narrator's developing art—the widow attracted by his reputation as a ragtime player, the burning witnessed as he begins a project to study southern black music—and, in fact, they lead to his giving up that art. His ambition, the "improvement" of ragtime by the introduction of elements from white classical music, is seen as a kind of artistic miscegenation, and in a society racist in its every part, this is no more acceptable than the "leprosy" of mixed marriage (125).[59] Thus one aspect of Johnson's novel is a critique of Du Bois's optimistic invocation of the "trivium and quadrivium"; the ex-colored man has set out to begin his education at Atlanta University, but he never gets there. What intervenes is the matter of the novel: his recognition of the inexorable pressures to "pass" and abandon Afro-American identity and art.[60]

An important variation on this same theme appears in an urban novel by a black woman, a novel contemporary with the writings of Du Bois and Johnson. On the surface, Pauline Hopkins's *Contending Forces* (1900) presents the same hopeful ideal of cultural uplift which we have seen in the early Du Bois. Indeed, her male hero, Will Smith, gets a degree from Harvard and studies at Heidelberg, perhaps mirroring Du Bois's own academic career; and her female protagonist, Sappho Clark, is genteel and self-educated. The home Hopkins wants for her two main characters is a civilized city.

That city seems to be Boston, a place of culture and the former locus of abolitionism. Hopkins sprinkles her text with quotations from Shakespeare, Gray, Goldsmith, Tennyson, Whittier, and others, and as she especially admires Emerson she chooses him for her epigraph: "The civility of no race can be perfect whilst another race is degraded."[61] Perhaps she is alluding to Emerson's own metaphor of America as the City of the West,[62] but in any event Boston symbolizes the hope of that "civility" being realized where the link with the past is so auspicious: "Here in the free air of New England's freest city, Sappho drank great draughts of freedom's subtle elixir" (115). This allusion to the medieval German proverb "City air makes you free" suggests that America might by looking to Boston as an example overcome a history in which blacks were "degraded."

Yet despite her praise for cultured Boston, Hopkins often focuses on an invisible city, one so tied up with the everyday that it could exist anywhere there were black people. Although she invokes the ideal of Harvard, her texture of urban life involves ice-cream socials, church fairs, and sewing circles, not the university. For this reason, when the terrible past erupts into the present the common life is what holds things together. And what gives the novel its curious combination of realism and romance is that odd mixture of sunny present and nightmarish past, the sense that at any moment even "modern" Boston might revert to the south of Simon Legree. Sappho's life—so placid and ordinary on the surface—is shrouded in mystery that hinges on the primal crime of slavery. The villain, John Pollock Langley, repeats the sins of his ancestor by attempting to rape Sappho. He himself is college educated and a lawyer, so Hopkins is noting that lessons in "civility" and/or the law are not something black people can count on. What they rely on instead is Ma Smith's boardinghouse. That house and its cozy rooms (in which Will and Sappho become lovers and Dora and Sappho friends) is the direct ancestor to the house on Opal Street in Jessie Fauset's *Plum Bun*; to the "intimate gate" leading to Janie's back porch which Pheoby will open in Hurston's *Their Eyes Were Watching God* (1937),[63] and to the kitchen-centered world of Paule Marshall's fiction.

One interesting aspect of *Contending Forces* is Hopkins's ability to play with the idea of "civility," a word that ancient writers associated with the best features of city life. Although she clearly admires high culture—and divides her characters into those who speak "proper" English and those who utter malapropisms—it is the homely institution of Ma Smith's lodging-house where true civility resides. Its "musical evenings" bring together high and low, the middle and the lower classes, within the context of ordinary communal socializing. Here the essence of black culture is not the higher institutions, the universities or the libraries, but what happens when folks on the street get together. In this, at least, Hopkins sees a distinction between what we call "popular" and "elite" cultures; and in her emphasis on the life of the local community she foreshadows the works of the Afro-American women writers of the 1970s and 80s, particularly the novels of Toni Morrison.[64]

Speaking generally, Afro-American writers at the end of the nineteenth century were hopeful about urban life, perhaps largely because of the tradition of the city as a refuge and a new beginning which was inherited from the period of slavery. In one way or another they suggested that the promise of America as the city on the hill might be realized by the black community within a new, and primarily northern, urban matrix. The questions of what this community would be like and how it would be related to the white city were answered in terms of the hard-earned cultural background of these writers: it would have "Culture" with a capital "C," Du Bois's "trivium and quadrivium," both to uplift the black common people and, by implication, to make them acceptable to their white fellow citizens.

There were reservations, however, and writers such as Du Bois, Johnson, and Hopkins each hinted at an alternative invisible city— Du Bois's "Jubilee Hall," Johnson's Dionysian streets, Hopkins's haven of the home—as a cultural refuge, a saving remnant of Afro-American identity. The dilemma outlined in *Contending Forces* and *The Autobiography of an Ex-Colored Man*—the "contending forces" of high and low in black life—will continue to preoccupy black writers even as the ground is being laid for Alain Locke's vision of a city whose culture grows from a unified sensibility. In Jean Toomer's *Cane* (1923), that sensibility is seen as an extraordinarily difficult and tentative creation; the melding of high and low, north and south, city and country is depicted in images of disintegration and painful transformation. Locke understood Toomer's point about the need to join his city to a vital folk culture, but he ignored for the most part Toomer's cautions regarding how hard that would be to achieve. Young black writers in the late 1920s saw the difficulty quite clearly, however; novels such as Claude McKay's *Home to Harlem* (1928), Nella Larsen's *Quicksand* (1928), Rudolph Fisher's *Walls of Jericho* (1928), Jessie Fauset's *Plum Bun* (1929), and Countee Cullen's *One Way to Heaven* (1932) all deal thematically with the continuing division between high and low in Afro-American society and art. Even a later novel returning to Harlem Renaissance themes, Dorothy West's brilliant *The Living Is Easy* (1948), attempts to update Hopkins's Boston, only to come to Hopkins's conclusion via her protagonist Cleo Judson (*née* Jericho). "You really had to love Bostonians to like them," Cleo admits to herself in a rare moment of candor.[65] And because she loves the idea of being cultured like a Bostonian, she betrays a folk self and a folk culture that might have saved her. The house in which she glories becomes her undoing, as it reflects only her selfish ego and her warped class aspirations. An answer to *Native Son*, West's novel informs Richard Wright that being black, middle class, and a woman is not "easy" even when the urban "living" is done in Boston and not the Chicago ghetto. Yet one doubts that she disagreed with the Marxist assessment of class divisions within black life which Wright presented in "Blueprint for Negro Writing" published in 1938 in *New Challenge*, a magazine West edited, for they were the subject of her own novel: "Two separate cultures sprang up: one for the Negro masses, unwritten and unrecognized; and the other for the sons and daughters of a rising Negro bourgeoisie, parasitic and mannered."[66] Among the many acute social points in Ralph Ellison's *Invisible Man* is a critique of this conflict within the black community. In Ellison's novel, Bledsoe's college is a mixture of Washington's Tuskegee and Du Bois's Atlanta University, and they are both shown to be largely irrelevant to the life blacks must live in twentieth-century cities. Further, Ellison will emphasize that true wisdom comes catch-as-catch-can, from any number of sources. Living by one's wits means knowing how and when to use both Ralph Waldo Emerson and the blues of Peetie Wheatstraw, resources provided by the "high" and the "low."

CHAPTER TWO

City Cultures

You sonofabitch! It ain't always going to be this way! His mind
went abruptly blank. He could not keep on with that thought,
because he did not know where that thought led. He did not
know of any other way things could be, if not *this* way.
—Richard Wright, *Lawd Today!*

Beatrice she got a phonograph
But it won't say a lonesome word.
What evil have I done
Or what evil have the poor girl heard?
—Robert Johnson, "Phonograph Blues"

W.E.B. Du Bois's books at the turn of the century reflected the pi-
oneering work in the 1890s by sociologists such as Charles Booth and
Jacob Riis and foreshadowed later critics of urban life such as Georg
Simmel, Robert Park, and Louis Wirth, whose insights would be crucial to black writing about the city, both in the Harlem Renaissance
and after.[1] The first English translation of Georg Simmel's ground-
breaking essay "The Metropolis and Mental Life" appeared in 1902;
the essay stressed "the intensification of nervous stimulation" in the
modern city, which was also a dominant theme in Paul Laurence
Dunbar's novel *The Sport of the Gods*, published the same year.[2] The
"intensification" Dunbar describes in his New York setting arises from
two conditions: the first, already mentioned by Du Bois and others, is
the loss of familiar rural contexts for the immigrants to the city; the
second is the nature of city culture itself.

The Sport of the Gods offers a view different from the city of Du Bois
or James Weldon Johnson. Dunbar describes an urban setting from
which Du Bois's caterers, schoolteachers, and tailors are absent, and
where the mediation of a black middle class or its cultural institutions

hardly exists. Dunbar's view of the city finds its characteristic cultural elements not in the university or the library, but in the daily newspaper, in a musical-vaudeville act known as the "coon show," and in a bar called the Banner Club, gathering place for a wide range of semi-respectable and disreputable characters. Dunbar writes from a literary tradition that already treats the city as a complicated social dynamic—he knows Balzac, Baudelaire, Dickens, and perhaps even Dreiser's *Sister Carrie*. The city, for Dunbar, is a place different from the country not in degree but in kind.[3] His black characters in this milieu are moved and formed not by the august institutions of a "higher life" but by a pragmatic city expressed in popular forms consumed as information and entertainment. In this sense, in the way he treats the ordinary and painful collision of the black migrant with city culture, Dunbar anticipates a post–Harlem Renaissance world.

The background of Johnson's and Dunbar's New York is a world where the cultural hierarchies of which Lawrence Levine writes are hardening into shape, part of a great shift in American economic and social structures. Changes that began in the eighteenth century with industrialization and the creation of modern capitalist states rapidly accelerated in the United States in the decades following the Civil War. By 1900 continuing urbanization, immigration, the spread of literacy, and technological innovation in transportation and communications (initially in printing and publishing, later in electronic media) were changing American life in both the country and the city at an unprecedented rate. The factory system and economic specialization produced sharper class lines and rural-urban divisions; the professionalization of service occupations (e.g., medicine, law, social work, and teaching) promoted a new white-collar middle class that increasingly turned to official accreditation to control its membership and assumed a "regulatory" function between owners and workers in the society at large.[4]

Perhaps because new forms of culture developed along with modern urbanization, the terminologies of cultural difference descended from "highbrow" and "lowbrow"—commonly, "elite" or "high," "folk," "popular," "mass"—reflect not only class distinctions, but also a measure of urban adaptation. "High culture," generally identified with the bourgeois tradition canonized in the eighteenth and nineteenth centuries, is set against a "popular" or "mass" culture, defined as standardized "industrial" production based either on the remnants of rural ("folk") societies transformed by the environment of the city, or on a "debased" imitation of artifacts of high culture. Mass culture—consisting of semianonymous, commercially produced products of information and entertainment—increasingly came to define public, and even private, urban life after the turn of the century, with "mass media" as the link between this culture and what came to be called "mass society."[5]

The complicated relationship between mass culture, Afro-American city life and Afro-American literature is part of a more general set of problems which has preoccupied modern sociological and cultural studies. In brief, these studies have asked what effects mass culture produce in the complex social setting of the metropolis. Does it somehow "represent" the mass of the population and provide them with a social interconnectedness sufficient to maintain a polity, or at least a minimal public life? Or does its pervasive commercialism, the narrow base of its production, and the deliberate blandness of its social vision represent an extreme of cultural alienation?[6] Black artists, especially writers working before the 1960s, were caught in a dilemma because Afro-American culture—in particular, music—was a major source for the products of mass culture, but mainstream white America and cultural critics either denied that connection or denigrated that art. Afro-American influence was everywhere, but nearly always it was invisible. As Amiri Baraka's poem "In the Tradition" says, "Africa people, our fingerprints are everywhere / on you america, our fingerprints are everywhere."[7]

In the view of two groups of cultural critics who became influential in the 1940s, those fingerprints were merely part of the general smudging of mass society. The New Critics, southern and patrician, invoking a conservative social and canonical ideal in the mode of T. S. Eliot, were the primary literary inheritors of the gospel of high culture. Their unlikely allies in a disdain for the cultural products of mass society were a group of radical German exiles, the Frankfurt School. The latter produced, particularly in the writings of Theodor Adorno, the classic statement of the destructive ends of mass culture, maintaining that the general effect of mass society is to debilitate individuals' or groups' capacities to understand and criticize the social conditions in which they live. Adorno, however, tended to lump together all the contemporary products of mechanical reproduction as part of the "mass," and he also undertook a sustained defense of high culture—the bourgeois arts of the nineteenth century, and the avant-garde of the twentieth—claiming that they held a unique potential to inspire a resistance to those myths of class, race, and gender by which social power and the status quo are sustained.[8] In the 1940s and 50s a version of Adorno's cultural hierarchy, largely stripped of its radical elements, was adopted by formerly left-wing New York critics such as Lionel Trilling, Philip Rahv, and Dwight MacDonald; this meant that in the decades after World War II there was among influential critical voices in the United States something like a unanimity about the need to resist the blandishments of the mass or the middlebrow and to endorse the values of a "complex" art, the nineteenth-century European writers, the poetry of T. S. Eliot, and the novels of Henry James.[9]

Afro-American writers working in the 1940s and 50s, such as Ralph Ellison and James Baldwin, were influenced by this critical background. In some ways, as Irving Howe noted at the time, the differences between Richard Wright and these younger men have to do with Ellison's and Baldwin's adaptation to the atmosphere of the cold war years, a period when "complex" art often was understood to mean "nonpolitical" art.[10] But this adaptation didn't mean that Ellison or Baldwin stopped writing about the themes of Afro-American city life or that their writing was strictly nonpolitical. The matter of mass—or perhaps more accurately, popular—culture became a political subtext for them, one in which they differed crucially from Wright; they opposed to the images of white mass culture black popular art and folkways, a city culture of music, food, religion, dress, and language which was largely absent from Bigger's world. They also developed a view of mass culture implicit in Wright, asserting that it is to some extent mediated by those very populations it is meant to control, and that this process may create, in forms such as popular music, or even film and television, a new focus of resistance. Toni Morrison, however, growing up in a period when mass culture had become omnipresent, was again more critical of its destructive infringement on black identity and life; her novel *The Bluest Eye* treats this question in terms very similar to *Native Son*.[11]

The assumption of a distinct black way of life which underlies Ellison's and Baldwin's novels was noted, perhaps without being understood, in the 1950s; Afro-American separateness was not a choice but a condition, though one that had—by necessity and to a degree—long been valorized by black people. If they had escaped, at least par-

tially, the domination of mass culture and the loss of communal traditions, it was due to what Du Bois described as their seeing American
life through a "veil," a vision that filters their experience differently;
thus Du Bois's "double-consciousness" in *The Souls of Black Folk* becomes Alain Locke's "dual citizenship" in *The New Negro*, and this later becomes what Wright and Baldwin call the black person's position
both inside and outside Western civilization. From another point of
view, "escape" becomes "exclusion," of course, but the idea of culture
as *communal* resistance would assume crucial importance in the Civil
Rights movement and the Afro-American movements of empowerment in the 1960s and later.[12]

"Double-consciousness" has been most acute for the Afro-American middle class because of correlations between class identity and
racial identity which have extended down to the present day in the
United States. Black writers almost by definition have been frequently
involved in crossing those lines: to become middle class has meant
adapting to what can fairly be termed a white hegemony, and finding
reasons for doing so. To "cross over" inevitably means to "class off"—
the phrase is Zora Neale Hurston's—and, as we've seen, the gap between above and below troubled Du Bois even as he celebrated the
university as the city on a hill. Du Bois seemed to sense that the
"higher life" might easily become Jonathan Swift's flying island of
Laputa.

This problem was particularly troubling for writers because the
continuous contest between "high" and "low," "in" and "out," represents the process through which canon definition takes place, and
that process is substantially determined by unacknowledged extralit-
erary matters, everything from personal friendship to class, gender, or
racial prejudices.[13] That definition is, literally, a matter of existence or
nonexistence for a writer, and historically it has denied virtually all
black writers. Around 1900 the position of Du Bois, Johnson, Hopkins, and Chesnutt was to explicitly accept the majority culture's
judgment as to the value of the canon.[14] This was perhaps an inevitable realism for them, given their class positions and the racial definitions of the society they lived in, but it meant valorizing a high
culture that was essentially white culture. It meant further that what
they accepted as the "best" was a tradition that had almost universal-
ly excluded them, that denied not only their intellectual equality but
their very humanity. This contradiction is something Morrison re-

turns to consider in *Beloved*, notably in the definition of civilization by which "schoolteacher" justifies his degrading of Sethe.

Alain Locke, building on Du Bois, attempted to get around this same question by upholding high culture but also claiming that some black arts were *almost* on the level of high art, as for example in his essay "The Negro Spirituals," included in *The New Negro*. Because the four post–Harlem Renaissance writers I will discuss chose to write primarily about characters and milieus outside the middle class, high culture as a problem in black identity almost disappeared for them. It was mass culture and the media that were central to their work, even when they were not preoccupied with these matters, because mass culture and the media became a way of measuring both the Afro-American's connection to American society and his or her alienation from it. Largely self-educated, these writers would assume a cultural breadth that asserts intellectual equality, but their fictional subjects would remain firmly attached to Afro-American common life and the historic problems of the milieu Paul Laurence Dunbar first treated in 1902.

Dunbar's *Sport of the Gods* is constructed around a series of opposites and parallels: city-country, north-south, black-white. In the south a black man, Berry Hamilton, is accused of stealing money on the Oakley plantation where his family works. He is jailed and his family forced to migrate north to New York City, though in fact the theft was carried out by the plantation owner's youngest son, Frank, who decamps to Europe. The thread Dunbar draws through all these oppositions, tying them together and eventually resolving the story, is the character of a white newspaper reporter, Skaggs, of the New York *Universe*. It is Skaggs who within the novel represents most exactly the nature of the city.[15]

The contradictory *moral* nature that Skaggs comes to symbolize, Dunbar expresses directly in a long Baudelairean passage describing the city's duality: the forces that push and pull, the emotional responses that range from love to hate, from pleasure to loathing:

> To the provincial coming to New York for the first time, ignorant and unknown, the city presents a notable mingling of the qualities of cheeriness and gloom. If he have any eye at all for the beautiful, he cannot help experiencing a thrill as he crosses the ferry over the river . . . and catches the first sight of the spires and buildings of

New York. If he have the right stuff in him, a something will take possession of him that will grip him again every time he returns to the scene and will make him long and hunger for the place when he is away from it. Later, the lights in the busy streets will bewilder and entice him. He will feel shy and helpless amid the hurrying crowds. A new emotion will take his heart as the people hasten by him,—a feeling of loneliness. . . . After a while he will find a place and give a sigh of relief as he settles away from the city's sights behind his cozey [sic] blinds. It is better here, and the city is cruel and cold and unfeeling. This he will feel, perhaps, for the first half-hour, and then he will be out in it all again. He will be glad to strike elbows with the bustling mob and be happy at their indifference to him, so that he may look at them and study them. After it is all over, after he has passed through the first pangs of strangeness and homesickness, yes, even after he has got beyond the stranger's enthusiasm for the metropolis, the real fever of love for the place will begin to take hold upon him. The subtle, insidious wine of New York will begin to intoxicate him.[16]

Within the passage is Baudelaire's *flâneur*, Georg Simmel's centrifugal world, and Dreiser's "tropism." Dunbar sees the city from multiple points of view, aware that one is drawn to it like an alcoholic to wine ("tropism"), alternately attracted and repelled by the crowd's "indifference," at times delighting in the freedom to "study" the city's swarming masses, at other times repelled by an appalling sense of Durkheim's "anomie."[17]

But those themes hardly exhaust the richness of the passage. Dunbar begins by associating the human aesthetic response with the city: the "eye . . . for the beautiful" is linked to a cityscape, not nature. Dunbar uses the phrase "the right stuff" to suggest a finer manifestation of human potential than the ordinary, and he again links it to the capacity to respond to and absorb the wonders of the city. Yet the phrase is not without its touch of irony: one "hungers" to consume the gaudy as well as the beautiful, for in the modern city the two are intertwined. And although the city's wonders appeal to and can create a finer human being, they are also overwhelming, and lead to confusion, fear, exhaustion, and loneliness.

Dunbar does not describe a black city within a city; rather, like Johnson in *The Autobiography of an Ex-Colored Man*, he talks about areas that are specifically black: "Twenty-seventh Street" (84), where the Hamilton family rents rooms in a boarding house; or the Tenderloin, where the entertainments associated with lowlife (clubs and theaters) are located.[18] One has the sense of an Afro-American community in the process of evolution, where black migrants who arrive in the metropolis find pockets of black people but no localized sense of community. Furthermore, Dunbar defines the Hamiltons' experience partly by contrast not only with the plantation life of their origins but also with the life of an elite society, the Paris to which Frank Oakley has run away.

Frank Oakley has gone to Paris to become an artist, but he is seduced by the city, and by a woman who becomes his mistress and whose expensive tastes he cannot support. The artist's life and the dangerous attractions of Bohemia are a theme from Baudelaire to Maugham, but Dunbar doubles Frank's urban fate with the fate of Joe Hamilton, who is not an "artist" but a victim of the fake glitter of the city's "theater," the view of New York's never-ending parade he can see from the window of his family's flat.[19] As Joe's final degradation in the city comes in his murder of Hattie Sterling, so Frank's is the cowardly theft of his brother's money, an act that in its many ramifications is also a kind of murder. Dunbar emphasizes the parallel by juxtaposing the two chapters on the men and the erotic dimensions of their downfall: each has a *femme fatale*. Joe disappears into prison, and Frank evidently vanishes into the Paris underworld: their ends are parallel, but not equal—Joe is in effect enslaved, while Frank remains at large.

The Hamiltons in New York try to define their own reactions to the city, "its advantages and disadvantages, its beauty and its ugliness, its morality and immorality" (96), but the city is not a neutral condition to be observed and understood; it imposes its standards and values through an urban culture that is already economically established and professionally produced. The Hamiltons' urban guide, Mr. Thomas, takes them to a "coon show" almost as soon as they are settled, and their reactions show the power of the city to alter traditional viewpoints. The coon show is a black musical, part of the entertainment circuit, including both vaudeville and "legitimate" theater, that grew up in the second half of the nineteenth century; by the time of Dunbar's novel it was an established popular urban art form and a kind of proto–mass culture, and Dunbar himself, as well as James Weldon Johnson, wrote both skits and songs for that stage.[20]

An essential part of this musical was the stereotype of the "coon," a rural southern Afro-American racially characterized by association with "chickens, razors and watermelons."[21] The racial stereotype was blended into a mix of song, dance, and comedy which both evoked and parodied the plantation tradition. The dichotomy of country and city was a constant theme of the coon show (e.g., the title of a vaudeville act such as *Back to Hicksville*), taking account of the human attachment to the past and at the same time reminding its audience that the past was gone. (Sometimes, however, the coon show focused on a distinctly urban setting, as in *A Trip to Coontown* [1898] and *The Sons of Ham* [1900].)[22] The method of the show was standard satire—caricature and exaggeration—but the element of technically produced spectacle and the degree of generalization, packaging the past for mass consumption, made the show modern. The coon show made the past more attractive by sentimentalizing it, while the packaging process called attention to the falsity of the spectacle:

> At first she [Ma Hamilton] was surprised at the enthusiasm over just such dancing as she could see any day from the loafers on the street corners down home, and then, like a good, sensible, humble woman, she came round to the idea that it was she who had always been wrong in putting too low a value on really worthy things. So she laughed and applauded *with the rest*, all the while trying to quiet something that was tugging at her away down in her heart. (105–6, my italics)

Ma Hamilton has at least three separate responses in this passage: disdain, then shame at her imagined ignorance, and finally, the "tugging," the evoking of "home" despite (or even because of) the coon show's artifice. Her response is critically innocent in comparison with that of the audience around her, yet that audience too is "innocent," in that it too is being drawn into the performance, sometimes—like Mrs. Hamilton—against its own will. In any event, Dunbar is also aware of how a more sophisticated person, such as Mrs. Hamilton's daughter Kitty, can be attracted by mass culture, suspending her judgment of the singing-dancing figures because she is beguiled by the metamorphosis wrought upon reality by the theater.

The other city institutions in *The Sport of the Gods* are similarly ambiguous phenomena. The Banner Club is filled with men like Sadness and Joe Hamilton, whom the circean city turns to swine, but it also welcomes Skaggs, a sleazy reporter, whose eye is so refined by the urban milieu that he can see in Joe's drunken story the possibility of a sensational scoop. When Skaggs travels south and enters the Continental Hotel to catch his rural flies with some sugary lies, Dunbar comments that his folly can't be separated from his "genius": "He had as yet formulated no plan of immediate action and with a fool's or a genius' belief in his destiny he sat down to await the turn of events" (220). It is the urban trickster who successfully controls his own "destiny," relying on his ability to discover a causal sequence within the confusion of an incomplete, apparently random tableau; more importantly, it is the newspaperman, that agent of the media, who brings about the plot's denouement.

Skaggs's ambiguous character is related to the ambiguous nature of the city. Dunbar calls him a "monumental liar," yet he brings the truth to light. So too, the city's artifice is both fiction as fiction and fiction as another level of truth. When Skaggs argues to his editor that the innocence of the elder Hamilton is "as clear as day," the editor responds, "Yes, it looks plausible, but so does all fiction" (219). Skaggs's story looks "plausible" *only* as fiction at first, but like any good artist he manipulates this "fiction" for his own ends and to illustrate the truth. In Skaggs's case those ends are both sordid and noble, as is the city that supports him.

Skaggs never loses the mixed character given to him by that city. (His name is deliberately ugly-sounding, echoing "Wragg is in custody" in Matthew Arnold's comment on the hideousness of Anglo-Saxon names and the callousness of English newspapers.) He belongs to a literary tradition that links the urban detective and the newspaper reporter. Dostoevsky saw that newspapers made some sense of the entangled web of the modern city and urged a correspondent to read them "in order that the visible connection of all matters, public and private, may become constantly stronger and clearer." Similarly, Balzac perceived Paris as a patchwork of disconnected colors and fragments, whose actual "clandestine" connections only the shrewdest observer could make out.[23] It is not by accident that the figure of the urban detective, Monsieur Dupin in Poe's "The Murders in the Rue Morgue" or Detective Bucket in Dickens's *Bleak House*, emerged in the nineteenth century, for the modern city came to be treated as a labyrinth (Balzac also compared it to James Fenimore

Cooper's wilderness) and the detective a kind of modern Theseus. His is the eye that can see an invisible city, though one closer to Marx than to Augustine.

Skaggs today would be called an "investigative reporter," combining functions of detective and reporter; and in his role Dunbar marks the difference between public information in the village and in the city. An individual can pass along information in a small community, and this village storyteller may depend upon a shared morality as well as something more intangible for the authenticity of his voice: an intimate familiarity, or a sense of "knowledge" of circumstances made possible by the size and interrelationships of a local community. Whether or not this "knowledge" is true, it is at least based on immediate experience. However, the crowd in the anonymous city, part of a large, indefinite community, cannot have "experience" of many actions outside its own locale, nor can "word of mouth" reports be very effective with large numbers and long distances. So the newspaper, the "news," becomes the source of urban "experience," or at least of the kind of experience likely to inspire some communal judgment. In this situation the news reporter necessarily becomes an ambiguous figure, because in mediating between anonymity and morality he assumes a power easily corrupted, either for his personal ends or for the commercial requirements of his employers.[24] Writing in 1900, Dunbar was close to the controversy over the role of the Hearst newspapers in fomenting the Spanish-American War, and to the new phrase "yellow journalism," which described a media moved by megalomania and greed.[25] The city explains Skaggs's character, for as Irving Howe has noted, quoting Balzac on the subject of urban paradox, "the city . . . 'is corrupt *because* it is eminently civilized.'"[26] This contradiction intrigued Balzac in such novels as *Père Goriot* and *Lost Illusions*: the city was amoral—to survive or rise in it, one adopted a pragmatic ethic that destroyed moral sensibility—and yet it glittered with romance and human possibility. (Robert Park, as we will see, put ideas similar to this in sociological terms.) We perceive this paradox in *Sister Carrie*: the protagonist both falls and rises, losing a moral center yet experiencing human transcendence. And it is not a simple matter of rising to fame or achieving happiness; the unhappy Carrie is a more fully aware human being at the novel's end than she ever would have been had she remained in Wisconsin. In an observation based on this same urban paradox, Walter Benjamin notes that the urban detective's intellectual clarity is grounded in a low opinion of human nature, for he knows that "'in a thickly populated area . . . an individual is, so to speak, unknown to all others and thus does not have to blush in front of anyone.'"[27] It goes without saying that this moral anonymity is shared by the detective himself.

The self's reaction to the city is replicated by a communal change that is both loss and gain. In the nineteenth century, the modern city alters how the collective human animal behaves, and what was once the moral voice of the community is replaced by the indifference of the crowd. Instead of acting as a voice of disapproval or approval, the crowd is emotional and fickle. Sometimes it protects the criminal and sometimes it turns him over to the police, but the element of morality hardly enters into its decisions.[28] This means that oppressive traditional relationships can be escaped, but it doesn't mean that new, equally arbitrary oppressions won't be established: the city's media finally free Berry Hamilton, but the city's freedom destroys his son. Dunbar notes that although "the *Universe* was yellow . . . it managed to do a considerable amount of good, and its yellowness became forgivable, even commendable" (237). Its drive to expose the truth can't be separated from its desire to sell copies of its early edition, and when Dunbar seems ready to make this separation, as when he praises the *Universe* for freeing Berry Hamilton, he suddenly reminds us of the other side of the newspaper's character. Freed from prison, Hamilton is told by Skaggs that he must come to New York, but he is not told the reason: "Now that the *Universe* had done its work, it demanded the right to crow to its heart's satisfaction" (243–44). The newspaper's odd mixture of virtue and publicity is a reflection of the city's new mass culture: primarily commercial, and essentially amoral even though it invokes a traditional morality.

Dunbar makes it clear that country and city are not the same; in every case, his plot hinges upon a new human context, the city, and this context affects even the pastoral world of the Oakleys. Skaggs is a key character in the novel because the mass media are a key element in modern life: Skaggs is important *because* he is a reporter for the New York *Universe*. Dunbar sets the mixed blessings of mass culture (the newspaper) against the evils of the plantation tradition, and chooses the former. Wright, Baldwin, and Ellison will make it clear that their black protagonists are shaped in part by the mass culture Dunbar first depicts, but their evaluation of it will be much more critical; Toni Morrison's depiction of the nineteenth-century newspaper's relationship to black life in *Beloved* will be the harshest of all. The recognition of the city's moral ambiguity would become an ongoing black tradition—LeRoi Jones's observation to Ron Lowinsohn in 1959 could serve as an epigraph to Dunbar's novel: "N.Y. City (to those of us hooked on it) is jewel stuck up elephant's ass. Love jewel, no elephant dukey . . . but it is, like they say, inextricable."[29] This is close to Dunbar's description of the newcomer's reaction to New York in 1902, though put more pungently. Moreover, Dunbar's novel represents a black urban literary tradition that is an alternative to Du Bois and James Weldon Johnson. When he describes the migrants to the city "breaking like waves against a rock" (213), he puts the city within the context of human cost, one that will shape later fiction such as William Attaway's *Blood on the Forge* (1941), Ann Petry's *The Street* (1946), and Willard Motley's *Knock on Any Door* (1947).

The difference between the urban world of Dunbar's novel and the urban world in the writings of Du Bois, Johnson, or Hopkins is one of contrasting visions of black culture and community. In Du Bois, especially, there is an elite, Arnoldian conception of Culture, one that underlies the connection between city and civilization, as well as the obligation of those above (the privileged, educated few, or "Talented Tenth") to help those lower down.[30] Although Hopkins and Johnson qualify that viewpoint, they still accept its general substance. Dunbar's city, however, is based on the prototypes of "mass culture" and/or "popular culture," a world where desire and aspiration originate in the glitter of the music hall or the promiscuous exchange of the anonymous streets.

There is another important division in Afro-American views of the city which will be continually reappearing, and which is a primary version of the utopia-dystopia conflict. It is especially prominent in the break between the Afro-American city novels of the 1920s and those after Richard Wright, and it has a sociological source in a crucial difference of emphasis between Robert Park and his student Louis Wirth.[31] Both Park and Wirth saw the city as an ecological organism, growing and changing shape like an amoeba; and both used the expression "a mosaic of little worlds" to define its often confusing terrain. Park's famous essay of 1915, "The City: Suggestions for the Investigation of Human Behavior in the City Environment," characterizes urban life in terms somewhat reminiscent of Dunbar's novel:

> Not only transportation and communication, but the segregation of the urban population tends to facilitate the *mobility* of the individual man. The processes of segregation establish moral distances which make the city a mosaic of little worlds which touch but do not interpenetrate. This makes it possible for individuals to pass quickly and easily from one moral *milieu* to another and encourages the fascinating but dangerous experiment of living at the same time in several different contiguous, perhaps, but widely separated worlds. All this tends to give to city life a superficial and adventitious character; it tends to complicate social relationships and to produce new and divergent individual types. It introduces, at the same time, an element of chance and adventure, which adds to the stimulus of city life and gives it for young and fresh nerves a peculiar attractiveness. The lure of great cities is perhaps a consequence of stimulations which act directly upon reflexes. As a type of human behavior it may be explained, like the attraction of the flame for the moth, as a sort of tropism.[32]

Like Simmel, whom he had studied with care, Park lists the pros and cons of city life, noting how the modern city destroys the cohesiveness of the small community but allows individuals to develop their full potentialities, especially rewarding the exceptional person, either genius or criminal. Park is aware that the city creates pockets of communal identity, but he emphasizes individuals' "mobility" rather than their "segregation." Aware of the self-destructive potential of urban life, Jacques Loeb's "tropism" applied to the social organism of the city—a theme that would fascinate Dreiser in *An American Tragedy* (1925)[33]—Park still suggests that the fundamental impulses drawing certain people to the city are not "primitive" atavistic impulses, but the desire of a species to evolve and become more complex (urbane). Park repeats a point made by Simmel in "The Web of Group Affiliations"; the intricate network of human relationships in the city allows the human personality to expand and develop in ways that would not be possible in a rural context, because it allows the person communication with groups and persons for which there would be no room or tolerance in a small town or village: "In a small community it is the normal man, the man without eccentricity or genius,

who seems most likely to succeed. The small community often toler-
ates eccentricity. The city, on the contrary, rewards it."[34]

It is not difficult to see how Park's ideas about city life are relevant
to the optimism expressed in Alain Locke's *New Negro*.[35] Harlem is
both village, with its storytellers, and cosmopolitan city, connected,
as it is, to the intellectual stimulus of New York. This, of course, is the
theme of James Weldon Johnson's essay "The Making of Harlem," in
the March 1925 issue of the *Survey Graphic*, which Park would quote
in his revised version of "Human Behavior in a City Environment."
In *The City* (1925), Park discusses "nascent neighborhoods and neighborhoods in process of dissolution," quoting Johnson to show that
Harlem belonged to the former, not the latter: it "is rapidly becoming
a very intimate and highly organized community."[36] Yet it would be
the cosmopolitan aspect of Park's thought which would intrigue the
writers of the Harlem Renaissance. What would be "eccentricity" in
the village (read: being black in the racist south) might flourish in the
city. And who would want to be a country eccentric if by moving to
the city he or she could become a "genius"? The "revolt from the village" theme in American literature, including the manifestations in
the Afro-American literature of the 1920s, is partially indebted to
Park's insight, especially as his ideas were well known to black intellectuals such as Charles S. Johnson and E. Franklin Frazier, both of
whom had been his students. This does not mean, however, that the
idea was always accepted uncritically.[37] It could be celebrated in Walter White's *Flight* (1926) but treated ironically in Jessie Fauset's *Plum
Bun* (1929) or in Wallace Thurman's *Infants of the Spring* (1932), where
the character representing Alain Locke is named "Dr. Parkes."

The passage from country to city could be repeated within the city
itself, in the individual's opportunity to traverse spatial boundaries,
"to *pass* [my italics] quickly and easily from one moral *milieu* to another," as Park says. Black writers such as Walter White, Nella Larsen,
and Jessie Fauset probably saw that Park's theme of crossing ("passing") boundary lines within the city could also be applied to a racial
theme: "passing" for white in the city might mean going not only
"from one moral *milieu* to another" but also from one existential condition to another.[38] In 1928, Park published another essay ("Human
Migration and Marginal Man") in which he utilized Simmel's idea of
the "stranger" as someone who occupies a space between two
worlds.[39] Some people who come to the city, Park argued, remain

"marginal men," caught between the world of custom and community they leave behind (the village or the ghetto of another city—or indeed, of the same city) and the modern, chaotic city to which they never quite adjust. Not surprisingly, Park saw the Jewish intellectual and the mulatto as obvious examples of this kind of modern urban nomad. His point was that this "stranger" lived permanently in a state of transition in the big city, as though the act of migration that had brought him or her there remained his existential condition.

Park saw that this condition was both a blessing and a curse. On the one hand, the "marginal man" is "cosmopolitan," enjoys the "freedom of the cities," and hence has a kind of protean power, changing shape as often as the city changes its shape, a theme that Walter White had illustrated in his heroic city mulatta Mimi Daquin (in *Flight*). On the other hand, the "marginal man" has "secularized" his life and spends much of his or her time drifting between or within cities, like Helga Crane in Nella Larsen's *Quicksand* (1928), or Angela Murray in *Plum Bun*.[40] Yet if Park thought that "mobility" could be a measure of the city's excitement and a possible source of personal freedom, his student Louis Wirth was much less optimistic. For Wirth, urban mobility was more illusory than real, and to the extent that it was real it became a primary cause of social angst. The difference between *The New Negro* and Richard Wright's *Native Son* is encapsulated in Wirth's departures from the Park thesis.

Wirth, who was a close friend of Richard Wright,[41] is famous for his statement in "Urbanism as a Way of Life" (1938) that "size, density, and heterogeneity" are the terms that define the modern city, and that this mix of elements creates "the forms of social action and organization that typically emerge" and give the city its distinctive flavor. What is notable, however, is that whereas Park puts an emphasis on the individual's potential to traverse spatial regions, to in fact live in diverse worlds, Wirth focuses upon the city as made up of molecules in conflict.

> Diverse population elements inhabiting a compact settlement thus become segregated from one another in the degree in which their requirements and modes of life are incompatible and in the measure in which they are antagonistic. Similarly, persons of homogeneous status and needs unwittingly drift into, consciously select, or are forced by circumstances into the same area. The different

parts of the city acquire specialized functions, and the city conse-
quently comes to resemble a mosaic of social worlds in which the
transition from one to the other is abrupt.[42]

Wirth's last sentence describes Bigger's trip to the Dalton house in
Native Son: "the mosaic of social worlds" in the city now encompasses
so much difference that in his ten-block passage to this wealthy white
neighborhood, Bigger feels he has walked off the face of the earth
onto another planet. His pilgrimage also illustrates Wirth's comment
(made in another context) that "whereas in an earlier society it was
unusual to meet a stranger, under the conditions of life in great cities
it is an equal rarity to meet someone who is familiar."[43] In Wright's
novel this "strangeness" applies to Bigger's "friends" as well—Gus,
Jack, G. H., and Bessie. They hardly represent more of a community
for Bigger than does the Dalton family. It is on this point that Baldwin, and later, Morrison, will divide themselves from Wright's view of
Afro-American urban life.

It is Wirth's city, however, with its emphasis on isolation, lack of
mobility, and nightmarish unfamiliarity, that strikes us as modern.
For Park in 1915 the city has not yet become a metaphor (as it has for
Wirth in the decade of the Depression) of hidden forces that manipulate human consciousness; Park still thinks of the newspaper in terms
of a substitute for the village storyteller, whereas Wirth will identify it
with the corporate powers that control the city.

The Harlem Renaissance writers recognized the problem that
would be exemplified in Wirth's differences with Park: the city is "an-
tagonistic" to black people, and since they are an easily identifiable
group, they are easily marginalized by racist social practices. "Passing" had a very different significance for Afro-Americans—as for
James Weldon Johnson's ex-colored man—than it had in Park's thesis
about urban contexts. And "passing for white" was a double-edged
problem, as Johnson understood. One edge defined the Afro-American's relationship to the white culture, the other his relation to his
own. After the success and controversy of *The New Negro* (1925) and
Van Vechten's *Nigger Heaven* (1926), much Harlem Renaissance writing turned its attention away from racist conditions at large, and toward black society and the divisions *within* it on the basis of color

lines, gender, and especially class and cultural splits. The renaissance had initially hoped to reconcile and fuse light and dark, high and low, at least within Harlem; but as Countee Cullen's brilliant novel *One Way to Heaven* (1932) illustrated, this was a doomed project. And while virtually all of the important writers of the renaissance were educated members of the black middle class,[44] many of the major postrenaissance writers—Wright and Baldwin, for example—were from the black underclass and would write at length about the pain and difficulty of crossing over that class line.

Locke's program in *The New Negro* was pragmatic in that it was shaped by the racist atmosphere of the times and by a need to satisfy both the old intelligentsia and a new generation of writers who admired the masses and thrived on the rhythms of modernity. What *The New Negro* illustrates is not how consistent or prescient Locke was but rather how tenuous was the fusion between elite and mass, high and low.[45] In his various introductions to the sections of his anthology of Negro art and writing, he defined an aesthetic platform that mediated between artist and audience, masses and intellectuals, folklore and high art, Dionysius and Apollo. The modern city was to be the home in which a harmonious, symbiotic relationship would exist between this mix of opposites; the new Harlem was to restore the "common consciousness" lost in the diaspora.[46] It was to be a "province" (in a Roycean sense) but not provincial; its inhabitants were to be Harlemites but also New Yorkers (cosmopolitan); and its artists would sing from within their race rather than singing about it from the distance of an elite class.

Locke's anthology is the summation of an Afro-American effort to try to understand the new phenomenon of the city: the changes that it wrought in human behavior, in class relationships within the race, and in the institutions within black life. Locke made use not only of the sociological critiques of Robert Park but also of the visionary prophecies of Randolph Bourne and Lewis Mumford. He tried to reconcile the contradictory elements within the race, and also to fuse elements of urban theory from both black and white writers. But although he recognized that the masses had a voice—that, indeed, the free air of the city would encourage its expression—Locke never quite believed that oral or performance art could be as "articulate" as legitimate poets in print. Blues or jazz could never measure up to

"Florentine ease and urbanity," an ideal that indicated a model for the invisible city that Locke preferred.[47] This was the invisible city defined by a past literary tradition; it was a locus in which he placed himself, and from which he could praise Rudolph Fisher's individual talent as being reminiscent of both Uncle Remus and "the art of Maupassant."[48] Locke never shied away from the vitalism of the common people—indeed, he took every opportunity he could to recognize and praise it—but the ultimate expression of this energy needed to be transformed, as Langston Hughes transformed blues lyrics into blues poetry. Locke never relinquished his view that true art was "high art." He would become angry when people accused him of holding this view, and yet, finally, this was what he meant. His utopian Harlem would be centered around a secular cultural equivalent of the medieval cathedral, a "temple of art";[49] and the most important characteristics of this culture would be its "Florentine . . . urbanity" and humane cosmopolitanism.[50]

Indeed, when putting together *The New Negro* for publication in book form, Locke made major changes in its earlier version, which had appeared as the March 1925 issue of the *Survey Graphic*. Those changes shifted the book's main focus from the situation of the common people in Harlem to the elite cultural institutions within black life. In the original magazine anthology, Locke had included an article on the Negro church; this he replaced in *The New Negro* with his own essay "The Legacy of the Ancestral Arts." In his deleted *Survey Graphic* article, George Haynes had observed that "the Negro church is at once the most resourceful and the most characteristic organized force in the life of the Negroes of the Northern cities as it was in the Southern communities from which they come."[51] Looking at some of the other *Survey Graphic* articles Locke left out of *The New Negro*, it is not hard to understand why a church-centered black community remained important in Harlem. Winthrop Lane's "Ambushed in the City" (subtitled "The Grim Side of Harlem") documented the many ways in which the masses are "gouged" in the city, from high rents to "bad whiskey" to poor health care ("In 1921 . . . mortality among Negroes was 67 per cent higher [than that of whites] in the cities" [714]). And Kelly Miller noted in "The Harvest of Race Prejudice" that "the most gigantic instance of racial segregation in the United States is seen in Harlem" (683). But it was a black woman, Eunice Roberta Hunton, who pinpointed the historical significance of this segregation: "Harlem," she said in "Breaking Through," is "a modern ghetto. True, that is a contradiction in terms, but prejudice has ringed this group around with invisible lines and bars" (684). Hunton in her essay tries to find a positive side to the situation (e.g., "Education is the way out of the ghetto") but in the last paragraph she prefigures the bleakness of Richard Wright: "It takes rare courage to fight a fight that more often than not ends in death, poverty or prostitution of genius" (684). Her statement concerning "invisible lines" took on an added poignancy when her article, as well as Winold Reiss's "Four Portraits of Negro Women" (685–88) was omitted from *The New Negro*.

The invisible city of the masses, the invisible city of black women—these were things that Locke wanted to keep invisible, or at least obscured, in *The New Negro*. In "The Legacy of the Ancestral Arts," not only was art to symbolize the new cathedral in the city, but that art would be "classical" and masculine. What black American artists could learn from their ancestral past was that African art illustrated the universal values always associated with high art: discipline, style, technique, and restraint. Locke wanted to open the canon to include African art, but he did not want the door opened too widely. He wanted a world that was both protected and accessible—protected from the barbarians at the gate (the "uncultured"), but accessible to the New Negroes of New York. One reason he declined to republish some of the articles from the *Survey Graphic* is that over and over the words "bound" and "boundaries" appeared in them, emphasizing how excluded much of Afro-American life was from the general culture of the city.[52]

Locke replaced Kelly Miller's unflattering portrait of Harlem as an impoverished ghetto with Miller's flattering portrait of Howard University, the black intellectual center in the nation's capital. Miller's attitude in the *Survey Graphic* article had been patrician—the segregated Harlem community, cut off "from the general life of greater New York," has few inner resources—yet he had at least attempted to deal with the reality of the black masses directly. Miller's new article, "Howard: The National Negro University," was now one of a trilogy focusing on the significance of the black middle class; the other two parts of the trilogy were Robert R. Moton's "Hampton-Tuskegee: Missioners of the Masses"; and E. Franklin Frazier's "Durham: Capital of the Black Middle Class." This cast an odd light on Locke's opening pronouncement that the "rank and file" led the way to Harlem, but

Locke covered the apparent contradiction by remarking that the common people were not "articulate as yet."[53] Although the intellectuals
had followed the masses to the city, they were "articulate" (as a book
like *The New Negro* showed) and hence had the responsibility—or in
Moton's sense, a mission—to describe what the new black urban experience meant.[54]

It is J. A. Rogers's essay on jazz and blues music, "Jazz at Home,"
included in both the *Survey Graphic* and *The New Negro*, that best reflects the ambivalence toward popular culture felt by many black intellectuals in the 1920s. Certainly, if proof were needed that the masses *were* "articulate," if only through their artists, this essay would be
the place to provide it. And indeed Rogers seems to proceed in that
direction, praising blues and jazz as authentic expressions of black life
and arguing that their infectious energy has rejuvenated the music of
American civilization. The rub comes when he has to deal with the
"vulgarities and crudities" of the lowly origins of that music. The
home of jazz is the "mob-level" of the juke joint and the cabaret, and
so, Rogers implies, "jazz has a great future" only if it can be "subli-
mated." Fortunately, Paul Whiteman and Vincent Lopez are beginning to realize the "finer possibilities of jazz music." In *The New
Negro*, the folk and their culture are always recognized as valuable,
and then passed over for something that will be "developed" in the
future, something beyond the art forms of the common people.[55]

Locke's *New Negro* represented an attempt to define a culture, the
new Afro-American urban culture, in terms of institutions, and Locke
focused on the university and the "temple of art" as this community's
substitute cathedrals. The idea of a cathedral—that is, the idea that
the new black city should have a center—is not limited to black
American literature of the 1920s. When, for instance, Jean Toomer
predicted in "Blue Meridian"—a poem begun in 1921–22 but published in 1936—that Americans would become a "cathedral people,"
he was paying homage to all those intellectuals—Van Wyck Brooks,
Randolph Bourne, Waldo Frank, Sherwood Anderson, Paul Rosenfeld,
Hart Crane, Lewis Mumford, and William Carlos Williams—who had
tried to find a "New World" equivalent for Chartres.[56] If Royce's
Beloved Community was to be realized, they believed it must crystal-
lize around some social institution both visible and invisible. None of
these men wanted high culture by itself, for they were all rebelling in

some way against the "genteel tradition." And while they didn't wish to return to the Middle Ages, each lamented the loss of a center in modern life which the cathedral symbolized for the medieval city. Frank's "anonymous group culture whose soul still stands expressed in the Gothic cathedral"; Bourne's "democratic Gothic civilization of the Middle Ages"; Rosenfeld's folk artist who "sings" as does "every upspringing, aspiring stone of Chartres"—these voices all found an echo in *The New Negro*.[57] They tried to recenter the city in terms of the "curveship" of the Brooklyn Bridge (Crane); the "altar" of Alfred Stieglitz's salons known as, "291" and later "An American Place" (Frank, Rosenfeld); the "usable past" of a New England town (Mumford); or the invisible city of the Aztecs, Tenochtitlan (Williams).

The writers who imagined these substitute cathedrals all recognized the new facts of the American city, and knew that it was the home of the masses—immigrants from southern and eastern Europe, the dispossessed from the countryside. Yet unlike Henry James and T. S. Eliot, elegists for the passing of a homogeneous and elite city culture, they embraced the possibility of the common people building a new, pluralist culture from the ground up. And unlike Henry Adams, they did not see the cathedral as the symbol of a closed, hierarchical society, one that was at odds with the modern world. Their vision of Chartres could be expressed by the ending of Sherwood Anderson's *A Storyteller's Story* (1924), in which the cathedral is viewed in terms of the nameless craftsmen who built it and the promise that this work holds for an American storyteller.[58] This secular re-centering of the City of God is often found in the writers of the Harlem Renaissance and is an indication of the common intellectual background of Afro-Americans and home-grown American modernists in that decade, and of their reciprocal influences. Indeed, so ubiquitous was this re-centering that Wallace Thurman could have fun with it in *Infants of the Spring* (1932), satirizing the idea of a substitute cathedral through the spatial construct of "Niggeratti Manor."

Yet however they attempted to transform or reimagine the meaning of Chartres, whatever new institution or context they replaced it with, something of elite culture, still privileged, lingered about the allusion. As with Theodor Adorno's critique of jazz, one has primarily a sense of inescapable assumptions and unconscious, or at best semi-conscious, prejudices. These ambiguous attitudes carried over even to Langston Hughes, who was not only a lover of the city but also a lover of the city's funk. That love is nowhere better illustrated than in *Fine Clothes to the Jew* (1927), Hughes's second volume of poems, which Arnold Rampersad has claimed did for black poetry what Walt Whitman's *Leaves of Grass* did for white: liberated it from the curse of Literature by legitimizing the vernacular.[59] However, Hughes's vernacular was never to be his only voice, and in the 1920s he spoke for both high culture and Bohemian intransigence. In his famous 1926 *Nation* article "The Negro and the Racial Mountain," the mountain in the way of the black artist is ostensibly the black middle class, bogged down in its gentility and economic ambition. But Hughes alludes also to the vision of the old Testament prophet Ezekiel, who saw the restored Jerusalem from a mountain, and the last lines of the essay echo Ezekiel's vision of the rebuilt temple: "We build our temples for tomorrow, strong as we know how, and we stand on top of the mountain, free within ourselves."[60] The implication is that although the temple of art has been desecrated by the philistines, young artists will rebuild that temple from within themselves; despite Hughes's democratic intentions, his position finally sounds like a variation of "art for art's sake." Appropriately, in 1925 Hughes considered writing an autobiography with the title "Scarlet Flowers," which has a distinctly fin-de-siècle flavor.[61]

Hughes was already predicting that his real audience would be the black masses, but he continued to use the image of the cathedral, or temple, to express an idea of art. In 1946, in his *Chicago Defender* column, he tells the out-of-town visitor that New York has "a lot of culture to store away in his mind's eye," and one example is "the Cloisters, the least visited yet the most beautiful of New York's many museums":

> As its name implies the Cloisters is built in a series of cloisters, courtyards, and outdoor gardens. And it shelters some of the finest medieval art in the world—ancient French tapestries, wooden virgins, and massive carved doorways from the churches of the Middle Ages. The view of the Hudson River and the Palisades from the high gardens of the Cloisters is one of America's loveliest sights.[62]

Hughes, of course, could subvert these images of high culture in his own poetry and stories (the medieval cathedral would become the "Pennsylvania Station"; the "outdoor gardens," Simple's street corner; the "courtyards," the blues palace in *Not without Laughter* [1930]); yet he also had a New Yorker's pride in the treasured icons of Western civilization, and it was a pride he would maintain throughout his tenure as a journalist with the *Chicago Defender* (1942–66).

As I have suggested elsewhere, in the 1920s Hughes and other black writers of the Harlem Renaissance knew that they were writing for a middle-class audience, black and white, even if the black middle class was embarrassed by the candor of Hughes's poetry and the whites did not truly understand it (those who thought they did still reshaped his views into a simplified form, that of the exotic Negro).[63] Later Hughes would unabashedly write for the masses in the *Chicago Defender*, and Wright and Baldwin would aim confidently at a sophisticated audience that was not just American but international. However, this did not mean that the questions of different classes of literature or of separate black and white cultures disappeared. The Depression of the 1930s introduced, especially through Wright, a class-conscious analysis of art which put the relation between "high" and "low" into a new perspective: the possibility of fusing them or even of linking the two, which black critics of Locke's generation had already been mocking, was no longer seen to be straight-forward or innocent. Paul Whiteman became the exemplar of an appropriation in which cultural elements such as jazz music or vernacular language at the popular level were incorporated into the products of a rapidly developing mass culture.

While the new media culture that began to flourish in the 1920s would dissolve some of the differences between high and low, it did little to break down racial barriers between blacks and whites. American society remained essentially segregated, by law or by custom, by force or by benign neglect; and the growing awareness of how absolute this separation was eventually changed the use of the cathedral/temple figure by Afro-American writers.[64] In 1945 Richard Wright invoked the image again: "Will the Negro, in the language of André Malraux, find a meaning in his humiliation, make his slums and his sweat-shops his modern cathedrals out of which will be born a new consciousness that can guide him toward freedom?"[65] Here a "new consciousness" means not a secular substitute for Chartres, but a completely different orientation to the idea of the Cathedral. For Du Bois and James Weldon Johnson, the image of the cathedral is of a functional institution serving to "uplift" the common life, and it is understood that Western civilization's Culture is the goal of uplift.

But the implication of Wright's "modern cathedrals" is that they will be part of a new democratic culture, one set in the common life.

In James Baldwin's 1953 essay "Stranger in the Village," this revision goes a step further: he sees the civilization of the cathedral as a symbol not of cultural wholeness but of cultural exclusion. Baldwin realizes he is speaking at the end of a long tradition in which Chartres is used as a symbol: of the Age of Faith (Lowell, Adams, Eliot), and of institutional coherence in the city (Bourne, Mumford, Frank). His observations illustrate not only the gap between him and this tradition but also the gap between the writers of the Harlem Renaissance and the postrenaissance writers. "The most illiterate" person in the Swiss village he is visiting, says Baldwin, "is *related* [my italics], in a way that I am not, to Dante, Shakespeare, Michelangelo, Aeschylus, Da Vinci, Rembrandt, and Racine; the cathedral at Chartres says something to them which it cannot say to me, as indeed would New York's Empire State Building, should anyone here ever see it."[66] Contrast this to Du Bois's Atlanta University, where Du Bois is at "home" with Shakespeare and Homer, or to Locke's Florentine allusions, and a generational chasm opens up. Note too that Baldwin rejects the idea of a secular cathedral—the Empire State Building. It is just as foreign, just as alien, an object as Chartres. Let us not indulge in facile illusions, Baldwin implies: slavery and its aftermath created a division between black and white that cannot be bridged by imaginative constructs such as Locke's idealized Harlem, which ignore the constrained reality of black life in America—the reality, as Wright put it in *Black Boy*, that Negroes "lived somehow in" Western civilization but did not partake "of it."[67] This view will be underscored by Toni Morrison in her essay "City Limits, Village Values." She opens with epigraphs from both Henry Adams (*Mont-Saint-Michel and Chartres*) and "The Stranger in the Village," noting how the "ideal" of Chartres for Adams becomes a black hole for Baldwin:

> Baldwin could not ruminate elegantly and with subjective pride in the achievement of Chartres as Henry Adams could—not because of any want of intellect or skill, but because the intimacy between writer and the historical artifact that Adams felt did not exist in the same way for Baldwin, and neither did the impetus to relish whatever was fine in those achievements.[68]

In her essay Morrison will reject both the Swiss village and Chartres, arguing that Chartres does not exist for the modern black writer. All that does exist for certain is his or her black village within the white city.

Yet it should be noted that Baldwin does not say he is *incapable* of reading Chartres. What he says is that it is a different text for him than the one read by the inhabitants of the Swiss village. The villagers

> are struck by the power of the spires, the glory of the windows . . . I am terrified by the slippery bottomless well to be found in the crypt, down which heretics were hurled to death, and by the obscene, inescapable gargoyles jutting out of the stone and seeming to say that God and the devil can never be divorced. I doubt that the villagers think of the devil when they face a cathedral because they have never identified with the devil. But I must accept the status which myth, if nothing else, gives me in the West before I can hope to change the myth.[69]

In Chartres Baldwin the outsider sees the "obscene" side of Western civilization and, by implication, of American culture. He is insisting upon an identification with the "devil" as a first step in the achievement of definition, both of himself and of the black community. The significance of this reading of Chartres is connected to his brilliant book of film criticism, appropriately called *The Devil Finds Work* (1976), in which he deliberately misreads those cultural artifacts that belong to the world of mass culture.

After the 1930s, as I've noted, black intellectuals became more conscious of the effects of mass culture on black city dwellers. For one thing, by the 1930s Hollywood film—that modern image of an earthly city based on material consumption—had become ubiquitous, a presence in black life that could not be ignored. There is nothing in 1920s black writing like Richard Wright's *Lawd Today!* (1936; published posthumously, 1963), a novel that documents how thoroughly the popular press, the radio, and the cinema—they seem indistinguishable in their effects on the human psyche—manipulate Jake Jackson's responses to the world. It should not be surprising that this was Baldwin's favorite Wright novel, or that Ellison steals a passage from it, or that some of Morrison's characters are Jake Jackson's descendants.[70] For Wright, Baldwin, Ellison, and Morrison, a crucial issue will be whether the products of "mass culture" can be read in new ways that can help build the invisible city or whether the diabolic magic of these products will overwhelm black sensibilities, as the promise of transcendence bestowed upon cosmetics destroys Hagar in Toni Morrison's *Song of Solomon* (1977).[71]

All four of the black writers I look at in the following chapters are grounded in the literature of Western civilization and literary modernism. Morrison wrote her master's dissertation on Virginia Woolf and William Faulkner; Wright, Baldwin, and Ellison grew up on Henry James, Hemingway, Eliot, Faulkner, Pound, Stein, Malraux, and others. Note as well that all four are also steeped in the "popular culture" of their race—the language and music of the black streets. So, too, each knows that the Depression pulled the plug on a "renaissance" based upon an independent, self-sufficient polis. Not only did the Depression deflate the balloon of "Florentine . . . urbanity"—how could there be such "urbanity" if there were no Florence—but it also gave birth to Wright's bleak assessment of black life. Cut off from their homeland and excluded from the "full spirit of western civilization," black people lived in a kind of Dantean netherworld where the positive qualities of community—"those intangible sentiments that bind man to man"—did not exist.[72]

Each of the later writers attempts to come to terms with Wright's postrenaissance judgment; it bears the same relationship to black modernism as Eliot's *Waste Land* does to white modernism. Each writer asks the question, what fragments are left to shore against what ruins?—and each arrives at a different answer. They come to either reject Chartres or modify its meaning, and they try to come to terms with the products of mass culture, a culture that most black writers of the past had generally avoided, ignored, or dismissed with contempt.[73] They recognize how insidiously those cultural products shape black lives, from Bigger's fascination with movies to Pecola's desire for a pair of blue eyes like those on a Shirley Temple doll; but they are not content to stop there, to simply lament the pernicious effect that mass culture has on the Afro-American community. All four see that in the modern world the fragments to be shored against the ruins of black life come in all forms and shapes and can be reassembled into new wholes, new "imagined communities." Even the packaged products of mass culture can be repackaged, robbed of their sting (or given a new sting) by being made over in the minds of those who use them, as Toni Cade Bambara's Hazel (*Gorilla, My Love* [1972]) restores Hollywood's racist "gorilla" to an image of pastoral innocence.

As Wright saw, Hollywood films, like the newspapers, magazines, and television commercials in a capitalist society, promote the earthly city in terms of consumer consumption; they create a desire for the "things" that drive the machine. Yet because wealth in this society is not distributed evenly, and because those lowest down have not the means to purchase the "things" invested by the media with power, the only means left by which people might deal with these projections of fantasy is the power of language. If language fails, one is left with only anger and frustration; but if the linguistic imagination is active, one is capable of reinvesting the image with new power, changing Macon Dead's fetishistic Packard (*Song of Solomon*) into a hearse. As Kenneth Burke suggests, language as a form of symbolic action may restructure reality: the negative applied to the Packard robs the commodity of its power.[74]

Thus any aspect of print culture, even the most vulgar, can be a means by which the imagined community is reimagined. At another level, print culture can manifest itself in the nation's "sacred papers," which Ellison points to in *Shadow and Act*; the shadow that falls between historical reality and America's lofty ideals creates not only "an unease of spirit" within the American scene but also an interstice within which the invisible city can be said to exist.[75] In other words, because of the existence of those "sacred papers" we begin to imagine a world elsewhere. The Depression and its harsh economic realities would bring down the utopian view of Harlem that Locke had expressed in *The New Negro*, but once the dust had cleared, the outline of the invisible city would be traced again. It would be traced again, because versions of it had been there all along, marked like palimpsests in the pre–Harlem Renaissance literature.

Or, for that matter, in the literature of the Harlem Renaissance itself. Jean Toomer's story "Theater," from the middle section of *Cane* (1923), opens with an evocation of an invisible world within Washington, D.C.:

> Life of nigger alleys, of pool rooms and restaurants and near-beer saloons soaks into the walls of Howard Theater and sets them

throbbing jazz songs. Black skinned, they dance and shout above the tick and trill of white-walled buildings. At night, they open doors to people who come in to stamp their feet and shout. At night, road-shows volley songs into the mass-heart of black people. Songs soak the walls and seep out to the nigger life of alleys and near-beer saloons, of the Poodle Dog and Black Bear cabarets.[76]

The exchange of "life"—of songs, dance, and language—between the street and the "road shows" has its vortex at the Howard Theater, where the black energy of *outside* seeps into the walls, saturating them as influence; at the same time, mass culture—in the form of the "road-shows" that visit the Howard—works its influence from *inside* to outside, its songs then becoming the songs of the pool halls, streets, and cabarets. And there is a further processing of mass culture within the theater, one that eventually finds its way even into white society. After the "jazz songs" from the street "soak" the "walls" of the Howard Theater, its manager shapes these "songs" and those who dance to their rhythms into "movements, appropriate to Broadway" (52). Commercial culture takes what it needs from street culture, homogenizes it, smoothes its rough edges, and packages it in terms of a military drill: "Its three counts to the right, three counts to the left and then you shimmy—" (54).

Toomer shows different forms of Afro-American art in the city, their complex interrelationships, and the black artist's ambiguous relationship to all three in the meeting between the "writer" John and the culture of the burlesque, an exchange constantly qualified by John's abstraction and sense of superiority, his class difference. The song-soaked walls of the theater represent the energy of the city's black culture, expressed directly in the ecstasy of Dorris's dancing, an art that both attracts John and frightens him. John's and Dorris's judgments of each other are class *and* race judgments reflecting a confusion of desires, sensual and romantic and material. John converts Dorris into a fantasy ("Dorris dances . . . John dreams" [55]) and imagines that her art infuses his, imagines reading to her his writing about her dancing. "Theater" not only sees how all kinds of art mix in the city, and how the different kinds cater to class tastes, it also poses the problem of the black writer's relationship to those tastes.

The complex questions asked by *Cane* were to find their way into postrenaissance literature. But more importantly, the image of the invisible city reflected in the reciprocal relationship between street and theater would also suggest possibilities for that city's continued redefinition. After the Harlem Renaissance the concept of the invisible city would become plural in ways that most writers of the Harlem Renaissance could not have imagined.

CHAPTER THREE

The City without Maps
in Richard Wright's *Native Son*

Ah! but in some low and obscure nook,—some narrow closet
on the ground floor, shut, locked and bolted, and the key flung
away,—or beneath the marble pavement, in a stagnant water-
puddle, with the richest pattern of mosaic-work above,—may
lie a corpse, and still decaying, and diffusing its death-scent all
through the palace! The inhabitant will not be conscious of it,
for it has long been his daily breath!
      —Nathaniel Hawthorne, *The House of the Seven Gables*

We have in the oppression of the Negro a shadow athwart our
national life dense and heavy enough to satisfy even the
gloomy broodings of a Hawthorne.
            —Richard Wright, "How Bigger Was Born"

Me and the Devil was walking side by side.
            —Robert Johnson, "Me and the Devil Blues"

The movement of black people from the south to the cities of the
north, which had been a series of small waves since 1900, became a
flood with the entrance of the United States into World War I. The
war meant jobs because of a shortage of workers in northern industry,
and thus there was reason and opportunity for blacks to move. The
Chicago Defender, which for all its criticism of conditions for blacks in
the south had never advocated immigration, changed its editorial
policy in 1916: the new word was "Come on up."[1] "From 1916 to
1919," James Grossman states, "between fifty and seventy thousand
black southerners relocated in Chicago," and thousands more would
continue to arrive year by year in the decade of the 1920s, most following a route along the Mississippi River via Memphis and St. Louis
which blues singers would describe in countless songs and eventually

make symbolic of all the transient conditions of modern life.[2] One unexpected result of this migration is that now in Florence, Italy, there can be heard groups of young German (or English or Swedish) musicians painfully pronouncing a list of railroad lines, highway numbers, juke joints, women and long-abandoned plantations along that route. This is a "Florentine urbanity" in reverse, one only partially glimpsed by Alain Locke and by most of the black intellectuals of the 1920s. Not only were blacks going to be changed by the city and its new mass culture, they were going to contribute hugely to the making of that culture.

When Alain Locke's *New Negro*—the manifesto of the Harlem Renaissance—was published in 1925, Richard Wright was a young man halfway to Chicago. His migration, from Mississippi via Memphis, fit the archetypal pattern exactly, and in fact it was Wright rather than any contributor to Locke's book who would be the "New Negro." The Great Depression would be the breaking point, the obdurate historical fact set between Wright and the writers of the Harlem Renaissance. Not only did Wright differ from these writers in background and situation, but the Depression meant that he would come to live in a city where the desperate conditions for blacks could no longer be ignored. These conditions, the invisible city of economic relations made all too visible, would demand new explanations and a new sociology, and Wright's Marxism would in turn lead him to depict the urban life of blacks from the underside. *Native Son* was a novel from which there was no going back; Wright made it impossible for anyone to make an important statement on black urban life without considering the racist social setting of the city. In this sense, Irving Howe is absolutely right: "The day *Native Son* appeared, American culture was changed forever."[3]

There is another divide between Wright and the Harlem Renaissance which perhaps because of his social focus is less evident: for literary models Wright looked to a generation of writers who were only tangentially influential upon most renaissance authors. In 1937 Wright published in a magazine called *New Challenge* an essay that amounted to a small *ars poetica* for his work:

> . . . for the life of the Negro people is not simple. The presentation of their lives should be simple, yes; but all the complexity, the strangeness, the magic wonder of life that plays like a bright sheen

over the most sordid existence, should be there. To borrow a phrase from the Russians, it should have a *complex simplicity.* Eliot, Stein, Joyce, Proust, Hemingway, and Anderson; Gorky, Barbusse, Nexo, and Jack London no less than the folklore of the Negro himself should form the heritage of the Negro writer.[4]

"Blueprint for Negro Writing" is an effort to theorize about the necessary political dimension of black literature, but the authors Wright invokes include Gertrude Stein, T. S. Eliot, Marcel Proust, James Joyce—the pantheon of the great modernists. In Wright's view, there is no contradiction between social themes and modernist technique for the black writer: "Every iota of gain in human thought and sensibility should be ready grist for his mill." Even political works require a "remaking": "The relationship between reality and the artistic image is not always direct and simple. The imaginative conception of a historical period will not be a carbon copy of reality."[5] Wright is usually placed in the tradition of literary naturalism or "realism," yet his "realism" is a quite different matter from that of a Walter White or even a Jessie Fauset, and his "naturalism" often expresses a "divided stream" of the facts and the fantastical.[6]

In actuality, *Native Son*'s documentary realism is almost always spilling over into myth.[7] In "How Bigger Was Born," Wright describes Chicago in terms of two kinds of myth, one related to the history of the city and one that emerges from an archetype:

> Then there was the fabulous city in which Bigger lived, an indescribable city, huge, roaring, dirty, noisy, raw, stark, brutal; a city of extremes: torrid summers, and sub-zero winters, white people and black people, the English Language and strange tongues, foreign born and native born, scabby poverty and gaudy luxury, high idealism and hard cynicism! A city so young that, in thinking of its short history, one's mind, as it travels backward in time, is stopped abruptly by the barren stretches of wind-swept prairie! But a city old enough to have caught within the homes of its long straight streets the symbols and images of man's age-old destiny, of truths as old as the mountains and seas, of dramas as abiding as the soul of man itself![8]

The city is "fabulous" and "indescribable" and mythic like the heavenly city—as well as being a specific, historical city with extraordinary extremes of weather, an odd mixture of peoples, "high idealism and hard cynicism," and an indomitable will to succeed in a place where no sane person would believe a city could be founded, much less flourish. In this passage, Wright surely has in mind Carl Sandburg, Chicago's epic bard: "out of prairie-brown grass crossed with a streamer of wigwam smoke— / out of a smoke pillar, a blue promise— out of wild ducks woven in greens and purples— / Here I saw a city rise and say to the people round the world: Listen, I am strong, I know what I want."[9] However, one key theme in *Native Son* is that the city, despite its strong will (or perhaps because of it), does *not* know what it wants. That confusion of intention or motive that Wright describes is part of the mythic dimension of the modern city, the city as Pandemonium or as Babel; it is, as with Dunbar's immigrants, the vision of the city seen by the outsider, which of course is what Bigger is. Bigger's vision is not his alone, however; it stands as well for the social fragmentation that is the general condition of modern urban civilization.

One fact in Chicago's history directly linked the city to the mythic; not only was this "fabulous" city young even by American standards, but it had been rebuilt since the great fire of 1872. It is no wonder that Wright was fascinated by *Crime and Punishment*,[10] for Petersburg was a city like Chicago, created de novo from the egg of the intellect.[11] Just as Peter the Great's platonic conception of the city emerged from the marshes in Western dress, so too Chicago sprang into being after the great fire on the shores of Lake Michigan. Much of this city was abstracted from the heads of architects and city planners, having little to do with the living reality of people like Bigger. Living in a rootless city, Bigger, like Dostoevsky's Raskolnikov, is a rootless man attracted to whatever electrical currents pass through the city's streets. For Wright, the city was also "fabulous" in the manner in which Dreiser had depicted it in *An American Tragedy*. According to Ellen Moers, Dreiser had complained in 1921 of the "dead end at which American realism had arrived." He saw the urban landscape as the means by which the "power of the imagination" might be revived, for the modern city in American life was something out of the Arabian Nights: "If there are all the chain cigar stores, chain drug stores, haberdasheries, movie theatres, and big hotels in Manhattan, here are also Hell, Heaven and Purgatory of the soul, which Dante would have found. . . . He would have gone beyond mere realistic description and shown us the half-monstrous proportions of our city like a giant sphinx with wings."[12]

Although it is true that *Native Son* is a "proletarian novel," the only time that we see Bigger actually working is in the context of a fairy-tale situation: he has a twenty-five-dollar-per-week job (during the Depression), with a room of his own in a rich man's house, and his only duty (besides tending the furnace) is to chauffeur the princess of the castle around the town. Here is the "fabulous" city that seduced Clyde Griffiths, one whose magnetic poles (positive and negative) Wright also felt when he came to Chicago: "There is an open and raw beauty about that city that seems either to kill or endow one with the spirit of life. I felt those extremes of possibility, death and hope, while I lived half hungry and afraid in a city to which I had fled with the dumb yearning to write, to tell my story."[13] Bigger also feels those extremes, death and hope, and in *Native Son* Wright will connect Bigger's possible fates to the two faces of the "fabulous" city he lives in, the demonic city that belongs to State's Attorney Buckley, and the paradisal city of community that his lawyer Boris Max offers Bigger at the novel's end.

Wright's attitude toward Chicago suggests that what is "real" about this "unreal city" (as he called it in *American Hunger*, thinking no doubt of *The Waste Land*) cannot always be pinned down. Indeed, his first impression of the actual city was that its "houses . . . were sinking slowly into the dank prairie."[14] The implications of this insight are important for *Native Son*. If the material city seemed fantastic, then Max's vision of a city of democratic community at the novel's end cannot be dismissed as Marxist doctrine or utopian fantasy. It is as "real" as the City of the Big Shoulders, the city of might. For as Wright said in *American Hunger*, the idea of community was a human need, made even more acute if one were "a Negro in America": "The problem of human unity was more important than bread, more important than physical living itself; for I felt that without a common bond uniting men, without a continuous current of shared thought and feeling circulating through the social system, like blood coursing through the human body, there could be no living worthy of being human."[15] The outlines of Max's utopian city trace, though faintly, the shapes of the city of *caritas* (Paul and Augustine), the city of civilization (Cicero), and the city of light and openness (Book of Revelation). The allusions to community are a reality beneath layers of chaotic impression; but myth and metaphor, as Kenneth Burke observed in a book that Wright owned (*Permanence and Change* [1935]),[16] move us with as much force as do empirical facts, because they give life a sense of purpose.[17] To Wright, Chicago's "straight streets" are empirical facts that lead us in the direction of myth and metaphor, even as the order of an urban pattern is deceptive because it doesn't reveal the disorder of urban life. As Wright says of Bigger, "Sometimes, in his room or on the sidewalk, the world seemed to him a strange labyrinth even when the streets were straight and the walls were square."[18] What Bigger doesn't know, but Wright does, is that Chicago's grid, laid out in accordance with the Land Ordinance of 1785, is not neutral but contains within its apparent rationality a secret record of money, power, and racial prejudice. As Mario Gandelsonas has shown, an invisible wall separates "north Chicago from south Chicago, white Chicago from black Chicago. This wall [is] implied from the fact that the monumental north-south axes seem to come to an abrupt end at the point where the streets change their name from north to south, marking a significant shift in the social geography of the city."[19] Even though Bigger finds his way around some of Chicago's walls, others equally invisible will effectively exclude him.

Bigger's sense of the city as labyrinth is as much an existential perception as a spatial one: a vision of the immigrant lost in the welter of conflicting cultural messages, straight streets leading nowhere, square walls that dissolve into a collage of bright social images, billboards whose real texts remain hidden. The question becomes, urgently, how to perceive coherence or find a way through the labyrinth. Or, from another viewpoint—Wright's—is there some coherence being imposed whose form is an apparent disorder? Wright's friend the Chicago sociologist Louis Wirth, who elaborated on the theories of his teacher Robert Park, attempted to answer that latter question in 1938. Because the modern city is made up of heterogeneous, segmented worlds, each with its own spatial and moral regions, "the masses of men in the city," said Wirth, remain isolated from each other and hence "are subject to manipulation by symbols and stereotypes managed by individuals working from afar or operating *invisibly* behind the scenes through their control of the instruments of communication" (my italics).[20] Those in control of the city's "instrumentalities" are masters of illusion: through newspapers and movies, they forge a myth that the city is still a homogeneous whole, still a village of shared values. It is a myth that disguises their own power, their attempt to reduce urban complexity to a manageable "normality," yet it is a myth that is attractive because it so closely imitates an invisible archetype of community—the heavenly city in the Book of Revelation, for example—that men and women desperately want to believe in.

The manipulators of the media pretend to a sense of community and a cohesive moral order that in fact has no basis in urban experience, especially in the experience of urban blacks who, like Bigger, recognize that the myth of a moral order is a mask for social control. But although mass media become the means by which moral order is contrived, control through their agency is always problematic, for there is something intrinsically subversive about these media. In particular, the appeal newspapers and movies make to a democracy of desire challenges the illusion of moral order and exposes the segmented, class-ridden city. As H. L. Mencken observed of Hollywood morality in an *American Mercury* book review: "The astounding thing is not that there are so many young criminals; but that there are so few. The public school, with its witless goose-stepping, is a natural hatchery of them. The newspapers and movies help, not so much by teaching that crime pays, as by teaching that virtue doesn't. The rich, it appears, do not have to obey the laws."[21] Since Wright was reading "the *American Mercury* from mid-1926 on,"[22] he might have recalled this observation as he imagined Bigger's response to *The Gay Woman*, a film Bigger sees shortly before he goes to work at Mr. Dalton's house.[23] For the moral lesson that Bigger remembers from the movie, despite its moralistic ending, is that "the rich . . . do not have to obey the laws." The Hays Code of Film Production (1934) demands that the gay woman return to her deceived husband and that her immorality be displaced onto a convenient scapegoat, a Communist bomb-thrower, but the movie's most potent meaning is the meaning Bigger takes away from it: Hollywood's heavenly city is a city of capitalist consumption. The word *gay* in the movie's title refers to the desire for pleasure that the movie instills in its audience; its visual luxury is the real message: "Then came *The Gay Woman* in which, amid scenes of cocktail drinking, dancing, golfing, swimming, and spinning roulette wheels, a rich white woman kept clandestine appointments with her lover while her husband was busy in the offices of a vast paper mill" (26). Bigger receives a message intended for a white, middle-class viewer rather than for him, for although the geographical boundary lines of the city are firmly fixed, movies and newspapers cross those lines, and their messages are registered and reworked in the minds of those who represent an invisible audience and who recreate an invisible city of desire.[24]

This moral ambiguity within the city's media points to the moral ambiguity of the city itself, which from the nineteenth century on has been the scene of America's great integration, the "melting pot" where various immigrant groups were more or less Americanized. In this century the means of integration has increasingly been a mass culture that, through the instruments of the media, has produced the popularizing, leveling, and homogenizing to make people of very different cultural backgrounds alike. But Wright's *Native Son* is in one sense a story of the failure of integration (though that failure is paradoxically a kind of salvation), and it is a failure phrased in terms of city space, city maps, horizons and perspectives, and views from windows. By extension, those views could even be said to include scenes framed by the motion picture screen or the advertising billboard. In the most general terms, this means simply that the city Bigger sees and moves through is a *different* city than the one Wright's white characters perceive.

The urban geographer Kevin Lynch has coined the phrase "cognitive map" to describe an individual's unique but limited view of his or her environment, a view importantly determined by social divisions of class, gender, race, or age. The perception of a city is "an active transaction between person and place," said Lynch, noting that "self-identity" seems to be "reinforced by a strong identity" with place.[25] In *Native Son*, Bigger boasts that he knows "the South Side from A to Z," (126), but the historical and cultural intention of the city's monuments escapes him. Thus, cognitive maps cover not only districts, streets, or houses but also other, less tangible, cultural formations. In *Native Son*, perception becomes an index of one's relationship to the city, and although Chicago's monuments are part of a "featureless environment" (Lynch's phrase) as far as Bigger is concerned, he perceives the city's media in ways that would shock its ruling class.

In "How Bigger Was Born," Wright said that "Chicago's physical

aspect—noisy, crowded, filled with a sense of power and fulfillment—
did so much more to dazzle the mind with a taunting sense of possible achievement that the segregation it did impose brought forth
from Bigger a reaction more obstreperous than in the South." Yet Bigger's mind is dazzled primarily by the media, for, Wright added, "the
environment supplies the instrumentalities through which the organism expresses itself," and Bigger's urban world is circumscribed by the
"instrumentalities" he is allowed to perceive: "It was when he read
the newspapers or magazines, went to the movies, or walked along
the streets with crowds, that he felt what he wanted: to merge himself with others and be a part of this world, to lose himself in it so he
could find himself, to be allowed a chance to live like others, even
though he was black."[26] His city's "instrumentalities" are not Du
Bois's university, or even Wright's Memphis library. He may share a
desire for community, but his desire is mediated by movies, magazines, and newspapers rather than by the library and the university.

However, because of his race Bigger is an outsider even from the
ersatz village of the media; and pushed by the desires the media create, he is left to try to find his way in a jungle of illusion. Throughout, the invisible city in the form of a labyrinth confines Bigger in a
world of darkness and misapprehension. In "Fear," book 1 of the novel, the antithetical "rhythms" of Bigger's personality—fluctuating, as
it does, between violence and nonviolence, silence and anger,
"brooding and intense desire"—emanate from a "far-away invisible
force": "He was like a strange plant blooming in the day and wilting
at night" (24–25). Later, outside Ernie's Kitchen Shack, Bigger backs
away from Mary Dalton "as though she were contaminated with an
invisible contagion" (62). In book 2, entitled "Flight," after the murder, he feels the he has "shed an invisible burden" (97), that he is no
longer "enclosed in the stifling embrace of an invisible force" (127).
Or as Wright's narrator says of Bigger, *after* he has killed Mary: "For
the first time in his life he moved *consciously* between two sharply defined poles: he was moving away from the threatening penalty of
death, from the death-like times that brought him that tightness and
hotness in his chest; and he was moving toward that sense of fullness
he had so often but inadequately felt in magazines and movies" (127;
my italics). The irony of this passage is that although the murder
frees him from the labyrinth of his powerlessness and places him in

that media world he associates with power and success, he is now even more helpless, because a fugitive.

One visual image that is intended for black Chicago, and that world alone, is the movie-screen-sized face of State's Attorney Buckley on the billboard outside Bigger's apartment building. Indeed, Buckley's piercing eyes are cinematic, seeming to follow the viewer until they disappear "like a movie blackout" (11). Underneath Buckley's face is the inscription "IF YOU BREAK THE LAW, YOU CAN'T WIN!" (11), but Bigger intuitively understands this poster in light of his reading of the movies. The poster argues not for a universal code of moral behavior but for one directed at black people alone; it is, as Bigger recognizes, an instrument of power—a perception revealed in Bigger's cynical, "You let whoever pays *you* off win!" Buckley *could* be an honest official—Bigger has no way of knowing that he is corrupt—but Bigger's perception of Buckley depends on the same observation Mencken made: what Bigger has learned from the movies is that only the poor have to obey the laws. And who wants to be poor? Instead of rejecting Buckley out of hand as morally reprehensible because he belongs to a corrupt world, Bigger identifies with him. He wants what Buckley has—money, power, and pleasure, the city of material consumption that hides behind the billboard or glitters beneath the Hays-code text of *The Gay Woman*.

Against the city as labyrinth or as desire is set Max's city of a utopian future, one that has both a Marxist and an American foundation. Throughout *Native Son*, Wright flirts with the possibility that the ideals of the Republic will become incarnated within the city, that they will forge the connecting link between city and civilization. Like Ellison, Wright believed that the nation's sacred documents do not go unnoticed even by its lowliest citizen, and "that every man and woman should have the opportunity to realize himself, to seek his own individual fate and goals, his own peculiar and untranslatable destiny. I don't say that Bigger knew this in terms in which I'm speaking of it; I don't say that any such thought entered his head. His emotional and intellectual life was never that articulate. But he knew it emotionally, intuitively".[27]

Yet it is precisely here that Wright differs from Ellison, who would complain that Wright never gave Bigger the imagination that he, Wright, possessed.[28] That is, in fact, Wright's point: Bigger, unlike Ellison's invisible man, cannot tell his own tale, because the city is never made real to him in the full extent of its mythic possibilities. Unlike Ellison's protagonist, Bigger cannot articulate his conception of American ideals in any other terms *but* those of the movies, magazines, and newspapers. Ironically, in the novel's conclusion Wright will enclose Bigger's story within the frame of Hollywood's cinema, but will rewrite that story's ending to fit a life that is more authentic—more truly "pious," to use Kenneth Burke's term—than those lived on the silver screen.

George Steiner has observed that the setting of the Gothic novel in the nineteenth century changed from the country mansion house to the "encroaching vastness of the city."[29] At the end of "How Bigger Was Born," Richard Wright links *Native Son* to the Gothic tradition in American literature because of the ongoing "oppression of the Negro": "If Poe were alive, he would not have to invent horror; horror would invent him."[30] What Wright does in *Native Son,* as Poe did in "The Man of the Crowd," is use the city as the setting for a contemporary horror story in which both the city and the city's creation, Bigger, are labyrinths that do not permit themselves to be read.[31] And in this sense, Wright is writing not only a Gothic novel, but also a detective story in which the ultimate crime remains unsolved.

At first, Bigger can read his own surroundings only in terms of somebody else's moral map: "Thou shalt not." This restriction is lifted when he kills. When, before the murder, he walks the ten blocks to the Dalton house, he is lost in a strange new world, trapped in a displaced country mansion whose separate rooms replicate a social power-structure he cannot comprehend. By the act of murder, imposing the negative upon others, he begins his long journey toward self-definition, a journey partly measured by his reordering of social space.

Wright employs a technique from "The Man of the Crowd"—the description of views from a window—to represent various attempts by characters in the novel to see the city as a whole. Yet seeing the world through a frame always yields an unreliable image, one that makes a direct appeal to experience, to *seeing*, but discounts the way in which the frame itself restricts the view. Ultimately all attempts to see a single pattern to the city fail, but not all fail in the same way or to the same degree. Indeed, Wright forces us to judge his characters in terms of what pattern they see in the city's mosaic. Thus Kevin

Lynch's "cognitive map" is connected to what Kenneth Burke calls the different levels of power in the novel and their "interrelationships,"[32] for power reflects class and race, and class and race determine what one sees in (and of) the city. For Wright, there is no purely "aesthetic" view; each "cognitive map" is a reflection of a political stance and a social placement in the urban world.

In an early scene in "Fear," Jan and Mary are in a car with Bigger on the Outer Drive, and the two white lovers, full of themselves and the beauty of the evening, look at the city's skyline through the car's windows:

> "Isn't it glorious tonight?" she asked.
>
> "God, yes!" Jan said.
>
> Bigger listened to the tone of their voices, to their strange accents, to the exuberant phrases that flowed so freely from their lips.
>
> "That sky!"
>
> "And that water!"
>
> "It's so beautiful it makes you ache just to look at it," said Mary.
>
> "This is a beautiful world, Bigger," Jan said, turning to him. "Look at that skyline!"
>
> Bigger looked without turning his head; he just rolled his eyes. Stretching to one side of him was a vast sweep of tall buildings flecked with tiny squares of yellow light.
>
> "We'll own all that some day, Bigger," Jan said with a wave of his hand. "After the revolution it'll be ours. But we'll have to fight for it. What a world to win, Bigger! And when that day comes, things'll be different. There'll be no white and no black; there'll be no rich and no poor."
>
> Bigger said nothing. (59)

Bigger says nothing because he doesn't see what they see; he can find his way to the Outer Drive, to Adams Street, then to Lake Street in the Loop, but he has no "cognitive map" of that world. If, as Lewis Mumford has said, architecture is "legible script,"[33] then Bigger is confronted with a sign system that he cannot read, for he has been excluded from the "symbols and images" of Jan and Mary's civilization (353), as Wright continually reminds us. To Bigger, the skyline is simply made up of "tall buildings," but to Jan and Mary the buildings are symbols within an urban text, symbols that are immediately recognized. Not only are these "buildings" particularized but only some of them are "tall" or even buildings. Jan and Mary would see the Wrigley Building and the Tribune Tower and possibly the Buckingham Fountain, the aquarium, the planetarium, and Soldier's Field. And hidden from view would be the Chicago Art Institute, the Chicago Public Library, and the home of the Chicago Symphony Orchestra. For Jan and Mary, these are all monuments to high culture—even the sports venue of Soldier's Field, with its classical architecture—and they would all be part of Chicago's skyline.[34]

The lovers see the city's skyline as beautiful because they have inherited an urban aesthetic tradition that has taught them to see the city as static and pictorial.[35] And buried in the image of Chicago's skyline is the legendary history of Chicago itself: the Columbian Exposition of 1893 and its famous White City, and Daniel Burnham's 1897 plans to remake Chicago into "Paris by the Lake."[36] Architecture was to have an important place in Chicago's cultural ambitions at the turn of the century, and one building built in the 1920s deserves particular mention: the Tribune Tower. In 1922, the *Chicago Tribune* ran a competition among architects for the design of the Tribune Tower, and even solicited suggestions from its readers; yet the competition was more or less determined beforehand, because what the *Chicago Tribune* preferred as a model was the medieval cathedral—even though one artist's rendering of the tower depicted it as a huge Doric column. Whether the motif was to be Gothic or classical, the calculated effect was to be the same: the Tribune Tower (1925) would express the values of Western civilization and guarantee their "guardianship" by the media.[37] In Wright's novel, the *Chicago Tribune* will give its demonizing account of Bigger's capture and trial, and that, too, may be a reflection of some of those values.

This, of course, points to the underlying irony of Jan and Mary's enthusiastic raptures over Chicago's skyline. Jan may be a Communist, and Mary a Communist sympathizer, but they are still full members of Western civilization. Products of an elite middle-class culture, Jan and Mary perceive the skyline in terms of the "picturesque," perhaps the most bourgeois of all visual perspectives because it implies an immense satisfaction with the status quo. What this aesthetic perspective ignores, of course, is that the skyscrapers represent the power of Dalton's economic system, and their obverse is the slum where Bigger lives. Replacing the skyscrapers' owners with new owners is a neat rhetorical slight of hand, a revolutionary trompe-l'oeil, as it were, but it does not touch the reality of Bigger's poverty or his myopia. In this context, Bigger is like John Locke's imaginary child who cannot see the skyline because he grows up in a house with no doors and no windows; but Jan and Mary are blind as well—outside the frame of the panoramic view of Chicago's skyline is the enclosed space of Bigger and his family's "kitchenette."

The limits to Mary's map of the city become apparent when Jan turns off the Outer Drive and into Bigger's neighborhood. Looking through the car window at "tall, dark apartment buildings looming to either side" of the car, Mary innocently comments to Bigger, "I've long wanted to go into those houses . . . and just *see* how your people live" (60). Although plainly meant to be sympathetic, her remark triggers an internal rage in him, making him wish he could "stand in naked space above the speeding car and with one final blow blot it out" (60). What Bigger responds to is the same pictorial perspective that allowed Mary to see the skyline in a certain way, although, in this context, the pictorialist becomes a voyeur. Because Bigger knows the misery of his own world so intimately, he perceives the obscene element in Mary's wish. Bigger's inarticulate rage represents a felt knowledge of existence that Mary is not privy to, hence his rejection of the kind of sympathy Mary has to offer: she only wants to *see*.

So extreme is Bigger's reaction that he remembers Mary's precise words on four separate occasions in the novel, and Wright seems to link his killing of her to those words. His anger represents a long history of enforced separateness which Mary's "innocent" remarks cannot begin to broach. On this history, Sam Warner, Jr., notes that in the nineteenth century the word *slum* began to be used to express the growing spatial divisions within the modern city. As poor people became more and more segregated, and hence isolated from what was seen to be the only authentic way of life (that is, middle-class life), the word *slum* took on a metaphoric and exotic character. A "slum" was like a foreign country that could be visited, as by tourists; it was also a place set apart, having no connection to "normal" life: "No one went slumming when the poor lived on the alley behind her or his house." Moreover, the word *slum* tended to hide the possibility that there might be an economic cause for such a place: "Slums were just there, facts of life, found objects." As such, slums "assumed a special role in contemporary ideological structure . . . [and] performed what Roland Barthes called the task of 'denomination.' The new symbol, by separating the slums from the conditions of urban employment, told us that the slums were a part of English and American cities, like smoke, or bricks, or saloons. By denomination, an historical event, something of a specific time and place, was transformed into a general fact of life."[38]

Wright anticipates Warner's remarks when he refers to Bigger's world as "this *prescribed* corner of the city" (97; my italics). The word *prescribed* suggests a fact of life so permanent that it was ordained *before* it was written down, thus justifying that "corner's" inclusion within the official, written map of the city. It is no wonder, then, that Bigger looks at the white people who prescribe him to *his* "corner of the city" not as human but as "a sort of great natural force" (97). The word *prescribed* also suggests that "space has absolute properties. . . . that structures, people and land parcels exist in a manner that is mutually exclusive each of the other in a three-dimensional, physical (Euclidean) space."[39] What enrages Bigger is the contrast he perceives between his fixed place in three-dimensional, physical space, and the fluid space of the cinema (or of an airplane), in which he can imaginatively move at will. And what he will end up doing is rearranging the space of the Daltons' house, making their space his own. Not only does he usurp the space of Mary's room by killing her, but after her death he transforms the basement—his space in the social spectrum—into the symbolic center of the house.

When Bigger first comes to the Daltons' neighborhood, its space is like that of a foreign land, "a cold and distant world; a world of white secrets carefully guarded" (37). He is bewildered, hesitating at the front door, wondering if he should use the rear entrance, which he cannot find. When he is ushered into the living room by Peggy, the Daltons' cook, he is again made anxious by the cold elegance of the house, which has nothing of the opulence he has come to expect of the rich of the movies: "He had not thought that this world would be so utterly different from his own that it would intimidate him" (39). His experience of this alien space continues to disorient him until he ends up accidentally trapped in the house's most forbidden enclosure, the daughter's room, and he kills her. After Mary's death, the spatial focus within the house completely changes. Before, movement and activity are concentrated in the living room and kitchen: ordinary domestic space. After the death, the house begins to revolve around the furnace, the sun of Bigger's new system. Peggy, Britten (a detective), the Daltons, and the reporters are all drawn like satellites to a new planet, and the social hierarchy of the house's space is reversed; now the invisible basement where the black servant works becomes its center. Bigger has drawn himself a new map of the house, and it is at last a map he can read.

The slum is only an image in Mary's mind, one that provokes a sympathetic tear or an anthropological interest (both motivations are behind Mary's desire to "just *see* how your people live"). Yet ironically, in wishing to close the gap between the segmented worlds that make the city difficult to comprehend as a whole, Mary also feels both Bigger's frustrated response to living in "a strange labyrinth" and his desire to "understand it" (204). In this desire to find a map to the whole city, rich and poor almost meet. Wright, however, never lets us forget that Mary's activism is that of a dilettante. Although she is different from her father, who shuts his eyes to the real nature of the economic arrangements of the city, she has none of the understanding of Max, who recognizes that Bigger's alienation from society cannot be overcome by gestures of goodwill alone.

Wright also emphasizes that Bigger's struggle to make sense of the city is linked to an existential question—"Who am I?"—while Mary's curiosity is that of the tourist who will never have to concern herself with a final destination, never have to give an answer to an overwhelming question. From Bigger's perspective, she is a careless meddler: what she wants to *see* is an obscenity that should remain hidden; what she wants to expose is a raw wound that she has no way of healing. For Bigger, blotting out the car means returning the world to blank space, to a primal emptiness, where all "prescribed" conditions disappear.

Like his daughter, Mr. Dalton also treats the slums he creates as a "general fact of life." He hides his relationship to Bigger's neighborhood by devoting himself to philanthropy and owning a car that is not a Rolls Royce or a Cadillac but only a dark-blue Buick sedan. Dalton's reluctance to consume conspicuously is not a moral choice, however, but a moral obfuscation: he pretends, even to himself, that his millions are neutral millions. The house is a symbol of power used to hide power, and in this sense it belongs to the world of the movies Bigger watches, the "democratic" medium that celebrates wealth and power at the same time that it claims to censure them.

Mr. Dalton also hides behind a legal fiction. Even as holder of "the controlling stock" of a corporation called the South Side Real Estate Company, he can tell himself that he does not exploit people, for his corporation operates in an amoral realm that doesn't touch individuals but only abstractions: supply and demand, his competitors, and so forth (277). A corporation is a kind of parody of the Beloved Community, for as Alan Trachtenberg has noted, a corporation is an "association . . . understood as strictly contractual, not necessarily comprised of people acquainted with each other or joined by any common motive other than profit seeking."[40] Moreover, it is a single "body" (from the Latin *corpora*) in which the whole is greater than the sum of its parts. "The advantage that the corporation has over the individual entrepreneur," said Louis Wirth in a moment of rare humor, " . . . derives not only from the possibility it affords of centralizing the resources of thousands of individuals or from the legal privilege of limited liability and perpetual succession, but from the fact that the corporation has no soul."[41] One can be sure that Wright, in his depiction of Mr. Dalton, didn't let this paradox slip by. Mr. Dalton washes his hands of any responsibility for Bigger's fate because the standards for Bigger's housing are set by the soulless corporation, a legal "body." Thus the reversal of the Christian paradox: in giving his soul to the corporation, he has lost it—he has become an abstract "body." Later in the novel, Max will pun upon "corporation" and "corpse" in the trial scene, trying to draw a connection between Mr. Dalton's attempt to distance himself from Bigger's life through a legalistic form, and Dalton's responsibility, because of this act, for his own daughter's death.

Bigger's compulsive gesture, blotting out the mapped universe, is an unconscious response to the invisible forces that govern his life. After he has killed both Mary and Bessie, he stands at the window of an empty apartment building gazing upon the city under snow, seeking for the pattern that continually eludes him:

> The snow had stopped falling and the city, white, still, was a vast stretch of rooftops and sky. He had been thinking about it for hours here in the dark and now there it was, all white, still. But what he had thought about it had made it real with a reality it did not have now in the daylight. When lying in the dark thinking about it, it seemed to have something which left it when it was

looked at. Why should not this cold white world rise up as a beautiful dream in which he could walk and be at home, in which it would be easy to do and not to do? If only someone had gone before and lived and suffered or died—made it so that it could be understood! It was too stark, not redeemed, not made real with the reality that was the warm blood of life. He felt that there was something missing, some road which, if he had once found it, would have led him to a sure and quiet knowledge. (204)

The snow outside the window destroys the last aura of Bigger's dream, a dream that had hinted that a pattern of the city's labyrinth could be found. For the white snow, which obliterates all shape, all pattern, is the city that Bigger lives in, a world that denies him a map. That Bigger lives outside the "symbols and images" of civilization means that he lives in a blank space, and the resurrected Christ cannot substitute for the dream: Christ's warm blood will not thaw the city's snow, or reveal the invisible City of God beneath the formless surface of the city. Indeed, the burning cross set to intimidate Bigger when he is forced to return to the scene of the crime is Wright's reminder that Christ's compassion is exclusive. The real Chicago is governed by myths that the Buckleys and the Daltons have imposed—these substitutes for God have created a mockery of community whose substance is the cold, white snow. Only Mary's death momentarily convinces Bigger that he is free to read the invisible traces and, like Prometheus, to challenge the gods of the city, to answer power with power.

The last section of the novel (book 3, "Fate") brings Bigger into the toils of Chicago's judicial system, a heart of darkness where the city's contradictions become flesh in the characters of the agents of the state. Calculating that he can be reelected if Bigger is executed for murder, Buckley visits Bigger in his cell, hoping to obtain a confession. He "led Bigger to a window through which he [Bigger] looked and saw the streets below crowded with masses of people in all directions. 'See that, boy? Those people would like to lynch you. That's why I'm asking you to trust me and talk to me. The quicker we get this over with, the better for you'" (258). Of all the window views of the city in *Native Son*, Buckley's is the most essentialist, reducing society to the expression of brute force. And Bigger yields momentarily to the voice claiming to explain the city, for it explains a city of power he himself has recognized and embraced. By the window Buckley manipulates Bigger's fear by exposing him to the people's monolithic wrath; at the trial, Buckley will arouse the people's fear by depicting Bigger as a beast, demonizing what is different. The intention of both rhetorical occasions is to freeze by means of terror the city's protean potential for change.

That Buckley is Bigger's sinister "double" is made clear early in the novel, when Buckley's face on the billboard glares at Bigger, and Bigger glares back. Buckley is both antagonist and doppelgänger—that is why Bigger reads the image on the billboard with such accuracy. He identifies with Buckley because he understands that the empirical reality operating in the city precludes the possibility of virtue being rewarded. In book 2 of the novel, the sense of freedom and release which Mary's murder gave to Bigger is quickly diffused among the city's conflicting, ephemeral narratives. Because of Bessie's chance mention of the sensational Leopold-Loeb case, Bigger associates his own situation with that half-known story, seeing a means to defend himself and to exploit his single act of identity. But here, as elsewhere, Bessie defines the nature of his estrangement more absolutely than any other character in the novel: his brutal murder of her illustrates that the only new identity he can conceive of assuming is the godlike persona on a movie screen or billboard.[42] In a city where the only maps trace circuits of power, Buckley is all that Bigger can imagine becoming.

At the trial, Buckley's relationship to the world of power is subsumed in his role of defender of the laws of the city, the written code that gives the city its formal rationale. Wright reminds us of the falsity of this legal assumption not only by alluding to Paul ("The letter killeth. . . .") but also by connecting Buckley's histrionics to the moralistic endings of Hollywood movies. The laws that Buckley stresses in his courtroom speech all illustrate what he calls God's "thunderous 'NO'!" (344). His civilization is defined in terms of negatives, and his strategy is to make Bigger nonhuman, "a rapacious beast," a "maddened ape," and so forth—he will ensure the safety of the city by destroying the beast that threatens it.

But the beast that Bigger stands in for, of course, is the scapegoat. In *Permanence and Change*, Kenneth Burke says that society's choice of a scapegoat often reflects a metaphor gone wrong. For, like a window frame, a metaphor is a way of seeing, an orientation; and "a way of seeing is also a way of not-seeing." Laying the city's sins upon a scapegoat should allow the city's residents to see that there but for the grace of God go they—the sins that Christ takes upon himself are humanity's sins. But making Bigger the scapegoat blinds the citizens of Chicago to the true nature of their society and its problems, an effect that Burke refers to as "trained incapacity."[43] Buckley's metaphor of the beast frames a Manichean view of the urban landscape, one that distracts the hearer's attention from the economic and political facts, just as the sublime aesthetics of the skyline sublimates questions of practical power.

Both Buckley and Dalton symbolize invisible forces that freeze the city's potential for change. The empty, skeletal buildings on Chicago's South Side are objective correlatives of Dalton's wintry world, illustrations of an architecture that, in Lewis Mumford's words, no longer reflects the "living functions" of an organic society.[44] The dead buildings in Mr. Dalton's slums are the reverse side of the gleaming classical architecture in the White City of the Columbian Exposition of 1893; they call into question the values ostensibly expressed by the city's Gothic cathedrals. They are what high culture divorced from the *demos* has created, a Gothic nightmare, where the freeze-frame of Buckley's face on the billboard (only the eyes move) overlooks a necropolis.

This connection between power, stasis, and death is emphasized at the inquest by the character of the coroner (literally, the agent of the *corona*, the crown) who presides over corpses. He obscures the story of power by constructing an alternative myth out of scattered icons. At the inquest, Bigger looks up to see on a table

> the pile of white bones . . . beside them lay the kidnap letter, held in place by a bottle of ink. In the center of the table were white sheets of paper fastened by a metal clasp; it was his signed confession. And there was Mr. Dalton, white-faced, white haired; and beside him was Mrs. Dalton, still and straight. . . . Then he saw the trunk into which he had stuffed Mary's body, the trunk which he had lugged down the stairs and had carried to the station. And, yes, there was the blackened hatchet blade and a tiny round piece of metal. (265)

The last is Mary's earring, which the coroner focuses upon to build, step by step, a symbolic history. Encouraged by the coroner, Mrs.

Dalton describes the ancestry of this pair of earrings (only one of which was found in the furnace), observing how they were passed down from generation to generation within her family.

The coroner's rhetorical strategy is obvious, but it involves much more than a sentimental picture of the Dalton family. He uses the earring to construct the moral history of what he conceives to be civilization, his method that of the archaeologist, a search for an *archē* (beginning). Where does civilization begin, he is asking, in what place and with what intimate gestures? For him, the scattered objects on the table illustrate the desecration of the sacred. In this sense, they are like objects in a museum in that they attempt "to give by the ordered display of selected artifacts a total representation of human reality and history." The museum implies a static world, a "Newtonian model [that] moves from point of presence to point of presence and does not have, intrinsically, a temporality that describes systems as changing."[45] It is a nineteenth-century metaphor for order, for things being in their place; it will be replaced by the twentieth-century furnace, a metaphor for things once solid melting "into air." In the furnace, objects go "from a differentiated state to an undifferentiated state."[46] Such change, which removes all difference, all distinctions between things, is an apt metaphor for the urban experience of "leveling," the transformation of culture caused by a predominantly commercial motivation. Hence there is a basic contradiction between the coroner's myth of stasis, stability, and the ordered march of civilization, and the corporate powers behind Mr. Dalton which create and manipulate the city's mass culture. The furnace in *Native Son* obliterates the Dalton family narrative. Mr. Dalton's daughter has literally melted into air in his own basement, and this is what Wright perceives the true meaning of the earring to be. It is a deeply ironic, and frightening, conception of the "melting pot."

In his summation speech at the trial, Max, too, wants to remove all illusion of difference, to look at a new "map." Those "colonists" you romanticize, he tells the jury, "were faced with a difficult choice: they had either to subdue this wild land or be subdued by it. We need but turn our eyes upon the imposing sweep of streets and factories and buildings to see how completely they have conquered. But in conquering they *used* others" (328–29). Wright, perhaps following Lewis Mumford, links the first city-builders in America and the white settlers' westward movement with naked aggression.[47] Theirs, continues Max, was "the imperial dream of a feudal age," the ultimate irony of a civilization that claimed to be based on the natural rights of man. The pilgrims and pioneers had fled the "cities of the old world where the means to sustain life were hard to get or own," but they became like the people who had oppressed them, for in creating their "streets and factories and buildings" they had themselves oppressed others. Late in the novel, Max will try to get Bigger to see how his present discontent contains a future promise, how dead stone might be reanimated by living spirit; but in his summation speech he confronts the city's citizens with the horror of a civilization that claims to be a uniquely just human society but has in fact simply repeated the sins of the past.

The point he makes to the city's citizens is that there *is* a beast in the city, but it is the creation of their civilization's failure. And that beast is a corpse that will not stay dead: "It still lives! It has made itself a home in the wild forest of our great cities, amid the rank and choking vegetation of slums! It has forgotten our language! In order to live it has sharpened its claws! . . . By night it creeps from its lair and steals towards the settlements of civilization!" (331). Wright takes Eliot's "Dog . . . that's friend to men" in *The Waste Land* and reworks it for use in another "Unreal City." Eliot's dog digs up the corpse of corruption beneath the placid philistine surface of the city, and in so doing is transformed into an agent of doom, James Thomson's "hound of heaven."[48] The city of Chicago is still close to the forest, the word *settlements* reminding us how recent, tenuous, and fragile its walls are. Dalton rejects any connection to this "forest," but the connection is made by the corpse of his daughter, who suffers the indignity of imitating how Bigger lives. Bigger cannot squeeze her into the trunk, having to bend her legs to make her fit, and later must cut off her head to make her fit into the furnace. The literalization of the Procrustes myth comments on Mr. Dalton's blindness; in death, Mary's body mirrors the physical and spiritual bends that he inflicts upon the black people who live in his buildings. Those "settlements" are built upon corpses, and the civilization they project is as illusory as a picture on a movie screen.

It is at the invisible boundary line separating civilization from wilderness that Wright wants the city to confront itself. The city, he insists, is lost within an illusion of its monuments, of its institutions, of its dreams of becoming a Paris on the Lake. It pretends that its

white city is an accurate measure of its status as a culture, that the facade of its classical and Gothic architecture reflects a city of *civitas*.
But throughout his novel, Wright has underscored a connection between power and high culture, greed and elegance. Those like Mr.
Dalton who represent high culture are self-deceived, because they
refuse to acknowledge their connection to power, and those like
Buckley who represent power hide their greed behind a myth of civilization, the city's skyscraper skyline.

When Jan and Mary attempt to speak to Bigger, despite their left-
ist rhetoric they unconsciously employ the symbolic image of the
skyline. But Bigger can't see that city, because he has been excluded
from it. When Max finally succeeds in communicating with him, it is
because Bigger's fear has been transformed, first to an illusion of power, then by a collapse into despair. For Wright tells us at the beginning of the novel's third book that the identity Bigger created for
himself by the negative act of murder has failed him, and that he exists in a kind of moral limbo, his only desire to sink into the "dark
face of ancient waters" (234). At this point Max approaches him by
indirection, as part of a professional interrogation that by degrees
leads to uneasy friendship. The questions Max asks about Bigger's
background and motivation have the unintended effect of causing
Bigger to try "to see himself in relation to other men, a thing he had
always feared to try to do, so deeply stained was his mind with the
hate of others for him" (306). Indeed, so successful has Max been in
stimulating Bigger to think of himself in terms of others that Bigger
has a vision of community that bears some resemblance to Max's final appeal. He sees himself "standing in the midst of a vast crowd of
men, white men and black men and all men, and the sun's rays melted away the differences, the colors, the clothes, and drew what was
common and good upward toward the sun. . . . Had he been blind all
along? . . . Was there some battle everybody was fighting, and he had
missed it?" (307). Wright's image overcomes the terror of the furnace
that melts down difference: the sun discovers a common humanity
beneath that difference. But if Max's vision already lies dormant in
Bigger, why then doesn't Bigger respond to it in the novel's final
scene?

In fact, the novel's third book begins in a way that anticipates a
Christian ending, or at least one whose themes are reconciliation, ac-

ceptance, and humility. Bigger's despair seems to demand an upward ascent, the one expected by the Christian-oriented literature of Western civilization. And indeed Max seems to play the part of Dante's Beatrice, who will lead Bigger out of his despair to a higher moral awareness, because his questions cause Bigger to probe the meaning of his own life and to connect it to something more lofty than mere ego. The scene is apparently set for a kind of Marxist and/or Christian redemption at the novel's conclusion. But there is a paradox here.

Even Max must use the "symbols and images" of a civilization that had betrayed the values that they stand for. If Mumford is right that the architecture of a civilization is a "sure index of what the people are subjectively,"[49] then is it possible to free the Wrigley Building from the chewing gum, or the Tribune Tower from yellow journalism? Max implicitly rejects Jan and Mary's picturesque view of these buildings—they will only be beautiful, he tells Bigger, when their stone is reanimated, not merely repossessed; his point is that humanistic values can be recovered when the "symbols and images" that express them are reconnected to an Ur–impulse: the passion to create an egalitarian society. Max wants Bigger to see the *figura* of the future buried within American civilization's frozen architecture;[50] but as Max implies at the trial, the prime mover behind these buildings, even if some of them look like cathedrals, was not God but the Faustian thrust of greed and power. This conflict between what is and what ought to be points to the tragic dilemma of the novel's final scene.

After the governor has refused Max's plea for clemency, the lawyer goes to Bigger's cell for a last meeting. Anxious for more than consolation, Bigger says to Max, "How can I die!" but he is asking in essence, "What did my life mean?" (354). Max tries to make Bigger see that he must join the human community in spirit if he is to understand that meaning. He takes Bigger to the window of his cell in the Cook County Jail, and Bigger sees "in the distance the tips of the sun-drenched buildings in the Loop" (356).[51] He tells Bigger that "those buildings sprang up out of the hearts of men. . . . Men like you." Human desire for fulfillment, Max continues, "keeps those buildings in their place. . . . What you felt, what you wanted, is what keeps those buildings standing there. When millions of men are desiring and longing, those buildings grow and unfold" (356). But a few men, he continues, have gotten control of the buildings and blocked the entrances; and the buildings "can't unfold." The meaning of Bigger's life, Max posits, is seeing himself in relationship to those "men like you [who] get angry and fight to re-enter those buildings, to live again" (357). Max wants Bigger to see his life in terms of living architecture, in terms of the vital polis, in terms of the *archē* of a true civilization. And he wants Bigger to join, if only in his imagination, with others in humanity's struggle to fulfill itself, a theme also implicit in the epilogue to *Invisible Man*.

Max's visionary portrait of the redeemed city is a classic statement of humanistic ideals, Christian and pagan. The vision from the window is like the vision Ezekiel sees of the New Jerusalem from high atop a mountain, and it also echoes the Book of Revelation, the ending of Milton's *Paradise Lost*, and book 6 of the *Aeneid*.[52] In this final scene from *Native Son*, we are reminded, as Maynard Mack has said in another context, of "man's recurring dream of the civilized community only one of whose names is Rome."[53] If Max gives his redeemed city a Marxist bias, Wright makes sure that readers see it in a more universal light through its archetypal setting.

Why then does Bigger reject Max's visionary city, especially since it reflects an image of community which he desperately seeks? Wright's answer is that one can imagine a holy city only if one perceives that the real city bears some resemblance, no matter how slight, to the archetype. Yet as Wright says of Bigger, in lines that precede Max's imaginary rendering of Chicago as an image of community and civilization: "He had lived outside of the lives of men. Their modes of communication, their symbols and images, had been denied him" (353). Just as he could not *see* Chicago's skyline as an image and symbol of civilization (having been excluded from that civilization), so too he cannot perceive the figura in Max's buildings. In order to make the cognitive leap to Max's buildings, Bigger would have to have some unifying principle in his mind to pull together the disparate images that exist there, and this would only be possible if the ideals of America's sacred documents had been made real to him *as ideals*. In other words, Max exists as Dante's Virgil for Bigger, showing him the various levels of Hell, but he cannot become Bigger's Beatrice. The only city Bigger knows is Chicago, and that city is either a maze or a prison; the only ideal city he can imagine is the one given to him by the mass media.

To look at the ending in another way, Wright makes it clear that

Bigger is a political animal in an Aristotelean sense: he feels the need to belong to a polis. Indeed, that need is so powerful, Wright said in "How Bigger was Born," that it might have taken the form of either fascism or communism. The problem is, America presents Bigger with no viable form of the polis that he can believe in, so that when Max's heavenly city is presented to him at the novel's conclusion, it appears to him not as something abstracted from his own experience but simply as an abstraction. Paradoxically, Dalton's and Buckley's urban abstractions—corporations and laws—are more real to him, because they cloak motivations that he knows all too well. As Wright reminds us in an oft-quoted passage from *Black Boy*, the human values we take for granted must be learned:

> How hollow our memories, how lacking we were in those intangible sentiments that bind man to man. . . . Whenever I thought of the essential bleakness of black life in America, I knew that Negroes had never been allowed to catch the full spirit of Western civilization, that they lived somehow in it but not of it. And when I brooded upon the cultural barrenness of black life, I wondered if clean, positive tenderness, love, honor, loyalty, and the capacity to remember were native with man. I asked myself if these human qualities were not fostered, won, struggled and suffered for, preserved in ritual from one generation to another.[54]

This passage has been criticized as too narrow an interpretation of black life, specifically black folk culture, yet we might consider it a just interpretation of Chicago in *Native Son*.[55] Within Chicago, Bigger sees the invisible cities of economic power and the mythologies of mass culture, but he doesn't see "tenderness, love, honor, loyalty and the capacity to remember . . . preserved in ritual from one generation to another," because *that* heavenly city does not exist in Chicago. And there is perhaps a deeper ironic level than this: in *Native Son*, Bigger lacks those "intangible sentiments that bind man to man" because he mirrors a city that in turn is a mirror of a nation that never caught "the full spirit of Western civilization." In this sense, he is the native son of *both* Chicago and America. That Wright was a student of Van Wyck Brooks, Waldo Frank, and Lewis Mumford, as well as H. L. Mencken, is significant here; these critics had also pointed to an undeveloped American culture, and in *Lawd Today!* Wright had used epigraphs from both Brooks and Frank which reflected on the absence of the Beloved Community in black urban culture, in Chicago, and in America at large.[56]

Hence Bigger opts for what he knows, his own experience, which in itself is difficult to pin down. (Wright is determined to leave no easy answers.) As Emerson saw, self-reliance is a vague concept: "Speak rather of that which relies, because it works and is."[57] Behind Emerson's transcendental philosophy is a tough-minded pragmatism, and this too is what Bigger accepts when he tells Max, "what I killed for, I *am*!" Bigger's sense of self "relies" upon "what I killed for," that is, upon desire made manifest through action. As a person excluded from American culture, Bigger is only able to define himself in opposition, by the act of murder, and that definition becomes so important to him that he will not give it up. Paradoxically, like any good American, Bigger "wanted to be happy in this world, not out of it" (302), yet his concept of happiness was shaped by the "instrumentalities" that his urban environment provided. Bigger authenticates himself by murder, and the only city he can imagine at the novel's end is one that created his life as a criminal, shaped it, and gave it meaning. And in choosing individual identity over community—a decision, we might say, that paradoxically marks him as an American—Bigger also fulfilled Kenneth Burke's definition of the truly "pious" life.

"What I killed for, I *am*": in Burke's terms, the "what" defines the man; it is the substantive pronoun, the "sub-stance," that "stands under" the human. Bigger killed to live—that is, in essence, the "what" that he killed for. In *Permanence and Change* (1935), Burke insists that true piety is *"the sense of what properly goes with what"*;[58] and Bigger's decision to remain true to his "sense of what . . . goes with what" explains why he rejects Max's vision. That vision does not express Bigger's sense of personal propriety: "When I think about what you say I kind of feel what I wanted. It makes me feel I was kind of *right*" (358). That is, "right" in terms of "what properly goes with what": right to kill, right even to die in the electric chair. To accept Max's vision as his own—to see himself as belonging to a community of human beings all striving to achieve utopia—would deny the rightness of actions that make up the pattern of a life he can understand. It is right that he die in the electric chair, because this sense of an ending makes him read his life as a whole text for the first time. The electric chair is a fitting conclusion to a life that was one long act of rebellion against what society officially considers pious.

Native Son's Gothic ending is indebted to Poe, Hawthorne, and Conrad—all favorite authors of Wright's—but it was also shaped by Hollywood movies. (As Michel Fabre tells us, Wright was an inveterate moviegoer; "he sometimes went to as many as three movies a day").[59] The debt is an indirect one, yet there is a suggestive coincidence of chronology, character, theme, and narrative maneuver between Wright's novel and the gangster movies of the 1930s. After 1934 the Hays code legislated that Hollywood would not depict gangsters in a favorable light; they had to die as a lesson to the supposedly impressionable audience, sometimes with just the hint of Christian redemption.[60] A film that fulfilled all the nominal requirements was *Angels with Dirty Faces*, released in 1938, while Wright was working on *Native Son*. The general structural similarity of plot (the poor boy turns to crime, has a brief success, and comes to a bad end), as well as Wright's use of the name "Buckley" (a crooked police captain in the movie) and other details make it possible that Wright had *Angels* in mind while writing *Native Son*.[61] But whether he had or not, the distinctive parallels between the ending of the novel and that of the movie help illuminate the last scene of *Native Son*.

Angels is a gangster movie set during the Depression; its locale is the city during hard times, and it focuses on those hit hardest by hard times, the poor. Thus it makes a claim on our conscience as we watch one bad boy, Rocky Sullivan (James Cagney), grow up in a tough neighborhood to become a gangster. Parallel to Rocky's glamorous rise from reform school kid to mobster is the humble vocation of the local parish priest, Jerry Connolly (Pat O'Brien), who was Rocky's boyhood chum. Although he and Rocky had engaged in petty crimes together as juveniles, he is determined now to save the teenagers in his parish from Rocky's influence and his fate. The movie ends with Father Connolly asking Rocky to die a coward in the electric chair so that the impressionable kids of their old neighborhood will despise his memory. Connolly's argument is that although Rocky's life is over, Rocky can perform one Christian act before he passes from the scene: to save the kids by not giving them a defiant and rebellious image to admire. Although Rocky at first resists so outrageous a request, he whimpers and whines in the death room, and the camera zooms in to a close-up of Connolly's face as we hear Rocky's weeping in the background. In the Rembrandt lighting that Hollywood in the 1930s reserved for Christians and virgins, Father Connolly is shown thanking God for the mysterious ways in which his wonders are performed, and the movie ends on this saccharine note. What began as a criticism of the city as social system ends as a celebration of Christian piety and of the triumph of good over evil.

The movie's ending would have appeared to Richard Wright as an example of Hollywood immorality, and when he came to write the ending of his own novel, he allowed Bigger to complete the cycle of piety, to frame his life in his own terms, in a way Hollywood's gangsters were never allowed to do. However, what makes *Angels* particularly interesting in reference to Wright's novel is that the movie's ending could be understood as very similar to the conclusion of *Native Son*. The penultimate shot of the film suggests that Connolly's motivation has been not a love of Christ but a love of power, and that it is as a figure of power that he has replaced Rocky in the boys' hearts. This shot is low-angle, looking upward at Father Connolly, who is wearing a fedora at a rakish angle and standing at the top of the basement stairs with bars of light behind him, as he ostensibly confirms Rocky's "yellow" behavior in the death chamber.[62] What this shot actually confirms is that beneath the Hollywood story line there has been a dark, *film noir* side to Father Connolly's behavior through the entire movie. He sees himself competing with Rocky for the boys' admiration, and he resents the infatuation of Lori Martin (Ann Sheridan) with his rival: it is at that point that he suddenly "converts" to active opposition. He quickly becomes a media figure and a power broker, using radio and newspapers as effectively as any propagandist and, incidentally, making once again the point of mass culture's moral ambiguity—Rocky has been (like Bigger) partially a creation of "the news." But Connolly is driven to his evangelical fury by a barely visible web of unpriestly motivations—jealousy, envy, lust, and the desire for power. Michael Curtiz, the film's director, seems to know exactly what he is doing; he tells one story for the Hays-code censors and tells another story, through innuendo and visual imagery, for whoever in his audience cares to see.[63] It is easy to imagine that if Bigger Thomas were in the audience watching *Angels*, he would have understood Connolly's will to power just as he understood Buckley's.

It is Rocky, not Father Connolly, who is truly pious in Kenneth Burke's sense. Rocky's contempt for the law, his will to succeed, his refusal to be anyone's dupe, and his arrogant mannerisms—these give him a consistency of character that only his bravery in facing the electric chair could complete. Rocky, like Bigger, is held up as a grotesque by the newspapers, but both men draw an invisible sustenance from their caricatures, becoming more and more like poisonous flowers, deadly nightshades, that gain their strength from being planted in dung.

The newspaper campaigns against Rocky only revitalize him, making him all the more determined to go out with guns blazing. What destroys his own sense of piety is an appeal made to him on the basis of another kind of piety. He allows Connolly to manipulate him, to use their boyhood friendship for his own ends; hence Rocky violates the sacred space of his own making, which is based upon rebellion, and resistance to a hypocritical city.

In *Native Son*'s original version, Wright has Bigger die in the electric chair like Rocky, though without Rocky's feigned cowardice. The published ending is more effective. Indeed, the slamming of the "far door" in the prison is one of the most terribly final conclusions in American literature. We recognize that the door is closing not only on Bigger's life but also on a myriad of hopes and illusions of American civilization, and it is ironically appropriate that we can measure the extent of our loss by comparing Bigger's end to Rocky's. In *Native Son*, Wright gave Bigger a much greater threat to his integrity than a hypocrite like Father Connolly; he made him square off against an honest man, one who represents a vision of the city that Bigger already wants to believe in, the idea of a Beloved Community in which a true democracy prevails. The heavenly city that Connolly presents to Rocky and the neighborhood kids is Dalton's corporation, a hierarchy with Connolly at the top (as shown by the *film noir* final shot). The tragedy of *Native Son* is that Bigger ultimately can only resolve the dilemma by choosing self-definition over a community with others. But it is, of course, no solution, because as Bessie's death clearly illustrates, by accepting "why all the killing was" (358), Bigger places himself beyond the pale of *caritas* and of the Beloved Community. The novel's tragic center is the fact that Bigger's definition of self include not one but two corpses, one murder "accidental," the other done in cold blood.[64] And it is that last murder that places him outside any refuge within the black community. Yet it is that definition of self based on murder which is the only thing in his life that makes sense: "What I killed for must've been *good*! . . . I didn't know I was alive in this world until I felt things hard enough to kill for 'em" (358; my italics). If there is a tragedy in *Native Son*, as one critic has argued, then both the reborn Bigger and the idealized city must be seen as *good* at the novel's end. For if the novel is a tragedy, then we need a tragic dilemma. And a tragic dilemma is one in which there are no satisfactory solutions.[65]

Through Bigger, Wright accepts the Lockean (even Hobbesian) implications of America's past. Bigger is a native son because, like other Americans, he lacks the cohesive glue of tradition, the *substance* that might close the large gap between the ideals contained in the nation's sacred documents and the quotidian world that he experiences. As Lewis Mumford had argued in the *American Mercury* in 1926, the American was a "stript European." The pioneers and puritans who emigrated to these shores were no longer "buoyed up by memorials of the past." They were modern men who shed the rich and varied intellectual heritage of the medieval-Renaissance world view and had only their Enlightenment grids to replace it. Coming to America, they wandered in the wilderness without a spiritual guide "to lead them . . . and here they have remained in exile," Mumford adds with a touch of understatement, "a little more than the Biblical forty years."[66] The diaspora for blacks was even longer and even more culturally traumatic. The problem of Max's vision of the city on the hill, and perhaps of John Winthrop's as well, is that it belonged to the piety of another time, another place.

At the end of *Native Son*, Max tries to counter the naked id with a vision of the Beloved Community, and we might say that through both Max's vision and Bigger's rejection Wright is speaking for us. It is precisely here that he anticipates, but with a different emphasis, Ellison's famous last sentence of *Invisible Man*: "Who knows but that, on the lower frequencies, I speak for you?" Ellison would have us identify not only with the invisible man's alienation but also with his desire to reconnect himself to the American polis. In the epilogue the invisible man hints that he is going to leave his cell, "since there's a possibility that even an invisible man has a socially responsible role to play." Because the city, whose true founder is Proteus, has taught him to be protean, he hopes to make the "sacred papers" live in and through him. Bigger, too, intends to be more than a disembodied voice at the novel's end: "What I killed for, I *am*" means that in accepting himself as a murderer, he has refused society's definition of him as an invisible man. But this means that, again paraphrasing Poe's "Man of the Crowd," he is a text that not only can't be read but also remains somewhat opaque even to himself: "When I think of *why* all the killing was, I begin to feel *what* I wanted, *what* I am" (358; my italics). Even Bigger cannot reconcile the paradoxical relationship between murder and creation; all he knows at the end is that the vision of the ideal place is unsubstantial compared to the places in the heart where he has in fact lived.

In *Native Son*, Wright accepts the Romantic paradox of Cain, who is both a homeless pariah and the first city-builder. The American Cain defined himself by rejecting somebody else's definition of him, but he in turn used others to build his city—aggression became its foundation.[67] Max fails at the novel's end not because his vision of the redeemed city is a pretty picture but because it is a picture that has no Cain in it. Bigger only knows the city at the bottom, and thus Cain's city is the only city he knows: "Bigger was gazing in the direction of the buildings; but he *did not see* them. He was trying to react to the picture Max was drawing, trying to compare that picture with what he had felt all his life" (357; my italics).[68] Max, too, is speaking for us through this "picture," but he leaves Bigger's cell with his eyes "full of terror," because he is brought face to face with the fact that the Founding Fathers' dream of "a more perfect union" may be an illusion. For Max, like them, is a rationalist who believes in humanity's capacity to recognize evil and remove it. This ultimately is the basis of his appeal in the courtroom: the corpse we have created can be put to rest if we ourselves can be brought to see its true nature. In the novel's final scene, Max is like Joseph Conrad's Kurtz, who has looked into the abyss and confronts a truth at the heart not only of this civilization but, perhaps, of all civilizations: there are no civilized cities. Each is based on a primal crime that cannot be eradicated. The true implications of his courtroom speech come home to him as he leaves Bigger's cell, for in describing Bigger's history he has also described the history of civilization and of its cities.

CHAPTER FOUR

The Ever-Emerging City
in Ralph Ellison's *Invisible Man*

> Memory is redundant: it repeats signs so that the city can
> begin to exist.
>
> —Italo Calvino, *Invisible Cities*

> And when you hear me howling in my passway, rider,
> Please open your door and let me in.
>
> —Robert Johnson, "Stones in My Passway"

In a 1945 review of Gertrude Stein's *Wars I Have Seen*, Richard Wright made a startling observation. He said that in "a Black-Belt basement" he had read aloud Stein's "Melanctha" to a group of "semi-literate Negro stockyard workers" and "they had understood every word": "Enthralled, they slapped their thighs, howled, laughed, stomped and interrupted me constantly to comment upon the characters."[1] Did Wright realize the implications of what he was saying? Here was a difficult story written by a high priestess of modernism, and it was accessible to those who were outside the "full spirit of Western civilization." Earlier, of course, in "Blueprint for Negro Writing," Wright had insisted that blacks had an authentic culture of their own: "Blues, spirituals, and folk tales recounted from mouth to mouth; the whispered words of a black mother to her black daughter on the ways of men, to confidential wisdom of a black father to his black son; the swapping of sex experiences on street corners from boy to boy in the deepest vernacular; work songs sung under blazing suns."[2] Both of these positions—belief in a common culture, and belief in the accessibility of high culture to the lowly—seem to contradict the ending of *Native Son*.

For what the ending of *Native Son* tells us is that if a sense of community is based on the common life, that common life does not exist for Bigger, any more than does the city's architecture, Mumford's "index of civilization." The only thing Bigger is connected to outside himself are the instruments of mass culture, out of which he forges a conception of his own life. Thus when the door slams on Bigger at the end of *Native Son*, Wright slams it shut upon the men in the basement "enthralled" by "Melanctha," as well as upon the world of popular culture: the communal response to Stein's "characters."

But it is precisely this world of give and take among Wright's stockyard workers that will fascinate Ralph Ellison, so he will focus in *Invisible Man* not upon the theme of cultural exclusion but upon cultural fusion. In *Invisible Man*, Ellison will show the multitudinous ways in which blacks survive and adapt to the city and even express, in unexpected modes, the "ideals" of the national culture. The similarity between Wright and Ellison is that both writers believe in the existence of these "ideals" in the layers below the commercial civilization; but it is Ellison who insists that they still function even in daily life. For Ellison believes that there is in "the American scene" a kind of "linguistic" Everyman who embodies "the idealistic action of the American Word as it goads its users toward a perfection of our revolutionary ideals."[3] Significantly, those "users" in *Invisible Man* dwell in the seemingly divided but actually related worlds of high and low cultures.

What goes on in *Invisible Man* is a tension between the philosophic and political ideals of the Republic and the chaos of everyday life. This tension is paralleled by a prose style that operates at different levels— the comic, extravagant expression of quotidian reality or wild puns and literary allusions ranging from famous American authors to myths and heroes of classical literature. Indeed, this interplay between high and low creates a dense prose texture that is conspicuous, whereas *Native Son*'s complexity is hidden behind a mask of surface "realism." And Ellison's protean prose style is a reflection of the novel's themes: the invisible man, the book's nameless protagonist and narrator, is condemned to live in multiple worlds, and he must learn to thrive within their diversity. As we shall see, he must become Proteus without becoming either Ras or Rinehart.

In this sense, Ellison will create a character who by the novel's end will be an answer to Bigger. In the epilogue, the invisible man knows what Ellison knows: that a divided universe can be overcome by a

fusion of high and low cultures into a single whole, and by the creation of a sensibility that will be able to traverse the distance between
the two worlds. And the key element in the process of creating this
fusion and recognizing its significance is popular culture, a world
mostly absent from *Native Son*. For unlike Wright, Ellison will put his
complete faith in the little man hidden behind the stove in the
Chehaw Station, in the "semi-literate Negro stockyard laborers" in
the basement. They are the ones who not only will forge the "uncre-
ated conscience" of their race but will express at the same time the
"revolutionary ideals" of the Republic. Yet for Ellison the key word is
always *movement* toward a perfection. At the conclusion of *Invisible
Man*, all signs point to a reenactment of a myth of emergence in
which the narrator seems to be acting out the "origin" stories of several cultures within the American scene, including John Winthrop's
famous "city on a hill" address, given in midpassage to homeless migrants who had not yet landed. Ellison never says that his narrator
has left his hole—rather, "I'm coming out"—yet the idea of his ascension is as real a "thing" as an actual exit.[4] For in his well-lit hole, he
paradoxically mirrors those Founding Fathers who "dreamed" a world
out of the "darkness" (433). That world was corrupted by its incarnation, yet the dream is no less valid for that fact. What the invisible
man dreams is a cosmos that takes into account the history of that
corruption, but it is a history with the dross drawn off. His dream involves a fusion of high and low cultures, and American and European
sources, and a participation in the remaking of the total culture at all
levels, local and national. This, he now realizes, has been the hidden
democratic meaning of his memoirs: participation in the act of creating the Beloved Community. When the invisible man contemplates
coming out of his hole, the invisible city also begins to reveal itself.

Ellison's novel opens with Wright's "wisdom of a black father" being passed down, as the invisible man's dying grandfather tells him
"to overcome 'em with yeses, undermine 'em with grins, agree 'em to
death and destruction, let 'em swoller you till they vomit or bust
wide open" (13–14). Folk wisdom from a deathbed, involving both a
theory and a method—it will haunt the invisible man through the
novel and into the epilogue, where he will still be turning over his
grandfather's words. In one sense the meaning of the novel is his
learning what those words mean, a learning that Ellison makes clear

is experiential, not an abstract lesson. It is also wisdom that points to a version of what Enlightenment civilization has regarded as the "highest" wisdom: "'Agree 'em to death and destruction,' grandfather had advised. Hell, weren't they their own death and their own destruction except as the principle lived in them and us?" (434), the narrator finally reflects. The "they" who have tried to render him invisible and nonexistent do not themselves exist without "the principle." If the principle itself turns out to be the grandfather's deathbed "yes," what exactly does that mean? Throughout the novel, in his attempt to come to terms with his grandfather's "yes," the narrator embraces a number of false ideologies—from a morally blind pragmatism (Bledsoeism) to an abstract idealism (the Brotherhood)—but he only begins to have a clue as to what "yes" means in the context of a cityscape.

When the industrialist Mr. Norton reappears in the epilogue to ask him the way to "Centre Street" in a subway station beneath the city, the narrator responds, connecting geography to identity: "If you don't know *where* you are, you probably don't know *who* you are" (436). As in *Native Son*, the city can be a maze or a grid in which there is no center, but here the lost man is a rich and educated white American who thinks of the city as his own. Norton does not remember the narrator because he does not "see" him, as he does not see the rich diversity within the American scene. In Henry James's famous phrase, he has reduced the "complex fate of being an American" to a few street signs, just as he earlier reduced the complexity of Ralph Waldo Emerson to a few handbook maxims.[5] He is lost because he does not have an adequate map to the center of the civilization in which he lives.

Knowing the meaning of grandfather's "yes" means knowing *where* the city's center is located. It is definitely not located in revenge, which, the narrator discovers, leaves you in a dark place no matter how bright the light of your rage. "Yes" is the invisible word lurking beneath those "sacred papers" of the country's founding; it is not the visible documents themselves, but the documents as a hint, a motion *toward*. "Yes," then, is the invisible light shining through those documents as a beacon, sometimes contradicting the words of the documents themselves. We come back to John Winthrop's famous allusion to Matthew 5:14–15, made long before those "sacred papers" were written: "Ye are the light of the world. A city that is set on a hill cannot be hid. Neither do men light a candle, and put it under a bushel, but on a candlestick; and it giveth light unto all that are in the house." Remembering in his underground hole beneath the city the events of his (and his race's) past, the narrator begins to perceive repeatable signs in remembered phenomena that speak of an invisible city. Although the narrator has had his invisibility confirmed "again and again"[6] in every version of the earthly city, that invisibility in the epilogue becomes a key to a map of a spiritual city beneath (and within) the tangible one. Reflection leads to a discovery that "the principle" is this city, for he now sees that the struggle in his own life to determine what the "yes" means was an unconscious attempt to make "the principle" visible. He finally decides to emerge from his hole because he wishes to claim a place at this essential city's center, at the same time realizing that this "center" will always remain elusive, just beyond reach—as, indeed, will be any final definition of the self.

The very tentativeness of the definition of what the "yes" means in the epilogue also indicates the difficulty of envisioning the invisible city. That tentativeness implies that the invisible city is a process, not a final realization. Perhaps, the narrator thinks at one point, since the sacred principle was "dreamed into being out of the chaos and darkness of the feudal past," it could be *separated* from its concrete, often corrupt, manifestations in history; yet he is not happy with that interpretation of his grandfather's deathbed "yes." Maybe, then, the old man meant

> that we had to take responsibility for all of it, for the men as well as the principle because no other fitted our needs? Not for power or for vindication, but because we, with the given circumstances of our origin, could only thus find transcendence? Was it that we of all, we, most of all, had to affirm the principle, the plan in whose name we had been brutalized and sacrificed—not because we would always be weak nor because we were afraid or opportunistic, but because we were older than they, in the sense of what it took to live in the world with others and because they had exhausted in us some—not much, but some—of the human greed and smallness, yes, and the fear and superstition that had kept them running. (433–34)

The invisible man at first distinguishes between essence and the accidental, between principle and its incarnation, but then he realizes that the conception of the ideal cannot be separated from accidental experience, no matter how terrible that experience may be. In the incest story that Jim Trueblood tells to Norton and the invisible man, accident and essence, high and low, are inextricably mixed. Trueblood can endure the unspeakable by "speaking" it, by using the forms of a culture of adversity—storytelling and blues music—that Norton lacks. In this sense, Trueblood is "older," knows more of "what it took to live in the world with others," because he and his "low" culture understand that "truth" is to be found in "blood," in the very suffering that Norton tries not to face. The white industrialist, for all his material power, has nothing to protect him from the shock of Trueblood's narrative, except of course his paper money.

Precisely what "the principle" means can perhaps never be expressed in verbal terms, but this failure to pin it down does not invalidate it. Not surprisingly, Kenneth Burke is Ellison's favorite cultural thinker,[7] for Burke's distinction between "existence" and "essence" explains why Ellison puts so much faith in something that the logical positivists would say isn't real. Burke observes:

> While I was puzzling over Santayana's way of distinguishing essence from existence, a six-year-old solved the problem for me when he explained, "There *is* an Easter bunny, but he isn't *real.*" I saw the application immediately: the Easter bunny has a *being*, or *essence*, but he does not *exist*. Or put it this way: there is a *character* called the Easter bunny, since it is distinguished from all other characters; yet the Easter bunny is nowhere to be found in the realm of material substances. Here clearly is an essence that did not exist.[8]

And he continues, "If it did exist, it would be subject to the flux of existence," yet "in its sheer *character* as Easter bunny it can be contemplated *in itself.*" Moreover, the Easter bunny, even as "essence," has an effect upon the "real," material world. A child expecting him on Easter Sunday will arise earlier that morning, thus disrupting the "normal" behavior of his or her parents. Rinehart disrupts the invisible man's life in a similar manner: he never actually meets Rinehart, yet "I know I don't have to know him, that simply becoming aware of his existence, being mistaken for him, is enough to convince me Rinehart is real. It couldn't be, but it is. And it can be, is, simply because it's unknown" (376). That is, "it" (Rinehart's existence) becomes known to the invisible man as "essence," yet that essence effects action as much as a tangible presence would.

Like the Easter bunny or Rinehart, "the principle" also operates as an essence that produces accident, and of course the words evoked in its name sometimes result in ambiguous action. There is first the Ur-essence and then the verbal enactment(s) that give(s) it expression. Once expressed, an essence such as "the principle" is never totally an essence again. It is incarnated in language, and that is both a blessing and a curse. On the one hand, language can pervert an essence; on the other, there are no hints of what an essence might be without linguistic expression. For Burke and Ellison this paradox has strong moral implications. The incarnation of an "essence" will never be a perfect expression of it, because it is now limited by its enactment, and because it exists in a world of flux. That very imperfection, however, demands the continued pursuit of the ideal, the adjustment of human circumstances to new conditions.

Of course, a basic means by which humans make this adjustment is language. Ellison (following Burke) calls the process a form of "symbolic action":

> Words that evoke our principles are, according to Kenneth Burke, charismatic terms for transcendent order, for perfection. Being forms of symbolic action, they tend, through their nature as language, to sweep us in tow as they move by a process of linguistic negation toward the ideal. As a form of *symbolic* action they operate by negating nature as a given and amoral condition, creating endless series of man-made or man-imagined positives. By so doing, they nudge us toward that state of human rectitude for which, ideally, we strive.[9]

Burke's point is that there are no negatives in nature: sickness, death, and decay are "positive conditions," no different within the natural context of organic phenomena than health and growth. The negative is a human invention, and it is like the Easter bunny in that it lives in the world of essences. And it, too, affects "the world of everyday finite experience," for every human context is a form of negation: "the world of *positive* things like apples, houses, people is in the Spinozistic vocabulary a world of 'negations,' because each such positive thing is *determined*, and the determined is that which has its boundaries marked by other things, in brief by things which this particular thing is *not*."[10] In short, apples are *not* oranges; houses are *not* cars; people are *not* bears; and the invisible man is *not* Rinehart, no matter how much he resembles him.[11] And since we are all creatures driven by hope and desire, we use the negative to express where we would like to be placed (determined) within space. Consider the position of the immigrant lost in the city. He or she may in fact wish to be elsewhere; as the invisible man discovers time and again, to his dismay, he's not at the place he wants to be or expected to be. And conversely, "The only way whereby one can *not be* at one place is for one to *be* at some other place."[12] Perhaps Bigger Thomas would make the first remark, but he would surely not make the second. The first statement indicates a reaction to the outside world; the second, consciousness reflecting upon itself and moving toward the proposition "I *am* somewhere else—what can I do about it?"

One reason that the invisible man wishes to be "at some other place" is that the places in which he finds himself are often determined by a debilitating conception of the verbal negative. For the paradox of the negative is this: in resisting the tyranny of nature's "positive conditions," human beings are capable of imposing a new tyranny on themselves through the negative. (Is this not Bigger's dilemma?) And these new "determinations" become somebody else's tyranny and so must be negated in turn: the Founder's college is a city "founded" upon the negation of the pernicious consequences of slavery (history's "determinations"), but in turn it has nurtured a tyrant named Bledsoe, who tells his students, "Thou shall not." An important contradiction develops in the novel, arising from the paradox of the negative. Ellison leads the invisible man again and again into this contradiction which is expressed in the figure of the running man.[13]

Running ("in the direction of that promise which, like the horizon, recedes ever brightly and distantly beyond the hopeful traveler" [145], as Bledsoe euphemistically puts it) is frustration; running (toward "the principle") is also the only fulfillment the invisible man can ever know. Both possibilities involve the urban trope, for running as frustration always ends in either an urban labyrinth or a walled city; and running as fulfillment is always toward a heavenly city that fulfills as it recedes. It is easy to see in the novel the theme of running as frustration (as in "Keep this Nigger-Boy Running" [26]); it is more difficult to see running as fulfillment, and in fact we hardly see it that way until we reach the epilogue. But there we realize, along with the invisible man, that to be here, in this place which suddenly has a future, it was necessary to have been in those other places where we didn't want to be. In other words, "running" from them meant unknowingly running toward something of invisible worth. The future only exists within a context of process, and process is always passing, is ephemeral in incarnation. As Kenneth Burke says, a principle is something that draws us forward (something toward which we run), and the act of running itself is like "the principle" in that it cannot be said to exist: "One never expects to see a verb exist as such. One doesn't expect to see a running or an eating. One expects to see some particular thing or other running, eating, etc. Or you might put the matter thus: you can picture many kinds of houses; but you can't picture housiness, which is sheer principle, the name of 'an ideal way of being a house.'"[14]

Because of the indefiniteness of the act of running, the nature of the running man is unfinished, always ambiguous. There will always be a gap between the "ideal and the actual, between the perfect word and the errant flesh," and thus the quest itself will forever remain something of a "mystery." In a sense, the epilogue in *Invisible Man* could be considered a figurative running done in the mind, a running toward "ideals grounded in a vision of perfection that transcends the limitations of death and dying." For Ellison, that action is essentially human. "Power ceases in the instant of repose," said his namesake Ralph Waldo Emerson; "it resides in the moment of transition from a past to a new state."[15] Emerson is talking about standing still and running in a figurative sense, repose and movement as expressions of the basic rhythms of the universe. Yet the key word for Emerson is *power*, and Ellison's running man is like Emerson's protean man, changing shape to realize himself, but only realizing himself at the moment of the metamorphosis. Therefore his potential for empowerment, in every sense, depends on his continuing to "run."

For Ellison, as he says in "The Little Man at Chehaw Station," the "ideals grounded in a vision of perfection"[16] can only be realized in the act of striving for them. We run toward "perfection," "the principle" being a source of energy and a *telos*, but because it cannot be pictured we often embody it in some concrete form that reflects our self-interest. This embodiment is at once inevitable and contradictory.

Through most of the novel the invisible man cannot see, so he collaborates with those who refuse to see him and who manipulate him for their own purposes. Bledsoe's letters to the northern executives, intended to undermine the invisible man's prospects, merely push this hapless traveler in a mistaken direction in which he was already going, but paradoxically his haplessness and mistakes eventually seem necessary. If he is a fool, he is William Blake's fool, persisting in his folly. "Self-reliance" is necessary, but it is only part of the social constitution of the human animal, and the invisible man continually rediscovers the American capacity for reducing self-reliance to self-interest. The past *promises* the future but doesn't guarantee it, as David Hume noted in a different context.

"National beginnings," which Ellison associates "with Edenic promises," are less important than running toward national endings. Moreover, the gratuitous invocation of those promises allows for a kind of metaphysical bulimia: "we Americans are given to eating, regurgitating, and, alas, re-eating . . . our sacred words."[17] These texts that represent our body politic are taken in yet never absorbed to become part of the body. In Ellison's novel, the word made flesh literally chokes the invisible man after the "battle royal," when he regurgitates Booker T. Washington's famous Atlanta Exposition Speech. That speech even when it was first delivered was a plea for a meager accommodation for Afro-Americans—Washington understood that to be the best which could be hoped for; but by the time the invisible man—battered, bloody, and debased—repeats the speech, its meaning is wholly changed. The hope of accommodation becomes the opportunity for blacks to destroy each other fighting for a small prize of money. Yet even in *this* deconstructed speech there exists, negatively, the presence of the ideal. Ellison always sees another side to the incarnated word, the incarnated dream. True, "the principle" is usually corrupted when incarnated, but in its incarnation, no matter how corrupt, it still shines through as though in a palimpsest: "Hell, weren't they their own death and their own destruction *except* as the principle lived in them and in us?" (my italics).

The utopian impulse in *Invisible Man* suggests Burke's definition of *entelechy*, "the title for the fact that the seed 'implicitly contains' a future conforming to its nature, if the external conditions necessary to such unfolding and fulfillment occur in the right order." Burke is drawing, of course, from Aristotle, and so the connection is made between Ellison's thought and the long mainstream tradition of Western philosophy. Another variation appears, for instance, in Eric Auerbach's theory of the figura in the Middle Ages, "the idea that earthly life is thoroughly real, with the reality of the flesh into which the Logos entered, but that with all its reality it is only *umbra* and *figura* of the authentic future, ultimate truth, the real reality that will unveil and preserve the *figura*."[18] This same idea is expressed again by Fredric Jameson in his analysis of Ernst Bloch's conception of utopia: "a kind of allegorical structure is built into the very forward movement of the Utopian impulse itself, which always points to something other, which can never reveal itself directly but must always speak in figures, which always calls out structurally for completion and exegesis."[19] These are all attempts to explain the recurring problem in Western thought of the connection between the ideal and the real; in *Invisible Man*, this problem is one major theme in the novel, from the invisible "spook" of the opening lines to the invisible radio waves of the last sentence. Ellison's comic genius delights in depicting the various kinds of interplay between the real and the ideal, as he attempts to demystify *and* mystify, to unveil and veil, or, as Rinehart's handbill declares, to "BEHOLD THE INVISIBLE" and present "THE SEEN UNSEEN" (374). And always, even within the agents of mass culture, a utopian impulse is lurking somewhere.

Like Burke and Ellison, Fredric Jameson stresses the importance of the negative in the utopian impulse, the invisible presence of the future contained in the present. Utopian literature is significant, says Jameson, not because of the literal forms of the future that it predicts but because it represents a "stubborn negation"[20] of the present, the present that tends toward what Burke would call the "bureaucratization of the imaginative," the hardening of fluid life into stone.[21] Thus, for Jameson, the response in the presence of the utopian impulse is "astonishment," the emotion felt at something that exists in the interstices between the shadow and the act. The problem with human beings, Burke and Jameson would agree, is that in their rush to understand the world they try to fix it in rigidity; they impose stable forms upon chaos without allowing for its most essential quality, mutability.

Mutability is the general problem of utopias, and in Ellison's *Invisible Man* there are repeated attempts to deny "the principle," to tie Proteus down, to contain the energy of the running man within a frozen tableau. The novel's major critique of these attempts takes the form of an antipastoral, an extended sequence that really involves two separate critiques. The pastoral is perhaps the most rigid sort of utopia, as well as the most socially unrealistic. Historically it has been used as a vehicle to attack the corruptions of urban life; the Golden Age of rural innocence in the garden, gentle love between shepherds and shepherdesses, could remind the decadent courtiers of what they had lost. In American history one version of the pastoral image is transformed into the frontier, an image of freedom from maps, from the labyrinths of human cities and societies. The virtue of this un-bounded garden is the expanse it might give to individual human ex-pression, perhaps the perfect dovetailing of setting and telos for Rousseauean man "born free." Even after 1890, when the frontier was declared to have been closed (and, incidentally, when the momen-tum of black migration to the north began to grow), this rural-urban, good-evil dichotomy continued in the cultural imagination.

The pastoral is important in Ellison's story not only as it represents a frozen utopia but also because of its relation to black myth and black history. The primary myth is of the plantation tradition, with its happy, singing "darkies" and its implications of an "organic" soci-ety in which hierarchy is the "natural" expression of the innate quali-ties of races and individuals. (This sort of social organicism, of course, is always defined from the top down.) The pastoral is also connected to the major event of Afro-American history in the twentieth century, the Great Migration by blacks from the rural south to the northern cities. As I have noted, that migration was not limited to the decade of World War I or the 1920s or 30s. World War II produced a greater attraction of black people to the north than even World War I had, and between 1940 and 1950, when Ellison was beginning to write *In-visible Man*, the net migration of blacks exceeded the total for the pre-ceding thirty years. The reasons for this movement remained virtual-ly the same in 1950 as they had been in 1920—greater economic opportunity in the north, as well as some freedom from the south's system of segregation, the separate and unequal society. Ellison's in-visible man, in moving from Alabama to New York,[22] follows one classic pattern of migration for blacks, just as Bigger did in moving from Mississippi to Chicago, but it's not money or freedom that moves Ellison's protagonist. Fittingly for the pastoral tradition, he leaves because he is expelled from the garden.

As in the garden myth, he is tossed out because of what he knows—though in Ellison's ironic modulation of narrator and character, the invisible man doesn't yet know *that* he knows. He demolishes the idea of a pastoral world in either the rural countryside or the garden of the university, without quite realizing what he has done; but at the end of the episode he is on a bus headed north. The narrator remembers the college in terms of a dual perspective, alternately the innocent who relives the experience and the sadder but wiser man who reflects upon it. Ellison mixes his narrative means, keeping us off-balance at every turn. To the innocent, the college is an enclosed garden; but to the memory-laden narrator, it is a garden with real toads in it:

> It was a beautiful college. The buildings were old and covered with vines and the roads gracefully winding, lined with hedges and wild roses that dazzled the eyes in the summer sun. Honeysuckle and purple wisteria hung heavy from the trees and white magnolias mixed with scents in the bee-humming air. I've recalled it often, here in my hole: How the grass turned green in the springtime and how the mocking birds fluttered their tails and sang, how the moon shone down on the buildings, how the bell in the chapel tower rang out the precious short-lived hours; how the girls in bright summer dresses promenaded the grassy lawn. Many times, here at night, I've closed my eyes and walked along the forbidden road that winds past the girls' dormitories, past the hall with the clock in its tower, its windows warmly aglow, on down past the small white Home Economics practice cottage, whiter still in the moonlight, and on down the road with its sloping and turning, paralleling the black powerhouse with its engines droning earth-shaking rhythms in the dark, its windows red from the glow of the furnace, on to where the road became a bridge over a dry riverbed, tangled with brush and clinging vines; the bridge of rustic logs, made for trysting, but virginal and untested by lovers; on up the road, past the buildings, with the southern verandas half-a-city-block long, to the sudden forking, barren of buildings, birds or grass, where the road turned off to the insane asylum. (27)

The movement of the paragraph follows the movement of the novel which will take place as the narrator leaves the garden for the industrial city, the dynamo in the garden foreshadowing Lucius Brockway's boiler room; and the home economics cottage, the "efficiency" that operates within the "small city" of Liberty Paints. The passage also moves from themes of order to themes of disorder, from sunshine to darkness (foreshadowing Jim Trueblood and the Golden Day), to a world where "southern verandas" are "half-a-city-block long" on the road to the insane asylum.

An important point about the college is that it is *not* either the rural world or a real garden. Behind its flowers, trees, and cottages is hidden the powerhouse of the modern industrial city. One can appreciate Ellison's satiric touch: the home economics cottage appears "whiter still in the moonlight," that is, in contrast to the darkness of the night, but behind it and down the road is the dynamo that drives it, for the home economics movement (or "domestic science," as it was sometimes called) was linked to Taylorism and the factory system.[23] The cottage's enhanced whiteness beckons like the genteel middle-class life the students imagine they are destined for, though the clear indication is that their preparation is meant to fit them smoothly into Norton's industrial scheme; the dynamo is associated with "a dry riverbed," a "virginal" bridge—not incapable, but unused—and finally, madness. Thus the "Economics" house is the purpose of Bledsoe's college, its static order the opposite of the disorderly but neighborly house run by Mary Rambo in the invisible city of New York.

For Ellison, Bledsoe is "the black powerhouse" at the heart of a demonic city. The myth of the Founder's mission, so eloquently described by Homer Barbee in his speech, disguises a very urban "power set-up" (110), with Bledsoe at the controls. Appropriately, when Bledsoe summons the narrator to his office to tell him he is being expelled, Ellison deliberately uses *film noir* lighting for this dark, big-city scene: "When I went in he was wiping his neck with a blue-bordered handkerchief. The shaded lamp catching the lenses of his glasses left half of his broad face in shadow as his clenched fists stretched full forth in the light before him" (106). The expressionistic lighting, continued throughout the scene, echoes the odd mixture of light and darkness used to describe the black powerhouse, "its windows red from the glow of the furnace." Bledsoe is the sun's dark double in the pastoral world, a gangster in the garden, the man who manipulates the manipulators from the urban north. He is the ultimate urban pragmatist, winning the city and ruling it ruthlessly but no longer knowing why he does so: "I don't even insist that it was worth it, but now I'm here and I mean to stay" (111). In order for him to stay, the invisible man, the unintentional unveiler, has to go.

The image of Bledsoe as an academic gunman is a logical end for the series of reversals and confutations out of which Ellison builds this section. The immediate cause of the invisible man's downfall was his being assigned, as a trusted student, to chauffeur Mr. Norton, a rich white trustee, through the countryside near the college. On their trip they meet Jim Trueblood, and the episode turns into a black parody of the classical pastoral (e.g., that of Theocritus) in which an urban sophisticate traveling in the country overhears a rural love song. Trueblood's "song," of course, relates a horrific tale of rape and incest, not what the city man was prepared for, and not providing the easy and obvious moral the city should get from the "simpler" life of the country. The tale is a complex tour de force of narrative styles and rhetorical strategies, and it also happens to open onto Mr. Norton's personal abyss, where lies a buried self that he wishes to keep buried. At the story's end a shaken Norton gives Trueblood a one-hundred-dollar bill, thus updating the pastoral illusion: the city pays the country to project an ideal, though in this case not the naive swain or lovable "darkey" but the libidinous beast. Most importantly, by paying the storyteller for his story, Norton commercializes his own relationship to it, creating a safe distance between vicarious experience and his own unexamined desires.[24] The episode concludes with a trip to the "pastoral village inn," a bar/bordello appropriately called "the Golden Day," in order to "rejuvenate" a spent Norton. Here he meets the real inhabitants of the countryside, the lunatics from the insane asylum, counterparts in the country to the "lunatics" who attend the college. Ellison's two-part critique of the pastoral ideal—the college as an ersatz garden, and rural life shown in a desperately realistic light—recalls the New England farmer's remark "Things ain't so good as they used to be, and they never were."[25]

There has been yet another ironic level in this narrative, however; Trueblood begins his unnerving story by recalling his "Mobile days," briefly evoking a Mark Twain nineteenth-century Mississippi pastoral that seems entirely alien to the world of Bledsoe and Norton. In that river world, the ephemeral events of the everyday are valuable as they happen. Trueblood is open to the momentary and the accidental, as in his recollection of watching a pretty woman walk down a country road; and in this openness is the protean flexibility that Norton or Bledsoe lacks. Trueblood's storytelling differs radically from the speech Homer Barbee delivers shortly afterward at the college convocation, and as always with Ellison, a linguistic difference represents a real and significant difference.

Barbee's style is versatile, his allusions ranging from high culture to low culture, but his epic theme is not. Epics, as we know, deal with the founding of cities, and *Homer* Barbee is the epic celebrator of the college's founding. As the epic bard, he celebrates Bledsoe as the Founder's Ascanius, who finished what Aeneas did not live to finish. The Founder's "dream," says Barbee in his famous sermon, "conceived in the starkness and darkness of slavery, [is] fulfilled now even in the air you breathe" (93). The Founder's past "seeking," he tells the students, has resulted in the "bright horizon which you *now* enjoy" (93; my italics).

In a sense, however, this patriarchal city was already completed at the first moment of its conception, and it does not promise to be flexible or open to change like Trueblood's river world. Because the epic posits a world determined by a single event in the past, the founding of a city, its reality, as Mikhail Bakhtin says in an appropriate metaphor, is always "walled off" and can only be approached with "reverence." The epic deals with a past that is completed, and it imposes its completed condition upon the present, for "the epic world knows only a single and unified world view." Yet "laughter," adds Bakhtin, "destroys epic distance," and "the dialogic imagination" of the invisible man's other urban perspective, his New York basement, makes us look at this sermon in several lights, not just one.[26] This implies something about Ellison's "principle"—it is not the epic's single voice celebrating a homogeneous city but rather the multiple voices of an open city.[27] Moreover, Ellison's novel as an expression of Bakhtin's "dialogic imagination" tends to confirm rather than deny (via satire) the idea of a heavenly city in Barbee's sermon. That sermon is *both* a corrupt version of "the principle," and the figura that reveals its presence in American culture, the city on the hill. This double vision explains why the sermon is both a satiric exposure of three scoundrels (the unholy trinity of the Founder, Barbee, and Bledsoe)[28] and, as Barbee says, "a beautiful story" (92). Although Barbee claims to be a witness, in the full biblical meaning of that word, to the Founder's life ("I knew him well and loved him, and I was there"

[96]), it is the story, not the man, that bears witness: it describes an ongoing quest for a city not yet found or founded.[29]

The import of Barbee's sermon is that it displays in miniature Ellison's narrative method throughout *Invisible Man*: satire containing within it the seed of future fulfillment. Consider, for instance, the sculptural figure of the Founder lifting the veil from the eyes of a "kneeling slave." The satire is obvious: "I am standing puzzled, unable to decide whether the veil is really being lifted, or lowered more firmly in place" (28). Yet if we remember Auerbach's observation that the figura is both a veiling and an unveiling, then we see that Ellison intends the ambiguity and not the satire to be the real point of the narrator's memory of this scene. Although we see through a glass darkly, the glass is in another view an illuminated manuscript waiting to reveal itself.

In the novel's opening line, "No, I am not a spook like those who haunted Edgar Allan Poe; nor am I one of your Hollywood-movie ectoplasms" (3), the figura of the spook is a kind of ghostly presence representing the many literary figures who hover behind Ellison's text. One of the most important of these is Ralph Waldo Emerson, whose writings appear as intellectual specters every time his name is evoked.[30] When Norton claims that the invisible man is Norton's "fate," meaning that he is a part of Norton's plans, we think of the Emersonian essay "Fate," in which a restrictive determinism is confronted and overcome through a protean will and intelligence. Similarly, the allusion to Edgar Allan Poe might recall his brilliant story "The Man of the Crowd," in which there appears the urbanite who refuses to be read. The actions of Poe's man of the crowd cannot be fathomed because he is a phantom, blown about by the random impulses of the city. He is a modern man in the modern city: mercurial, unsubstantial, his character a perfect mirror of the electrical energy running through the London streets. Yet what is a horrible revelation to Poe's narrator (and perhaps to Richard Wright) is a source of delight to Ralph Waldo Emerson. For Emerson would have us all be "spooks" in the sense of ectoplasm: "matter reduced to extreme thinness." Behind the delicate skein of skin of a human being is a world whose laws make those of crude cause and effect seem puny. "Power," says Emerson in "Experience," "keeps quite another road than the turnpikes of choice and will, namely, the subterranean and invisible tunnels and channels of life."[31] Emerson's urban metaphors foreshadow the invisible man's revelation in the subway about the boys in zoot suits who are "outside of history" (331–33).

The coming together of these allusions, or perhaps they are only vague suggestions or hints, is part of the method of Ellison's novel. Like Emerson, Ellison argues that life is largely a matter of making music out of things around you, out of the messiness of your own life, if need be. The narrator is forced to "make music out of invisibility" (11)—to *improvise*, an important word in Ellison's lexicon.[32] For in assembling and reassembling the various parts of your life, you may discover an invisible harmony. The tension between chaos and order, which is such a major theme in Emerson's essays and in *Invisible Man*, is reconciled by the twin (and related) figures of Orpheus and Proteus, the one harmonizing the world to match the self, the other changing the self to deal with the world.

Proteus, a figure who looms large in *Invisible Man*, was an important figure for the Renaissance precisely because he was associated with creating "cities on earth." The Renaissance believed that "man is not Protean because he is civilized; he is civilized because he is Protean."[33] Proteus is multisided like the city, living in many realms at once like Ellison's little man at Chehaw Station. In *Invisible Man*, it is only by becoming Proteus that the narrator can begin to read the signs of yams and leg irons. Paradoxically, it takes a civilized intelligence to make sense of something apparently simple. Yet living in the city's liquid reality, as he does, makes him dangerous because unpredictable. He can change at a moment's notice, as the city changes from instant to instant.

There is always a risk in such change, but the alternative is worse: the human tendency to choose one of Proteus's many shapes and call it the ultimate reality—hence the walled city and Bakhtin's monomyth. Burke's analysis of the rage for order explains all those formerly fluid, now fixed, states of being in *Invisible Man*: "An imagined possibility (usually at the start Utopian) is bureaucratized when it is embodied in the realities of a social texture, in all the complexities of language and habits, in the property relationships, the methods of government, production and distribution, in the development of rituals that re-enforce the same emphasis." We would be doomed to live with this cake of ice were it not for protean humans' unpredictable tendency to open the icebox. Consumer capitalism, for instance, strives to impose itself upon all aspects of American life, but until we have "a monetary equivalent for everything, until every last bit of material exchange among friends [is] done for profit, until every casual greeting [is] given at a price," there are still cracks in the seams of the official ideology. If there is a perverse propensity in human nature to bureaucratize the imaginative, there is also a propensity to resist bureaucracy—to insist that the city's gates be swung open.[34] Burke's analysis of the failure of bureaucracy to thoroughly bureaucratize everything is part of the reason that, in the epilogue, the invisible man thinks of emerging from his basement. As long as there is one Peter Wheatstraw (Ellison's version of "Peetie") in the city's streets, the "imperial city" has failed in its quest to imperialize.

For Ralph Waldo Emerson, the more cracks in the seams the better, but he, too, is haunted by the twin themes of order and chaos, the centripetal city versus the centrifugal. Resisting a completely open city, he argues for an invisible city with its own unique center.[35] In a passage that may have been one source for *Invisible Man*, Emerson speculates in "Experience" on the subterranean pattern that lies behind our protean quirks: "Bear with these distractions, with this coetaneous growth of the parts: they will one day be *members* and obey one will . . . Underneath the inharmonious and trivial particulars, is a musical perfection, the Ideal journeying always with us, the heaven without rent or seam. Do but observe the mode of our illumination."[36] It's a hard line to walk between the ideal and the real, the perfect and the particular; and Emerson most often steps over into idealism. For Ellison, however, as for Kenneth Burke, William Carlos Williams, and, ultimately, Aristotle, it is equally important that there is no ideal without a host of real particulars. He is a true modernist in this, because one of modernism's important aims is to valorize particulars, no matter how disparate or ugly they may be. Emerson theorizes, but it is Whitman, his contemporary, who immerses himself in the world. The invisible man, like Whitman, lives and moves by the particulars of his world. This orientation implies a division between "high" and "low" which not only is theoretical but is also reflected in society's economic structure and in its cultural systems, the distinction between "elite" and "popular" art forms.

When the invisible man reaches New York, one of the first things he does is to go to a movie, "a picture of frontier life with heroic Indian fighting and struggles against flood, storm, and forest fire, with the out-numbered settlers winning each engagement; an epic of wagon trains rolling ever westward. I forgot myself (although there was no one like me taking part in the adventures) and left the dark room in a lighter mood" (130). The western movie is an epic form of mass culture and, as in Bakhtin's epic, historical time in this cinematic genre collapses into one moment: that instant when the attempted settlement in the wilderness clashes with the forces of "lawlessness and savagery" (Indians, outlaws, and so forth) that are still strong enough to threaten it.[37] This moment, as we have seen, is similar in its monomythic dimensions to the epic moment in Barbee's sermon when the Founder confronted and overcame his figurative Indians. The western simplifies history, reducing it to a single epic moment, in the same way that a product of mass culture simplifies its subject in an effort to maximize its potential audience. But mass culture's conception of its audience is a limited one, and the invisible man defines an Afro-American's relationship to Hollywood by noting, "I forgot myself (although there was no one like me taking part in the adventures) and left the dark room in a lighter mood." The point of the pun is that the only way Afro-Americans can attach themselves to that epic wagon train is by becoming white.

In a sense, the rest of Ellison's novel explores the possibility of *not* joining the wagon train. Until the epilogue, however, it does so always in terms of depicting that not-joining as a failure. The invisible man does his best to fit in and find acceptance, yet in the end he is rejected by all the institutions of society. And that is his redemption: try as he may to embrace the earthly city, he can never quite figure out how to do it, and each step he tries to take toward those towers of visible success in fact leads him toward the invisible city whose inhabitants only he can see shuffling by him in the streets.

So, just in time, along comes Peter Wheatstraw, Ellison's own version of an epic hero and city-builder, he of the many voices and many blueprints, singing a song about a woman of parts who looks like a sphinx.[38] Peter Wheatstraw stands in perfect opposition to the western movie, as chaos does to completed form. He is an assortment of odds and ends, from his Charlie Chaplin baggy pants to his crazy-quilt blues song. Indeed, even the blueprints in his wheelbarrow are not of a piece—they consist of "everything"—"cities, towns, country-clubs. Some just buildings and houses. I got damn near enough to build me a house if I could live in a paper house as they do in Japan. I guess somebody's done changed their plans" (133). In fact, Barbee's sermon and the movie's myth of the white man's conquest illustrate the change from "plans" to "plan." It will take the entire novel for the narrator to realize that Peter and those groundlings like him are America's true ground. Although the name "Wheatstraw" seems to allude to "chaff," to the discarded part of the wheat, Peter will in fact be the seed from which the invisible man's new consciousness will grow. He is the straw that gives a brick coherence. The blueprints left behind are the worlds of possibility now discarded; they contain "the principle" struggling to emerge into form. These blueprints are aspirations shrouded in mystery, in "astonishment" (characterized by Jameson as the response to the utopian impulse), which the narrator feels but cannot say why he feels. Peter himself speaks like an oracle, asking questions ("Is you got the dog?") without giving answers. Whatever *the* dog is, the narrator clearly doesn't have it, not even the common sense to sniff out faulty plans and bad faith. When the narrator tells Peter that it is important to stick to one "plan," Peter knows that the invisible man needs a good lesson in how dogs behave.

But there is something else going on here as well. Slavery may be in the past, but the bloodhounds are still in hot pursuit, and Ellison seems to suggest that the only way to beat them is to become one. According to the anthropologist Edmund Leach, dogs occupy a "special category" in our civilization in that they slide up and down the scale of human evaluation. On the one hand, "to call a man a dog is an obscenity," a low-level metaphor that Leach might have illustrated by blues lines: "Ain't going to be your dog," or "Don't dog me around." On the other hand, "in seventeenth century English witchcraft trials it was very commonly asserted that the Devil appeared in the form of a Dog—that is, God backwards."[39] Robert Johnson's famous blues song "Hellhound on My Trail" implies both the demonic and the mysterious that we associate with supernatural powers. To be a "hound," as the blues singer "Hound Dog Taylor" knew, could convey a certain nobility.[40] Barbara Babcock has noted a similar ambiguity regarding the coyote in "trickster" tales, a creature whose nature— half hero, half charlatan—defies human classification; the trickster remains "invisible" because he is neither this nor that.[41] When the invisible man meets Peter, the city has freed him from previous categories, and Peter, in asking him if he *has* the dog, seems to be telling him he can now start from scratch: he can become the "dog" of his choice. And eventually the city provides that lesson, though the invisible man must first confront a series of false cities, beginning with the "small city" (149) of Liberty Paints, where he goes to work.

Liberty Paints as an earthly city is an example of Burke's "bureaucratization of the imaginative," for it literalizes the city of light in the Book of Revelation. In mixing the prize-winning paint called "Optic White" (with its echo of the White City of Chicago's Columbian Exposition of 1893), the narrator unintentionally becomes "the nigger in the woodpile," putting the wrong dope in the vat. The figura shines through that act, as the narrator for the moment unknowingly emulates Peter Wheatstraw, Mary Rambo, Tarp, and a host of others. For the White City of America could look white only if black people were there as the "ground" ("10 drops" [152] of black paint dope) but were not visible—they were literally excluded from Chicago's White City Exposition. Yet Ellison understands that their absence implies their invisible presence: when the Optic White comes out slightly gray, it is as if an act of industrial miscegenation has taken place. In fact, Liberty Paints hides a black man, Lucius Brockway, away in a hole where he makes the "vee-hicle" (as he calls it), the "base" of the paint. He has chosen to remain buried in the cellar, to define himself as the end of possibility, with one blueprint of reality in his mind, the blueprint of the building foundations of Liberty Paints. He is set against all change, though he was once a Proteus who did seize an opportunity and turn it to advantage, into *his* shape. Because of that act the future still shines through him, dimly as in a boiler room darkly, for now he is the king of an underworld city, the emperor of Dis.

The invisible man's descent into that underworld literally explodes his illusions; he falls from innocence into experience as Brockway kills his old self and sends him to a surreal hospital where he is prodded, shocked, and defined as not fit for "industrial conditions" (187). The implication is that he should go "home" to a pastoral life; and so, ironically, he has, though not in the way the doctors meant. Confined in their box in their hospital, the invisible man hears "a sweet-voiced trumpet rendering 'The Holy City' as from an echoing distance" (178). The music arises from his memory of the college but persists as a reminder of a future that is continually making itself known in the present. For locked in their "machine," he is buffeted with memories of his racial history and his own life. At a crucial point the question comes to him, "WHAT WAS YOUR MOTHER'S NAME?" (183). His identity scrambled, he is released amid images of rebirth to return to Harlem and be taken in by a new mother, Mary Rambo.

He ends up at Mary Rambo's boarding house because when he returns to his old lodgings, the Men's House, an urban annex of Bledsoe's college, he sees everything there in a new light: "The moment I entered the bright, buzzing lobby of the Men's House I was overcome by a sense of alienation and hostility. My overalls were causing stares and I knew that I could live there no longer, that that phase of my life was past. The lobby was the meeting place for various groups still caught in the illusions that had just been boomeranged out of my head" (194).

The city has begun to give the invisible man lessons in earnest, and when he almost by reflex empties a full spittoon over the head of a man he mistakes for Bledsoe, he has "boomeranged" himself back to a "cultural zero" at which point he is excluded from the Men's House, (a world of aspirants to fake gentility, "with their homburgs and Chesterfields, their polo coats and Tyrolean hats worn strictly as fashion demanded" [195]) but not included in any other world. Or not yet aware of which world he is included in, for his experience of the city will be a series of collisions with people and scenes that gradually lift him from his zero point, though paradoxically this experience will leave him marooned in a cellar with a briefcase full of junk. As he observes about city life, "In the South everybody knew you but coming North was a jump into the unknown. How many days could you walk the streets of the city without encountering anyone who knew you, and how many nights. You could actually make yourself anew" (377). The remark resembles in its ambivalent reaction to the city Dunbar's characterization of the urban effect in *The Sport of the Gods*.

Most of the invisible man's encounters with people in the city are singular: he meets people once and they vanish, disappearing back into the anonymous mass, though their impression remains with him. In 1921 Ezra Pound made an acute observation about the city experience, suggesting how making oneself anew might be a source of a new kind of urban order and not a descent into chaos: "The life of a village is narrative; you have not been there three weeks before you know that in the revolution, et cetera, and when M Le Compte et cetera, and so forth. In the city the visual impressions succeed each other, overlap, overcross, they are 'cinematographic,' but they are not a simple linear sequence. They are often a flood of nouns without verbal relations."[42] Like Walter Benjamin, Pound saw that modernity had rendered the traditional storyteller obsolete, for the storyteller implied a cohesive community of listeners who helped supply the connecting links (verbs) of a story. The structure of the organic community ensures that there is a common bond of experience to act as a "ground" for narrative comprehension. In contrast, there is no common bond of experience in the city, the newspaper being its symbol of the way events are communicated—fragmented, overexplained, and repeated again and again—because the newspaper cannot assume a background as a storyteller can.[43] Yet Pound saw that the city itself might create its own kind of storyteller, who, if he were able to manipulate the protean world he lived in, could tell a new kind of story.

A year after Pound made his remark, *The Waste Land* was published, and Eliot applied Pound's technique (availing himself of Pound's editing help) to the "Unreal City" of London. Yet Eliot's poem depicts a personal reaction to the malaise of modern urban life and a strong cultural distaste for its crowds and artifacts without finding more hope in that life than a handful of quotations by long-dead writers. Eliot can only desire to reconstitute a past frozen in obsolete forms, describing the protean world he fears but never redeeming it. For Ellison, however, the city must be redeemed in terms of the present and immediate experience must be remade to promote a usable future, because for black Americans the past cannot be a refuge.[44] It must be remembered but it cannot be relived.

After moving to Mary Rambo's house, the invisible man is walking a Harlem street when he smells a familiar and delicious smell and sees at the end of the block a small cart where the yam man sells hot roasted yams, "bringing a stab of swift nostalgia" (199). He buys and eats this food from his past, and moved by memories and a sense of freedom they bring, he buys more of them. Yet he realizes: "Continue on the yam level and life would be sweet—though somewhat yellowish. . . . The freedom to eat yams on the street was far less than I had expected upon coming to the city. An unpleasant taste bloomed in my mouth now" (202). The past is not enough, even with its echo of the Golden Age ("yellowish"), and the narrator's redemption must be a "running," a coming to terms with things as they happen.

In the novel's final section, as Harlem is being torn apart by the riots, and black people are being victimized by the opportunistic politics of Jack and the Brotherhood, the storytellers are busy putting their world back together out of the broken fragments. This city narrative is "cinematographic": out of the darkness of the Harlem screen comes Dupre, he of the "thrice hatted head" (he has stolen three Dobbs hats from an expensive men's store), looking like the Pope as he baptizes his own apartment with kerosene. He becomes the center of a group whose members are already telling tall tales of the night's doings, already formulating frames that will be passed down to others as inherited wisdom about this night when, as one says, "I seen some things I never seen before" (424). One of those "things" is Ras the Exhorter, whose exploits one storyteller in this group of storytellers (and Ellison emphasizes the democracy of the situation) proceeds to describe.

In the previous section of the novel, which deals with the narrator's involvement with the Brotherhood, Ras, a West Indian with the charisma of Marcus Garvey, has been a formidable antagonist to the invisible man. An epic figure on the order of the Founder, Ras, too, wishes to found a city, one based upon race. The storyteller, though, describes him not with an epic vocabulary but with a vocabulary that comes out of vaudeville, a form of mass art in which, as in the cinema, "impressions succeed each other, overlap, overcross." In a sense, Ellison is echoing Eliot's original title for *The Waste Land* ("He Do the Police in Different Voices"), for the storyteller speaks of Ras in different voices, moving him through a series of transformations, partly heroic, mostly bathetic.[45] He is first depicted as Genghis Khan ("He had him a big black hoss and a fur cap and some kind of old lion skin or something over his shoulders" [424]), then as a cowboy, then as something out of a comic-strip apocalypse: "And 'bout that time some joker with a big ole Georgia voice sticks his head out of the window and yells, 'Ride 'em cowboy. Give 'em hell and bananas.' And man, that crazy sonofabitch up there on that hoss looking like death eating a sandwich, he reaches down and comes up with a forty-five and starts blazing up at that window" (424–425). The storyteller next turns Ras into a medieval knight matched against the mounted city police ("He reached back of his saddle and come up with some kind of old shield"), and as Ras moves toward the police, one of his followers hands him a spear—"You know, one of the kind you see them African guys carrying in the moving pictures" (425).

At this point in this "cinematographic" story, we are interrupted by an intermission. Someone asks the storyteller, "Where the hell are you?" and his answer is appropriate to the material: "Me? I'm over on the side where some stud done broke in a store and is selling cold beer out of the window. Done gone into business, man." When Ras charges the police, the storyteller changes metaphor again: "He's got his head down low . . . like Earle Sande in the fifth at Jamaica" (425). What ensues is a mock-heroic battle out of Cervantes' *Don Quixote* or Fielding's *Tom Jones*, but appropriately adapted to the modern city. Ras escapes, shooting "up the street . . . like Heigho, the goddam Silver!" (426). What makes this scene work is the storyteller's ability "to make it new" (as Pound advised the moderns) again and again, as Ellison applies Eliot's "mythical method" to Harlem, fusing folklore, mass culture, and classical allusion. The effect of this passage is a comic diminution of the "hero," but not only that: the storyteller, mirroring Ellison's "dialogic imagination" in the many voices of the city, mocks the hero's absurd pretension while managing, in a backhanded way, to affirm his resistance.

For Ellison the modern city is a symbol of chaos, and at the heart of that city is Harlem—"nowhere," as he called it in an essay entitled "Harlem Is Nowhere." In that essay he turns Richard Wright on his head, writing, "For if Harlem is the scene of the folk-Negro's death agony, it is also the setting of his transcendence."[46] That is, "nowhere" is also utopia, and in *Invisible Man* Ellison ends the section on the Harlem riots with an image of the storyteller who does more than shore fragments against ruins. He is Proteus the rebuilder, anticipating what the invisible man will do in his hole when he creates a "city of words" out of his memories and so, by the act of writing, mirrors a larger reconstruction. Uprooted and dislocated, African slaves had to remake a culture, and they did so by any means possible. "When we began to build a sense of ourselves," Ellison said in an interview, "we did it by abstracting from the Bible, abstracting the myths of the ancient Jews, the early Christians, modifying them as we identified with these people, and projecting ourselves. . . . This was a creative process. . . . this was the *reunification* of a shattered group of people."[47]

Within this section of *Invisible Man* is another allusion, elaborated in terms of both classical epic and modern comedy, which deals specifically with the idea of "reunification." Ellison plays with a paradox crucial to the meaning of Virgil's *Aeneid*: "Rome [was] founded not by a conqueror but by a defeated man."[48] The invisible man's excursion with the middle-aged white woman named Sybil has the flavor of a Mack Sennett comedy, with the narrator putting her in a cab to send her home only to find her again—drunk, incoherent, and full of lust— on another streetcorner. (Later, when he is finally rid of her, it occurs to him that she may have been the person responsible for the Harlem riots.) But this encounter and the one between Aeneas and his Sybil in book 6 of the *Aeneid* have parallel meanings. Until that prophetess guided the Trojan hero through Hades to his dead father, Anchises, Aeneas had wandered across the world without direction; only in Hell does Anchises give him a firm sense of geography and mission: he is to found a city in a new world. The narrator in *Invisible Man* is also haunted by a spiritual father's presence as he wanders the city; and it is only in his underworld that he discovers the meaning of the deathbed "yes." Saying yes to "the principle" means saying yes to a vision of civilization. This was what his grandfather had been trying to get him to see: that he would have to lose his sense of direction before he found it. And this means not looking back, but looking forward, for like Aeneas, the invisible man cannot go home again—"his is no homecoming or *nostos*, like that of Odysseus. . . . The real tragedy is that he is not and cannot be an Odysseus. He can never go home."[49] It also suggests that those who have been "defeated" are best able to understand the need to reunify this nation of the lost.

What Ellison makes of the classical allusion to Sybil illustrates in miniature what he does through the novel with many of his major characters. She begins as a comic figure, a caricature based on the traditional ingredients of age and gender and an incongruous lust, but ends as mysterious as her classical antecedent: who is that woman who keeps turning up on street corners? When the narrator leads his intoxicated Sybil through the streets of New York, they stand before a building whose carvings recall those on the gates of Apollo's temple at Cumae: "We tottered before an ancient-looking building, its windows dark. Huge Greek medallions showed in spots of light upon its facade, above a dark labyrinthine pattern in stone, and I propped her against the stoop with its carved stone monster. She leaned there, her hair wild" (399–400)."[50] This Sybil is now frenzied like a prophetess; the carvings are the work of Daedalus; the labyrinth, that of King Minos, built to house the Minotaur. The carvings narrate Daedalus's escape from Crete after he helped Theseus destroy the monster, and the invisible man will soon find himself in Harlem's labyrinth, in a hole where he must grapple with his own monsters before he can become a storyteller like Daedalus.

To Ellison's mind, the situation in which Aeneas, or Daedalus, finds himself is not only the archetypal American experience but that of modern man as well. This is why the novel, as a genre, is a modern art form: "Before the eighteenth century, when man was relatively at home in what seemed to be a stable and well-ordered world . . . there was little need for this change-obsessed literary form." The novel may be "changed-obsessed," but its theme, Ellison insists, is the search for home in terms of "nationhood"—not the nationhood of Matthew Arnold's culture but the nationhood of what Ellison calls "a 'familiar' experience."[51]

What Ellison means by "familiar" can be explained by Kenneth Burke's criticism of Lord Raglan's *The Hero*.[52] Ellison admired Raglan's book—he was reading it as he was writing *Invisible Man*—[53] but he would have agreed with Burke's point that Raglan "seems to underestimate the role of the people in the development of mythic figures."[54] Raglan assumes that myth and ritual in drama were created by and for aristocrats and remain unfamiliar to the common folk, but Burke argues that the "kingly symbols" depicted on stage trickled down and were recreated and reinterpreted within the folk in terms of everyday life. Ellison may have noted this criticism, for his own novel illustrates Burke's thesis: high culture doesn't just remain with the upper classes. And although Ellison's hero follows the pattern that Raglan describes for the traditional (aristocratic) hero—going first to a "far country" (city), undergoing trials with giants (Jack the Cyclops), descending into an underworld, and being born anew—this hero has been democratized.[55] In terms of Ellison's metaphor, he is "speaking for you" and to you via invisible radio waves—that ubiquitous instrument of mass culture—on a frequency unrecognized by the Federal Communications Commission.[56] His program features the hidden talents of the riffraff of the city, who embody the protean capacity to transcend what they appear to be—or perhaps what they appear to be is what they are, *if* "you" have the perception to see and hear them. As Emerson said in "Experience," choosing an urban metaphor, Christ can appear "in the neighborhood" at any moment "hidden among vagabonds."[57]

Similarly, Ellison has a most democratic conception of culture: everything fits in somewhere for him, even the comic-strip character Popeye ("I am what I am"[201]). If he is fond of quoting "Heraclitus' axiom" that "'Geography is fate,'" his "fate" seems to include most cultural items from most times and places.[58] It is no surprise when Hart Crane's bridge turns up near the novel's end—fleeing the invisible man's tormentors, who would treat it as mechanical instead of symbolic. We "pontificate," as Burke says, not only to control reality but also to move through its different levels.[59] Ellison, like Burke, is fascinated by the kinds of language, not always verbal, which we use to try to bridge disparate worlds and to mediate between self and society. So another identity the invisible man takes on (partly by allusion throughout the novel to Jack the Bear from black folklore) is the bear, which lives in two worlds (above and below ground) and is a mediator between private and public, between spirit and flesh, between all those dualisms that beset humanity.[60]

The trick is to feel at home in the world without making that home a prison. One wants to be part of a culture without being its prisoner, and this involves a perception of the invisible machinery behind the face of the clock. "For to be profoundly representative of a culture," Burke said in 1948, a person should "imitate" not "its mere insignia but the principle behind the *ordering* of those insignia." That is, each age of a culture has a unique surface, which should "convey," says Burke in the same book, "an invisible, intangible idea in terms of visible, tangible things."[61] What the perception of this requires, argues Burke, is street sense, the ability "to see around the corner of everyday usage."[62] At the novel's end, we find Ellison's narrator echoing Burke's urban metaphor as he, too, begins to understand the various dimensions of reality, both personal (memory) and public (low and high culture), which he not only lives in but must bridge: "It was as though I'd learned suddenly to look around corners" (383).

So it is appropriate that Ellison in the epilogue links the hibernating invisible man to the bear, a creature associated in myth with the rebirth of a self and the entrance of a people into a new world. For as Proteus, the invisible man will enter the world of "infinite possibilities" (435), the city that lies just above the limbo of Hart Crane's cellar in the poem "Black Tamborine". Crane's poem, which depicts the Afro-American as caught between two worlds, presents a tragic dilemma, but Ellison sees that Crane's depiction can be looked at in another way, as a situation of infinite potential, since being in a nether world means that you are neither this *nor* that and hence are free to become anything. As an outsider, the invisible man exists at society's lowest level and in ambiguous circumstances (as Hart Crane saw), yet this "nowhere" contains the potential for becoming its opposite. In "nowhere," the narrator has, for the moment, escaped the definitions of the walled city, and he has managed it in such a way as to save himself from the fate of Richard Wright's Bigger. Both characters end up enclosed in cells, physically constrained, although with some kind of psychological freedom. But Bigger's is a negative freedom, based on the supposition Jean Genet describes: "Every young American black who writes is trying to find himself and test himself and sometimes, at the very center of his being, in his own heart, discovers a white man he must annihilate."[63] The invisible man, even in his cellar, is able to escape this conclusion by discovering the possibility of remaking his culture. He does so not by killing the white man in his heart but by re-viewing and reshaping the "gifts" of the white man's civilization.

At first glance, the invisible man sees the zoot-suiters in the subway as Richard Wright would: "A body of people came down the platform, some of them Negroes. Yes I thought, what about those of us who shoot up from the South into the busy city like wild jacks-in-the-box broken loose from their springs—so sudden that our gait becomes like that of deep-sea divers suffering from the bends" (332). As Michel Fabre notes, when Ellison read Wright's *Twelve Million Black Voices*, he agreed with Wright's analysis of the urban experiences for blacks coming from south to north: "The trauma of passing from the country to the city of destruction brought no anesthesia of consciousness," he wrote to Wright, "but left our nerves peeled and quivering."[64] But as always with Ellison, there is a great deal of punning and word play in the passage from *Invisible Man*, and this ultimately makes Ellison's vision of the city different from Wright's. In employing Burke's "comic frame," he diffuses the tragic implications of the sudden jolt from country to city. This is not to say that the passage is robbed of its seriousness, for good comedy is always serious, but the wordplay extends Wright's vision into other realms of meaning. By this time in the novel, we have seen various transmutations of the "box" ("wild jacks-in-the-box"), the north being as willing as the south to put black people in barracoons, ranging from the boxing ring of the "battle royal," to the college, to the box in the factory hospital. And there is always someone willing to replace their springs with strings, as Tod Clifton grimly shows with his Sambo doll. Moreover, if the Brotherhood does not make these "jacks" (with a pun on "servants") dance to its tune, it squeezes them onto a Procrustian bed.

Yet Ellison's metaphors finally spill out of the enclosed box—the "jacks" simply refuse to be servants, demanding instead to have their own faces. The narrator separates three boys from the crowd of zoot-suiters and considers the way in which they have integrated a diversity of sources into a single amalgam—conked hair, porkpie hat, peg pants. He has to admit that he "has never seen their like before," and it suddenly occurs to him: "What if history was a gambler, instead of a force in a laboratory experiment, and the boys his ace in the hole? What if history was not a reasonable citizen, but a madman full of paranoid guile and these boys his agents, his big surprise!" (333). Ellison is not just rejecting the Brotherhood's Marxism but is looking for an alternative to Wright's Chicago-based sociology (that of Robert Park, Louis Wirth, and Robert Redfield). He is also turning Eliot's fear of an unpredictable history on its head, finding hope there rather than despair.[65] This means, of course, deemphasizing the actual history of the "zoot suit riots" of 1943, in which clothing was symbolic of racial difference and racial conflict.[66] In contrast, Ellison places these zoot-suiters in a metaphysical rather than a historical context. Although they have "the bends," their humanity is not diminished. They are not cultural distortions; rather, they are the "bearers of something precious." They have merged a "country glamour" (332) with an urban style, shedding useless skin as they emerge into something new. To Ellison the culture of the people, the popular culture, is resilient because it is as flexible as the people themselves.

Adaptability in pursuit of "the principle" is the key to the invisible man's discovery of himself and where he belongs. He must also find the personal level of that principle, a manifestation of it intimate enough to support emotionally his return to the world. He has portions of this in his encounters with Peter Wheatstraw, with the yam man, with Mary Rambo, and with his memory of Susie Gresham, another "bearer of something warm and vital and all-enduring" (89)— true denizens of an invisible city of the Beloved Community. It is in the invisible man's epiphany in the snowy street that the most important part of this understanding emerges, and where Ellison's urban vision is most exactly separated from that of Richard Wright. The representative of the Brotherhood who follows the narrator after his speech for the evicted old people tells him that he should waste no sympathy on them ("They're . . . dead" [220]) and that he must lose his "old agrarian self" (221) in the city. Ellison may have been thinking of Wright's *Black Boy*, in which the city and its "undreamed-of shores of knowing" created an unbridgeable gap between Wright and his peasant father.[67] The spokesman even comes up with a neat phrase for what has happened to the old folks: "*A Death on the City Pavements*"—a title, he says, of "a detective story or something I read somewhere" (220). It is of course the title of chapter 3 in *Twelve Million Black Voices*, a book that Ellison knew well and admired.[68] What Ellison objects to is the limitation of Wright's vision, in which the old folks were no more than objects of pity, because they were anachronisms in the modern city.[69] For Ellison, they are clues to a "detective story" that still needs to be solved.

For they, too, are bearers of something precious, as the narrator realizes when he stands looking at the possessions of the evicted lying in the street:

> I turned and stared at the jumble, no longer looking at what was before my eyes but inwardly-outwardly, around a corner into the dark, far-away-and-long-ago, not so much of my own memory as of remembered words, of linked verbal echoes, images heard even when not listening at home (207).

This is Proust's *mémoire involuntaire*: lying beneath conscious memory, these images also lie outside history, like the boys in the subway. At the center of this unremembered world now remembered is the narrator's mother, who opposes the patriarchal Founder of conscious memory:

> *And why did I, standing in the crowd, see like a vision my mother hanging wash on a cold windy day, so cold that the warm clothes froze even before the vapor thinned and hung still on the line, and her hands white and raw in the skirt-swirling wind and her head bare to the darkening sky—and why were they causing me discomfort so far beyond their intrinsic meaning as objects. And why did I see them as a veil that threatened to lift, stirred by the cold wind in the narrow street?* (207)

The metropolis, as Walter Benjamin notes, speaking of Baudelaire's poetry, "inflicts" its "stigmata" upon what is loved and remembered.[70] The invisible man feels an unease of spirit because the frozen clothes are so many inauthentic selves hung out to dry. He has already betrayed his mother in two patriarchal cities (the college and the paint factory), yet these "objects" swirling in the wind are also like a "veil that threatened to lift." For at the center of the remembered moment is the mother who is the figura, the loved object who bears the aura. Kenneth Burke answers the question posed by the last sentence of the narrator's remembrance of lost time:

> We think of the present as "growing out of" the past. Yet if we "begin with" the present and next study the documents of yesterday, then those of the day before, etc., the past would "gradually emerge" for us "out of" our starting point in the present. The successive disclosures of the ever remoter past would thus be a constantly unfolding future, so far as our particular process of revelation was concerned.[71]

Hence the paradox in the novel: the more glimpses the narrator has of the past, the more he will have of the future. In this bildungsroman, Ellison does not provide a childhood for his hero (except for his grandfather's deathbed "yes") because he wants this childhood (personal, racial) to be presented as fragments, just as in the epilogue the heavenly city will be glimpsed in tentative statements about "the principle." Moreover, the reencountered past attempts to *unveil* the present in terms of the figura—the more he remembers of a treasured past and not an imprisoning one, the more the future promises to reveal itself in the present. Those objects lying out there in the city's snow, for instance, hint at "the principle" when seen in the context of his mother's continuing love.

I say "continuing" because the image of the mother, before it was awakened by mémoire involontaire, was, like the clothes, frozen in the memory. Like a movie projector, the narrator's mind releases his mother's image from the freeze-frame of the past to become part of a continuing context with the evicted old people. Country and city are not divided, nor are the past, present, and future. In making the connection between the objects in the snow and his mother hanging clothes on a cold day, the invisible man has added "verbs" (movement) to the total recall of memory. He also has evoked the invisible city from those pitiful fragments of an earthly one. When this act of sympathetic understanding becomes intentional, voluntary, the invisible man will be able to see himself in the invisible city as well.

His understanding becomes intentional, however hesitantly, in the novel's epilogue. The memorabilia in his briefcase—his high-school diploma, Tarp's leg irons, a Sambo doll, a broken piggy bank—become icons with a significance that must be read.[72] Some he rejects and some he keeps, and ultimately the icons that are kept are those whose penetrated meanings provide him with the will to ascend and affirm "the principle." One might say that the icons are the origins of the invisible city. They symbolize a past whose aura foreshadows a future, just as Tarp is both a reappearance of the grandfather and a foreshadowing of his continuing existence. For the narrator considers leaving his hole because he knows that he will meet Tarp's manifestation (with its full religious implications) again.

The mosaic of seemingly unrelated objects in the briefcase is like the mosaic of unrelated worlds in the city (Park's urban thesis) or, for that matter, in the nation (*pluribus* without the *unum*). On the surface there seems to be no connection between the objects, but since the invisible man lives in separated worlds, Ellison believes that he can find the invisible threads that make them one. Stimulated by his briefcase full of odds and ends, the invisible man looks backward only to realize that the utopian moment was embodied in some of the objects he kept (for whatever inarticulate reasons). These pointed to a future that has yet to be realized. As Tarp says of the portrait of Frederick Douglass, "He belongs to all of us" (286). By absorbing Douglass as part of their collective history, all Americans contain within themselves the figura of the future.

The authentic icon itself has no single meaning—it, too, is protean. Seeing Mary Rambo's broken piggy bank anew in his basement, with its grotesque, smiling, obsequious black face and the inscription *"feed me"* below it, causes the narrator to reassess its meaning. It is first an object of embarrassment, and he means to throw its broken fragments away, but then he puts them in his briefcase, perhaps unconsciously realizing that the bank will say something about (and to) him. Ellison has called attention to the fact (noted as well by Michel Fabre) that his novel was influenced by Burke's concise description of the movement of symbolic action: purpose, passion, perception.[73] That is to say, "action leads to passion (or suffering of the opposition)—and passion leads to revelation."[74] We might say as well that the iconic bank recapitulates the novel's structure. In his own efforts to acquire power and prestige (purpose), has not the invisible man, with the same thoughtless smile on his face, devoured other people's ideas (passion)? Yet instead of rejecting this symbol of his past, he sees (perception) that the bank is the figura of what needs to be done to make the invisible city come alive. For does not the bank also suggest the possibility that what is eaten may one day be transformed into nourishment and growth?

In his basement, the invisible man learns that he must continue to devour experience (passion) if he and the country are to have a sense of purpose. Hence the formula of purpose, passion, and perception can repeat itself again and again without being reduced to an exercise in frustration, just as the act of "dreaming" is not limited to one time, one place (the Founding Fathers). The Republic must be dreamed into being with each generation, an ongoing process that Burke in another context calls "the dancing of an attitude."[75] So, in his cellar, the invisible man perceives and acts simultaneously, and Emerson's "Man Thinking" becomes the man who will emerge. Running, with its connotations of forced exile and/or uncontrolled motion, now becomes movement. For the man who will emerge is not only new (Proteus) but renewed spiritually, having found "the Rome term to which all roads lead"[76] Rinehart has shown the invisible man that all things are possible, but the other face of possibility is chaos, and chaos can only be focused by the pursuit of the elusive "principle," something that can reside both within the folk and within the nation.

The tentativeness of the epilogue's solution is the logical (or paradoxical) result of a very tentative formula: "the principle" is something pursued, not something arrived at. In writing the epilogue, Ellison, as a writer, engages in the same form of risk taking that he is asking of his protagonist (and of "us"). He knows that for writers, too, a thin line divides cannibalism from a healthy appetite: "We Americans are given to eating, regurgitating, and, alas, re-eating . . . our most sacred words." The same ambiguity exists in the novel's key trope, running, for *Invisible Man* skewers not only the American propensity to rush in where others fear to tread but also the American mentality that condemns the Afro-American to run toward a horizon that recedes forever into the distance. Yet Ellison finally believes that we have no choice: we run, or we stagnate. Moreover, like Plato, he thinks that informed desire separates a seeming good from a real good, that to "know where you are" is to "know who you are." And although geography, that is, knowledge of one's location, may be fate, it, too, is protean: "knowing where you are" means knowing that there are multiple "wheres." Finally, geography for Ellison is the telos, the city on the hill whose distant light tells us where we are headed.

"Perhaps at the root of our American fascination with the humorous story," he said in an essay on Stephen Crane, "lies the awareness that if we don't know *where* we are, we have little chance of knowing *who* we are, that if we confuse the *time* we confuse the *place*."[77] On the one hand, we must recognize that there never was a single time in the past that we can return to, a recoverable lost Eden; but on the other hand, we must make use of, and not lament, the complex present with its many times: "Ours is the tempo of the motion picture, not that of the still camera."[78] Although we are condemned to live in the fast-paced, technological twentieth century, we must explore what that time gives us, and if it gives us life as a motion picture, then we must look for illumination within this matrix. What we find is that the running man is like the moving pictures; we find his meaning not in freezing the frame—this is what Hollywood does— but in paying close attention to the figura that shines through the kinetic energy. What that tells us is that the true metaphor for the nation has never been the exclusive, static, enclosed garden that we lost but rather the open city toward which we run: "Our fate," concludes the invisible man, "is to *become* one, and yet many" (435; my italics).

For, finally, the *open* city of the Book of Revelation is the city Ellison believes in—not open in terms of defenselessness or chaos, but open in terms of "speaking for you."[79] Eliot, we might say, speaks for the elect, the chosen; Ellison, for the potential Proteus in "Boobus Americanus." Like H. L. Mencken, whom he admires, Ellison satirizes the booby bird in the American scene—his novel is filled with boobies of various plumage—but he never loses faith that the booby may become the phoenix, even the eagle. The city as labyrinth, then, does not terrify him as it does Eliot, for its mapless state points to an unmapped America, one that existed before, and continues to exist invisibly within the Enlightenment grid. Nor does the mass culture of the city disturb him as much as it does Richard Wright.[80] Finally, Ellison's unmapped city is an unfinished city, in which the self-reliant individual is continually negotiating his connection to the living polis, a process that is blessedly never complete.[81]

CHAPTER FIVE

The Watchman on the Wall
in James Baldwin's
Go Tell It on the Mountain

> I looked down the line,
> And I wondered.
> —James Baldwin, *Go Tell It on the Mountain*

> Standing at the crossroad, I tried to flag a ride.
> Didn't nobody seem to know me, everybody pass me by.
> —Robert Johnson, "Crossroad Blues"

James Baldwin was a native New Yorker, not from the deep south like Richard Wright or from a border state of the midwest like Ralph Ellison; he was born in Harlem Hospital in 1924, the year Alain Locke began putting together the issue of *Survey Graphic* which would become *The New Negro*. Baldwin was, however, just barely a native son of Harlem; when he was born his mother had only recently moved north from Maryland, and he understood that the Great Migration had placed him at the same cultural crossroads as Wright and Ellison: "I was born into a Southern community displaced into the streets of New York." He probably knew that his remark echoed the opening sentence in the final chapter of Wright's *Twelve Million Black Voices*: "We are the children of the black sharecroppers, the first-born of the city tenements."[1] Baldwin's stepfather was a working-class man from Alabama and a preacher in storefront churches, who may himself have been born in slavery.[2] The family was large and poor, representing that majority part of Harlem which Locke's picture of Afro-American urban life had pushed into the far background, a class subsisting only marginally for whom the racial climate in the north was often scarcely distinguishable from that in the south. Remembering his life as a young man coming of age, Baldwin spoke more angrily than either Wright or Ellison; he spoke without Ellison's humor or Wright's dispassionate sociological distance: "I was icily determined—more determined, really, than I then knew—never to make my peace with the ghetto but to die and go to Hell before I would let any white man spit on me, before I would accept my 'place' in this republic."[3]

In those lines from *The Fire Next Time* (1963) sound the echo of Bigger Thomas, or perhaps of another remark by Baldwin: "No American Negro exists who does not have his private Bigger Thomas living in the skull."[4] But that private self, Baldwin came to believe, was a suicidal one, both socially and existentially. For him Bigger was only one road at the crossroads, and he felt that in considering how blacks survived in the city Wright had ignored an important "dimension," in particular "the relationship that Negroes bear to one another, that depth of . . . unspoken recognition of shared experience which creates a way of life."[5] Most black people, Baldwin argued, find a mode of compromise, some kind of accommodation to the intolerable conditions within racist America. He himself chose the "gimmick" of the black church as a necessary haven, "to lift him out, to start him on his way."[6] Looking backward from the vantage point of adulthood in *The Fire Next Time*, he realized that the church was a necessary halfway station for him, a resting place in the city of destruction.

Baldwin always claimed to be a "city boy," and *Go Tell It on the Mountain* is his autobiographical (and best) novel about the city. Although filled with flashbacks, the novel has the unity of time, place, and action of a classical Greek play, and like a Greek play its conflict pits an individual against a city. On the day of his fourteenth birthday, John Grimes makes a pilgrimage through the streets of New York, and Baldwin depicts the view through the young boy's eyes, a vision that includes both the desire of the adolescent to possess the world and the realization of the outsider that he is excluded from it. In this exclusion Baldwin and Wright both recognized the terrible weight of the past upon the present, how the heritage of slavery paralyzes action in the present through its limited perspectives, through the burdensome (though understandable) puritanism of its religion. Yet in the last sentence of *Go Tell It on the Mountain*, John Grimes does not say, "It is finished," but instead proclaims, "I'm ready . . . I'm coming. I'm on my way."[7] Baldwin, like Ralph Ellison, wants to show a way out of the locked cell, to uncover a potential to remake oneself: in his first novel he intends to demonstrate that there are possibilities in "the great, unfinished city" (his favorite phrase for New York)[8] and that some of these possibilities exist within Afro-American culture, constrained or despised though it may be. Bigger rejected the "shared experience" because what was shared was a world view that made it impossible to live in this world; Baldwin would argue, through John Grimes, that what was shared was also an inherited communal wisdom that could help people to survive in the earthly city.

In the famous attack on *Native Son* in *Notes of a Native Son*, Baldwin's method is satire, and the technique used is one that is basic to the satirist: reduction. Baldwin reduces *Native Son* to "protest" literature and Bigger to a one-dimensional character. Yet as perverse as these essays are in some ways, the devil (as Baldwin well knew) speaks in more than one voice. When Baldwin compares Wright to Milton, claiming that Bigger "prefers, like Lucifer, rather to rule in hell than serve in heaven," we suspect that his admiration for *Native Son* is greater than these essays imply.[9] That admiration, and influence, are unmistakable in Baldwin's adaptation of the structure of *Native Son* to his own work. Wright's division of *Native Son* into three books—"Fear," "Flight," and "Fate"—is reflected in Baldwin's structuring of his own novel into three parts: "The Seventh Day," "The Prayers of the Saints," and "The Threshing-Floor." The plots of the novels are very different, yet the narratives are very similar in their rhythmic movement: a section of thesis, one of antithesis, and a synthesizing conclusion. This isn't an uncommon form for a novel, but the resemblance in this case is not likely to be accidental. Baldwin gave the impression in *Notes of a Native Son* that the gap between himself and Wright was greater than it actually was—he once said, "As writers we were about as unlike as any two writers could possibly be."[10] But his version of urban life almost always corroborates Wright's, despite such remarks, and even though he "misread" *Native Son* in order to have his protagonist "swerve" from the self-destructive path that Bigger traveled.[11]

The language of the section titles in the two novels, however, suggests one difference between the urban visions of the two writers. Wright's titles name psychological states, almost physiological ones, which imply inexorable and reflexive action. Baldwin's, on the other hand, are specifically biblical and mythic. John's story will be conceived in terms of a kind of "pilgrim's progress," and told in a prose style that echoes the King James Bible in image and rhetoric. In *Go Tell It on the Mountain*, while Baldwin acknowledges every truth that Wright saw about the American city, he revises these truths to fit his personal myth of emergence.

John Grimes would seem to be more closely parallel to the invisible man of Ellison's epilogue, who finally says, "I'm coming out" of the underground than he is to Bigger, because both John and the invisible man deny the closed door of Bigger's cell, which represents a separation from any community. Those denials, however, issue out of very different contexts. Leading up to the invisible man's remark, Ellison includes a long allusive passage in which he refers both to Louis Armstrong and, immediately before that, to the opening of Eliot's *Waste Land*: "There is a stench in the air, which, from this distance underground, might be the smell either of death or of spring."[12] Such a reference will be impossible in the world of John Grimes, a ghetto child islanded within the world of Harlem, and that difference makes an important distinction between Baldwin's novel and Ellison's. Both men were widely read, with access to a great range of cultural sources;[13] Ellison chose to use as many as possible, while Baldwin restricted his frame mainly to the background of black ghetto life. The difference seems to be, and is, a choice of approach, a difference of intention, but it also implies different understandings of the nature of the invisible city. For Ellison, "the principle" is a civilized ideal that, however it is misused in practice, includes all of the cultural forms and elements an individual might be exposed to; for Baldwin, "principles" grow out of one's survival of the conditions in the city of destruction. His character doesn't have access to the materials of high culture, but he finds in Afro-American popular culture resources that, in his view, are sufficient.

John Grimes's choice of the black church at age fourteen not only will give him refuge but, in the words of Baldwin's epigraph, will *renew* his "strength":

> They that wait upon the lord shall renew their strength;
> they shall mount up with wings like eagles;
> they shall run and not be weary, they shall walk and not faint.

In the novel's first section, John looks "down the line" (3), and he finds the view terrifying, for to look down the line is to become aware of the aggressive malevolence and bewildering complexity of the two earthly cities of Harlem and New York. Coming of age for a black male means (in addition to sexual awakening) that he is now a potential target on the city's mean streets. It is quite literally a "threshold" experience, for the child crosses into the world of threatening, unmapped public space. It will take an adult to discover on what terms, if any, that space can be defined, in what terms the "unfinished city" can be finished.

In all of his writings, fiction or nonfiction, Baldwin emphasized these overwhelming conditions of American city life and especially of life in the city of his birth. Unlike Paris, his adopted city, New York evoked his strongest emotions. This passage from *No Name in the Street* (1972) is a pointed example:

> If I had ever loved New York, that love had, literally, been beaten out of me; if I had ever loved it, my life could never have depended on so long an absence and so deep a *divorce*; or, if I had ever loved it, I would have been glad, not *frightened*, to be back in my home town. No, I didn't love it, at least not any more, but I was going to have to survive it. In order to survive it, I would have to *watch* it. (my italics)[14]

Divorce, frightened, and *watch* are key words in this passage, because they indicate the nature of Baldwin's ambiguous feelings toward New York. His is a quarrel with a city he wants to love, and his relationship to that city is a parable of his torturous love affair with America: the "unfinished" city is a mirror image of the "unfinished" country, which, at its most strange and frightening, is like "another country" (hence the title of his third novel).

Paris is a finished city. Baldwin has no illusions about the "City of Light," as he illustrates over and over in his essays (in *Nobody Knows My Name* and *No Name in the Street*), in his novels (*Giovanni's Room* and *Another Country*), and in his short stories (e.g., "This Morning, This Evening, So Soon"), but the alienation he and his characters feel is caused by the sense of estrangement that affects them outside their native land. He is free in Paris, because the city is comparatively indifferent to him. Like all of France, it is a world already made up, already created, "fixed"; and his relationship to it is essentially that of a visitor.[15] He says in his essay on Chartres that he feels excluded from the civilization of either Paris or New York, but whereas in Paris he is frightened because he doesn't know the rules of the game (see "Equal in Paris" in *Notes of a Native Son*), New York frightens him because the city is "shapeless, unspeakable."[16] As Hall Montana says in *Just above My Head* (1979), the streets are both "familiar, and yet unfamiliar," and no one in New York knows the rules of the game, not even the white New Yorkers.[17]

One reason for this confusion lies in what Henry James perceived as the city's architectural transience: "I build you up but to tear you down."[18] Indeed, Baldwin's view of New York often sounds as though he is seeing the city through the lens of *The American Scene*:[19]

> No other city is so spitefully incoherent. Whereas other cities flaunt their history—their presumed glory—in vividly placed monuments, squares, parks, plaques, and boulevards, such history as New York has been unable entirely to obliterate is to be found, mainly, in the backwaters of Wall Street, in the goat tracks of Old and West Broadway, in and around Washington Square, and, for the relentless searcher, in grimly inaccessible regions of the Bronx. . . . No plaque indicates that Harlem was once a Dutch province, with two *a*'s to its name, or that the movie house, on 42nd Street, the New Amsterdam, bears the name the city was given when, again by means of the Dutch, it entered recorded, or acceptable, history. The Dutch lost the city to the English, who, being passionately devoted to a city on their island named York, decided this was *New* York. The name of the island, an Indian name, Manhattan, was never changed.[20]

But Baldwin is also making another point, one made by urban geographers such as Kevin Lynch.[21] In a city with recognizable "public space" or place markers, citizens can construct their cognitive maps from both public and private experience, but New York, a city that has tried to hide its history (or to pretend that it has none), leaves its citizens to their own devices. It is, as he says in *Another Country* (1962), a city that is public without being civil:

> New York seemed very strange indeed. It might, almost, for the strange barbarity of manner and custom, for the sense of danger and horror barely sleeping beneath the rough, gregarious surface, have been some impenetrably exotic city of the East. So superbly was it in the present that it seemed to have nothing to do with the

passage of time: time might have dismissed it as thoroughly as it had dismissed Carthage and Pompeii. It seemed to have no sense whatever of the exigencies of human life; it was so familiar and so public that it became, at last, the most despairingly private of cities. One was continually being jostled, yet longed, at the same time, for the sense of others, for a human touch; and if one was never—it was the general complaint—left alone in New York, one had, still, to fight very hard in order not to perish of loneliness.(230)

Yet in a strange way New York's failure to preserve its past could be a blessing. Its very transience and insubstantiality, its overwhelmingly *public* character, forces New Yorkers to come to terms with their present lives, to face up to their "loneliness." Its continual voiding of the past *might* allow a LeRoi Jones to escape his defined heritage (as hinted by his lines about New York's Gansevoort Street, discussed in chapter 1, above), and this, finally, is a reason that Baldwin remained so ambivalent about New York and wrote so passionately about it: "Whoever is born in New York is ill-equipped to deal with any other city: all other cities seem, at best, a mistake, and, at worst, a fraud."[22] Despite his often-professed hatred of this city (and it is difficult to find anything he wrote in which this hatred is not expressed), he continued to see the "unfinished" city as a city of possibility. The ending of *Another Country*, for instance, is not completely ironic. In that novel, New York has chewed up the lives of most of the major characters, yet for Baldwin love between two individuals has the potential to redeem the city. Knowing that Eric awaits him within its walls, Yves "strode through the barriers, more high-hearted than he had ever been as a child, into that city which the people from heaven had made their home"(436).[23]

The context of Baldwin's use of that phrase "unfinished city" points also to a larger, ironic, but still hopeful meaning. He applies the phrase to New York in *No Name in the Street* as he is desperately seeking to leave the city; yet his destination is the "Southland" of his nightmares, and his purpose is to begin his engagement with the Civil Rights movement, that effort to complete the establishment of the American "principle." The private also inevitably becomes the public, for the Beloved Community is both public and private and Baldwin's action represents, in a sense, his public counterpoint to John Grimes's words at the end of that first novel: "I'm on my way."

Baldwin's novels document people who are either destroyed or seriously compromised by the urban carnage, but he also creates survivors, made stronger by being seared in the city's furnace. At the end
of *If Beale Street Could Talk* (1974), Fonny, in prison, builds a table, anticipating a future life with Tish and their child. This action is a portrait of the artist whose descent into the domestic is a triumph of the
spirit; the extraordinary is phrased in terms of human ordinariness,
without allusion to any frame beyond Fonny's cell. Against this image of a potential home, Baldwin juxtaposes Tish looking out of a
window onto New York's "dreadful streets," as the baby in her womb
seems to ask: "*Is there not one righteous among them?*"[24] In *Beale Street*,
despite its ambiguous ending, Baldwin answers that the city's redemption comes through the links between Tish and Fonny and
Tish's family. Writing about the city, Baldwin gives us people who try
to create their own invisible city in the alien space of the "dreadful
streets." Whether they succeed is usually determined by their capacity to love, and so transform the space of a room or a tavern or a jail
cell into sacred space.

In *Just above My Head*, the "harsh" New York sunlight outside is
"softened . . . by the curtains at the bar window" in a room of a tavern transformed by the narrator Hall Montana's newly discovered affection for Sidney.[25] This image of intimate space set against the im-
personal city appears so often in Baldwin that it's not surprising he
was an avid reader of Dickens, especially admiring *A Tale of Two
Cities*.[26] When he tells his nephew in *The Fire Next Time* that "your
countrymen . . . have caused you to be born in conditions not very
far removed from those described for us by Charles Dickens in the
London of more than a hundred years ago," he is not only comparing
two bleak urban landscapes but also indirectly revealing how one
theme in Dickens has influenced his own treatment of the city.[27] As
Alexander Welsh notes of *Great Expectations*, "nowhere in literature is
the modern segregation of hearth and city, of personal life and business, so sharply and consciously drawn."[28] In his fiction Baldwin has
absorbed this Dickensian antithesis of hearth versus city, private life
versus public life, into his personal vision and used it to define the
conditions of black urban life.

It is here that we should draw a distinction between Henry James
and Charles Dickens in terms of their influence on Baldwin's urban
vision. James spoke to Baldwin's sense of exile, to his sense of his na-

tive city's "incoherence" as seen from the perspective of one both outside and inside the culture. In contrast, Dickens spoke to a less cerebral side of Baldwin. If James urged a civilized perspective upon the uncivilized city, Dickens spoke to Baldwin's sense of the city's debilitating dangers and of the vulnerability of those very people—the city's outsiders and immigrants—who bewildered Henry James. True, James himself could feel like a foreigner in a city he thought was home; *The American Scene* describes his ambivalent feelings toward those others—the Russian Jews on New York's Lower East Side, for example—who helped create the chaos of modern New York.[29] Yet Baldwin was too completely shaped by that chaos to assume James's urban detachment, for he lacked the distancing provided by the older writer's Brahmin background. Baldwin would ultimately choose Dickens over James—his last novel, *Just above My Head*, is a loose, baggy monster in the Dickensian mold—because Dickens knew what Richard Wright knew: that the layers of the city were littered with corpses, that those corpses spoke of hidden crimes that would elude even Detective Bucket, the resolver of mysteries in *Bleak House*.

Consider, for instance, Baldwin's "Notes for a Hypothetical Novel" in *Nobody Knows My Name*, an essay that sets out to describe a Jamesian novel and ends by doing something else. Baldwin begins by imagining a "pretend" novel, "a very long novel . . . concerning the people or some of the people with whom I grew up."[30] The novel he imagines writing will deal with the "complex fate" of being an American (the Jamesian theme of *Nobody*'s opening essay). And perhaps, as he describes this "pretend" project, he is looking sideways at the Jamesian novel he is actually writing at the time, *Another Country* (1963). In any event, Baldwin makes it clear that he doesn't want to be a reductive, sociological novelist like James T. Farrell or Richard Wright (147), or a garrulous, editorializing Victorian one like Dickens. He wants his "people" to speak for themselves, with neither an ideology nor an author's moral views imposed on them: "I want to impose myself on these people as little as possible. That means that I do not want to tell them or the reader what principle their lives illustrate, or what principle is activating their lives, but by examining their lives I hope to be able to make them convey to me and to the reader what their lives mean" (142).

Yet Baldwin compromises this Jamesian detachment almost immediately when he informs us of the "thread" that links these people together. Although their lives are all unique and complex, Baldwin as imagined author comes back to the thing that binds them: "What does it mean to be an American?" (149). On the surface, the answer to this question is the Jamesian theme of American "incoherence," which all Americans share, but we soon find out that this theme is tied to the country's inability to face up to the "fact of color" in its history. And the metaphor Baldwin uses to describe the significance of this "fact" tells us something about his literary ancestors other than James:

> Let us say . . . that I have a friend who has just murdered his mother and put her in the closet and I know it, but we're not going to talk about it. Now this means very shortly since, after all, I know the corpse is in the closet, and he knows I know it, and we're sitting around having a few drinks and trying to be buddy-buddy together, that very shortly, we can't talk about anything because we can't talk about that. No matter what I say I may inadvertently stumble on this corpse. (150)

This "corpse," of course, is the corpse at the heart of *Native Son*, the historical nightmare that refuses to go away. And as we listen to Baldwin talking about his childhood memories in this essay, we soon discover what that corpse means in terms of his own history: "I have not known many survivors. I know mainly about disaster" (147). Despite Baldwin's artistic desire to write like Henry James, he would be drawn to Richard Wright and Charles Dickens—Wright, for his sense of terror based on "the fact of color"; Dickens, for his creation of intimate space within the walls of the terrifying city. Perhaps Baldwin's most successful treatment of these twin themes is "Sonny's Blues."

In this justly famous short story, a child sits in a room listening to the voices of old people—parents, grandparents, friends, and relatives—as the afternoon fades into the darkness. The voices are comforting to the child: "He hopes that there will never come a time when the old folks won't be sitting around the living room, talking about where they've come from, and what they've seen, and what's happening to them and their kinfolk." Yet he only obscurely knows the reasons for the talk: why and when it begins, why and when it will stop as the darkness outside begins to fill the room. For when someone in the room turns on a lamp, flooding the room with light, the talk does stop, and the child mysteriously knows then "that every time this happens he is moved just a little closer to the darkness outside. The darkness outside is what the old folks have been talking about. It's what they've come from. It's what they endure. The child knows that they won't talk anymore because if he knows too much about what's happened to *them*, he'll know too much too soon, about what's going to happen to *him*."[31]

No Afro-American writer in modern literature conveys better the sense of menace lying in wait in the urban streets "outside." Words such as "menacing," "dreadful," and "unspeakable" are Baldwin's choices for describing those streets, not because he wishes to be sensational but because, like Edmund Burke, he understands that what is truly terrifying is that which is indescribable. The old people know from their own experience that the world "outside" is a world without maps; hence their conversation is calculated to give the child just as much of a map as he can use. No matter what they talk about, it is information he can store away for the day that he must leave this room for the "outside." The conversation among themselves—"where they've come from, and what they've seen"—is pushing the child toward a world that he must one day walk through, and so their stories function as a preparation for him in the same way (the narrator discovers) that Sonny's music functions for the adults in the nightclub. The child is being prepared to enter the city of destruction; the adults are strengthened to return to it. Sonny's blues, the old folks' conversation—these are stories that bear witness, that create community, and make the world, if only for the moment, less hostile. And as always with Baldwin, these stories and this music are expressions of love that transform empty space (a room, a tavern) into the great, good place. Small, intimate spaces, Baldwin suggests, are what black people have instead of the cathedral at Chartres or the Brooklyn Bridge in New York.

The failure to create sacred space in the city is an equally significant theme in Baldwin, and people who fail in this say something about the urban temptations and pitfalls that John Grimes must face. Rufus Scott in *Another Country*, for instance, is what John Grimes might have become, someone without a refuge in the city. Baldwin places Rufus on a balcony overlooking New York, as though he were "standing on a cliff in the wilderness, seeing a kingdom and a river which had not been seen before. He could make it his" (20). The scene is an exact parallel to one in which John looks down at New

York from a hill in Central Park, but Rufus, lost in the wonder and glory of the view, is without a guide through its labyrinth; alone, he lacks the strength to bear "the weight of this city" (4). He ends his life jumping from the city's white cathedral, the George Washington Bridge, because "he could never go down into the city again" (87). Baldwin's characters are endangered, or betrayed, by being caught in the open, suffering a kind of spiritual agoraphobia. The aspirations of Rufus's sister Ida are cynical; she treats the city as a "whorehouse," determined to climb to the top, "to be the biggest, coolest, hardest whore around, and make the world pay you back that way" (347).[32] She would prey on the city's plentitude instead of being overwhelmed by its confused, changing variousness, yet, like Leo Proudhammer in *Tell Me How Long the Train's Been Gone* (1964), she finds that she "had conquered the city: but the city was stricken with the plague."[33] The urban plague is cynicism, alienation, and isolation, and no individual in Baldwin's fiction is immune.

These two themes intertwine when Baldwin writes about the city: the Dickensian emphasis on the need for intimate space amid incoherence, and the Augustinian suspicion of a city so perilous it needs to be continuously "watched." But "watching" has a complex meaning in Baldwin's city. "Watching" is pragmatic survival; if you don't read the street signs, you die young: "I come out of streets where life itself—life itself!—depends on timing more infinitesimal than the split second, where apprehension must be swifter than the speed of light."[34] Then, in a passage quoted earlier ("in order to survive it [New York], I was going to have to watch it"), he joins personal survival to "watching" in a biblical sense, alluding to the "watchman" in Jeremiah (6:17), Ezekiel (3:17–21), and Hosea (9:8), the figure on the city wall who both observes the city and watches for its enemies. Individually, that is, the "watchman" looks both outside and inside; the city can kill, or corrupt. But a further implication is that the watchman is watching the social city, the public life of the community at large. Baldwin in his nonfiction writings filled that role many times *vis-à-vis* American culture. Like Jeremiah he chastised the members of the polis with an aim to encouragement, pleading that they restore the city to righteousness; and like Juvenal, he grimly catalogued the sins of the Republic which made its city seem past redemption: as Julia preaches in *Just above My Head*, "'Except the *Lord* watch the city, the watchman watcheth but in vain.'"[35]

All of these meanings of the "watchman" on the city wall have a place in *Go Tell It on the Mountain*. The watchman watches because the city (New York) is corrupt, and he must protect himself from its treachery. However, if Christ has graciously shown him the "way," then the city is his own soul, the paradise within, which he must protect from everything outside *and* inside the walls of the self. As the Book of Proverbs (25:28) puts it, "A man without self-control is like a city broken into and left without walls." In the novel the city to be guarded is also the black church, the community of true believers who do daily battle with the frightening reality of Harlem. "The Temple of the Fire Baptized" stands on a corner "facing the hospital to which the criminal wounded and dying were carried every night" (59). The hospital is an apt symbol, for Harlem is the earthly city sickened unto death, and therefore stands in contrast to the black church, which promises "the way" to the heavenly city. Hence Baldwin's decision to title his novel after the Afro-American spiritual "Go Tell It on the Mountain":

> When I was a sinner, I prayed both night and day;
> I asked the Lord to help me, and He showed me the way.
>
> When I was a seeker, I sought both night and day.
> I asked my Lord to help me, and He taught me to pray.
>
> He made me a watchman upon the city wall;
> And if I am a Christian, I am the least of all.[36]

The line, "And He showed me the way" foreshadows the novel's last sentence, in which the "way" for John is the way of the black church—that road which leads to the heavenly city.

The route that Baldwin describes, however, is not a direct one. The novel's first section, "The Seventh Day," takes the young John Grimes through multiple cities, all existing within New York, filled with the terrors and attractions opening up to the boy. This narrative depends for part of its effect on a confusing of cultural levels and meanings, an effect that imitates the mixture of images and ideas the city presents as John walks through it. It ends, significantly, with the boy going to a movie, in which those uncertainties are reenacted as a reaction to a Hollywood narrative. Baldwin, like Wright and Ellison, gives the movies a crucial role in his urban culture.

In a long essay, *The Devil Finds Work* (1976), Baldwin expressed his admiration for films of the 1930s, especially for two that had the greatest impact on him as a young man: *A Tale of Two Cities* (1935) and Fritz Lang's *You Only Live Once* (1937). He said of Lang's film that it had a "genuine indignation" that "was very shortly to disappear out of the American cinema, and severely to be menaced in American life. In a way, we were all niggers in the thirties" (25). It was the theme of the outsider, and especially the outsider living within an urban milieu, that appealed to Baldwin. In his remarks on Dickens's Madame Defarge, he identifies with an unsympathetic character because of her urban credibility:

> In the novel, *A Tale of Two Cities*, it had been Madame Defarge who most struck me. I recognized that unrelenting hatred, for it was all up and down my streets, and in my father's face and voice. The wine cask, *shattered like a walnut shell*, shattered every Saturday night on the corner of our street, and, yes, Dickens was right, the gutters turned a bright and then a rusty red. I understood the knitted registers as hope and fate, for I knew that everything (including my own name) had long been written in The Book: *you may run on a great long time but great God Almighty's going to cut you down!* I understood the meaning of the rose in the turban of Madame Defarge as she sits knitting in the wine shop, the flower in the headdress meant to alert the neighborhood to the presence of a spy. We lived by such signals.(12)

Baldwin could have included another movie in *The Devil Finds Work*, but he may have omitted *Of Human Bondage* (1934), the Hollywood version of Somerset Maugham's novel, because he had discussed it earlier—it's the film John Grimes will go to see at the end of "The Seventh Day."

John Grimes's Harlem is a city of Madame Defarge's wine-stained streets, where the boy's earliest memories are of walking to Sunday morning service with his family and seeing the men and women who "had spent the night in bars, or in cat houses, or on the streets, or on rooftops, or under the stairs" (5). These people haunted the Sunday mornings like disturbed spirits: "They talked, and laughed, and fought together, and the women fought like the men." One time he and his brother Roy "had watched a man and woman in the basement of a condemned house. They did it standing up. The woman had wanted fifty cents, and the man had flashed a razor" (5). This is the city as nightmare.

As John approaches manhood, his confused feelings about his stepfather, his home, and himself manifest themselves in reactions to that outside world. He hates his stepfather, Gabriel, who he believes is his real father, yet he continually seeks his approval, not understanding why his "father" should dislike him. "Set thine house in order" reads Gabriel's favorite passage from the Old Testament, but John can never set Gabriel's house in order, though every Saturday he is assigned to clean it. Like Sisyphus he is given an impossible task, because the house is a metaphor for Gabriel's morally untidy life, and John's pointless labor illustrates the circles of deception and self-deception which surround the father's authority. The image of John's entrapment partakes of the world of myth, resembling a fairy tale in which the protagonist lacks some bit of knowledge needed to escape. John doesn't know that he is not Gabriel's real son, and so he cannot fathom the emotional tangles around him. He knows that he is an outsider in the city, but not that he is also one in his own house.

Moreover, John has unconsciously accepted Gabriel's view of human nature as naturally sinful, and this conflicts now with a New York that he desperately wants to believe in, a city that promises everything and withholds nothing. If Harlem is the city of night, New York is the city of brightness, some of it sunshine, some neon. This is the New York "skyline" he sees on his fourteenth birthday, a sight that brings "exultation and a sense of power" (35). As he runs to the top of his favorite hill in Central Park to view this "shining city," it seems to summon him as it had never summoned his "ancestors."[37] John wants this earthly city in order to escape Gabriel's circumscribed world, but he cannot help seeing this city through Gabriel's eyes. He cannot make the judgment of Gabriel's real son Roy, who tells his mother (in language meant for Gabriel), "You think that's all that's in the world is jails and churches" (24); nor is rebellion and the choice of the streets an answer for John. Roy, however, like Wright's Bigger, is set on a doomed path, coming home wounded from knife fights, yet determined to go back and make his place in that brutal world.[38]

John believes that his intelligence will be a passport to "another life," but everywhere he goes, the injunctions of Gabriel go with him.

The school principal had praised his work, and her esteem and the admiration of others "rose in his mind like a great brass gate, opening outward for him on a world where people did not live in the darkness of his father's house, did not pray to Jesus in the darkness of his father's church, where he would eat good food, and wear fine clothes, and go to the movies as often as he wished" (15). New York is open space, a city whose gates are open, as in the Book of Revelation; but will *that* city open its gates to a child whose face is black? In *The Devil Finds Work*, Baldwin recalls the ironic ending of *You Only Live Once*, when the voice of the dead priest speaks to the dying Eddie Taylor as though in a dream: "*The gates are open*" (26). Baldwin's response at age fourteen—"I knew damn well the gates were *not* open" (26)— showed that he understood that the voice merely taunted an already doomed Eddie, an outcast condemned to remain outside the city's gates and on the road ("down the line") until society picked its moment to kill him. The voice of Gabriel is like the voiceover on the movie's soundtrack, reminding John of the city's closed gates even as the adolescent rushes toward what he conceives to be the way out.

John also hears in the voice of his stepfather the final reminder of his own mortality: this city would bring John's soul to "perdition" (36). Broadway, the street whose name implied a world more expansive, now calls forth a biblical meaning: "The way that led to death *was* broad, and many could be found thereon; but narrow was the way that led to life eternal, and few there were who found it" (36). The city John desires is Gabriel's city of sin, though the son tries to resist that vision:

> But he did not long for the narrow way, where all his people walked; where the houses did not rise, piercing, as it seemed, the unchanging clouds, but huddled, flat, ignoble, close to the filthy ground, where the streets and the hallways and the rooms were dark, and where the unconquerable odor was of dust, and sweat, and urine, and homemade gin. In the narrow way, the way of the cross, there awaited him only humiliation forever; there awaited him, one day, a house like his father's house, and a church like his father's, and a job like his father's, where he would grow old and black with hunger and toil. The way of the cross had given him a belly filled with wind and had bent his mother's back; they had never worn fine clothes, but here, where the buildings contested

God's power and where the men and the women did not fear God, here he might eat and drink to his heart's content and clothe his body with wondrous fabrics, rich to the eye and pleasing to the touch. (36–37)

It is a brilliant passage because it reveals the full range of John's ambivalence, as well as the limits of his imagination. The buildings *contest* "God's power," unlike the buildings of Max's speech to Bigger in *Native Son*, which represent the struggles between men. The people *here* do not "fear" God, but John cannot help but think that they should. The way of the cross is the way of humiliation, but is not humility the way to the true city? Yet this "city was real," John argues with himself, whereas the glories of paradise were "unimaginable" (37).

The ironic comedy in this is that John imposes an *imagined* glory ("rich to the eye and pleasing to the touch") on this "real" city. The language he uses to describe the real city is secondhand, having as its source the King James version of the Song of Solomon or the florid texture of the historical romances he has been reading, and by placing his stepfather's life in a biblical context (humiliation, humility), he even gives Gabriel an unintended dignity. The scene on Fifth Avenue further provokes his literary and cinematic fantasies: "In summer he had seen people riding in . . . carriages, looking like people out of books, or out of movies in which everyone wore old-fashioned clothes and rushed at nightfall over frozen roads, hotly pursued by their enemies who wanted to carry them back to death. '*Look back, look back,*' had cried a beautiful woman with long blond curls, '*and see if we are pursued!*'—and she had come, John remembered, to a terrible end" (38). What John (and Baldwin) is remembering are Lucie Darnay's lines from Dickens's *Tale of Two Cities*, when she cries out to Jarvis Lorry while fleeing with her drugged husband (Charles Darnay) and her mentally enfeebled father (Dr. Manette) from Paris.[39] John euphorically identifies with the aristocrats, but he also tacks on a conclusion not in Dickens—"she had come . . . to a bad end." It is not Lucie and Charles Darnay who come to a terrible end, but Sydney Carton, the novel's Christ figure. John misremembers because *he* is the one being pursued in the city of destruction, by his stepfather's reminder that he will "come to a bad end."

Gabriel comes to possess John's imagination completely. These people who are so beautiful and fashionable have *no* church, John tells himself: "They were in the world, and of the world, and their feet laid hold on Hell" (39). Besides, "niggers did not live on these streets," John thinks. Nor were they allowed to enter the wonderful shops and apartments: "Not today, and he heard his father's laugh, *'No, nor tomorrow neither!'"* (40). Gabriel is a narrow-minded tyrant, but in this case, he is right: for John to think that the world is his because it *seems* so would be to seriously mistake the world: "Niggers did not live on these streets." Gabriel's mistake, which the child cannot perceive but Baldwin does, lies in the finality of his pronouncement *"No, nor tomorrow neither!"* And it is a judgment suffused with malice, for Gabriel wishes to inflict upon John his own blighted life. Baldwin is not so naive as to think that the world will necessarily change (though it might), but John may grow beyond the apparent potential of his origins, if he can survive his early years in the ghetto.

When John walks over to Forty-Second Street, the spirit of his stepfather does not follow him. "He loved this street," Baldwin says of John, "not for the people or the shops but for the stone lions that guarded the great main building of the Public Library, a building filled with books and unimaginably vast" (41). In the novel, John's church, "the Temple of the Fire Baptized," stands in direct opposition not only to the hospital but also the public library, and this represents the black church's antiintellectualism, which Baldwin, like Wright, sees as a disabling constraint. Yet we see how Baldwin differs with Wright's viewpoint when John is afraid to enter the Forty-Second Street library. To him, it is like the bewildering city, "a maze . . . [in] which he would be lost and never find the book he wanted" (41). John is still too young to find his way in the "unfinished" city; he needs a city *with walls*, precisely what his real father, Richard, did not have. It is this scene that connects John to the father he never knew.

The final episode of John's visit to the earthly city is the movie *Of Human Bondage*, with its strong performance by Bette Davis as Mildred, the tough, arrogant little cockney who haunts the crippled Philip (Leslie Howard), effectively complicating his progress toward a happy middle-class life. (In *The Devil Finds Work*, Baldwin says that what "held" him to Bette Davis was "the tense intelligence of the forehead, the disaster of the lips: and when she moved, she moved just like a nigger"[7].) John Grimes enters the theater prepared to identify with Philip—"a fool like him in every family," declares the movie poster—but in the course of the film he finds himself irresistibly drawn to the vulgar blonde woman who says, "You can kiss my ass!" to the world (42–43). Like Baldwin and Madame Defarge, John and Mildred have some empathetic connection. Mildred has emerged, fighting, from the depths of the city, and claws her way, for a while, up to the levels John has observed in his walk. Initially John likes both her bitter contempt and her marginal success in escaping her origins.

Of Human Bondage is Hollywood melodrama, and it follows a well-worn narrative groove. It has a "bad woman," a "good woman," a "good" but misdirected young man, and a hypocritical bourgeoisie— basic elements of nineteenth-century popular fiction (or of Dunbar's *Sport of the Gods*)—and these elements interact in a story concluding with the bad woman's death and the young couple's redemption.[40] John Grimes's identification with the "bad woman," Mildred, comes out of her resistance and her role as an outsider; she embodies the contradiction that has built up in him during his city walk, the conflict of fear and desire. Thus the movie serves as a summary that in its melodramatic form can, as Jane Gaines describes, "accommodate both the address which assumes some power and the order of events which counsels resignation."[41] John will embrace first the power, then the resignation.

Bette Davis's Mildred initially wins him because of her urban insolence and self-assuredness. She is like Lucifer: "Perhaps her sin was so extreme that it could not be forgiven; perhaps her pride was so great that she did not need forgiveness." And he "wanted to be like her, only more powerful, more thorough, and more cruel, to make those around him, all who hurt him, suffer as she made the student suffer" (44). Obsessed with himself and his own suffering, John shuts out the image of Mildred as a cheap tart, the image that Hollywood deliberately stresses. Being used by others as she uses Philip, she is equally the city's victim, yet unlike Philip, who knows Mildred's faults, John identifies in her a persona that he needs for himself, one to deal with the three cities that threaten him: Harlem, white New York, and his father's church.

Mildred's fall from power in the movie (considerably simplified from Maugham's novel) returns John to himself. Confronted by death, the tuberculosis-ridden girl seems bewildered, all her pride counting as nothing compared with "the place where she was going" (45). Hollywood makes the death sordid enough to give any audience a "lesson," yet sitting in the theater at the movie's end, made miserable by the thought of eternal damnation, John still "struggled to find a compromise between the way that led to life everlasting and the way that ended in the pit" (45). But by Gabriel's scenario he must choose between two cities (jails and churches), and only while Mildred rises in *Of Human Bondage* and "assumes some power" does John choose New York over his father's church; when she falls, New York becomes Babylon and Bette Davis its whore. John's conversion to Christ in the novel's last section will be his "compromise," a "resignation," yet also a middle way that allows him to humanize the demands of one city (heavenly) and to keep at a distance the dangers of the other (earthly).

When Baldwin constructed the scene in the movie house, he may have been drawing on the memory of his own adolescence, discussed in *The Devil Finds Work*, but he was also aware of the famous scene in *Native Son* in which Bigger sees *The Gay Woman*. Like John, Bigger is impressed by a rebellious woman who seems to break the rules with impunity. The gay woman is wealthy and white, and can afford to be promiscuous; she represents the city's power and possibilities, and in a sense she is what Bigger "killed for." She is the city's prize—not literally, but as a symbol of what the city promises to all but only gives to most people vicariously, in the movies. Bigger misreads the film by judging its people in terms of what they do, not what they say. He doesn't accept the repentance at the movie's end because he knows, perceptive movie critic that he is, on one level, that repentance is not what most American movies are really about. The term "Hollywood ending" describes the sort of conclusion that the Hays code demanded of commercial movies after 1934: any action that might "lower the standards" of morality had to be corrected or punished, whether or not that correction or punishment provided a believable ending for the film.[42]

Bigger probably *would* have believed the moral conclusion given in *Of Human Bondage*, not because of its morality but because of its realism. Mildred's only power is Philip's obsession with her, which she can't use to ensure her own survival. Bigger would have understood the fate of the powerless in the earthly city, as well as Philip's redemption through the intervention of middle-class friends and a timely inheritance. Philip's class connections ensure his survival. John Grimes, on the other hand, while he may appreciate Mildred's resistance to her condition as a kind of social resistance, finally sees her death in the absolute moral terms of Gabriel's religion: "It was the Lord who had led him into this theater to show him an example of the wages of sin" (45).

Although Bigger and John read films differently, neither reads them "innocently," that is, as a white middle-class audience ideally would. Wright, Baldwin, and Ellison, in fact, all use a movie scene in their novels to differentiate their black characters from the white mass culture that dominates the public life of the cities.[43] The mixed and contradictory message of Hollywood is both "Consume" and "Be good," and that contradiction shows most clearly in the view from underneath. Hollywood presents the upper middle class as the measure of what is worthwhile (cars, houses, and clothes) and at the same time enjoins modest behavior which is seriously at odds with those levels of consumption. Wright has Bigger read only the message "Consume," while Baldwin has John fixate on the moral rule "Be good." Ellison's difference from either writer illustrates the different terms of his city, for the invisible man goes to see a western, a film not about the urban condition but about the myth of escape from the city to the frontier. This involves a different contradiction, for to identify with the conquest of the American west, the invisible man must validate a history that ignores his own existence ("there was no one like me taking part") as well as the destruction of the native "Indians." But although Ellison sees the epic ironically, it is still in epic and picaresque modes that he views the city, and that view differs essentially from both Wright's drama of race and class and Baldwin's tale of domestic conflict.

The house, the room, and the family or extended family and its life in the city: these are the concerns of Baldwin's fiction. He said that when finishing his first novel in Europe he was isolated in a small Swiss village with a typewriter and two Bessie Smith records, one of them "Back Water Blues" (1927), which includes the lines "My house fell down / And I can't live there no more."[44] The background of the song is the great Mississippi Delta floods of the 1920s, but the lines Baldwin focuses on as "a great achievement" might also summarize his fictional themes. The house, as we have seen, is set within and against a city; and a stultifying patriarchal presence hovers over both, yet Gabriel is only one "father" among a group of relatives who influence John's life. The section of *Go Tell It on the Mountain* called "The Prayers of the Saints" tells of four people (Florence, Gabriel, Elizabeth, and Richard, John's real father) whose stories cast a shadow over John. Each story represents a house that has "fallen down," a failure of domestic support that excludes the character from a nurturing community. In terms of the black spiritual to which Baldwin alludes in his title, each person has been a "seeker" whose quest for the ideal city has been ironically fulfilled.

As these characters pray in "the Temple of the Fire Baptized" on the night of John's birthday, each is haunted by his or her own past, and trapped within his or her own ego. They seem incapable of hope, because their portraits are already drawn; their memories are fixed like moral *exempla* taken from the lives of the saints. However, the landscape of their memories is not merely factual, for each history is based upon a metaphorical city.

Florence's city belongs to the material American dream: it is the place where one goes to become rich. From the enclosed world of southern racism and her own people's parochial outlook, she brings to New York the ambitions and virtues that ensure success, yet the city defeats her. Despite (or because of) skin whiteners, Negro Uplift, and her worship of frugality, industry, and gentility, she becomes inflexible and incapable of compromise, drives her husband away, and, now an old woman, works cleaning offices in one of the city's towers. Dying of cancer, she is haunted by guilt and a rage against the past: her abandoned mother, her ruined marriage, and her brother Gabriel, whose hypocrisy she bitterly dissects even as she seeks refuge in his church. Equally bitter is Baldwin's irony in these "exempla"; the "saints" are fallen, and their "prayers" are curses.

Gabriel has avoided the material city, for he is afraid of his own imperfect self-control. As a young man he "hated the evil that lived in his body, and he feared it, as he feared and hated the lions of lust and longing that prowled the defenseless city of his mind" (120). Thus the urban significance of his character is internal, the self vulnerable in the manner of an undefended city;[45] all his metaphors (city, mountain, and house) are ironic, though he believes that God's *house* ("Set thine house in order") has supplanted his defenseless id, providing him with solid ground on which to stand. Yet the walls of his "house" prevent him from looking into the recesses of his own heart and isolate him from everyone around him, even his wives, sons, and mistress.

Gabriel's self-deception appears in his sexual affair with Esther, whom he invites to his church and then preaches to so passionately that she is pleased "as though she were at a theater" (159). Without realizing it—for he cannot allow himself to realize it—Gabriel had staged his sermon for Esther's benefit and transformed the church, the fortress protecting Christians from the earthly city, into Vanity Fair. His text that day in church reinforces the irony: "the story of the young Ahimaaz who ran too soon to bring the tidings of battle to King David" (156). The comedy of his "seduction" of Esther arises from both "running too soon," and a dangerous enclosed space. Finding himself alone with her in her employer's house, he helps her to lock up, and as he runs through rooms and doorways in his haste to leave the house and temptation, he discovers that the only exit left is through the kitchen, where Esther waits. The protected space of the house, which was to be his defense, has made him its prisoner. His treatment of Esther, whom he abandons; of her son Royal, whom he refuses to recognize as his son and thus condemns to death; and of the tainted Deborah, whom he marries as a visible proof of his spiritual purity—these acts illustrate that his "ordered" house has collapsed. His denial of the earthly city is as ineffectual as Florence's pursuit of it.

Elizabeth's New York is the biblical city of refuge. Like Florence she flees the limitations of rural life, leaving her small town in Maryland not from ambition, however, but for love. Her husband-to-be, Richard, is drawn to the city by its cultural gravitation; to him it represents the intellectual and aesthetic heritage of Western civilization, something to which (like Richard Wright or the invisible man, or like Baldwin himself) he wants access. Of course, both Elizabeth and Richard discover the hidden snare within the city's freedom, for while no one watches them, no one cares about them, either: "Here, in this great city . . . where people might live in the same building for years and never speak to one another, she [Elizabeth] found herself, when Richard took her in his arms, on the edge of a steep place: and down she rushed, on the descent uncaring, into the dreadful sea" (219). From that mountain, there is no Pisgah view of the Promised Land; rather, one sees a vast emptiness.

Richard had been trying to both work and go to school, so they remained unmarried. On Saturday afternoons he would take Elizabeth to the Museum of Natural History or the Metropolitan Museum of Art. In the latter, he gazed, "with such melancholy wonder" upon "an African statuette, or totem pole" that Elizabeth was bewildered by his adoration of "things that were so long dead" (224). She sensed that they gave Richard "a kind of bitter nourishment, and that the secrets they held for him were a matter of his life and death. It frightened her because she felt that he was reaching for the moon and that he would, therefore, be dashed against the rocks" (224). Richard's attraction to the institutions of high culture as a refuge invokes a line of black aspiration that runs from Frederick Douglass and W.E.B. DuBois through the Harlem Renaissance and on into the first part of Wright's autobiography, *Black Boy*. It appears as the idea of "uplift," of being "civilized," sometimes of climbing via a stack of books into the middle class and/or to self-reliance. "City air makes you free" because in the city's cultural vortex anyone can find the elements of civilization and educate himself or herself to become an informed and rewarded citizen; "culture" is one of the invisible cities existing within the urban boundaries, at least in the ideal blueprint of the "New Negro."

There is a deep irony in Baldwin's novel, for Richard's fate will be similar to Bigger's rather than to that of the Richard Wright of *Black Boy*. He is mistakenly arrested for the robbery of a grocery store, and the store owner cannot distinguish him from the robbers because, to him, Richard is just another "nigger." In the white man's city, the problem for the "New Negro" is that he is still black. There is a further suggestion to this incident, for when Richard insists to the owner that he "wasn't *there*" (232), he is right in just the way Ellison understood. No matter how brilliant his intelligence, it doesn't verify his existence in the white man's world, and he remains in the position of the invisible man. Unlike Ellison's character, however, Richard is destroyed by this shock of recognition.

Elizabeth is left alone with their new baby, John, and one afternoon she encounters Gabriel at Florence's home. She will marry him because in the wilderness of her city he now seems like a "hiding-place hewn in the side of the mountain" (253). It is a place of fear and denial, as well as protection. When they met, a phonograph record of the blues was being played in an adjacent apartment, and

John instinctively responded to it "by wriggling, and moving his hands in the air, and making noises, meant . . . to be taken for a song" (248). But to Gabriel it was the "Devil's music," as to most white Americans in the 1920s it would have been "nigger music." With John's innocent response Baldwin represents a rejection not only of Gabriel's puritanism but also of the majority culture's racist standards; he also suggests a connection between that puritanism and the racist viewpoint. Afro-Americans, defined as "other," as subhuman, have been compelled to "prove" their humanity according to the values of whites, and the church's puritanism becomes a refuge from a white demonization of a racial "otherness." Gabriel's fear internalizes the culture's traditional view of Afro-Americans, which the baby John, of course, knows nothing about. The infant's response to the music is like Richard's response to African sculpture in that it moves outside the "hiding place" of Gabriel's religion;[46] but it also touches another sphere, popular black art, which is freer from the intervention of a white institution such as the museum.

Though whites hardly exist as characters in Baldwin's novel (in fact, none are given proper names), they represent a background, a force, the implied cause behind events, as in Richard's death. The triangle of identity formed between Richard, Gabriel, and John, and mediated by the museum, the church, and the blues, illustrates the perilous and ambiguous nature of Afro-American culture. As with Bigger and the invisible man, and as we will see with Toni Morrison's characters, the problem is establishing an Afro-American point of view within a white culture that has always devalued it.

Baldwin's image of the blues coming through the walls of a ghetto apartment resembles two earlier figures by Afro-Americans writing about their popular culture: Du Bois on the Jubilee Hall at Fiske, and Jean Toomer describing the Howard Theater's song-soaked walls. There is a line of descent from Du Bois's institutionalization of the Sorrow Songs, to Toomer's metaphor for the interchange between popular and mass culture, to Baldwin's perception of culture absorbed at ground level.[47] The baby John hears the blues through the walls. Culture is a ubiquitous presence, absorbed as if with one's mother's milk, Baldwin implies, and while it must become a conscious need at some point (his taking Bessie Smith's records to Switzerland), its original source is the experience of the common life, whatever that may be. John will carry on his real father's good fight in his own way. He will confound Gabriel by his conversion, and that conversion will also illustrate the truth about God's "house" which Gabriel has denied: "In my Father's house are many mansions" (John 14:2). Some of these mansions are juke joints rather than churches.

In the middle of Saturday night service at "the Temple of the Fire Baptized," John is possessed by "the spirit" and falls to the floor of the church. At first, an "ironic voice" in his mind tells him to "rise . . . and, at once . . . leave this temple and go out into the world" (262). Otherwise, he would "become like all the other niggers" (263). This is the voice of the earthly city, urbane and cynical, the voice of Bette Davis in the movie he has seen that afternoon. The "ironic voice" is insistent but weak, because John is now convinced, albeit subconsciously, that the appeal of that earthly city is overshadowed by its uncertainties. This fear, learned from Gabriel, can only be a starting point, however, if the boy is to be born again not only into the church but into the world.

That process in John's imagination is vividly portrayed in the visionary sequence of his conversion. He sees himself walking with Gabriel through the streets of a mysterious city. The buildings are narrow, "rising like spears into the sky, and they were made of beaten gold and silver" (268). But this is not the heavenly city of the Bible, for "John knew that these buildings were not for him—not today— *no, nor tomorrow, either!*" The echo of his stepfather's voice in his mind reminds us of his earlier journey that day on Fifth Avenue. Continuing their walk through this street, Gabriel and John encounter an ugly old hag. Gabriel points to her: "You see that? That's sin. That's what the Devil's son runs after" (269). Gabriel threatens to beat the whore of Babylon out of John, and the young boy "looked about him for deliverance; but there was no deliverance in this street for him" (269). This is the moment of John's vision of death. "The knife came down," his father thrusting him outside the community of the faithful, making him "a stranger there" (271). The dream sequence vividly states John's dilemma, caught as he is between the city and the church, which as defined by Gabriel thrusts him outside into "this street" where there is "no deliverance."

From that moment, the nadir of hope, John tries to rise up and thus begins a second series of visions. He observes the wretched of the earth in their pain and despair, and he realizes that their misery is his. Hearing the singing of the congregation, he recalls the words of John of Patmos:

> *I, John, saw a city, way in the middle of the air,*
> *Waiting, waiting, waiting up there.* (278)

He rejects the "ironic voice" that had urged him to rise above his people, but his rejection now grows not from fear, not from Gabriel's negative depiction of the city, but from an empathetic love for his people, the "other niggers." In his imagination, he joins the multitude as they "moved on the bloody road forever, with no continuing city, but seeking one to come: a city out of time, not made by hands, but eternal in the heavens" (278). The city "not made by hands" is also the church not made by Gabriel's "hands."

On one level, John's conversion resolves his troubled relationship with Gabriel. Finding God is an unconscious attempt to please his "father," but it also places Gabriel in a dilemma because his own righteousness is based upon a similar inner light, and this irony creates an important dramatic moment at the novel's end. When the family arrives home after the ordeal of the night, John asks Gabriel for the living word that would bind "father" and son in the name of Christ. Gabriel refuses to give it, and John warns him that he has found salvation on his own and that *his* God will protect him "against everything and everybody . . . that wants to cut down my soul" (282).

Yet what has validated John's separateness is paradoxically his realization of a new community within the church. Baldwin makes this point very specifically in describing John's return from his visionary dream:

> "Rise up, rise up, Brother Johnny, and talk about the Lord's deliverance."
>
> It was Elisha who had spoken; he stood just above John, smiling; and behind him were the saints—Praying Mother Washington, and Sister McCandless, and Sister Price. Behind these, he saw his mother, and his aunt; his father, for the moment, was hidden from his view. (279)

When Sister McCandless sings, "Lord I ain't no stranger now," in celebration of John's deliverance, the theme of the spiritual suggests Baldwin's complaint against Richard Wright: that Wright ignored in

Native Son "any sense of Negro life as a continuing and complex group reality."[48] Admitting that the black church could be as puritan and paranoid as Wright said, Baldwin nonetheless shows that John's impulse to commit himself to it is based finally upon love rather than fear. His wrestling match with Elisha has humanized the church in his mind, has made possible the intimate space that his own home, because of his stepfather's dominance, has been unable to provide. It hardly matters to Baldwin whether the passion between the two boys has its basis in Eros. Eros remains a necessary part of the community, even if it is denied by the white culture or suppressed by a black culture seeking legitimation in whites' eyes. In any case, Baldwin has shown in the story of Gabriel and Esther that suppression is no solution.

To John's mother, Elizabeth, John's conversion means the death of Richard's presence in her son, but her understanding of the event is skewed by the inflexibility of Gabriel's character and the tragedy of Richard's life. Ironically, she prematurely imposes a patriarchal narrative (beginning, middle, end) on John's life. For in associating the church with Elisha, and not Gabriel, John perceives it in terms of a transformation of gender in much the same way that the City of God became feminine for Augustine. Kenneth Burke notes how in Augustine's *Confessions* God the Father becomes, through the transforming power of love, "our Catholic mother." Thus for Augustine the idea of "citizenship" changes from a "political category to a religious one."[49] Citizenship in Rome is masculine; it is a public world of privilege, order, and agendas. Citizenship in the City of God is feminine, for it assumes that the binding element of a religious (from *religare*, meaning "to bind") community is something private (as in Paul's *caritas*, 1 Cor. 13:1–13), invisible, and nurturing. When John awakens from his vision, he is surrounded by the women of the church. His affection for Elisha is like Richard's for Elizabeth, but it expresses itself within the ordered framework of a safe haven, which gives the boys a chance to mature to face once again "the tigerish lights of the city" (220).

In one sense, John's fall into the black church is a turn to popular culture against the mass society of New York. He chooses the local and the small-scale over the splendor of the downtown world, and the local is a traditional institution that connects the boy's public and private lives. Despite Gabriel's presence, it seems a feminine institution, characterized by the "sisters," and it makes John's personal struggle with his "father" a public matter and allows him to return to his home with the new strength of a public and communal identity. The dangers of the city of destruction still accompany him, as he observes the street walking home: "The water ran in the gutters with a small, disconnected sound: on the water traveled paper, burnt matches, sodden cigarette ends; gobs of spittle, green-yellow, brown, and pearly; the leavings of a dog, the vomit of a drunken man, the dead sperm, trapped in rubber, of one abandoned to his lust." (295).[50]

The difference now is that John's conversion has created "an imagistic bridge" between two realms of being, the transcendent and the empirical, allowing him to see everything that threatened him before through the aura of a transcendent principle: love.[51] For Baldwin, if this is an illusion, it is a necessary one. So too is the illusion of a Beloved Community created by John's conversion.

That communal attachment represents an essential difference between John Grimes and Bigger or the invisible man. For Bigger, the determining institutions of his life are the public welfare agency and, later, the Chicago justice system. The invisible man's adventures comprise a series of encounters, all of them disastrous, with various American institutions. But while Wright's and Ellison's characters move and act in a primarily public arena, Baldwin's young boy, on the threshold of manhood, remains in all ways domestic; his life is worked out in the confines of family and church. This is not simply a necessary realism due to John Grimes's age. In Baldwin's later novels, all his major characters will have this close relationship, for better or worse, to domestic situations. Baldwin, in fact, sees the invisible city of true community as a domestic creation, a local habitation; thus the allusion to Ezekiel's New Jerusalem (Ezek. 40–48), with its restored "temple," in the Central Park episode is ironic because John's "temple" is restored in terms of space made intimate. That temple is not a memory of Chartres, a public ideal of social planning, or a philosophic condition of continual striving, but an actual home.[52] In *Native Son*, all domestic space is dangerous for Bigger, from his family's "kitchenette" (in which he kills a huge rat) to Mary's room to the final jail cell. The idea of home for the invisible man is the awareness that he has to keep moving. In a sense, Jim Trueblood's dilemma—"to move without moving"—is the invisible man's fate, as he realizes that "the principle" can only dwell within him (or he within it) when he travels an open road.

Baldwin's view of family as the entirety, or a substantial part of, an individual's fate links him to the important black female novelists who have emerged since the 1960s, and notably to Toni Morrison. It is a link Morrison has acknowledged more than once, a link that is based not only on a shared vision of the domestic origin of the invisible city but also on a biblical moral language secularized to make it "truly modern, dialogic, representative, humane." At his funeral, she described his gift to her in an appropriate metaphor: "You gave me a language to dwell in."[53] And equally important, both as a writer and as a citizen Baldwin engaged the history of his time in such a way as to connect him to the experience and values of Morrison's generation.

CHAPTER SIX

The Beloved Community
in Toni Morrison's *Beloved*

> Adam was therefore the father of both lines of descent, that is,
> of the line whose successive members belong to the earthly
> city, and of the line whose members are attached to the City in
> heaven. But after the murder of Abel . . . there were two fathers
> appointed, one for each of those lines of descent. Those fathers
> were Cain and Seth; and in their sons, whose names had to be
> recorded, indications of these two cities began to appear with
> increasing clarity in the race of mortals.
>
> —Augustine, *The City of God*

> When a woman gets in trouble, everybody throws her down,
> Looking for her good friend, none can be found,
> You better come on in my kitchen, it's going to be raining
> outdoors.
>
> —Robert Johnson, "Come on in My Kitchen"

> listen,
> you a wonder.
> you a city
> of a woman.
> you got a geography
> of your own.
>
> —Lucille Clifton, "what the mirror said"

Richard Wright began writing *Native Son* in the late 1930s; it was published in 1940. Ralph Ellison published parts of *Invisible Man* in 1947, and the complete novel came out in 1952. James Baldwin has recorded how he struggled to complete *Go Tell It on the Mountain* for several years, finally publishing it in 1953. The line from *Native Son* to *Invisible Man* and *Go Tell It on the Mountain* is direct. Not only had Wright's novel received more attention, and acclaim, than any previ-

167

ous work of fiction by an Afro-American, but Wright had posed in uncompromising terms the major social dilemma of American life— what was to be the fate of black people in the northern cities? That recognition of Wright's achievement and the acuity of his social analysis led Ellison and Baldwin to conceive their novels within the frame of Wright's themes.[1] Ellison and Baldwin both knew Wright, and he, in turn, had offered both men advice and encouragement as writers; but in a larger sense, the theme on which they all focused was one presented to them by history: the migration from the rural south to the urban north, which was the major fact of black life in this country between World War I and 1960. It was also a theme that, in one variation or another, was central for the writers of the Harlem Renaissance, and those writers, it is important to remember, were the black literary establishment when Wright, Ellison, and Baldwin began working. The renaissance was rejected in the political 1930s, and it would almost disappear from literary history for thirty years; nonetheless, one cannot read any of these three later novels without seeing their strong thematic connections to books such as Walter White's *Flight* (1926), Rudolph Fisher's *Walls of Jericho* (1928), Claude McKay's *Home to Harlem* (1928), Countee Cullen's *One Way to Heaven* (1932), and Jessie Fauset's *Plum Bun* (1929). Or to any of a half-dozen other novels written during the Harlem Renaissance.

From the publication of *Go Tell It on the Mountain* in 1953 to the publication of Toni Morrison's first novel, *The Bluest Eye*, in 1970, there is a gap of seventeen years, and they are perhaps the most significant and extraordinary seventeen years in the history of Afro-Americans in this century. Essentially, Morrison's first novel is separated from Baldwin's by the Civil Rights movement—everything from *Brown* v. *Board of Education* (1954) to the assassinations of Malcolm X and Martin Luther King, Jr. Richard Wright, absent in Europe, did not participate in the emergence of the major Civil Rights resistance, while Ralph Ellison was to be only tangentially concerned with the activism of the 1960s. Baldwin was obliquely critical of both men for their disengagement. He returned from Europe, saying, "Everyone else was paying their dues, and it was time I went home and paid mine";[2] and he spent much of the decade speaking out and sitting in, as well as writing about the movement.

In speaking of her relationship to some earlier black writers, Toni Morrison told an interviewer: "I always missed some intimacy, some direction, some voice. Ralph Ellison and Richard Wright—all of whose books I admire enormously—I didn't feel were telling *me* something. I thought they were saying something about *it* or *us* that revealed something about *us* to *you*, to others, to white people, to men."[3] Morrison is perhaps speaking here of the "public" orientation of Wright's and Ellison's writings. To say that they addressed themselves to others—white people and men—is to say that they spoke to the majority or to the elite groups of the society; not necessarily with that intention only, but as a necessary result of their desire to speak in terms of public policy and high culture. That was their chosen forum and their milieu. Morrison, with more formal education than any of the other three writers discussed here, has always set her fiction in the common life, not uncritically, but with the same concentration on domestic space, domestic relations, and the small-scale which characterizes Baldwin's novels. (Even on the cosmopolitan canvas of her novel *Tar Baby* [1981], she essentially focused on the "local habitation.") In her memorial address in honor of Baldwin's life and art, Morrison both paid homage to his engagement in the world ("the courage to live life in and from its belly as well as beyond its edges") and recognized the quality that their works shared, something like "intimacy" ("the courage to go as a stranger in the village and transform the distances between people into intimacy with the whole world").[4]

The intimate implies the domestic, and the themes that Baldwin and Morrison share—love, family relations, and the extension of these concerns into the larger world—revolve around the house. In *The Bluest Eye*, Morrison's characters remain, for the most part, isolated in their houses, debilitated in various ways by the devastating myths of white society. The bluest eye is Lacan's *invidia*, the gaze that petrifies. The black housekeeper Pauline Breedlove pours her passion into the house of her white employers, but the space of her own home lacks intimacy—its "furniture had aged without ever having become familiar."[5] In contrast, the narrator Claudia's house is space made place by the presence of love, yet that love remains insular, rarely crossing the threshold into the community. In *Sula*, Morrison begins to explore the possibilities of an autonomous community, but Sula dies alone in Eva's labyrinthine house; she is a pariah because the community has not matured enough to recognize her independent existence.[6] The community uses her to define its essence, but she cannot use it to locate herself. In *Song of Solomon*, communities (Not Doctor Street, Danville, and Shalimar) thrive, but the house still reflects the enclosed, often warped, egos of individual community members. Circe transforms the Butlers' ersatz plantation manor into a pigsty, but she herself is transformed into a grotesque by her own revenge; Ruth is "pressed small" by her father's huge mansion and in turn arrests her own son's spiritual growth; Macon Dead industrializes his house, setting his daughters to manufacture velvet roses for Gerhardt's department store; even Pilate's "open" house, despite (or because of) its association with nature, fails to give Hagar the structure she needs to save herself.[7] In Morrison's novels the house becomes an increasingly complex measure of individual well-being, and because it is the basic unit of the community, its relations to other houses become the measure of the well-being of an invisible city.[8]

In *Song of Solomon*, it is the street rather than the house that reflects the heart of the community. As Morrison remarks of the daily rhythm of black life, "One lives, really, not so much in your house as you do outside of it, within the 'compounds,' within the village, or whatever it is."[9] Nevertheless, the ideal community for Morrison is one based on common understanding and *caritas,* balanced between individual respect for communal ties and communal respect for individuality, and in her fiction this balance is played out between house and village. Discussing *Beloved* in a recent interview, she portrayed her own craft in a favorite metaphor from the world of housekeeping; her job as a writer, she said, was "to dust and clean off old words."[10] One might say that the residents of Not Doctor Street in *Song of Solomon* do the same thing with their language, and the process by which the street received its name suggests the possibility of the "neighborhood"—Morrison's usual term for the black community—being reconnected to the house.[11]

The renaming of Mains Avenue—Not Doctor Street— within the unnamed city of Detroit illustrates the way in which Afro-Americans make their own space intimate; they rename as a revolt against urban anonymity, against the colorless names whites have given their streets. The new names they choose mark their own communal history and reflect its changing situation. Thus the Southside's residents initially rename Mains Avenue "Doctor Street," out of respect for the first black doctor to live in their neighborhood, but when it turns out that the city officials insist on its official name, they rename their street again, as "Not Doctor Street." Yet behind this ironic response to the white authorities' sense of urban propriety lies another motive for the renaming: the doctor regards himself as superior to his neighbors and apart from the neighborhood. Thus "Not Doctor Street" is a paradoxical sign for the community's true feelings; its members, like Morrison herself, apply the dustcloth to the name they had coined, refurbishing it for a new circumstance. By this act they change the static, Euclidian cartography of the dominant culture—city space parceled and subdivided in terms of Enlightenment rationality and pragmatic real estate values—into a flexible, homely space. The map that once showed an abstract major artery within a spatial grid defined by economics is now a map of the local and the particular.[12]

The naming of *Not* Doctor Street illustrates Kenneth Burke's insight that the *negative* exists only within the human (verbal) world and reflects the desire of human beings to control the world of nature, which simply "is."[13] Since, as Morrison notes in *Sula*, black people often associate the behavior of white people with natural catastrophes such as droughts, floods, and plagues, the naming of Not Doctor Street symbolizes an attempt to establish a purposeful black context in the midst of an incomprehensible and hostile world.[14] Moreover, as we have seen, the naming itself is no absolute fiat establishing a fixed definition for all time. It is an existential act that manifests a vital community whose space is fluid, protean. That is, it shapes space into a particular *place* that "is constantly being created and remade by human activities,"[15] like the invisible man's discovery that saying "yes" may be saying "no" (and vice versa), that there is no one fixed plan for making "the principle" live.

Morrison has struggled in her fiction to integrate her characters into a usable conception of community. Her approach to the Beloved Community is always by way of individual experience and the commonplaces, better or worse, of Afro-American life. To her great credit, she has not cheated: in each novel she has investigated the conflicts within black life with great subtlety, recognizing that often the black community fails to establish itself as a viable matrix that nurtures the individual (*The Bluest Eye*), or that it may succeed and fail at the same time, creating Not Doctor Street while relegating its female members to the status of pariahs and prisoners within their own houses. In *Tar Baby*, Jadine flees the black community of Eloe, and her lover Son's seductive "dreams . . . [of] yellow houses with white doors which women opened and shouted Come on in, you honey you!" (119). She chooses, finally, the briar patch of New York and Paris because these large cities give her opportunities and room to breathe. Morrison's obvious sympathy for Jadine in this situation is based on the knowledge that the "yellow houses" of Eloe, attractive as they are, belong in part to a male fantasy; they are, after all, Son's "dreams" for Jadine. Yet despite these negative portraits of houses in her fiction, Morrison herself has identified with "a woman's strong sense of being in a room, a place, or . . . a house."[16] Indeed, she has pointed to the historical circumstances of slavery as an explanation for the ambivalence that black women may feel toward the house. Contrary to popular impressions, most black women "were not, by and large, domestics in the house"; rather, they were laborers in the fields with the men. This situation created a laudable comradery among men and women, but it meant that the women were deprived of houses, of being householders.[17] Hence Morrison's female characters often evince strong attachments to houses, even those that seem cursed, and instead of rejecting the house as an image of confinement or entrapment, as white women writers have often done, Morrison in her fiction shows a desire to redeem the house and reintegrate it into the community.[18]

In her first four novels, Morrison moves back and forth between these questions of individual and communal realization, a movement illustrated by the positions of Dr. Foster and Pilate in *Song of Solomon*. The doctor is black, but he is also a male, a professional, and wealthy far beyond the average of the neighborhood. His is an individual success that is admired or envied by other black people, yet he also represents an intrusion of white and patriarchal values into the community. He provides, albeit reluctantly, a useful service to his black neighbors, though actually he would prefer (and has in part) a white clientele. However, when his son-in-law Macon Dead inherits what is left of his wealth and property, even that minimal service vanishes. What remains is pure economic exploitation, as Macon Dead proceeds to become a black slumlord. At the opposite end of the nominal social scale, the old woman Pilate is an impoverished refugee, a remnant of the folk in the city, a witness whose stories go unheard. Reduced to the level of a bootlegger by a community that refuses to recognize her significance, Pilate is the potentially nurturing ancestor who can bring health to the black urban community. Of the myriad characters in *Song of Solomon*, only Milkman catches a glimpse of her full intrinsic worth.

With *Beloved*, her most ambitious novel to date, Morrison documents the redemption of the house, the origins of community, and the integration of the individual within the community's life-sustaining body. There is an important difference between this novel and Morrison's earlier work, and indeed, any of the other novels I have been discussing: *Beloved* is a historical novel set in the nineteenth century, an imagined narrative based on a particular incident in the past,[19] and its story is formed around the conditions of black life in the south and in the north, before and after Emancipation. This, of course, does not mean that it is a novel with no bearing on contemporary matters. Morrison goes into the past because she understands how crucially relevant it is to the present, and *Beloved* is, in a sense, by analogy, her most thorough consideration of the state of Afro-Americans in the 1980s and 90s.

In its historical and geographic setting, *Beloved* at first seems to deal less with urban than with rural experience, unlike, say, *Song of Solomon* or even *Tar Baby*. Yet we need only contrast Shalimar in *Song of Solomon* with the little community on the edge of Cincinnati in *Beloved* to see the difference between the two kinds of "rural" experience. Shalimar cannot be found on real-world maps, but unlike Not Doctor Street—also unrecognized by the mapmakers—it seems caught in an ahistorical time frame. Shalimar, despite its cars and crackers, exists for the most part in the timeless world of the pastoral, just as the flight of the legendary ancestor Solomon exists in the timeless world of myth. By contrast, the community on Bluestone Road in *Beloved* is the historical antecedent to Not Doctor Street: it is the "village" that has evolved within the historical frame of black migration to the northern cities.

From another perspective, *Song of Solomon* is about the failure of community based on heroic action or heroic myth; heroism is contrasted with Not Doctor Street, which looks forward to an alternative communal strength that will be the subject of *Beloved*. Solomon chooses to fly back to the "archaic mother" (Africa), and his descendants *name* their town (Shalimar: Solomon) in honor of his flight.[20] In a sense, his extraordinary act founds a city, yet the act itself represents absence and loss. His heroic individualism puts a blight on both "place" and community, and after him, the idea of community becomes increasingly problematic with each generation of his male descendants in the Dead family. Heroic individualism descends into helpless anger, selfishness, and, finally, solipsism.²¹ So Guitar, a member of the Seven Days terrorist group, says of Milkman that he "hang[s] out" but "don't live nowhere" (103), even as his own group's actions represent the impotence of violence to *create* community, to resolve placelessness. The *not* of Not Doctor Street, however, is an attempt by the neighborhood to identify the community with a nurturing matrix—the rejection of the doctor is also a rejection of a death-centered maleness. Members of the community rename Macon Dead's Packard "Macon Dead's hearse" and continue to call Macon's real-estate office by its older name, "Sonny's Shop."²²

In her perceptive essay "City Limits, Village Values: Concepts of the Neighborhood in Black Fiction," Morrison has discussed the significance of the urban village for the twentieth-century black writer. She argues that whereas a white American writer objects to the city because its social life destroys individualism, a black writer who writes about the city usually locates himself within the theme of community. For most black writers, what creates livable space in the city is not the absence of the machine but the presence of the ancestor, the person who connects past and present and embodies a sense of historical continuity and communal wisdom. For Morrison, too, the symbolic center of the city is the ancestor, not the cathedral of Chartres, which, as Baldwin saw, spoke to Afro-Americans in terms of a past they could not claim. Because of the ancestor, the hostile, centrifugal modern city can be reshaped in terms of a cohesive village. "The city is wholesome, loved when such an ancestor is on the scene, when neighborhood links are secure." Thus the city becomes "home" *if* the ancestor is a functioning source of power: "The ancestor must defy the system, be cautious of Chartres, provide alternative wisdom, and establish and maintain and sustain generations."²³

This is a big *if*, of course, as Pilate's ambiguous position in the "neighborhood" surrounding Not Doctor Street illustrates. Macon Dead perceives her as an embarrassment; Guitar's mother, as "the very last thing in pea-time" (7); Guitar, as a female Step-n-fetchit. Instead of assuming her rightful place as the neighborhood's healer and shaman, Pilate is reduced to practising a lesser kind of magic, making and selling cheap wine. The curse that lies upon her is a microcosm of the curse that lies on the Dead family and, by implication, on the black community: the curse of the diaspora, which is revealed in the darker implications of Solomon's flight. As a heroic male, Solomon, like Prometheus (or Bigger), challenges the will of the gods; yet his ascent is also a fall. His separation from Ryna evokes her scream, the anguish felt at the severing of humanity into parts as people become doomed to "fly on and off and leave a body" (209). In *Song of Solomon*, people are always leaving "a body": Solomon leaves Jake; Jake leaves Pilate and Macon Dead; Macon Dead leaves Pilate and Ruth; Milkman leaves Hagar; Guitar leaves Milkman. Hagar's clothing and cosmetics literally "leave" her body in the rain. She had hoped that they would help her to transcend her body, but the promises on the labels of the packages betray her. Her victimization by mass culture is Morrison's comment on an incomplete city, one whose foundations lack the presence of the "archaic mother."

In *Song of Solomon*, dystopia and utopia meet on Not Doctor Street, but this is also true of the community being formed on Bluestone Road in *Beloved*. For Morrison, the city is utopian because of the presence of *communitas*; this, for her, is the space of intimacy, the space where people make contact. Modernity means alienation, fragmentation, and bureaucracy, and whites have often fled to the suburbs to escape these conditions. Morrison sets her community on the periphery of Cincinnati as an ironic comment on "suburbia." Her community is banished to the periphery—its members have little choice in the matter—and it disappears into the underground (*sub*-urbia), becoming invisible. And if we think of an *urbs* as having well-defined boundaries, being located on a map, Morrison's "city" is sub-urban in that its center and circumference are, as the Apostle Paul says, "things not seen." Thus the "city" on Bluestone Road is generic; it will become not only the black community in any modern metropolis but also the origins of a spiritual community that defies the *mappe mundi*. And for Morrison's characters, this latter community will be the only "city" that matters.

In *Song of Solomon* Detroit is not even named, yet in presenting an account of the origins of the invisible city within or beyond the white metropolis, Morrison reminds us that Bluestone Road is tied to Cincinnati, just as Detroit's presence—in the form of Macon Dead's Packard, for example—is felt on Not Doctor Street. In *Beloved* the invisible city will be formed within the earthly city, if only because the invisible city's members are economically dependent on the earthly city—Sethe on Sawyer's restaurant, and Paul D on the city's slaughter-houses. And those members will always be subjected to civilization's racism, to its law, and to its burgeoning mass culture. Thus, although Morrison's utopian city is possible, its fate is perilous because of its inescapable connection to the earthly city.

As we have seen, by the time we get to Wright, Ellison, and Baldwin, dystopia has overwhelmed utopia: after Wright, the problem is to imagine means of escape or survival. In *Beloved*, Morrison puts the utopian theme back into black urban literature, but her version of this theme, unlike Ellison's, is distinctly local, intimate, and provincial. This is significant not simply because she wishes to focus almost exclusively on Afro-American life but also because she wishes to revise an earlier, more expansive view of the city. Du Bois's university on a hill, James Weldon Johnson's "Cultural Capital," and Alain Locke's cosmopolitan Harlem have now shrunk to a community of the lowly outside the gates of Cincinnati.

From *The Bluest Eye* to *Tar Baby*, Morrison's settings are more or less contemporary; their conflicts and social questions are seen primarily in terms of the black neighborhood's existence within a white city, though that neighborhood might be represented as an apparently isolated village utopia like Shalimar, or even an isolated black individual such as Jadine in New York. Conflict arises most often from tension between the values of a black "village" culture and those of the mainstream white society. In *The Bluest Eye*, the black community is fragmented and overwhelmed by the deluge of images from white mass culture. The opening passage of *Sula* describes the death of a black village: "In that place, where they tore the nightshade and blackberry patches from their roots to make room for the Medallion City Golf course, there was once a neighborhood."[24] The name "Medallion," ironically commemorating a moment in the past which is unique and not subject to change, figures a tension between what in a community endures and what is lost which the novel investigates. In *Tar Baby* Jadine is a "city girl" and New York "a black woman's town," because black women have been able to convert, with different degrees of success, the briar patch of the city into their own intimate space: "Talk shit, take none" is their motto. Because they have melted into the interstices of the city's political structures, they wield real power within the localized space of corporate institutions: "Con Edison" offices, "Household Finance," telephone companies, fashion magazines (222). This power has come at a price, however, as Morrison makes clear early in the novel by Jadine's encounter with the woman in yellow and her "unphotographable beauty" (46). One thing the consumer culture consumes is identity, and the ideal of beauty promoted for the cover of *Elle* may serve to negate other possibilities, which then become "unphotographable"; what haunts Jadine is her sense that her identity has shifted from a black ideal to a white one. In Morrison's first four novels this atomization, the splitting off of individuals from a local culture by the power and attraction of a market-driven mass culture, is a major source of conflicts—conflicts between self and other, male and female, house and neighborhood, village and metropolis. Those early novels, however, skirt the general problem of finding a usable past that might be a source for Afro-American cultural identity—something that could give strength and coherence to that identity—because they avoid essential historical questions rooted in black slavery. It is only in *Beloved* that Morrison sets out to narrate a story of the origins of Afro-American community which substantiates that community by recovering its lost history.

Two time sequences interweave in *Beloved*'s narrative: a present of 1873–74, and a past of 1850–55. The division is between the decade before the Emancipation Proclamation and the decade that followed it; but the earlier date also marks the passage of another crucial law, the Fugitive Slave Law of 1850, which put teeth into the original Fugitive Slave Law of 1793. Between 1793 and 1850, the Ohio courts, following the lead of Massachusetts and other New England states, had curtailed the federally-supported legal rights that southern slaveholders had when they tried to reclaim runaway slaves in a "free" state; the 1850 law reversed this progress by bringing "federal law-enforcement officials into the fray on the side of the masters." A United States marshall, for instance, could now *compel* whites to co-operate with the slave catchers by deputizing a *posse commitatus* in his district.[25] In *Beloved*, the vacillation in the legal status of the members of the black community on the periphery of Cincinnati pre-scribes the kind of community that was formed, and this vacillation remains a primary continuing fact of black life.[26]

The Fugitive Slave Law, Morrison has argued, would have been administrative folly had it not been for the high visibility of the runaway slaves, whose skin color made it possible to enforce the law.[27] That enforcement did not necessarily observe any distinction between freedman and runaway,[28] a situation that had a significant consequence for the black community: even those who were not escaped slaves were *visible* outcasts, who tended to band together as (in some sense) fugitives from society. Hence in 1855 the members of the black community outside of Cincinnati had yet to forge firm internal, *invisible* bonds. Their community, in Alain Locke's words, was based primarily upon a "common condition"; what its members lacked was a "common consciousness."[29]

The frailty of the bonds that link the members of the newly formed black community is made apparent on the day Sethe's pursuer, "schoolteacher," arrives in Cincinnati. Ordinarily someone would have sent a runner to warn the newly escaped Sethe, and her mother-in-law, Baby Suggs, of the appearance of slave catchers, but on that day no one did, and schoolteacher's unhindered entrance into Baby Suggs's garden results in a curse falling not only on the house but on the community as well. Why no one took responsibility for warning them involves a complexity of motives: fear of the whites, envy of Baby Suggs's relative comfort, the fact of Sethe's being a newcomer, and the "reckless generosity" of the party celebrating Sethe's reunion with her family. The neglect also involves a failure of communal memory: "They woke up the next morning and *remembered* the meal-fried perch . . . and got angry. . . . Too much, they thought" (my italics).[30] Somehow the members of the black community imagine that Baby Suggs has not suffered in slavery as they have suffered, and this ignorance of their mutual history makes mutual trust impossible. If, as Morrison has said, "the act of imagination is bound up with memory," then memory itself—both collective and personal—becomes central to the issue of true liberation.[31]

Morrison agrees with Alain locke that for a real community of the spirit to be established there must be a change of communal definition. When a community is shaped by a "common condition" it is shaped by forces from the outside, and even though some of those forces may be good, like the Emancipation Proclamation, they are inadequate foundations on which to build a city. The real foundation must be a sense of belonging that comes from a community's recognition that its members share a world in common. The community defined only by an opposition ignores its own internal needs; the experience of mutuality is subjected to external definition.

The black citizens who live in the suburban neighborhood outside the earthly city of Cincinnati will form their own spiritual city, one whose bonds are more permanent than those devised by human laws. In juxtaposing a bad law (the Fugitive Slave Law) with a good one (the Emancipation Proclamation), Morrison underscores the fact that even a good law is not good enough so long as the basic structures of oppression remain intact. Freedom, especially if it is contingent upon someone else's decision to grant it, is no more than a hollow vessel, an abstraction. The great power of *Beloved* lies in Morrison's delineation of the travails through which the slaves move toward filling that vessel by and for themselves.[32] The novel will also link the emotional ties between Paul D and Sethe to the emergence of this invisible city; the personal is an effective, though not a simple, analogue of the public.

The introduction of the theme of the invisible city comes in Morrison's epigraph, taken from Paul's Letter to the Romans:

> I will call them my people,
> which are not my people;
> and her beloved,
> which was not beloved.(9:25)

Those who were once abandoned now become "people"; those who were once unloved, now become loved. And in the novel the process occurs simultaneously, as Sethe, the outcast who has murdered her own daughter, becomes the founder of a city. In this sense, she belongs to an urban tradition of cities founded upon a primal crime, fratricide in the case of Cain and Romulus, parricide in the case of Theseus.[33] But in Western cultural traditions, how many women founded cities? Even Athens, founded in honor of Athene, was created by Apollo as an exaltation of paternal priority. Hence Morrison, while participating in an ancient tradition, also radically reverses and transforms that tradition by making her founder a black woman, the lowest of the low, from the perspective of the white hegemonic culture—indeed, a kind of "barbarian," the very emblem of dis-order. Morrison herself, then, like Sethe, founds a new kind of city, outside the bounds of the white, male-dominated tradition of civitas. *Beloved* is her house in every sense of that term—the site of a new lineage and social/literary order.

The "beloved" in the epigraph refers not just to Sethe's murdered and reincarnated daughter but also to Sethe herself. Paul D will come to see the real woman beneath the woman who murdered her daughter, or rather, to see that the two Sethes are inseparable. The strength of will that allowed her to kill her daughter in order to save her from the slave catchers is the same strength that enabled her to travel from Kentucky to Ohio, though starving, beaten, and pregnant. Her iron will matches her "iron eyes," and the shock of Paul D's recognition entails an awareness that in the long run she has been a better "man" than he has been.

Further, the black community centered around Bluestone Road can only become a "people" if they accept Sethe back within their fold. Their defensive pride—the fearful, ex-slave identity that made them neglect to warn Sethe and Baby Suggs of schoolteacher's arrival—is the measure of their community's incompleteness. In one sense, *Beloved* is about how space becomes place: the black community outside Cincinnati will become a city when it accepts Sethe not as different but as the same, and when it rejects an identification of "right" with law or convention. When Ella comes to the conclusion that "what's fair ain't necessarily right" (256); when Stamp Paid realizes that nothing has been fixed by his taking a new name—that "paying" does not mean that you don't have to pay again—then the community, escaping the walled city constructed by the white man's laws and embracing the open city of the book of Revelation, begins to see that Sethe's lot is also theirs.

The distinction between the Law and the Spirit, elaborated in Romans, is one that Paul makes elsewhere as well (e.g., in his Letter to the Galatians and in his two Letters to the Corinthians), but it has a special relevance to the Romans because these people, though Christians, were also citizens of the greatest earthly city the world has ever known. And Rome was a city, a civilization, that prided itself on its laws, as Cicero's *De legibus* and *De re publica* illustrate. The parallel to the United States is apt, because it, too, has prided itself upon its legal foundation. As Robert Ferguson has noted, the Founding Fathers were not only lawyers and lawmakers, but also children of the Enlightenment. Confronting "a continent unspoiled by human history," they believed that "man-made" law would work hand in hand "with the natural order around them."[34] The other side of this coin was a bit more pragmatic. Once "constitutional bonds" with England were severed, then the law would presumably be the only thing to protect the citizens of the new Republic from the savagery of nature, human and otherwise.

Morrison's representative of the voice of law in *Beloved* is schoolteacher, a darkly malevolent figure who embodies a perverse rationality that destroys all human feeling. When she named him, Morrison probably had Paul's famous lines in mind: "Now before faith came, we were kept under the law, shut up unto the faith which should afterwards be revealed. Wheretofore the law was our schoolmaster. . . . But after that faith is come, we are no longer under a schoolmaster" (Gal. 3:23–25). Like the culture that produced him, schoolteacher identifies slavery with "civilization" and its laws, which he deems necessary to prevent the transplanted Africans from reverting to "the cannibal life they preferred" (151), yet because he is so completely without compassion—and Morrison's depiction of him is worthy of Jonathan Swift—he himself creates the "jungle" he abhors. As a "pedagogical" lesson to his nephews on the "animal" nature of blacks, he sends them to milk Sethe. One boy holds her like a cow while the other suckles her breast, and the image that returns to her and remains as her humiliation is of his "mossy teeth" (78) biting at her.[35] This act is a product of schoolteacher's law, the logical end of the Fugitive Slave Law and of the whole rational order of his slave system. It is Stamp Paid who makes the ultimate indictment of the slaveholders as "chosen ones". Suddenly realizing the significance of a string of red ribbon he pulls from the bottom of the river, still tied to "its bit of scalp," he gasps: "What *are* these people? You tell me, Jesus. What *are* they?" (180). His replacement of *who* by *what* negates the humanity of a civilization based on laws that dehumanize, and that justify savagery by logic and by appeals to a "higher" level of culture.

In *Beloved*, "these people" are the damned, the Pharisees who seek glory in Augustine's earthly city but create the conditions of Dante's Dis. In using a passage from Romans as her epigraph, Morrison undermines the dominant civilization by re-centering one of its most valued symbols. The lowly ex-slaves, with a black female Christ figure in their midst, possess the capacity to create "the city on a hill" of the New Testament, once the utopian dream of the Puritans but now debased by white America's greed. Cincinnati, named after a heroic Roman farmer whose loyalty to the Republic could not be measured in money or fame, has by 1873 become "pig port" (154), the hog-butchering capital of the Midwest, but the "stench" (257) that it exudes has none of the epic grandeur Carl Sandburg will later bestow on Chicago.[36] Instead, it is the stench of money which contaminates every aspect of American life, changing "the city on a hill" into Cain's city and leaving the classical ideal of *hortus conclusus* an unweeded garden.

"Sweet Home," the plantation in the south where the novel's major characters begin, is a garden for its owner, Garner (his name also symbolic), but finally a hell for those blacks whom he was pleased to call "men."[37] (Indeed, Sethe suffers from an extreme topophobia— fear of place—long after she has left "Sweet Home.") Schoolteacher's entrance into "Sweet Home" to restore order after the chaos of Garner's permissiveness mirrors his entrance into Baby Suggs's garden when he comes to seize Sethe and her children. Baby Suggs feels his coming as though he were Satan, as indeed he is, coming into her "yard" (179). He is the serpent in the guise of civilization, the murderous side of a Republic that places all its faith in the principle of law as a basis of order. The legal code that schoolteacher enforces begins, "The slave is entirely subject to the will of the master"; by this law "the slave had no brother or sister, no husband or wife, no son or daughter, no ancestors and no posterity." The legal status of slaves is described as "social death," their relations to their families defined as "kinlessness" and "natal alienation"—they have no family, and the mother has no lawful attachment to her child.[38] This is the "natural" world schoolteacher's law creates, set against the "unnatural" act of Sethe's murder of her child—which, paradoxically, can then only be the destruction of the slavemaster's "property."

Even the abolitionist Edward Bodwin operates within this legalistic frame. He hates slavery, but he sees it simply as an aberration to be rectified by changing the laws of the land. His charity toward blacks is as abstract and detached as schoolteacher's cruelty. Schoolteacher makes lists of Sethe's animal and human characteristics to define her; and Bodwin, for all his decency, is also a lawmaker, a definer. In that sense, he, too, is an example of what the rebellious Sixo painfully learns: "definitions belonged to the definers—not the defined" (190). Bodwin believes that abominations like that committed by Sethe will not occur once the laws have been changed. He also believes in the absolute efficacy of a legal code, and Sethe is recalled only as the object of a political tactic; Sethe's daughter Denver, whom he doesn't recognize, is merely a new hired "girl." He remembers the time of the abolitionist movement as "good years . . . full of spit and conviction" (260), a time in which he felt most alive, and at the novel's end, when he comes to find his childhood toys buried in the backyard of 124 Bluestone Road, he comes in complete ignorance of the facsimile of black history that has been enacted in "his" house. It is a sentimental journey of memory, of "good years," leading back to a nostalgic house that has no connection, despite his life's work, to Sethe's "rememory." As noble as these abolitionists and their cause were, they inevitably remained distant from the horrors they sought to change. And the legal system of the Republic, swinging pendulumlike between the position of schoolteacher and that of Bodwin, never finally defines Afro-Americans as either slaves or citizens.[39]

Beloved focuses not so much on new definitions as on the invisible presences within the old ones. If the Bible begins with a garden and ends with a city, it is because both garden and city reflect the communal life. The line from Paul that follows the passage Morrison chose for her epigraph emphasizes a connection between the emergence of a "people" and restored "place": "And in the very place where it was said to them, 'You are not my people', they will be called 'sons of the living God'" (Rom. 9:26). Similarly, Morrison refers to the "site of memory" to emphasize memory's role in the restoration of place.[40] Thus garden and city—two "articulated" images that white Americans have appropriated for themselves to describe their relationship to the New World—will be reappropriated by the very "people" whom they have excluded from their defining terms.

There is a further refinement in Morrison's choice of an epigraph. Paul is actually quoting the Old Testament prophet Hosea (1:8–9), indicating that the passage should be understood in light of both the Old and New Testaments. Hosea's relationship to his wife Gomer parallels God's relationship to the Israelites, who have prostituted themselves by worshiping false idols. God commands Hosea to marry the prostitute Gomer so that their marriage will be a mirror image of the debased marriage between God and the people. The offspring of Hosea's and Gomer's marriage are called "Not my people" (the son) and "Not pitied" (the daughter), negatives that are doubly negative because they illustrate the spiritual estrangement between God and his people.

Yet the point of the parable is that the mystery of God's love is beyond measure. Just as Hosea will restore Gomer to his affection, and so remove the taint of the negative upon their offspring, so God will return his love to his people. Paul takes this situation from the Old Testament and subjects it to a bit of creative misreading. In transforming "Not my people" into "my people," God indicates to human beings that the idea of the "chosen people" is not local but universal: "What shall we say, then? That Gentiles who did not pursue righteousness have attained it, that is, righteousness through faith; but that Israel who pursued righteousness which is based on law did not succeed in fulfilling the law." The real "Israel," Paul argues, is not a historical people defined by a written covenant of the law, but a spiritual people created anew by the spirit of *caritas,* a Beloved Community that contains within it the *figura* of the heavenly city (Rom. 9:30–31).[41]

This distinction, of course, is the basis of Paul's famous attack upon the "written code," as opposed to the life-giving spirit ("the letter killeth, but the spirit giveth life" [2 Cor. 3:6]), but it is also the basis of other oppositions as well, all of which contrast the tangible with the intangible, the visible with the invisible. The law, the temporal, and the written word fall on one side of the ledger; the spirit, the promise ("Hope"), and the spoken, protean Word (or "sound") fall on the other.[42] The distinction that Paul makes here will become the foundation of Augustine's two cities, the one mortal, corrupt, and transient, the other immortal, spiritual (internal), and invisible.

If the visible is less important than the invisible, then it is not surprising to find that both Paul and Augustine talk about God's city in terms of the more intimate space of a house. Hence Paul: "For we know that if the earthly tent we live in is destroyed, we have a building from God, a house not made with hands, eternal in the heavens" (2 Cor. 5:1). And Augustine: "Here then the two cities are presented, one existing in actuality, in this world, the other existing in hope which rests on God. They come out, we may say, from the same door of mortality, a door which was opened in Adam."[43] Augustine's "door" and Paul's "house not made with hands" recur in revised form in both *Tar Baby* and *Beloved.* In *Tar Baby*, Morrison placed an emphasis on the "contentions" in the "house of Chloe," her epigraph from Paul referring to unresolved contradictions in both the black community and in her own "house" of fiction (Morrison's middle name is

Chloe); but in *Beloved*, those contradictions are resolved when Denver walks out of Augustine's "door of mortality" into the world of the black community and when Paul D comes back into Sethe's life by walking through the door of Sethe's house.

Using Paul and Augustine, Morrison wrote a ghost story in which the invisible city is another ghostly presence. The effect of Sethe's resurrection at the novel's end radiates outward to include house and community. (According to Augustine, the name "Seth" means "resurrection.")[44] This is what gives *Beloved* an epic scope, for establishing a heavenly city within is the first step to founding the heavenly city without. The "people" who will become "my people" are those who have been the victims of the law and in consequence have received the gift of grace, for, to paraphrase Baby Suggs's words, this is the only thing they have left to "imagine. . . . O my people" (88).

*B*eloved begins with a naked house, so naked in fact that it is referred to not as a house but as a number: 124. Morrison said she began her novel this way because she wanted to reproduce the original conditions of being uprooted:

> I wanted that sudden feeling of being snatched up and thrown into that house, precisely the way they were. They were picked up from anywhere, at any time, and removed without resources, without defenses, without anything, naked . . . Snatched just as slaves were from one place to another. . . . No lobby, no door, no entrance—a gangplank, perhaps (but a very short one). And the house into which this snatching—this kidnapping—propels one, changes from spiteful to loud to quiet, as the sounds in the body of the ship itself may have changed.[45]

The novel begins with the grotesque situation of two women trapped in a haunted house, but this fairy-tale situation has its origins in a historical nightmare: the house is a slave ship, one cause of the Union becoming "a house divided" (Lincoln's metaphor) during the Civil War. This symbolic geography carries another implication. The house's address, 124 Bluestone Road, is itself a recent addition to the city's cartography, the abstract number anticipating an expanding city and an extended grid. When Sethe's sons Buglar and Howard fled the house in the 1860s, "it didn't have a number then, because Cincinnati didn't stretch that far" (3).[46] The house exists first in undefined space, then in space defined by the outer society, as though its number were branded on a slave. Morrison's point, of course, is that the house itself recapitulates the slave's experience in the New World. That it has "no back door" (29) suggests that the people in this house are, despite slavery's official demise, still trapped within "the terror of history."[47]

Morrison has said that although she began writing *Beloved* with a contemporary theme in mind—the theme of "self-murder," the ways in which people destroy themselves "with good intentions"—she found herself being drawn to Margaret Garner, a figure from history.[48] Because of the enormity of Garner's actions, this historical figure, Morrison discovered, could not be separated from myth. She was neither Medea nor Lady Macbeth, but she was monumental like those figures, for her crime not only challenged "the peculiar institution" but offended the black community as well. The act of killing (or trying to kill) her own children was an expression of "non serviam" in its deepest sense: it declared to the slaveholding society: you may enslave me but not the best part of me, my children. It even, in a way, reclaimed her children by negating society's legal rule of "natal alienation." But it also shocked the black community by its violation of that community's own natural laws, even those of kin and tribe. No wonder, then, that Morrison felt that her material reproduced the conditions of "Greek tragedy . . . the heroic struggle between the claims of community and individual hubris."[49]

Morrison believed that the character of Sethe could not be approached through the limiting strictures of realism. For Sethe illustrated the classic tragic dilemma—if she had been less strong, there would have been no murder. Because she is heroic, she suffers on a heroic scale. Only an oblique approach could capture the monumental dimensions of such a protagonist, and Morrison's own comments on her novel connect it to the tradition of the American romance, a tradition that includes the genre forms of horror, detective, and historical novels. Morrison has observed that scholarly studies of slavery have always seemed to her "too big and flat."[50] They were like realistic novels that in trying to include all the facts missed the essence. Slavery in the New World is shrouded in darkness, in mystery, because its horror seemed literally unspeakable. The slaves themselves left no record, oral or otherwise, concerning the Middle Passage; the need to survive, psychologically, blocked out from the racial memory the traumatic experiences of the sea journey. Regarding what the voyages were like for the slaves who endured them, we only have hints from the memoirs of the ships' captains. Morrison felt that through the character of Sethe, she could penetrate the darkness at the heart of slavery. That involved eschewing the "flat" social realism of the English novel for the exploratory world of the American romance; she believed that by working within narrow limits instead of broad ones, she might be able to do "something deep."[51] The depth she is speaking of is the depth of the human heart, Sethe's heart, which in its misery contains the misery of the race.

Writing about the genre of the detective story, Fredric Jameson argues that "everything in it, events and sentences alike, draws its ultimate value and even its meaning from an event in the past, an event necessarily external to the work's structure." For instance, in the Oedipus myth, the archetypal detective story, the event is tied to the "very *darkness* or *incognito* of origins themselves."[52] For Morrison, in both *Song of Solomon* and *Beloved*, slavery is the primal crime, but in *Song of Solomon* slavery is not the source of "origins"; rather, the significant "event in the past" is Solomon's flight from slavery back to Africa. In discovering this fact in a Gullah folk song, Milkman, like Oedipus, solves the key riddle, thus linking past and present, city and country, Pilate and her father's burial place. But Milkman's solution remains very much within the domain of the *animus*, the male world of a Philip Marlowe or a Gravedigger Jones. By focusing upon Solomon's flight from slavery, as revealed in the folk song, and upon the intellectual detective who discovers the song's meaning, Morrison shifts the focus away from the darkness of slavery and the mystery of Ryna's scream. In *Beloved*, however, she attempts to retell the story, as it were, from Ryna's point of view and confront issues in the heritage of slavery which are more mysterious than the world of *Song of Solomon* allowed. As *Beloved* develops, more and more fragments (of memory, of fact) are revealed to us, but ultimately we—like Sethe and Paul D—know no more about why the plan to escape "Sweet Home" failed than we did at the beginning. Those facts, which belong to a detective story, are not finally the fragments that matter. The truly significant fragments are of an interior nature, belonging to that "mental landscape" of romance whose meaning will never be completely fathomed by the intellect, whether by historians or urban detectives.[53]

When Paul D appears in Ohio eighteen years after Sethe has fled "Sweet Home," his information about Sethe's husband Halle—that Halle went mad when he saw Sethe victimized by schoolteacher and his two nephews—becomes one of several catalysts whereby the past is made tangible a second time, incarnated in the form of the girl Beloved. Paul D exorcises the invisible ghost in the house with his blunt methods (furniture wrecking, screaming, and shouting), only to have the murdered child return in corporeal form, more powerful and dangerous. What seems to be a supernatural event is psychologically true: Sethe fights a losing battle to hold the past at bay, for her "rememory" frustrates any effort to establish a foothold in the present: "Her brain was not interested in the future. Loaded with the past and hungry for more, it left her no room to imagine, let alone plan for, the next day" (70).

In discussing the romance as a literary genre, Northrop Frye has observed that "the notion of a world of pure memory, where everything forever continues to be as it has been, is the core of the religious conception of hell." Thus the "recreation of memory" is essential to the "transformation of the past," which Frye sees as "distinctive of romance," and this recreation creates a redeemed place, an escape from the Hell of "a closed cycle of recurrence."[54] Morrison has discussed the need for the "recreation of memory" in similar terms. She has no interest, she claims, in art as social description, in a memory whose basis is Locke's mental *tabula rasa* passively filled by experience. For her, memory symbolizes a starting point, not an end: "Memory (the deliberate act of remembering) is a form of willed creation." It becomes a means to "improvisation" and "audience participation," not the basis of an artificial whole that is a sealed-off version of the truth (what Walter Benjamin called "information," the province of the newspaper).[55] And she resists the idea of "pure memory" in which one is trapped within the infinitely repeatable world of the enclosed past. For her, "creation" means shaping the contents of memory into new wholes that are protean, open-ended, and rooted in the community, as is Benjamin's "story." Indeed, she sees her role as a novelist in terms that recall Benjamin's "storyteller":

> If my work is to be functional to the group (to the village, as it were) then it must bear witness and identify that which is useful from the past and that which ought to be discarded; it must make

it possible to prepare for the present and live it out, and it must do that not by avoiding problems and contradictions but by examining them; it should not even attempt to solve social problems, but it should certainly try to clarify them.[56]

In *Beloved*, Sethe, too, must become a storyteller, but she can do this only if she finds a way to escape the prison house of "pure memory" in order that she might shape the past, an act that would make it possible for her to live in the present. And this requires as well a listener who will participate in the telling of her story.

In the novel's beginning, Sethe is trapped within "a closed circle of recurrence." Time has stopped for her; she is fixed by a past that returns first in the form of her daughter's ghost, then in the form of that ghost's reincarnation. The supernatural event of Beloved's appearance has a "closed," psychological explanation: because Sethe's love for her daughter had been "too thick" (165), so too is her guilt, and she unconsciously wills her daughter's return. At the novel's beginning, fornication with the stonecutter is an act of penance as well as payment for the engraving of the word *Beloved* on the headstone. That "would be enough," Sethe thinks (5), but as Stamp Paid says later, people pay and pay again for sins they have committed—or even not committed. The relationship between crime and punishment in this novel is ultimately mysterious, exploding all "closed" explanations, because Sethe's murder of her child echoes a primal crime whose original context and circumstances can never be fully known. And the force of human desire compounds the mystery. In order to survive under slavery, black people taught themselves to "love just a little," but mothers often could not learn the lesson.[57] Morrison's novel is about a woman who could not do so, and who paid for that inability *in extremis*; yet in loving too well, she has also loved wisely, as Paul D, echoing his New Testament namesake, will remind her at the novel's end. Sethe suffers because her love is profound, but love this deep ultimately connects with the generative principle at the heart of the universe, as Paul's epistles suggest.

In talking about *Beloved*, Morrison noted that the "past" paradoxically appeared to her to be "infinite," the future "finite."[58] That is, the past's recurrence in human memory can numb a human being with an infinite variety of horrors and thus negate the possibility of imagining a future. Moreover, the past can seem more real than the present. Sethe repeatedly says, "I do rememory that" (201), and her grammatical mistake, substituting a noun for a verb, precisely expresses a personal history that has overwhelmed her with nouns. For not only is her memory "infinite" in recalling things she thought she had forgotten, but the past impresses itself upon her with such vividness that it seems incarnated in space: "If a house burns down," she tells Denver, "it's gone, but the place—the picture of it—stays, and not just in my rememory, but out there, in the world" (36). The past is so importunate, taking shape at any time in her memory without warning, that "rememory" is a more appropriate word than "memory," for it suggests the continual *re*turn of what cannot consciously be willed away. "Sweet Home," for instance, indiscriminately floods her mind with pictures of "shameless beauty" (6) and unspeakable horrors, and the recurring images of her sons Buglar and Howard walking away from her turn her mind into a movie projector condemned to show the same sequence interminably. When Baby Suggs tells Sethe that the only detail she can remember of a baby taken from her was that the baby liked the "burned bottom of bread," Sethe responds: "That's all you let yourself remember" (5). In this respect, James Baldwin's observation on memory in *Just above My Head* (1979) might serve as an epigraph to *Beloved*: "The burden of memory is to clarify the event, to make it . . . bearable. But memory is, also, what the imagination makes, or has made, of the event, and the more dreadful the event, the more likely it is that memory will distort, or efface it." Sethe has her own word, "disremember" (118), to refer to the process of willing the past away, but disremembering is obviously something she can't do. For as long as imagination and memory work together to "distort" the past, Sethe will remain enslaved to it. In terms of the negative implications of Ezra Pound's comments about the modern cityscape, her mind will remain "cinematographic. . . . a flood of nouns without verbal relations."[59]

Baby Suggs may control her own memory, but she cannot control schoolteacher coming "in her yard" (179). The suppression of memory doesn't prepare either an individual or a community to deal with a present crisis. Baby Suggs has had each of her six children taken from her and sold; she is overwhelmed by brute reality: "bad luck"—that is, white people—is the only reality she can imagine at the end of her life. Forgetting is a reflex, an understandable one, but also a symptom of despair. She dies because she can no longer imagine a reason to live, "suspended," as she is, "between the nastiness of life and the meanness of the dead" (3–4). She is reduced to the pleasure of gazing on "harmless" patches of color, her attempt to detach life from a historical context and its consequences. In her despair, Baby Suggs has detached the patches of color from the living quilt, the Afro-American art of weaving together a whole piece out of fragments.[60] The quilt might be described as an enactment of what Henry Louis Gates, Jr., calls "(re) membering," putting the scattered "members" of the past into a new contextual pattern.[61] This broken Baby Suggs is not the heroic preacher who delivers the Word to a newly formed black community outside of Cincinnati, who urges them to "love" the separate parts of their bodies—their hearts, their necks, their livers, even their private parts—because "yonder they do not love your flesh" (88). The only grace "they could have," she tells her audience in the Clearing, "is the grace they could imagine," and the grace Baby Suggs imagines at the end of her sermon goes into her dance, the gesture that imaginatively puts together her fragmented parts, even her "twisted hip," into a new whole of intimate space.

But the "grace" that Baby Suggs urges the members of the new black community to imagine cannot yet be fully imagined. They have not yet recovered from the devastating effects of slavery, and the narrative technique of *Beloved* in a sense illustrates their fragmented social condition: the story is told in bits and pieces, through the thoughts of many different characters, with a discontinuous movement between the past (the 1850s) and the present (1873–74). A reader of the novel gradually accumulates enough information to understand the stories of the individual characters, and their relation to each other; the act of reading the novel then becomes the construction of the community's history, and the method imitates the way in which we actually acquire most social knowledge: by small stories, anecdotes, observation of everyday life, conversation, and gossip. And these interwoven stories suggest a third, *unseen* time, the present of the 1990s, because the present-day city conditions our perception of Morrison's past one.

The effect of these interwoven stories, like patches of color becoming parts of a quilt, is also to create a social context for Sethe's story, just as the "Prayers of the Saints" section of Baldwin's *Go Tell It on the Mountain* gives such a context to the life of John Grimes.[62] Yet whereas Baldwin organized his novel around a conventional tripartite structure, Morrison leaves out chapter headings—indeed, even chapter numbers—and moves her narrative freely between different times and places. In discussing the fate and meaning of the characters in Morrison's novel, we necessarily speak of their stories as completed in a way they never appear in the fiction; the critic's attempt at closure is always outside of a text that tries to remain open, like a visual text within one kind of Afro-American quilt.

Baby Suggs's fate is to be destroyed before her vision of community can be realized. Wherever she lives "sadness was at her center, the desolated center where the self that was no self made its home. Sad as it was that she did not know where her children were buried or what they looked like if alive, fact was she knew more about them than she knew about herself, having never had the map to discover what she was like" (140). Freedom on Bluestone Road allows her to see the traces of a map ("These hands belong to me. These *my* hands" [141]), but schoolteacher's invasion of the space of her house and yard (her intimate space) cuts short her attempt to unify all the parts of the self. Sethe's action against schoolteacher paralyzes Baby Suggs, who can neither approve nor disapprove of the murder, and Baby Suggs's withdrawal from life occurs at the same time that the black community ostracizes Sethe. What Baby Suggs has begun to build through the spoken Word and the dance will be left to others to finish.

When she preaches in the Clearing, she is in the process of imagining a "grace" that goes beyond fragments (love your hands, love your heart), but she never completes that linking of part to part. Her new freedom means that the parts can be recognized and loved, but her dance—"the prize" (89) that she offers to the members of her audience—symbolizes an integration of personal identity that only lasts for the dance's duration. Neither Baby Suggs nor the members of the black community in the Clearing can "imagine" a whole community whose parts are like the integrated parts of her body when she dances, because the end of the dance brings them back to a world defined by the Fugitive Slave Law and the constant threat of schoolteacher's arrival.

As Baby Suggs's sermon suggests, the question of personal integration and that of the individual's joining to the community are the most important versions of a recurring figure in the novel, the figure of "sections," of a whole seen or felt only as parts. More specifically, this is the figure of *dis-memberment*. The past invades Sethe's mind as fragments; Beloved fears falling into pieces; the rooms of the house are separated into parts, each with a memory attached to it. Indeed, Denver's parts shut down: when Nelson Lord confronts her with her past, she literally turns deaf rather than hear the young boy's rhetorical question verified by her mother. Paul D puts the pieces of his past—the cage in Alfred, Georgia, and "Sixo, schoolteacher, Halle, his brothers, Sethe, Mister, the taste of iron, the sight of butter, the smell of hickory, notebook paper"—"one by one" into a figurative tin box (113). Each noun, even the memory of Sethe seeing him with the bit in his mouth, represents a horror that he must hide away if he is to remain sane.

Paul D's tin box ("a tobacco tin") contains parts of his and his race's history, just as does the briefcase that Ellison's invisible man carries with him down to his underground refuge. The parts compose a symbolic narrative that each character must read as a whole story if he is going to understand who he is and where he is; yet keeping the narrative in unreadable fragments allows the characters not to see a whole that might be unbearable. When the invisible man, alone in his cellar, finally "reads" the contents of his briefcase, he reads them with a willful creativity that converts Tarp's leg-iron into Tarp's resistance: the transformation of the horrific past into the linked records of a continuous if partial fulfillment of the principle is an act of individual affirmation and integration. The invisible man takes the fragments of the lives of others and makes from them a whole identity for himself. In Morrison's story, however, the past of slavery is closer and more debilitating, and beyond the strength of the individual to overcome. Paul D is moved about the house by Beloved, an incarnation of slavery's past, until she finally forces him to an intimate contact in which sexuality becomes the metaphor of a history destructive in the extreme, a loveless reenactment of fear and terror.

Beloved's possession of Paul D's past, her breaking into his tin box, marks the vulnerability of the disconnected past; the facts that are isolated are also hidden, in that they are unknown each to each. Paul D begins to gain control over his past only at the end of the novel, when, in the company of Sethe, he suddenly remembers a remark that Sixo made about Patsy, the Thirty-Mile Woman: "She is a friend of my mind. She gather me, man. The pieces I am, she gather them and give them back to me in all the right order. It is good, you know, when you got a woman who is a friend of your mind" (272–73). Paul D sees that Sethe does the same thing for him that Patsy did for Sixo, but what Paul D also recognizes is that Sethe *is* Sixo, a whole person if she will only see it: "You your best thing, Sethe. You are" (273). The last image we have of Sethe and Paul D is that his "*holding* fingers are holding hers" (273; my italics). That is, his fingers can hold hers because his belong to one hand. Because of Sethe's presence in his life, his fingers are no longer separate, and he holds Sethe's fingers because hers now threaten, in her despair, to fall separately from her hand.

Yet when he finds her in the keeping room dying as Baby Suggs has died, she is "lying under a quilt of merry colors" (271).[63] He begins by rubbing her feet, and the ritualistic gesture of bathing her in "sections" ("Will the parts hold?" Sethe wonders [272]) is a prelude to an act of the imagination that he wants her to entertain: to see that the strength of her will, which caused her failures, is also the source of her redemption. In the world of the merely rational, school-teacher's world, the slaves fail miserably: their plans for escape go awry because their timing is off. Indeed, Sixo can never seem to get his timing right: neither his rendezvous with the Thirty-Mile Woman nor his cooking experiments with baked potatoes ever work out as planned, just as Sethe can only save her daughter in the temporal scheme of things by killing her. Both Sixo and Sethe are penalized by the earthly city for their failures to live within its framework, but what Paul D sees at the novel's end is that Sethe's strength of will is like Sixo's. Just as Sixo shouts "Seven-o" right before he is killed, because his seed has outwitted his enslavers, so Sethe's act is also, paradoxically, generative: not only does she deny schoolteacher another slave (her daughter), but she prevents him from taking her daughter back to "Sweet Home" to become another breeder for the system.

Even when the actions of Morrison's Afro-American characters seem hapless or self-destructive, they are paradoxically affirmative when they negate a white definition of Afro-Americans as "beasts" or merchandise. Sixo's essential human act is to imagine a future not his own, and Sethe's is to refuse the definition of her children as property. This necessary separation from the values of white culture is given a historical dimension in the episode with Amy, the young white woman who aids Sethe and then helps at the birth of Denver. Amy thinks of Sethe as only an unfortunate "nigger woman," though both are servants, orphans, and runaways; the white underclass finds its social distinction in the subordination of blacks, and the key difference between their two fates is that Mr. Buddy cannot pursue Amy to Boston the way schoolteacher is able to hound Sethe across the Ohio River.[64]

The meeting of Sethe and Amy also suggests the different cultural histories of the races by means of the lullaby, "Lady Button Eyes," that Amy sings to Sethe. Taught to Amy by her mother, the song echoes the fairies and moonbeams of Shakespearean comedy, and shows Amy, the daughter of an indentured servant, connected to a cultural tradition denied Sethe. There are multiple ironies in the song. Its subject is probably a doll (the eyes of nineteenth-century dolls were often made with buttons) that Amy's mother made to comfort her, while Sethe is haunted by her own memory of the mother she could not comfort in death. The lines "Through the muck and mist and gloom / To our quiet cozy home" mockingly foreshadow Sethe's escape: she will have twenty-eight days of a "cozy home" with Baby Suggs before schoolteacher arrives. Yet, more subtly, Morrison hints at the different cultural paths the two women are on by references to cloth. Amy's passion for Boston and for velvet is a passion for a developing mass urban culture which is already supplanting her own useful knowledge of folk medicine (spider webs) and midwifery. The likely fate of women like Amy in the late nineteenth century was to end as drudges in the company towns of New England textile mills. Behind this episode are not only the historical origins of the modern consumer culture but also the debate between Wright and Baldwin on the value of Afro-American culture as a means of resistance. Sethe, it seems, will retain a more authentic culture than Amy—she learned her lineage from Nan, and practical things from Sixo, which she never forgets; and the cloth by which she is defined is not a luxury good like velvet, but the handmade quilt.[65]

Sethe's first worlds to Paul D after not seeing him for eighteen years are "Is that you?" Her last words to him in the novel also take the form of a question: "Me? Me?" The differences between the two questions suggest how identity has changed for both of them in the course of the novel. The first question implies that Sethe is trapped in the past, the second that she has a possibility of a future. The second question also implies that Paul D has a new perception of Sethe. It takes him the entire novel to discover that she has an integrity and magnitude that he himself has lacked.

Paul D's epiphany regarding Sethe at the novel's end reverses the hint of a Hollywood scenario Morrison presents at the beginning, when she puts him in the role of the hero who will save the beautiful maiden from the haunted house. Paul D thinks that he is the man to play this part; he not only chases the ghost away but brags to Sethe that now that he is at 124, she can do anything: "Go anywhere you want. Jump, if you want to, 'cause I'll catch you. . . . 'fore you fall" (46). He has no idea that where Sethe is afraid to go—"inside," as she tells him—is a place of demons. He thinks that the "place" is distinct from the woman: "I knew it wasn't the place I was heading toward; it was you" (46). But the place *is* the woman, as Morrison makes clear when Beloved tells Denver, "This is where I am" (76). Beloved is the nightmare of Sethe's history which contaminates place, and Sethe can only be awakened from the nightmare by someone who will accept her history as her story. Only then might "place" be redeemed.

Paul D's bravado not only echoes a Hollywood scenario but also partakes of the common American illusion that one can dispense with the past and start anew. When he chases the ghost from the house, he rearranges the building's space; but he remains too naive to realize that the spatial arrangement of the house is a map of Sethe's history. His observation "I thought . . . there was some space for me" (45) is reasonable enough, but it reflects a kind of masculine innocence. He wants to enter Sethe's life without understanding it. Perhaps the most egregious manifestation of his male vanity occurs at the carnival, where he parades with his two women in tow as though he were the cock of the walk. And yet the stench of the "doomed roses" and Morrison's veiled allusion to the carnival as Vanity Fair foreshadows the end of his brief triumph.

In Bunyan's *Pilgrim's Progress*, Vanity Fair is the earthly city through which the pilgrims must pass on their way to the heavenly city. Some are seduced by the glitter of the fair, and some become martyrs there, beaten and put in cages to be held up to scorn by those who accept the false image of the true city. At the carnival in *Beloved*, Paul D confronts an atavistic double in a cage: "When Wild African Savage shook his bars and said wa wa, Paul D told everybody he knew him back in Roanoke" (48–49). The easy joke hides Paul D's past, one he keeps hidden even from himself: his cage in Alfred, Georgia. And the cage itself contains a cage: the "tobacco tin" that has replaced his "red heart."[66]

Thus his gaiety at the carnival is as false as his masculine bravado in the house. His rearrangement of the space of 124 Bluestone Road does not change the essential nature of the place. Each person in the house continues to live in an isolated cell of his or her own. With the ghost gone, Denver feels more lonely than ever; and when Beloved appears to replace the ghost, a door closes between Denver and Paul D. Beloved's appearance is caused not only by Sethe's guilt and by Denver's loneliness but also by Paul D's naive belief that the past can be put in a tin box. In terms of the romance tradition, Beloved is Paul D's *femme fatale*, the woman who reminds him that his masculinity is problematic.

If Paul is beset by insecurity, Sethe has never had any doubts about herself as a woman. Because she has a center that Baby Suggs is never allowed to have, she becomes the figure around which all the novel's transformations occur. Part of it is character (her "iron eyes"), and part is luck (she is allowed to make her own space intimate at "Sweet Home": the sprig of myrtle in the kitchen staking one claim, the rearing of her own children another). Her decision to murder her own daughter rather than have her return to a world that she "knows is worse" than death symbolizes a self that has the potential to imagine a different social order.

Paul D's manhood, however, has been given to him by Garner, and it is a gift dependent on place: "Sweet Home." The implications of this pastoral illusion are obvious: Garner plays God by treating his "niggers" like men, but the fiction of their manhood only exists on his "place" and only lasts as long as his life. When schoolteacher takes command of "Sweet Home," the definitions change, and the men become boys. On the day of the failed escape, Paul D comes face to face with his real ontological condition when, with the bit in his mouth, he sees a rooster, appropriately named Mister, laughing at him. As he later tells Sethe, "Mister was allowed to be and stay what he was. But I wasn't allowed to be and stay what I was" (72). Not having a firm "place" as a man, Paul D is later moved by Beloved "from place to place" within the house. The man who would catch Sethe if she fell needs someone to "place" him. Paul D's existential instability illuminates a larger issue in the novel. Paul D's cultural "place" is never settled because whites treat Afro-Americans arbitrarily, and the historical setting of Morrison's novel, the era from the Fugitive Slave Law to the closing of Reconstruction, illustrates this at painful length. American law operated by political expediency, and the social definition of blacks changed with the wind of every election and court decision, from the Fugitive Slave Law and the Dred Scott decision in the 1850s to the Supreme Court's negation of the various Civil Rights acts after the Civil War. The final withdrawal of federal troops from the south after the election of 1876 would leave the legal definition of blacks' social existence in the hands of the former slaveowners once again. Paul D could be called a "man" or chattel property—for census purposes before the Civil War he would be legally "three-fifths" of a man—but always the white man's definition of him is shifting, and, as he sees, he lacks even the certainty of self that a rooster possesses. Similarly, the Civil Rights enactments of the 1950s and 60s, which certified (again) the humanity of Afro-Americans, would be undercut by the racist images in the television commercials of the 1988 presidential campaign, shifting (again) the ontological status of a Paul D.

At the novel's beginning, Paul D's perception of Sethe is circumscribed by a masculine conception of heroic action. After he makes love to Sethe, the ugly "tree" of scars on her back reminds him of "Brother," the tree at "Sweet Home" around which Sixo and the other men gathered in comradery. "Now *there* was a man, and *that* was a tree," he thinks (22). The marks on Sethe's back do not compare with "Brother," nor does Sethe with Sixo, because Paul D is incapable at this point of reading the story that Sethe's "tree" tells. He sees it not as a text but just as a "mass of scars" (22). But Sethe's whole body— her "iron eyes," her breasts robbed of their milk, her back beaten into a tree—is a text that Paul D must read if he is finally to save himself.[67] At the novel's end, he sees that the tree on her back is a map of her life—that she is rooted, that she is a woman of intricate parts, that, to use Benjamin's word, there is an "aura" emanating from the events of her life. Appropriately, "he is staring at the quilt but he is thinking about her wrought-iron back" (273). The quilt and Sethe's tree both tell stories. The quilt emphasizes the communal experience (often several quilt makers work on the same piece); Sethe's tree expresses her private sufferings. Yet the weave of both tree and quilt marry the individual to the community and to something "unspoken" in the Afro-American past. Ellison's invisible man reads the artifacts in his briefcase to understand his life, but Paul D must read the living flesh of a lover in order to find himself. And the final gesture of his admiration for her takes the form of his desire to put "his story next to hers" (273).

Beloved begins with a maiden trapped in a house, trapped in a past of "eternal recurrence" that makes a present and future impossible, and the novel documents how narratives break that pattern of recurrence, changing the past to make a future possible. Paul D remembers that when Sethe saw him "collared like a beast . . . she never mentioned or looked at it," thus leaving him what remained of his dignity (273). That memory of her is something he can build on, and in reconstructing himself, he is able to begin reconstructing the house from the inside out. When he first appeared at 124 Bluestone Road, he brought his workaday masculine self into the house; and his songs, like himself, were too large for it. His revision of the past allows him to see the house from another angle. As Gaston Bachelard suggests, "In the intimate harmony of walls and furniture, it may be said that we become conscious of a house that is built by women, since men only know how to build a house from the outside, and they know little or nothing of the 'wax' civilization."[68] Like "wax," Sethe has held together and has held things together, and her example for Paul D is the basis of a new conception of what it means to be manly, a conception that transcends (even transforms) gender.

The community of two that Sethe and Paul D form has a significance for the larger community as well. Their lives have become "stories" because there is a listener for the storyteller; the events of a story told by a storyteller have meaning not because they lead to a happy ending but because they make a direct appeal to a community's collective understanding. Thus the sorrows present in a story are reshaped by the storyteller so that they take on significance as something more than mere sufferings. This is why (to paraphrase Isak Dinesen) such sorrows can be borne.[69]

Collective understanding grows most often from the communal exchange of stories, information, facts, and theories, and only rarely from a more direct process. The definition of community depends on the formal and informal structures by which people make sense of their own lives and the lives of others, the extension of a context for meaning beyond the self or the couple. The actions that will restore the house to the community in *Beloved* are reciprocal: the intervention of Stamp Paid from the outside, and the reaching out of the daughter Denver from within the house.

Stamp Paid tells Paul D of Sethe's crime, acting within the masculine ethos of one man warning another about a "bad" woman. But it is of equal significance that Stamp Paid gives as evidence against Sethe a newspaper clipping that Paul D cannot read. Reading it for him, Stamp Paid brings to bear against Sethe not his own judgment or the community's, but the external judgment of the white press of Cincinnati. It is an opinion Paul D knows better than to trust—"there was no way in hell a black face could appear in a newspaper if the story was about something anybody wanted to hear" (155)—yet the enormity of the claim shocks him into pursuing the matter with Sethe herself. She can only read part of the story, but knows "that words she didn't understand hadn't any more power than she had to explain" (161). Both Paul D and Sethe disclaim the possibility that the story could be accurate or true, yet both are affected by it. Morrison presents a kind of parable of the insidious nature of mass media, for in judging Sethe on the basis of an incident, the murder of her child, with no other context than a white newspaper, Paul D reveals how Afro-Americans may accept their own demonization. When he tells her that she has "two feet . . . not four" (165), he participates in *its* story of his and her past.[70]

Yet Stamp Paid is ultimately the catalyst whereby the community will reclaim its stories. Seeing Paul D suffer, and hearing the chaos within 124 Bluestone Road, Stamp remembers his own lack of charity to Baby Suggs after the death of her granddaughter, his lack of sympathy for her despair. He had changed his own name from "Joshua" to "Stamp Paid" after deciding *not* to kill the white man who stole his wife, Vashti; but the imperative, official voice of the verb *stamp* suggests a change different from the naming of Not Doctor Street. The sense of his own moral probity which he derives from that single act reduces his understanding to an Old Testament legalism, even in regard to Vashti, whom he has never forgiven or understood. Only Paul D's suffering reminds him of how, suffering himself, he took little notice of Vashti's pain.[71] In an expression of *caritas,* Stamp Paid visits Paul D a second time, telling him how much Sethe loved "those children" ("She was trying to outhurt the hurter") (234). This act of empathy restores him to his old name: in becoming Joshua again he blows down the walls of his and Paul D's masculine pride.

Denver is victimized by her own walled city. In her loneliness, she separates herself from others by retreating to the outdoor "emerald closet" (a ring of trees), the symbol of her "ontological insecurity" within the house.[72] The reincarnation of the demon Beloved is due as much to Denver as it is to Sethe, for not only is Denver lonely but she wants a second chance to protect a sister she has never known. Yet with Paul D gone, the three women create a grotesque parody of a family, an unholy triad of regrets, recriminations, and guilt. And Denver's isolation increases as Sethe and Beloved metamorphose into a distorted simulacrum of community: Sethe supplying the seed for Beloved's pregnancy (what new horror will emerge from the womb of the past?), Beloved preying like a vampire upon Sethe.[73] In addition to aspects of the historical and the detective genres, Morrison's novel has aspects of the Gothic.

Not only is Beloved a vampire (the past destroying the present), but in the world of this romance, she is also Denver's "demonic double."[74] The background of slavery has marked all familial relations, and Sethe will only be free of Beloved if Denver can free herself from her dependence on Sethe. This means stepping off the front porch and walking down the road to see her former teacher, Lady Jones: reestablishing that connection is Denver's first step toward emotional maturity. Denver's name means, paradoxically, "to strip bare" and "to restore."[75] Leaving the house means risking being stripped bare, but it also means that Denver begins to restore herself to herself, and Sethe to the community. She steps, at last, into the future. It is the memory of Baby Suggs which pushes her off the porch, into the yard, and out the gate. Baby Suggs—the ancestor crushed by schoolteacher's presence in her yard—now appears to Denver in the role of a protector and wise counsellor, urging her to have the courage to "go on out the yard" (244).

The double role of Baby Suggs as both helpless victim and wise ancestor points to the significance of the novel's second (and final) ending. As one critic has noted, Beloved is not only Sethe's dead daughter returned in the flesh as she might have been had she lived, but also the embodiment of all the abandoned and separated daughters of the diaspora.[76] Sethe's memory travels not only into her own past, finding what she thought she had forgotten, but into the unknown territory of the race's past, a horror so unspeakable that the race itself has repressed it in order to survive. Beloved "erupts into her separate parts" (274) at the novel's end because she symbolizes an unusable past. Here is "not a story to pass on" (274). Some things need to be forgotten because they cannot be assimilated by the tribe. Yet this conclusion is contradicted by the existence of Morrison's novel. Its relationship to the problem of remembering is, like Sethe's life, at first cautionary but finally exemplary; it moves by difficult means from an unredeemed state to the redeemed.

Morrison made her novel out of the hint of a life defined by abolitionist propagandists—in other words, a life recorded in terms of Bodwin's world. What she imaginatively reconstructs is the life lost to that world, a life to which she gives meaning that extends beyond the legal-political terms of Reconstruction, the common life that is within and yet outside of history. If the common life is what is forgotten, and history is what is remembered, then Morrison's novel, by reversing this order, overturns the culture's hierarchy of value. The components of community, the bricks of the invisible city, are not great events or large constitutional principles, but the everyday, the usual. Likewise, Morrison often levels the established literary genres of Western culture to the commonplace, as when Paul D remembers Sixo's "She *gather* me, man. The pieces I am, she *gather* them and give them back to me in all the right order." Here the pastoral image (gathering), whose official locus is Garner's garden ("Sweet Home"), becomes the intimate connection of two people who have no garden. So, too, Baby Suggs's garden is both her "yard," the threshold for Denver's entrance into the world, and also the place where the black community "gathers" for everyday gossip and cheer.

However, the everyday can be terrible. The novel ends with the hidden possibility of Beloved's return: "Sometimes the photograph of a close friend or relative—looked at too long—shifts, and something more familiar than the dear face moves there. They can touch it if they like, but don't because they know things will never be the same if they do" (275). The world of the photograph is the world of realism or normality, but the genre called romance takes for granted that the world of realism is never stable, dependent as it is upon human consciousness.[77] Romance posits a world where the photograph is itself a mirage, a moving image that threatens always to slip into a dream.

The surviving image of Margaret Garner from an abolitionist pamphlet depicts her in a melodramatic posture pointing to her dead child: in writing *Beloved*, Morrison re-imagines the story suggested by that picture. An experience that the individual or the community cannot endure in its own time, that has been misappropriated in its time, needs eventually to be restored to memory. As historians of the United States have attempted to rediscover the nature of nineteenth-century Indian wars, or the way in which the history of the post–Civil War Reconstruction was written to serve the ideology of white supremacy in the south, so Morrison's novel in a different way recovers an unwritten but essential memory of black life in America. The contradiction of Sethe's community forgetting and Morrison's novel remembering is only apparent; they are both necessary actions in their time. Paul's evidence of "things not seen" (2 Cor. 4:18) includes not only the innumerable human links of communal relationship but also the actions that compose "the terror of history."

One reason the past takes such a tangible form for Sethe is that Beloved is not only Sethe's guilt reincarnated as her daughter, but also Sethe herself, the daughter who suffers from an undefined guilt concerning her mother.[78] Haunted by the murder of her own child, Sethe also feels the loss of her shadowy relationship to a woman whom she dimly remembers as "one among many backs turned away from her, stooping in a watery field" (30). Beloved, likewise, can only see her mother's face through "the water where she is" (212). For both Sethe and Beloved, then, the memory of the mother is like a dream, an image seen through water, one that each is desperate to make flesh: Beloved, because she has never known her mother; Sethe, because she was unable to save her mother from being murdered. The ambiguous image of water in the novel, as both a dark mirror and a cleansing agent, reflects again the ambiguity of a past that can either paralyze or redeem the present.

Perhaps, too, the weight of the past implies a tragic frame for history. Events are not repeated literally, yet patterns of similarity seem to emerge. In choosing this subject, Morrison may have been struck by the uncanny resemblance between those periods one hundred years apart, 1850–80 and 1950–80; and by the similar fates in each

century of movements to legitimate black political and social existence within the United States.[79] That legitimation depends finally,
Beloved shows, on the Afro-American community, on the discovery,
or the restoration, or the creation, of the voluntary and necessary
bonds of the invisible city (the Beloved Community). Thus the conclusion of *Beloved* seems to offer an escape, however ambiguous, from
a hopeless repetition of action and memory.

Invisible Histories,
Invisible Cities

> Defeat goes deeper into the human soul than victory. To be in
> someone's power is a conscious experience which induces
> doubts about the ordering of the universe, while those who
> have power can forget it, or can assume that it is part of the
> natural order of things and invent or adopt ideas which justify
> their possession of it.
>
> —Albert Houroni, *A History of the Arab Peoples*

> But even in that thralldom, that dumb thrall, we built some
> actual things . . . we were not just full-of-shit tourists. We did
> take the city away from the lowest level, and if the next level is
> sickening, the task is of a higher order, and its solution is the
> current day's work.
>
> —Amiri Baraka, *The Autobiography of LeRoi Jones*

> She got a Elgin movement from her head down to her toes.
>
> —Robert Johnson, "Walking Blues"

This book began with W.E.B. Du Bois's *The Philadelphia Negro*,
published in the final year of the nineteenth century, and it concludes with Toni Morrison's *Beloved*, published in 1987. There is an
88-year span between the two books, a long time in the history of a
nation not yet 220 years old. In his book, Du Bois defined what, in
his view, was necessary to understand the life of Afro-Americans (or
any specific social group) in the city: "A complete study must not
confine itself to the group, but must specifically notice the environment—the physical environment of the city, sections, and houses,
the far mightier social environment—the surrounding world of custom, wish, whim and thought which envelops this group and power-
fully influences its social environment."[1] *Beloved* incorporates all of

Du Bois's demands, and its being a fiction rather than a sociological study doesn't lessen its value as a depiction of the real urban world. Neither does its being imaginatively located in a time *before* Du Bois wrote, and in a place unlike his model of the city. The city's unseen configurations, the interaction of countless unrecognized economic desires, choices, and actions, and the incorporeal net of human relationships, all exist in Morrison's novel. And as Alain Locke did in 1925, Morrison attempts to describe the necessary conditions for the Afro-American community to exist within a racist society; those conditions are local in the novel, but never only individualistic: the social point must be that nobody survives by him- or herself. Indeed, she confirms in different terms Cross Damon's realization in Wright's *Outsider* (1953): "Alone a man is nothing."[2] Given the fact that the fragmented condition of city life became more extreme after the 1920s, one could argue that since the 1930s the search for the Beloved Community has become an ever more urgent theme in Afro-American city novels. It is Morrison's *Beloved* that makes us see, of course, how the search for community has a history—is spread across time, diachronic—even if that history is buried or exists only by implication in other writers.

The novels of Wright, Ellison, and Baldwin were written in the midst of the Great Migration, which transformed black life from a primarily rural and southern experience to a northern and urban one. They are about the city life created by a huge demographic change that, as I noted earlier, seems now at last to have ended. There were 492,000 blacks in Chicago in 1950, 813,000 in 1960, and 1.1 million in 1970; by the 1986 count the number had increased to only about 1.2 million, and that increase was apparently due to natural population growth and not migration.[3] Among many other factors, the experience of racism in the north, reflected in the ghetto rebellions of the 1930s, 40s and 60s, made the social advantages of the migration moot.

The gap between the three male novelists and Morrison is a historical one, in intellectual context as well as time. Wright's, Ellison's, and Baldwin's first novels all deal with a view of black city life emerging after the collapse of the Harlem Renaissance ideal, whereas Morrison's books take their background from the Afro-American protest movement after Watts and before the Reagan administration, as well as from the social re-visions created by the black women writers of the 1970s and 80s. There is also an obvious difference in terms of literary genre. The novels of Wright, Ellison, and Baldwin have some relation to the genres of the proletarian novel, the picaresque novel, and the bildungsroman, respectively; *Beloved* is a romance. Yet the mystery of origins and the curse of the primal crime, the explicit themes of *Beloved*, exist in all four novels, and this, in a sense, makes them all romances. The true parent of the "son" in *Native Son* is the "terror of history," a past that, like Max's "corpse," will not stay dead. In *Native Son*, Chicago pretends to live in the sunlight of both tradition (classical and Christian) and modernity (its media dream of a superior civilization). The *Chicago Tribune* assures its white readers that these dreams have a history rooted in the logical development of Western civilization, but through that sunlit surface erupts the unrecorded, invisible past that lay buried, like the "corpse" in Hawthorne's Pyncheon house. The corpse in the furnace of Mr. Dalton's house, despite its realistic origin, is as much a reincarnation of the past as is the character of Beloved. In detective fiction, as David Trotter observes, "traces left by murder continue to bear witness to the violence that produced them."[4] In this sense, there is no such thing as an innocent corpse. Whether that corpse is Karintha's dead baby in *Cane* or the mysterious bale of cotton in *Cotton Comes to Harlem*, each speaks of an invisible past of agony, exploitation, and terror.

The theme of lost history appears in *Invisible Man* when Ellison's narrator asks in the prologue, "What Did I Do to Be So Black and Blue?" The invisible man is looking for a personal and collective past that remains a secret; Louis Armstrong's song points to an obvious condition, but also to an unknown and undiscovered previous condition, one that impinges on the present as a nightmare. Why is skin color a "sin"? Beginning in the prologue, Ellison, like Wright, draws our attention to the world of romance with his pun on the word *spook*: "No, I am not a spook like those who haunted Edgar Allan Poe." In the epilogue the ghost in the basement of the Republic vanishes into thin air, or, rather, it is translated into radio waves, speaking the shadowy "principle" to the city. Ellison's hero answers the question in Armstrong's song by penetrating the mystery of his grandfather's dying words—their meaning is that history is potentially redeemed by an affirmation inherent in the invisible origins of the nation itself. Ellison knows the separateness of black history, but only his novel, of the four here, says that connection between Afro-Americans and those national origins is likely, or at least possible.

In Baldwin's *Go Tell It on the Mountain*, the hidden history is the secret of John Grimes's parentage. Because he does not know that Richard is his real father, the forces of the unknown past oppress John in the present. Yet that past, like Ellison's and Morrison's, contains a redemptive seed: slave owners gave the slaves the Bible to keep them docile and subservient, but the black church at the ground level of popular culture transcends the limitations of those origins by its expression of the communal life. Ellison, Baldwin, and Morrison see the various manifestations of popular culture both as efforts to evoke a way of life lost in the move to the cities and as bits and pieces of a historical record that the community, at its on peril, has suppressed or forgotten. The crazy-quilt patchwork of the blues (Peter Wheatstraw), the fragments from the Book of Revelation (John's vision on the threshing floor), the odds and ends of a Gullah folk song (*Song of Solomon*)—these are collages that attempt to draw together the scattered parts of the diaspora into new wholes.

The attempt to recover history looks then for a cultural integrity that must be partly imagined, since it has been broken and scattered so many times. And the black middle class's conformity to the standards of "uplift" can't represent a guide to the city on a hill modeled on the New Testament, or to any possible *communal* transcendence, for the aim of those standards is individual material success.[5] The library, as a means of self-improvement, assumes a different importance for Richard Wright in *Black Boy* than it does for W.E.B. Du Bois in *The Souls of Black Folk*. For Du Bois, it is the center of an institution, the university, that promises the integration of the Afro-American within the full spirit of Western civilization. For Wright, the library, as an institution, is part of the fabric of a racist society that presents itself as "Western civilization," yet since the library harbors the answers to the mystery of identity, both personal and collective, its secrets must be stolen, as Prometheus stole fire from the gods. In *Black Boy*, Wright's relationship to the library is that of the heroic outsider, the "trickster," who is determined not to join *their* club but who will reread their texts to restore to the world a sense of context. Perhaps the clearest indication of Wright's distrust of the city's institutions occurs in *Native Son*. The South Side Boys Club—a veiled reference to the YMCAs so important to the urban dreams of the Harlem

Renaissance—is used by Bigger and his friends to plan robberies. Bigger's alienation from the city and its institutions exists at all levels, from the welfare agency's low-class service job, to Mrs. Dalton's plans for his continued education, to Max's utopian ideal of the heavenly city of a classless society.

Similarly, Ellison shows in detail the corruption and foolishness of all plans for black "uplift," from the university, to his various jobs, to the Brotherhood. What the invisible man experiences, however, is not Bigger's sudden immersion in a strange world; instead, his picaresque adventures recapitulate the history of black Americans since the Emancipation,[6] and if he is defeated, deceived, and frustrated by what happens to him, he is still ready at the novel's conclusion to begin anew. Ellison's point may be not only that Afro-Americans *have* survived all of these horrors, but also that the key to the invisible man's resilience is his having experienced and understood the history of all his people, not only the history of its elite class.

The middle class hardly exists in *Go Tell It on the Mountain*, but its absence is a significant fact in the novel. Richard is attracted to the city's institutions of high culture—and there is the allusion to Wright in his name—yet finally these institutions offer him no protection from the city's essential racism. Meanwhile, his son John is afraid to enter the Forty-Second Street branch of the New York Public Library, a fear related to Bigger's fear of the white city; but John finds security in the institution of the local storefront church. Baldwin acknowledged that he was drawn to Wright's work because "the life he described was the life I lived . . . the black middle class was essentially an abstraction to me."[7]

In Morrison's novel, the setting of the modern city, with its divisions within its Afro-American community, has apparently been abandoned for an imagined gathering of blacks living outside of Cincinnati in 1873; yet the historical metaphor that the narrative of *Beloved* represents joins that imaginary community of the past to the situation of the present. It has been suggested that there is a parallel between the 1870s—when the Thirteenth, Fourteenth, and Fifteenth Amendments, confirmed in the years immediately following the Civil War (1865–70), became legal dead letters—and the 1970s and 80s, when a conservative administration and U.S. Supreme Court began undermining the legal gains of the Civil Rights movement. The character of the abolitionist Bodwin might be matched with any number of white Civil Rights supporters of the 1960s who had fallen away by the 1980s.

Those historical references are necessary background to *Beloved*'s central concern with the nature of communal responsibility among the novel's black characters. Sethe's tragedy begins when her community deserts her, failing to warn of schoolteacher's approach. Since in the free states Afro-American resistance to the Fugitive Slave Law of 1850 was comprehensive and effective, the betrayal of Sethe is a kind of communal original sin more devastating than the infanticide.[8] Sethe's neighbors' decision to accept their obligation to her finally signifies the founding of the true city: their choice is a human reference point between the Augustinian city of biblical tradition and a contemporary urban culture that either ignores or demonizes its black citizens.

In *Beloved* the recovery of lost history is joined to the creation of a Beloved Community. In the twentieth century, arguments over the nature of the "peculiar institution" have been diverse, passionate, and informative, but they have been conducted for the most part from a perspective outside the experience of the slaves themselves. Morrison's Garner and schoolteacher are examples of a benevolent slaveholder and a cruel one, respectively, but their significance does not lie in whether they illustrate and/or debunk the historical theories of an Ulrich Phillips or a Stanley Elkins. Morrison is concerned with invisible worlds of the psyche, those worlds unrecorded in any visible documents: "unspeakable things unspoken," which only a literary artist can record. It is this attempt to document history from the inside, not the outside, that joins her with the three male writers of an earlier generation.[9] Although Ellison glories in an "unfinished" Reconstruction, seeing its open-endedness as a beacon from the city on a hill, all four writers recognize that the majority culture has failed to provide descriptive maps of the invisible cities within black life. True history, as these black writers recognize, can only be constructed by acts of the imagination. The romance is the common genre for all four novelists because it is the one literary form that directs our attention to the depths beneath the surface of American history and culture.

In the twentieth century, the visible city of American life became the urban world of mass culture, a phenomenon no modern writer has been able to ignore. American city novelists such as Dreiser and

Dos Passos were obsessed with this new culture, but even the south, to the great dismay of the Agrarian intellectuals of the 1920s, became more and more urbanized, leaving Faulkner and others to choose the elegiac themes of a disintegrating culture. Modernism, that elusive term, was European in origin perhaps, but had as a primary aspect the creation of art within a modern city and a commercial society that came to be thought of as particularly American. The advertising slogans that find their way into Eliot, Pound, Joyce, Stein, and Hart Crane were drawn from this new environment, and were unwelcome to those who, like Eliot, saw them as symptomatic of a breakdown and disorder that might eventually include the rising of the despised and excluded. Against the possibility of that ruin, the fragments of high culture were a shoring and a refuge, even as they were embedded in new cultural forms representing modernity's fearful transformational vortex at work.

High modernism as a cultural event helped confirm all Afro-Americans, not necessarily only Afro-American writers, in their continued invisibility. Migrants to the cities themselves, blacks barely participated in the high modernist literature created primarily by white urban immigrants between 1910 and 1940, and their absence is another paradigm of high and low, of a difference that modernity does not melt down. When Houston Baker, Jr., wrote *Modernism and the Harlem Renaissance*, he argued that within an Afro-American text any deviation from the norm of white writing constituted a modernist gesture. Baker wanted, usefully, to revise the reputation of neglected Afro-American writers by redefining modernism in terms of black culture; an enforced separateness becomes a literary virtue. Not all black writers recognized that virtue. As the biographer of Melvin Tolson notes, Tolson regretted that when he attended Fisk University he could not join in the discussions of the white Agrarian writers across the tracks, "arguing out their poetic and cultural credo at Vanderbilt only a short distance away. If he could have participated in these discussions, he often implied, his development as a modernist poet might well have begun years earlier."[10]

Ralph Ellison has suggested that Afro-American culture is "a part of the general American culture, the language itself," and argued against the idea of that culture as something separate, "ghettoized" from the majority. He speaks of the influence of blues and jazz on American music and the way Eliot could bring various bits of folklore into a poem that included everything: "high culture, popular culture, it's all mixed." The problem with this, of course, is that Eliot's use of such materials wasn't approving or neutral or even primarily humorous; those slogans, song refrains, and so forth ironically measure the degradation of contemporary society. As Michael North has shown, the example of black dialect language was important to Eliot and Pound; their use of black dialect, albeit an "Uncle Remus" variety, served to set them free from a European tradition they found intimidating. Eliot and Pound felt that the traces of that dialect in their American speech set them apart and even gave them access to innovative literary possibilities. They also felt, however, that a certain cultural inferiority attached to those traces, and the recognition of linguistic kinship never meant that white modernists saw Afro-Americans as equals in any sense.[11]

No one who thinks about it could doubt the essential contribution of Afro-American music to the world's culture, but that contribution hasn't been simply received or recognized. Black music has been ignored, censored, and stolen; it has become one of the most important ingredients of mass culture without essentially changing the position of Afro-Americans in the white society. What Ellison sees as the individual's heroic redefinition of cultural terms may become an impossible task when faced with a combination of received prejudice and social anomie. If, after years of travel, the city on a hill appears no closer, should we ask whether or not it's a mirage?[12]

From Josiah Royce's phrase "Beloved Community" and his call for its activist creation there is a direct intellectual line of descent that includes Randolph Bourne, Waldo Frank, Jean Toomer, Alain Locke, Richard Wright, Martin Luther King, Jr. and Toni Morrison.[13] There is another connection, less direct but still evident, to T. S. Eliot and the southern Agrarians of *I'll Take My Stand*.[14] The Beloved Community, in other words, could be a radical popular "rediscovery" of American democracy (as in Frank's *The Re-Discovery of America* [1928]) or a restoration of an elitist, hierarchical society with divisions assigned by race as well as class. Before 1940 the city seemed to promise democracy, and the country seemed to offer only a static hierarchy. For Afro-American writers from Du Bois to Richard Wright the influential social science was the study of urban sociology; for modernists such as Eliot and Pound, it was anthropology, though not the anthropology of Franz Boas (who exploded the theory of race), but rather, that of writers on "savage" culture and on the mysterious sources of religion, and race and cultural-history theorists such as Frobenius.[15] Black writers looked to urban studies to explain their city experience; Eliot and Pound looked to Western interpretations of other cultures to explain a malaise they detected in their own cities. Ironically, both groups wanted some escape from the modern city of destruction, and looked to an "organic" community as a refuge (e.g., Eliot's *Idea of a Christian Society* [1940]). Eliot, though an immigrant to Europe, thought that "on the whole it would appear to be for the best that the great majority of people should go on living in the place in which they were born."[16] In their native "place," Africans were acceptable, especially if they were part of the British Empire's Christian and hierarchical Beloved Community, but when they migrated to the city, as Eliot himself migrated from Saint Louis to London, then they became black savages. As Pound punned in a letter to Eliot in 1940, "neither of us likes sabages, black habits, etc."[17]

Ezra Pound's extremity in all things made him more outspoken than other high modernists on the tangent matter of blacks and a crumbling civilization. At times he wished to let "deh chinas and blackmen" into his conception of culture, and thus he admired Frobenius's description of Wagadu, the mythical "invisible" city of African folklore: "For, really, Wagadu is not of stone, not of wood, not of earth. Wagadu is the strength which lives in the hearts of men and is sometimes visible because eyes see her and ears hear the clash of swords and ring of shields, and is sometimes invisible because the indomitability of men overtired her, so that she sleeps."[18] As Hugh Kenner and Guy Davenport have noted, Pound was to use Wagadu in the Pisan Cantos as one of his "visions of lost order."[19] This was an answer, in part, to Eliot's "Unreal City" in *The Waste Land*, the earthly city of London after the Great War, whose bridges were "falling down." It was Pound's reminder, perhaps, that although modern civilization lay in ruins, man's capacity for renewal was eternal, and that the sources of that renewal could lie anywhere, even in a neglected African tale.

But as Pound's life so bizarrely illustrates, prejudice was not something easily given up. Although most of the kind treatment he received at the prison camp where he was held and where he wrote the Pisan Cantos came from Afro-American fellow prisoners, a few years later, while incarcerated at Saint Elizabeths, he was writing for and

working with a network of white supremacists who advocated violence against blacks in the south.[20] Given the sort of cultural schizophrenia shown by writers such as Pound and Eliot, it is not surprising
that most black writers' view of the invisible city since the Harlem Renaissance has been drawn not from Ellison but from James Baldwin's
essay on Chartres. Baldwin would not limit his definition of Western
civilization to that high icon, however; in *The Devil Finds Work* he
discusses in detail his own relationship as an Afro-American to the
movies, mass culture's most prominent icons, and explains very exactly how he is both "inside" and "outside" of mass culture. He is inside because, yes, he does begin understanding his life in reference to
Hollywood's stories: "My first conscious calculation as to how to go
about defeating the world's intentions for me and mine began on
that Saturday afternoon in what we called *the movies*."[21] He is outside
by the fact of his "calculation," and his judgment of what the movies
present as "truth" against his own experience (e.g., his reading of
Dead End, an American *film noir*).[22] In his own life, clearly movies
came first and Chartres much later, and then mainly for its symbolic
value. There is also in Baldwin's anecdotes an example of a reading of
mass society's media which *consciously* remakes those media, using
them to define *his* position in that society.

When Baldwin finally comes to Chartres, it merely confirms what
Fritz Lang's *You Only Live Once* had already taught him; if Chartres
symbolized civilization to Henry Adams, it only reminds Baldwin
that he is excluded from the values of that civilization. Morrison
finds Baldwin's response significant for the black writer in general; denied the symbolic meaning of the objects in the city which white
writers seize upon, the black writer has learned to perceive what it is
in the city that gives meaning to urban black life. What Morrison discovers is that the city has value only if the idea of the village is carried into the city. This was a possibility that Zora Neale Hurston had
explored in her novel *Their Eyes Were Watching God* (1937), a work
that Wright and Ellison accused of being politically unconscious. Yet
Hurston understood something about how black people could survive
in the modern city—something that she passed on to both Wright
and Ellison. Wright would call for a black literature that could trade
upon the strength of the folk, their capacity to transmute the alien
and threatening into "blues, spirituals, and folktales recounted from
mouth to mouth";[23] this, Hurston was to show, is the basis of the

strength of the black community, something that could resist or absorb the most extreme urban shockwaves.

A pertinent example is the story of the Eatonville streetlights in *Their Eyes Were Watching God*. Jodie Stark is from Atlanta, and as mayor of Eatonville he has high ambitions for his small country town—he intends to make it "de metropolis uh de state."[24] He sends off to Sears, Roebuck and Company for street lamps, and when they arrive, he ceremoniously installs them, using the occasion to give a speech that combines the metaphorical with the literal, the sacred with the profane, the wisdom of the folk with the modernity of the metropolis:

> Folkses, de sun is goin' down. De Sun-maker brings it up in de morning,' and de Sun-maker sends it tuh bed at night. Us poor weak humans can't do nothin' to hurry it up nor to slow it down. All we can do, if we want any light after de settin' or befo de risin', is tuh make some light ourselves. So dat's how come lamps are made. Dis evenin' we'se all assembled heah tuh light uh lamp. Dis occasion is something for us all tuh remember to our dyin' day. De first street lamp in uh colored town. (72–73)

As the gas lamps are lit, the members of the community break into song, singing a spiritual that metamorphoses the unfamiliar into the familiar:

> We'll walk in de light, de beautiful light
> Come where the dew drops of mercy shine bright
> Shine all around us by day and by night
> Jesus, the light of the world. (73)

Jodie provides the impetus, and the townspeople do the rest: technology from the outside world is absorbed into the mythology of the small town. As metaphor, the lamps are not only rendered harmless but contribute to the iconographic imagery that governs and gives meaning to the townspeople's lives. Hurston sees that the strength of the black community lies in its ability not only to keep chaos at bay but also to use chaos for its own ends. The community's *potential*— but not certain—response is to resist anomie and to refute prejudice.

The social question that remains, or in Royce's terms, "begins," is how to create or make secure the Beloved Community. Hurston's solution is an adaptive one, expressed in an already existing and

coherent village; but how is the "village" to "begin" in the chaos of urban ghetto life? As Baldwin saw, the more horrific the real urban conditions become, the more private and personal the invisible city has to
become. In a sense, after 1940 Ma Smith's boardinghouse in Pauline
Hopkins's *Contending Forces* (1900) replaces Du Bois's university as an
image of sacred, centering space in black life. The invisible city that
exists on the porch of Jodie's store now becomes a tavern (in James
Baldwin's "Sonny's Blues"), or a kitchen (in Paule Marshall's *Brown
Girl, Brownstones* [1959] and Toni Cade Bambara's *Gorilla, My Love*
[1972]), a streetcorner (in Langston Hughes's Simple stores), and even
a dance.[25] An abandoned house in a cemetery becomes "a small Manhattan" in June Jordan's *His Own Where* (1971), a title that in itself indicates the need for space to be made place. In contemporary black
American literature, the invisible city can be anywhere people gather
together—held together "in His name" (the black church) or by the
ancestor, or by something akin to Jules Romain's *unanimisme*, an electrical current that links self and other (e.g., Etta and Mattie in *The
Women of Brewster Place* [1982]). The omnipresence of these invisible
cities is what links together such diverse novels as Samuel Delany's sci-
ence-fiction fantasy *The Fall of the Towers* (1968), Chester Himes's detective thriller *The Real Cool Killers* (1959), Ishmael Reed's surrealistic
satire *Mumbo Jumbo* (1972), George Cain's Dantesque *Blueschild, Baby*
(1970), David Bradley's meditation on history *The Chaneysville Incident*
(1981), and John Edgar Wideman's narrative of memory, *Sent for You
Yesterday* (1983). No matter where the invisible city exists in modern
black literature, it must be entered by the "intimate gate" that Pheoby
passes through on her way to Janie's back porch. And the gate can
only be seen by those who know the city by its invisible signs, as in
Sent for You Yesterday, when Albert Wilkes knows he is back in "Homewood again" as he passes "through the deep shadow under the railroad bridge." Pittsburgh only exists in the novel as a beer ("Iron
City"), but Albert has a "cognitive map" of the only city that matters:
"This was the exact place, this daylight after the dark tunnel, this door
you pushed through to get into Homewood, this line you stepped
over."[26] Whenever the invisible city cannot be created, as in William
Attaway's *Blood on the Forge* (1941), Ann Petry's *The Street* (1946), or
Gayl Jones's *Corregidora* (1975), forces beyond human control have
prevented a "where" from being made "his [or her] own" space.

The house as focal point of community has become even more important in the literature written by Afro-American women in the 1970s and 80s. Sethe's steadfast refusal to leave her house when Paul D suggests that she move ("as though a house was a little thing—a shirtwaist or a sewing basket you could walk off from or give away any old time")[27] illustrates a determination to domesticate space that is somehow one's own. In the *Bluest Eye*, Morrison makes a distinction between "outside" and "inside": "Outdoors, we knew, was the real terror of life. . . .There is a difference between being put *out* and being put out*doors*. If you are put out, you go somewhere else; if you are outdoors, there is no place to go. The distinction was subtle but final. Outdoors was the end of something, an irrevocable, physical fact, defining and complementing our metaphysical condition."[28] She puns on the expression "put *out*." If you are white and happen to be angry ("put out"), you go elsewhere because the world beyond the house's threshold is still hospitable; if you are black and are "put out*doors*," you are faced with the street, which is *still* the destructive street of Richard Wright, James Baldwin, and Ann Petry. When in the twentieth century the city increasingly assumes for blacks the contours of a wilderness (or of a closed "system," as in LeRoi Jones's *System of Dante's Hell* [1965]), then the house becomes not only a refuge from the void and chaos outside but the only potential locus for the invisible city. In other words, Heidegger's *bauen* and *ich bin* come to refer not to the visible civilization but to a more intimate relationship between dwelling and existence. There is a direct connection between Bigger's failure to *see* Max's buildings *out there* in the city and Morrison's refocusing of a true civilization from the inside out.[29]

Recent black feminist criticism has put another emphasis on the "inside-outside" dichotomy. It has been argued that for black women writers the "personal is political"; for when inside space ("intimate space") becomes the black woman's province, it does not necessarily circumscribe her world.[30] A room of one's own often expands into an everywhere, assuming the same political significance, let us say, as Locke's phallocentric "temple of art" in the public arena.[31] The contrast between male and female perceptions of urban space lies in Paule Marshall's memory of her mother's kitchen as the center of a community of women, a place where conversation became a "magic rite," exorcising the "day's humiliations" and restoring people "to themselves." Thus she remembers the kitchen table "set like an altar in the middle of the room."[32]

Still, there needn't be an insistence on too rigid a distinction between male and female definitions of space, one that fails to allow for
commonality and exception.[33] House versus streets, neighborhood
versus city—these seem to be spatial issues that sometimes reflect,
sometimes transcend, gender differences. Ideally, as the writings of
Baldwin and Morrison indicate, sexual antagonisms and spatial definitions based on gender might be subsumed within the matrix of the
invisible city, a matrix including intimate space described by authors
of both sexes. Black male writers may depict enclosed space as fright-
eningly claustrophobic. Bigger finds himself trapped in Mary's room;
Jim Trueblood is caught in his dream of the bedroom of Mr. Broad-
nax's wife; and Gabriel Grimes finds his fate with Esther in a kitchen:
all three characters victimized by an enclosed space that is sexually
threatening. Nonetheless, this does not negate a male need for authentic intimate space. For male writers, too, the private and the political often become one, as shown by Wright's room in the Memphis
boardinghouse where he discovers "writers" who redirect his life, Ellison's invisible man in his underground room gathering himself to
reemerge into the world, and Baldwin's community of women beckoning John to testify that he now has found a home. So, too, Bessie
Smith sings not only to black women but also to Baldwin as well as to
LeRoi Jones' Clay (in *Dutchman*) when the latter realizes, a moment
before his death, that her lyrics are codes to an invisible city beneath
New Amsterdam.[34] Robert Hayden's poem "Those Winter Sundays,"
describes the mixture of fear and security a child feels regarding a
house and a father's love. The father rises to build a fire, and the child
wakes to

> hear the cold splintering, breaking.
> When the rooms were warm, he'd call,
> and slowly I would rise and dress,
> fearing the chronic angers of that house,
>
> Speaking indifferently to him,
> who had driven out the cold
> and polished my good shoes as well.
> What did I know, what did I know
> of love's austere and lonely offices?[35]

The "chronic angers" allude to the world outside, but the word *offices* reminds the speaker who reflects upon the past that private obligations are the real indicators of civilization.

"Offices" become private because they cannot be expressed by any public social ritual in a civilization that re-values all things as commodities and that trades on the public image of Afro-Americans as subhuman.[36] In one sense, the retreat to the house in recent black literature parallels the sense of public retreat in black history since the 1960s. The realization that the gains of the long Civil Rights struggle have been limited, if real, the failure to achieve genuine social, economic, or even legal equality, and the prospect of the indefinite tenure of a hostile government that endorses thinly veiled racist policies: all of these historical conditions no doubt encouraged Afro-American writers, especially women writers, to try to re-conceive, or re-imagine, their social perspective.

Their turn to the local and small-scale, however, isn't necessarily seen by these writers as a social panacea. Morrison's *Tar Baby* is a good example of how the heterotopias of modern black life are often in conflict.[37] The effect of mass culture in the city is to destroy the pluralisms of "provincial" life, as Wright saw in *Lawd Today!*, yet although Morrison shies away from the finality of Wright's point of view, she, too, recognizes the insidious impact of mass culture on the urban black community. But more than that, she also recognizes the narrowness of provincial life, even when it withstands or absorbs mass culture. Jadine can only find refuge in the briar patches of large urban centers (Paris and New York), where she can try to resist the mass culture on her own terms. The idealized small town, Eloe, has all the virtues of Hurston's Eatonville, yet its closed, inward-looking world is the "tar baby" of the novel (or one of several tar babies), and Morrison's obvious sympathy for Jadine's flight from this constricting local habitation qualifies any approval of the ideal village.

That conflict between individual and community, however, now seems increasingly submerged within the larger conflict between an expansive mass society and any local community at all. This was a point in Wright's early criticism of Hurston's *Their Eyes Were Watching God*: the nature of human community is being changed so rapidly in the twentieth century that "local habitations" are never safe from intrusion, and under this attack the defenses of the past are simply inadequate.[38] As David Harvey has observed, those in the postmodern world "who are relatively empowered to organize in place" are often "disempowered when it comes to organizing over space."[39] Eaton-ville's method of adapting to street lighting won't necessarily work to prevent an interstate highway from being routed through the village. Spike Lee's recent film *Do the Right Thing* dramatizes this dilemma in a way familiar from the fictions of Wright and Baldwin. Mookie's obsession with money, Buggin-out's outrage over his scuffed topsiders, Radio Raheem's dependence on his Gargantuan radio (its size a symbol of his ontological insecurity)—these items from the world of mass advertising and commercial culture represent modern space invading and usurping communal place. In *Do the Right Thing*, Spike Lee depicts Brooklyn's Bedford-Stuyvesant neighborhood as an embattled "village" within *and* against the city, in the very midst of a civil war that pits inside space against outside. And Sal's Pizzeria, an island inside Bed-Sty, shows also the invisible history and shifting boundaries that have left it the Afro-American community's functional center though it can never be its spiritual center. This contradiction accounts for Buggin-out's anger (the photographs on Sal's walls record only Italian history) as well as Mookie's contradictory behavior (both wanting to emulate Sal and wanting to tear down his business). Indeed, Lee's camera continually moves from inside Sal's pizzeria to outside, and vice versa, often shooting the street scenes through the windows, as though the two worlds are separate yet linked.[40]

The urban ghetto is always subject to subtle as well as unsubtle kinds of exploitation. It continues to give rise to cultural forms (witness the phenomenon of "Hip-Hop" in the 1980s), which are quickly taken over by the majority society outside; in fact, the rate of this appropriation seems to have accelerated in the past decades. How then does any subgroup escape becoming lost in "the catacombs of visible culture"?[41] Each of the authors I have discussed tries to answer this question, although Ralph Ellison implies that the confusion may be more apparent than real. Ellison would say that there is an essential "wholeness" to American culture, that the separate parts are not lost but merely recombined in an ongoing process. To the extent that this is true, it can't be much consolation for Afro-Americans consigned to the underclass and tacitly, even if now more cautiously, always made aware of their exclusion from a society they can't escape.

The similarity of black urban experiences from Dunbar to Morrison should be a historical anomaly. Cities have been the sites in which, for the most part, modern culture has been created, cauldrons in which the "melting down" of ethnic difference and the dissolving of traditional social ties have taken place. As countless writers have observed, all groups of rural immigrants drawn to the city have undergone the same kinds of trials, suffered the same kinds of losses, been forced to adjust their modes of life in much the same way. A major political argument in favor of industrialization, urbanization, and capitalism (collectively referred to as the processes of "modernity") has been that they produce more social equality; the economic aim of the ideal worker and consumer serves to erode group differences, religions, and ethnic, linguistic, and even gender or racial distinctions. If the solvent effect of the consumer society produces negatively what Pier Paolo Pasolini called "anthropological genocide," the destruction of cultural differences, it may produce positively a tolerance and social harmony impossible while those differences exist.

There are two problems with this potential positive effect. First, the erosion of old differences doesn't ensure that new ones based on fresh distinctions won't grow up; and second, the solvent has not in fact dissolved many differences. It is the second condition, of course, that has made the Afro-American experience of urban life unique: blacks have never been assimilated into the general life of cities in the United States. They have been forcibly separated from the rest of the population geographically, economically, and politically, and so have remained apart socially and culturally as well. While others have moved into ghettos and then out of them, Afro-Americans have remained largely segregated in the cities, southern or northern. This has been made possible, of course, by the simple biological fact of their different skin color and physiognomy. And if Africans' physical and cultural otherness made their enslavement seem more easily justifiable in the seventeenth and eighteenth centuries, the racist ideology that grew up to defend the property relations of the southern cotton kingdom in the nineteenth century has been the primary heritage of American race relations.

Black life in the twentieth-century city has been framed by that heritage. This history is commonplace, even if ignored or neglected by most of white culture, but it has been central for black writers, and it is the source of the underlying question for the Afro-American intelligentsia: "What is to be our relationship to the majority culture?" Frederick Douglass's amalgamation and Booker T. Washington's "self-improvement" and vocational training were forms of accommodation to that culture. With W.E.B. Du Bois, however, the matter of black separateness becomes important; it is a line of thought which runs through twentieth-century Afro-American writing and finally becomes central in the Black Power and Black Arts movements of the 1960s and 70s.[42] That separateness is recognized in each of the writers I have considered, in their treatment of history—a past that has been buried or lost, not once but twice, first in the Middle Passage and then in the Great Migration.[43]

In Raissa, "city of sadness," as Italo Calvino says in his poetic novel *Invisible Cities*, "there runs an invisible thread that binds one living being to another for a moment, then unravels, then is stretched again between moving points as it draws new and rapid patterns so that at every second the unhappy city contains a happy city unaware of its own existence."[44] The ending of Morrison's *Beloved* is an example of the invisible happiness that Calvino describes, and yet as a document that in a way defines the state of racial relationships in the United States at the end of the twentieth century, *Beloved* is hardly optimistic. In 1903, Du Bois had predicted that "the problem of the Twentieth Century" would be "the problem of the color-line." Morrison's *Beloved* indicates that almost 90 years later the line has been drawn even tighter. The city on a hill (Atlanta University) that Du Bois set as a model for his Talented Tenth and as a warning for the nation as well, has by 1987 become a small black community of the downtrodden living on the edge of the national "pig-port" of Cincinnati. The aristocratic and industrious Philadelphia Negro that Du Bois saw as the race's best hope has by 1981 become Morrison's Sidney in *Tar Baby*, who prides himself on being "a Phil-a-delphia Negro mentioned in the book of the very same name" but who by the novel's end is as morally ambiguous as the trickster rabbit of black folklore.[45] In the twentieth century, black people, like Sethe, have had a difficult time escaping the "endless pluralization of the episode,"[46] the repetition of oppression and injustice; yet strangely enough the "threads" of *caritas* that weave Paul D, Sethe, Stamp Paid, Ella, Denver, and Lady Jones into a "happy city" are perhaps the same that Du Bois thought in *The Souls of Black Folk* might connect high and low, rich and poor, black and white. That Morrison sees their existence only within the context of the fallen would not have surprised an Augustine or a Nathaniel Hawthorne or even a John Winthrop. Nor would it have surprised the older Du Bois.

Robert Johnson's "sweet home" was Chicago, a promised land that, like Moses, he probably never reached.[47] Toni Morrison's "Sweet Home" is a southern plantation, the site of an enslavement that her characters in *Beloved* escape, but then must spend the remainder of their lives trying to overcome, for it taints even the "home" that they claim for their own. Sethe's remark to Paul D conveys a bitter critique of American sentimentality (home, sweet home): "I don't have to tell you about Sweet Home—what it was—but maybe you don't know what it was like for me to get away from there" (161).[48] "Sweet Home" has circumscribed the two former slaves with a "name" they must negate if they are to begin anew.

While for Robert Johnson "sweet home" was a promise of the great, good place in a world elsewhere, the name has become horrifically ironic in Toni Morrison's novel, and this change casts light on Afro-Americans' experiences in the American city in the twentieth century. In the ambiguity of reference to "sweet home" is the tension between a *where* and a *no-where* which the word *utopia* conveys, for a utopia always has the potential to break down into its opposite, dystopia. The novels I have been looking at recognize the need for the invisible bonds of community to resist that breakdown and create a *where*, a home that overcomes placelessness. And they recognize that such creation is always, in Amiri Baraka's phrase, "the current day's work."

Notes

Introduction. Utopia and Dystopia

1. See Alan Greenberg, *Love in Vain: The Life and Legend of Robert Johnson* (Garden City, N.Y.: Doubleday, 1983), 226n.

2. Also see Houston A. Baker, Jr., *Modernism and the Harlem Renaissance* (Chicago: University of Chicago Press, 1987), 71–98.

3. See Amritjit Singh, *The Novels of the Harlem Renaissance* (University Park: Pennsylvania State University Press, 1976), 12, 13; Ernest Alleen, Jr., "The New Negro: Explorations in Identity and Social Consciousness, 1910–1922," in *1915, the Cultural Moment: The New Politics, the New Woman, the New Psychology, the New Art, and the New Theatre in America*, ed. Adele Heller and Lois Rudnick (New Brunswick, N.J.: Rutgers University Press, 1991), 48–68.

4. A series of limericks, "King Bolo and His Big Black Queen," exists in manuscript letters, primarily to Conrad Aiken and Bonamy Dobree, but has never been published. A few examples appear, however, in *The Letters of T. S. Eliot*, ed. Valerie Eliot (London: Faber & Faber, 1988), 42–43, 125–26. See also Conrad Aiken, "King Bolo and Others," in *T. S. Eliot: A Symposium*, ed. Richard March and Tambimuttu (London: Editions Poetry, 1948), 20–33; and Robert Crawford, *The Savage and the City in the Work of T. S. Eliot* (Oxford: Clarendon, 1987), 83–85, 193, 207.

5. Kenneth Burke, *Attitudes toward History* (1937; reprint, Berkeley: University of California Press, 1984), 290.

6. Toni Morrison, "Unspeakable Things Unspoken: The Afro-American Presence in American Literature," *Michigan Quarterly Review* 28 (Winter 1989): 11.

7. See David Harvey, *The Condition of Postmodernity: An Enquiry into the Origins of Cultural Change* (London: Blackwell, 1989), 122; Berndt Ostendorf, "Anthropology, Modernism, and Jazz," in *Ralph Ellison*, ed. Harold Bloom (New York: Chelsea House, 1986), 158. For the various ways in which the "hidden hand" has inscribed the surface of the city, see Mario Gandelsonas, *The Urban Text*, with essays by Joan Copjec, Catherine Ingraham, and John Whiteman (Cambridge: MIT Press, 1991).

8. Quoted from Kenneth L. Smith and Ira G. Zepp, Jr., "Martin Luther King's Vision of the Beloved Community," *Christian Century* 91 (April 3,

1974); 361. Both W.E.B. Du Bois and Alain Locke studied under Royce at Harvard; King read him in L. Harold DeWolf's course at Boston University School of Theology, and the phrase "Beloved Community" became a commonplace in King's sermons and speeches. See John J. Ansbro, *Martin Luther King, Jr.: The Making of a Mind* (Maryknoll, N.Y.: Orbis, 1982), see 187–97, 319n. Also see Josiah Royce, *The Problem of Christianity* (New York: Macmillan, 1913), 1:xxv, 172. Following the Apostle Paul, Royce stressed that the "Beloved Community" had not yet appeared—it remained for "the faithful" to "create" it (54): "It has not been my privilege to tell you where the true Church is to-day to be found. As a fact, I believe it still to be an invisible Church" (115). For the impact of Royce's idea on an important group of white intellectuals, see Casey Nelson Blake, *The Beloved Community: The Cultural Criticism of Randolph Bourne, Van Wyck Brooks, Waldo Frank, and Lewis Mumford* (Chapel Hill: University of North Carolina Press, 1990).

9. Alain Locke, "The New Negro," in *The New Negro*, ed. Alain Locke (1925; reprint, New York: Atheneum, 1969), 7. Locke found Randolph Bourne's secularization of the Beloved Community more attractive than Royce's Christian emphasis. And while critics of Locke have talked of Van Wyck Brooks and Randolph Bourne as if there were no differences between the two, or have emphasized Brooks's influence on Locke, Locke preferred Bourne to Brooks because of Bourne's sociological focus on the American city. More specifically, Locke found Bourne attractive because of the latter's analysis of immigrant urban culture and his view of the city as the new home of the Beloved Community. See especially Randolph Bourne, "Trans-National America," in *The History of a Literary Radical and Other Papers*, ed. Van Wyck Brooks (New York: Russell, 1956), 260–84. Bourne's essay was first published in 1916 in the *Atlantic Monthly*, and Locke borrowed freely from it. His borrowings ranged from specific phrases to the notion that the Beloved Community was a "higher ideal than the 'melting pot'" (261, 284). America was to fulfill herself through diversity, not uniformity; yet this "federated ideal" was to have a center in ethnic rootedness, a point Bourne also stressed in "The Jew and Trans-National America," *Menorah Journal* 2 (December 1916): 277–84. America's true destiny lay in the future, in "a spiritual welding" (284) that would be both "cosmopolitan" and provincial, centrifugal and centripetal. See Nathan Huggins's *Harlem Renaissance* (New York: Oxford University Press, 1971), chap. 2; S. P. Fullinwider, *The Mind and Mood of Black America* (Homewood, Ill.: Dorsey, 1969), 116–22. For an excellent discussion of Brooks and Bourne, see Blake, *Beloved Community*, 76–121. Also, see Charles Scruggs, *The Sage in Harlem: H. L. Mencken and the Black Writers of the 1920s* (Baltimore: Johns Hopkins University Press, 1984), 89–93. One should not overlook the influence on Locke's *New Negro* on Lewis Mumford, especially his *Story of Utopias* (1922), which like Bourne's essays attempted to place the Beloved Community within an urban context. In *Story of Utopias*, Mumford applied Brooks's idea of a "usable past" to a tradition of utopian thought in order to find the seeds of a possible American city/civilization that would inspire the present and provide direction for the future.

10. James De Jongh's *Vicious Modernism: Black Harlem and the Literary Imagination* (Cambridge: Cambridge University Press, 1990), a study of the images of Harlem in black writers from Alain Locke to the present, finds a mixture of dystopian and utopian images and notes a similar continuity of the ideal displaced from the public to the private arena: "Where Alain Locke had proclaimed the birth of a New Negro psychology in the promising emergence of black Harlem, the poets of the Black Arts movement were seeking an inner city of the spirit in the ashes of a riot" (208).

11. Sidney H. Bremer claims that the Harlem Renaissance writers "challenged" the commonplace American notion of "rural nostalgia"; see her "Home in Harlem, New York: Lessons from the Harlem Renaissance Writers," *PMLA* 105 (January 1990), 50. For an earlier view, claiming a strong pastoral element in the renaissance, see Robert Bone, *Down Home: A History of Afro-American Short Fiction from Its Beginnings to the End of the Harlem Renaissance* (New York: Putnam's, 1975).

12. See also Rom. 2:20. James Baldwin's last book is *The Evidence of Things Not Seen* (1985). Also see Houston A. Baker, Jr., "There Is No More Beautiful Way: Theory and Poetics of Afro-American Women's Writing," in *Afro-American Literary Study in the 1990s*, ed. Houston A. Baker, Jr., and Patricia Redmon (Chicago: University of Chicago Press, 1990), 136: "Our intellectual history privileges the unseen."

13. Robert Bone, *The Negro Novel in America*, rev. ed. (New Haven: Yale University Press, 1965), 107. Also see Hugh M. Gloster, *Negro Voices in American Fiction* (Chapel Hill: University of North Carolina Press, 1948), 193–95; and Sterling Brown, *The Negro in American Fiction* (1937; reprint, New York: Atheneum, 1969), 149: "Focusing upon carefree abandon, the Harlem school, like the plantation tradition, neglected the servitude. Except for brief glimpses, the drama of workaday life, the struggles, the conflicts are missing. And such definite features of Harlem as the lines of the unemployed, the overcrowded schools, the delinquent children headed straight to petty crime, the surly resentment—all these seeds that bore such bitter fruit in the Harlem riot [1935]—are conspicuously absent." The critical tradition that points to a lack of seriousness in the novels of the Harlem Renaissance continues into the present. See C.E.B. Bigsby, *The Second Black Renaissance: Essays in Black Literature* (Westport, Conn.: Greenwood, 1980), 16; James O. Young, *Black Writers of the Thirties* (Baton Rouge: Louisiana State University Press, 1973), 203.

14. See Young, *Black Writers of the Thirties*, chaps. 5, 6.

15. Two critics, however, have extended the Harlem Renaissance to 1940. See Michael W. Peplow and Arthur P. Davis, *The New Negro Renaissance: An Anthology* (New York: Holt, Rinehart, & Winston, 1975), xix–xxxi.

16. Roger Rosenblatt, *Black Fiction* (Cambridge: Harvard University Press, 1974), 21; Addison Gayle, Jr., *The Black Situation* (New York: Horizon, 1970), 202; David Levering Lewis, *When Harlem Was in Vogue* (1981; reprint, New York: Random House, 1982), 306.

17. Donald Gibson, "The City and the Black Writer: Mythology and Symbology," *Criterion* 8 (Spring–Summer 1969): 22, 25. Also see idem, "Individual-

ism and Community in Black History and Fiction," *Black American Literature Forum* 11 (Winter 1977): 126; J. Lee Greene, "Black Literature and the American Literary Mainstream," in *Minority Language and Literature: Retrospective and Perspectives*, ed. Dexter Fisher (New York: Modern Language Association of America, 1977), 26.

18. Thomas Byrne Edsall and Mary D. Edsall, *Chain Reaction: The Impact of Race, Rights, and Taxes on American Politics* (New York: Norton, 1991); see especially chap. 11 for differences in Afro-American income groups. Although the Edsalls' book is an excellent history of electoral politics, it has nothing to say about COINTELPRO, Fred Hampton, or George Jackson. Its assumption that voting patterns represent the central history of the United States between 1960 and 1990 seems inadequate set beside the history Manning Marable narrates in *Race, Reform, and Rebellion: The Second Reconstruction in Black America, 1945–1982* (Jackson: University of Mississippi Press, 1984).

More specific studies of Afro-American upward mobility are Bart Landry, *The New Black Middle Class* (Berkeley: University of California Press, 1987); and Landry's supplemental essay "The Enduring Dilemma of Race in American," in *America at Century's End*, ed. Alan Wolfe (Berkeley: University of California Press, 1991), 185–207. An historical survey of Afro-American living conditions is Reynolds Farley and Walter Allen, *The Color Line and the Quality of Life in America* (Washington, D.C.,: Russell Sage Foundation, 1987). For essays on the economic and legal situation by the end of the 1980s, see George W. Shepherd, Jr., and David Penna, eds., *Racism and the Underclass: State Policy and Discrimination against Minorities* (New York: Greenwood, 1991). Also see Adolph Reed, Jr., and Julian Bond, eds., "The Assault on Equality," (special issue), *Nation*, 253, no. 20 (December 9, 1991). Good sources of detailed statistical information are the National Urban League's annual reports; also a number of articles that appeared in the *New York Times*, March 16, 1989, Sec. B, p. 15; July 17, 1989, Sec. A, p. 11; September 27, 1989, Sec. A., p. 20, October 9, 1989, Sec. A, p. 8; and March 23, 1990, Sec. A, p. 17, all of which deal with the high infant mortality rate ("double that of whites"), poor health services, and short life expectancy. These references are only a few of many that could be cited; however, they should be sufficient to make the point that the crisis is no fiction.

19. A good introduction to this debate is David Lionel Smith, "The Black Arts Movement and Its Critics," *American Literary History* 3 (Spring 1991): 93–110. For a defense of professionalization, see Henry Louis Gates, Jr., *Figures in Black: Words, Signs, and the "Racial" Self* (New York: Oxford University Press, 1987), introduction and chap. 1. In discussing a 1977 Afro-American literature "conference of twenty-eight college professors grouped together at Yale," Gates says, "The conference itself, in short, represented an attempt to take the 'mau-mauing' out of black literary criticism that defined the 'Black Aesthetic Movement' of the sixties and transform it into a valid field of intellectual inquiry once again" (44). The problem with using a term like *mau-mauing*, of course, is that it is taken from a white neoconservative writer who employed it to discredit the black activism of the 1960s, the same activism that Gates

has earlier averred is "at least indirectly" responsible for his own academic position (xxvii). For an interesting juxtaposition of a left and a right political view of an important Black Arts writer, Larry Neal, see Amiri Baraka, Forward to *Visions of a Liberated Future: Black Arts Movement Writings,* by Larry Neal, ed. Michael Schwartz (New York: Thunder's Mouth, 1989); and Stanley Crouch, Introduction to Neal, *Visions of a Liberated Future.*

20. Alexander Cockburn, "Beat the Devil," *Nation* 252 (May 27, 1991), 691; also see Robert Hemenway, "In the American Canon," in *Redefining American Literary History,* ed. A. LaVonne Brown Ruoff and Jerry W. Ward, Jr. (New York: Modern Language Association, 1990), 62–72.

21. See Gerald Graff, *Literature against Itself: Literary Ideas in Modern Society* (Chicago: University of Chicago Press, 1979); and Frank Lentricchia, *Criticism and Social Change* (Chicago: University of Chicago Press, 1983).

22. Peter Dews, *Logics of Disintegration: Post-Structuralist Thought and the Claims of Critical Theory* (London: Verso, 1987), xv. Dew's book places the poststructuralists in the lineage of European thought after Hume, pointing out not only how they replicate positions of the followers of Kant but also how their adoption of Saussure's paradigms and terminology requires a significant simplification of both the questions and the qualified answers of their predecessors. See also Sibel Irzik, *Deconstruction and the Politics of Criticism* (New York: Garland, 1990). A wide-ranging and acute critique of the role of intellectuals in the "poststructuralist society" is O. K. Werckmeister, *Citadel Culture* (Chicago: University of Chicago Press, 1991).

23. Cornel West, "Minority Discourse and the Pitfalls of Canon Formation," *Yale Journal of Criticism* 1 (Fall 1987); 197–98. Walter Benjamin made a similar point in a more general context, "Before I ask: what is a work's position *vis-a-vis* the productive relations of its time, I should like to ask: what is its position *within* them" (my italics; I have not been able to locate the source where this quotation appears).

24. This historical crossroads became a matter of angry public debate in an exchange between the Afro-American scholar Joyce Ann Joyce and two prominent Afro-American critical theorists, Henry Louis Gates, Jr., and Houston A. Baker, Jr. Joyce objects to their turn away from the socially focused criticism of the Black Aesthetic writers, whom they nevertheless evoke as predecessors: "By referring to Larry Neal and LeRoi Jones's 'splendid' anthology *Black Fire,* Gates cunningly leads us 'black intellectuals' to believe that his own work shares the spirit, ideology, and purpose of *Black Fire.*" But, she continues, quoting Audre Lorde, "'the master's tools will never dismantle the master's house'"; for poststructuralism, its sophisticated linguistic arsenal notwithstanding, cannot touch the very real exigencies of black life (Joyce Ann Joyce, "'Who The Cap Fit': Unconsciousness and Unconscionableness in the Criticism of Houston A. Baker, Jr., and Henry Louis Gates, Jr.," *New Literary History* 18 [Winter 1987]: 376, 379). Joyce's "reply" to Gates and Baker belonged to a debate that took place in the pages of *New Literary History*: see Henry Louis Gates, Jr., "'What's Love Got to Do with It?': Critical Theory, Integrity, and the Black Idiom," ibid. 18 (Winter 1987): 345–62; Houston A. Baker, Jr., "In Dubi-

ous Battle," ibid. 18 (Winter 1987): 363–69. The debate was initiated by Joyce Ann Joyce's "The Black Canon: Reconstructing Black American Literary Criticism," ibid. 18 (Winter 1987): 335–44. The question posed by Joyce—can a "black family identity" and a black vernacular criticism be created from a body of critical theory that has its origins within the cultural matrix of Western civilization—has been the subject of further discussion by Baker, Gates, and Joyce. See Baker, "There Is No More Beautiful Way," 139–44; Henry Louis Gates, Jr., "Authority, (White) Power, and the (Black) Critic: It's All Greek to Me," *Cultural Critique* 1 (Fall 1987): 19–46; Joyce Ann Joyce, "Black Woman Scholar, Critic, and Teacher," *New Literary History* 22 (Summer 1991): 544–65. For outside perspectives on the subject, see James Snead, "Racist Traces in Postmodern Theory and Literature," *Critical Quarterly* 33, no. 1 (Spring 1991): 31–39; Harold Fromm, "Real Life, Literary Criticism, and the Perils of Bourgeoisification," in *Academic Capitalism and Literary Value* (Athens: University of Georgia Press, 1991), 183–200; Vera Kutzinski, "History, Literature, and the Problem of Synthesis," in *Reconstructing American Literary and Historical Studies* (New York: St. Martin's, 1990) 128–44; and Theodore O. Mason, Jr., "Between the Populist and the Scientist: Ideology and Power in Recent Afro-American Literary Criticism, or, 'The Dozens' as Scholarship," *Callaloo* 11 (Summer 1988): 606–15.

25. Both books depict the desperate straits of the Afro-American masses in the city, in terms of disease, poverty, crime, and unemployment. See Nicholas Lemann, *The Promised Land: The Great Black Migration and How It Changed America* (New York: Knopf, 1991), 282–83. And compare W.E.B. Du Bois, *The Philadelphia Negro: A Social Study* (1899; reprint, New York: Blom, 1967), chap. 10 ("The Health of Negroes"), with the *New York Times* articles cited in n. 18, above.

26. W.E.B. Du Bois, *The Souls of Black Folk* (1903; reprint, New York: Penguin, 1989), 69. My point will be made clearer in chap. 1, below. Martin Bulmer's "W.E.B. Du Bois as a Social Investigator," in *The Social Survey in Historical Perspective, 1880–1940*, ed. Martin Bulmer, Kevin Bales, and Kathryn Kish Sklar (Cambridge: Cambridge University Press, 1991) discusses the ground-breaking nature of *The Philadelphia Negro* as well as the indifferent reception it met. That experience probably discouraged Du Bois's belief in the relevance of academic work. In the 1920s Du Bois would wonder if any institution in America could escape the taint of bourgeoisification: "What do we want? . . . Do we simply want to be Americans? Once in a while through all of us there flashes some clairvoyance, some clear idea, of what America really is. We who are dark can see America in a way that white Americans can not. And seeing our country thus, are we satisfied with its present goals and ideals?" Quoted from Harold Cruse, *The Crisis of the Negro Intellectual: From Its Origins to the Present* (New York: Morrow, 1967), 43—Cruse has an excellent discussion of Du Bois vis-a-vis the Harlem Renaissance (39–43). The question Du Bois poses has relevance to a two-part article on Chicago's black ghetto by Nicholas Lemann: "The Origins of the Underclass," *Atlantic Monthly* 257 (June 1986): 31–55; 257 (July 1986): 54–68. Lemann's solution to the problems of the ghetto—that

those who can should escape into mainstream America—is itself problematic. Certainly economic security is a desirable goal, but are the white middle-class "ideals" that go along with it also desirable? The recent fiction of Toni Morrison, Paule Marshall, and Gloria Naylor often criticizes a black middle class that remains loyal to the "ideals" of a consumer culture that continues to oppress Afro-Americans. In his "radical" later years, Du Bois pointed to the same paradox regarding the black middle class. See Marable, *Race, Reform, and Rebellion,* 29–30.

27. *New York Times,* February 7, 1943, quoted in Allen L. Woll, *The Hollywood Musical Goes to War* (Chicago: Nelson-Hall, 1983), 124–25.

28. Thomas Cripps discusses the Hollywood meeting in his *Slow Fade to Black* (New York: Oxford University Press, 1977), 375–78.

29. Stuart Cosgrove, "The Zoot Suit and Style Warfare," in *Zoot Suits and Second-Hand Dresses: An Anthology of Fashion and Music,* ed. Angela McRobbie (Boston: Unwin Hyman, 1988), 4. The background for the discussion of the zoot suit and its relation to the urban riots of 1943 is taken primarily from Cosgrove's article. Chester Himes wrote an essay for *Crisis* in 1943 entitled "Zoot Riots Are Race Riots"; it was reprinted in Chester Himes, *Black on Black: Baby Sister and Selected Writings* (New York: Doubleday, 1973). The Los Angeles riots are reviewed in detail in Mauricio Mazon, *The Zoot-Suit Riots: The Psychology of Symbolic Annihilation* (Austin: University of Texas Press, 1984).

30. The phrase "coats long and hip-tight" comes from Ralph Ellison, *Invisible Man* (New York: Random House, 1952), 332.

31. This despite the fact that Twentieth Century–Fox claimed that they reshot one-third of the film to try to comply with the NAACP agreement. See Cripps, *Slow Fade to Black,* 378; and Woll, *Hollywood Musical Goes to War,* 129–30. An interesting sidelight to *Stormy Weather* is that an Afro-American composer who was the film's music supervisor resigned in protest, partly because of studio attitudes and partly because of the "crude" black music and "erotic" dancing (Daniel J. Leab, *From Sambo to Superspade: The Black Experience in Motion Pictures* [Boston: Houghton Mifflin, 1975], 122–25). The film's segregated setting is a given, and the "invisible man" of *Stormy Weather* is a chauffeur's "boss," presumably white, who never appears but whose car and racetrack visits provide the economic largesse that enables the black characters to succeed. This is perhaps an early version of the "trickle-down" theory.

32. Ralph Ellison, *Shadow and Act* (New York: New American Library, 1966), 266–67.

Chapter One. City Bound

1. Emmett J. Scott, *Negro Migration during the War* (1920; reprint, New York: Arno, 1969), 3. A more detailed evaluation of migration during the war is included in U.S. Department of Labor, *Negro Migration in 1916–17* (New York: Negro Universities Press, 1969), a series of government-commissioned reports originally published in 1919. For a bibliography of studies of the Great Migration which appeared earlier than Scott's, see George Edmund Haynes, *Negro*

Newcomers in Detroit (1918; reprint, New York: Arno, 1969), 41–42.

2. A brief summary of the study of Afro-American migration to the north is included in Joe William Trotter, Jr., "Introduction: Black Migration in Historical Perspective: A Review of the Literature," in *The Great Migration in Historical Perspective: New Dimensions of Race, Class, and Gender*, ed. Joe William Trotter, Jr. (Bloomington: Indiana University Press, 1991). The endnotes to Trotter's essay (pp. 17–21) are also a good bibliography for historical and sociological literature on the migration. Three studies that have been most important as background to my work are Carole Marks, *Farewell—We're Good and Gone: The Great Black Migration* (Bloomington: Indiana University Press, 1989); James R. Grossman, *Land of Hope: Chicago, Black Southerners, and the Great Migration* (Chicago: University of Chicago Press, 1989); and Nicholas Lemann, *The Promised Land: The Great Black Migration and How It Changed America* (New York: Knopf, 1991).

3. For a discussion and critique of the presentation of studies of black migration, see Trotter, "Introduction," and Grossman, *Land of Hope*, 4–9.

4. Gilbert Osofsky, *Harlem: The Making of a Ghetto. Negro New York, 1890–1930* (New York: Harper & Row, 1963), 18.

5. See Ralph E. Luker, *The Social Gospel in Black and White: American Racial Reform, 1885–1912* (Chapel Hill: University of North Carolina Press, 1991), 159: "America's black urban ghettos were already in embryo by 1900, when seventy-two American cities had black populations of over 5,000. Seventy percent of black people in the North lived in cities. Washington, D.C. had the world's largest black community, numbering over 86,000. By 1910, New York and Washington both had more than 90,000 Negroes; Baltimore and Philadelphia had black communities of more than 80,000."

6. Daniel M. Johnson and Rex R. Campbell, *Black Migration in America: A Social Demographic History* (Durham: Duke University Press, 1981), 71.

7. Robert Hall, "'Come Out from among Them': Black Migration and Urban Culture," *Research Reports in Social Science: Studies in Minority Relations* (Florida State University Institute for Social Research), November 1975, 61–62.

8. Lemann, *Promised Land*, 70.

9. R. D. McKenzie, "The Rise of Metropolitan Communities," in *Recent Social Trends in the United States* (New York: McGraw-Hill, 1933), 1:461. Also see Scott Donaldson, "City and Country: Marriage Proposals," in *The Shaping of Twentieth-Century America: Interpretive Essays*, ed. Richard A. Abrams and Lawrence W. Levine (Boston: Little, Brown, 1971), 49–67: "In the 1920s, suburbanization became a demographic process of real magnitude for the first time" (59). In the last thirty years or so, social historians and sociologists have revised their history of the American suburb, noting that it was not a recent development and did not have a uniform social structure. See Michael H. Ebner, "Rereading Suburban America: Urban Population Deconcentration, 1810–1980," *American Quarterly* 37 (bibliographic issue, 1985): 368–81; and Carol A. O'Connor, "Sorting Out the Suburbs: Patterns of Land Use, Class, and Culture," ibid. 37 (bibliographic issue, 1985): 383–93. Afro-Americans would not make the flight to the suburbs until recent times, and the treatment of

that flight as a theme in Afro-American literature is relatively new. See especially Nicholas Lemann, "The Origins of the Underclass," *Atlantic Monthly* 257 (June 1986): 31–55; 257 (July 1986): 54–68. Lemann argues that the Great Migration from south to north essentially came to an end in the 1970s, but up till then segregation forced most blacks, even those who belonged to the middle class, to live together in designated areas of the city. "The second migration," he continues, "began in the late sixties—a migration out of the ghettos by members of the black working and middle classes, who had been freed from housing discrimination by the civil-rights movement" ("Origins of the Underclass," 257 [June 1986]: 35). While Lemann's *Atlantic* articles stressed problems he identified within the Afro-American communities of the cities, his book-length study emphasizes the structures of white racism as the original source of those problems.

10. Johnson and Campbell, *Black Migration in America*, 152. Also see Grossman, *Land of Hope*, 19; and Charles S. Johnson, *The Negro in American Civilization: A Study of Negro Life and Race Relations in Light of Social Research* (1930; reprint, New York: Holt, 1970), 16.

11. Theodore Kornweibel, Jr., ed., *In Search of the Promised Land: Essays in Black Urban History* (Port Washington, N.Y.: Kennikat, 1981), 8.

12. See Johnson and Campbell, "Epilogue, the 1970s", in *Black Migration in America*; "Migration by Blacks from the South Turns Around," *New York Times*, June 11, 1989; Dernoral Davis, "Toward a Socio-Historical and Demographic Portrait of Twentieth-Century African-Americans," in *Black Exodus: The Great Migration from the American South*, ed. Alferdteen Harrison (Jackson: University of Mississippi Press, 1991), 10–13.

13. Alain Locke, "The New Negro," in *The New Negro*, ed. Alain Locke (1925; reprint, New York: Atheneum, 1969), 6.

14. Ralph Ellison, *Invisible Man* (New York: Random House, 1952), 332.

15. Charles Chesnutt's *The Marrow of Tradition* (Boston: Houghton Mifflin, 1901) is a fictional treatment of a related pattern: the black migration to the southern cities, which "more than doubled in the four decades from 1870 to 1910" (Johnson and Campbell, *Black Migration in America*, 73). Chesnutt calls "Wellington" (Wilmington, N.C.) a "city," not a small town—indeed, the word *city* is used throughout. Moreover, his treatment of the *Morning Chronicle*, Mayor Carteret's "yellow" newspaper, shows Chesnutt's understanding of how the mass media shape the public opinion of a population that is no longer that of a small town.

16. Frank Webb, *The Garies and Their Friends* (1857; reprint, New York: Arno, 1969). In Webb's novel, it is assumed that Philadelphia, despite its segregated worlds, is too intimate a place for a mulatto child to pass for white—hence he is sent to Sudbury, where he is not known. Even the metropolis of New York is not big enough for the secret to remain safe, a situation due in part to the requirements of Webb's melodramatic plot.

17. Robert B. Stepto, *From behind the Veil: A Study of Afro-American Narrative* (Urbana: University of Illinois Press, 1979), ix, 3–31. Stepto does not connect these themes specifically to the city.

18. I borrow this phrase from Donald Petesch, *A Spy in the Enemy's Country: The Emergence of Modern Black Literature* (Iowa City: University of Iowa Press, 1989), 38. Petesch sees the "documentation" of reality a continuing tradition within Afro-American literature.

19. Solomon Northup, *Twelve Years a Slave*, in *Puttin' On Old Massa*, ed. Gilbert Osofsky (New York: Harper & Row, 1969), 241; Harriet A. Jacobs, *Incidents in the Life of a Slave Girl*, ed. Jean Fagan Yellin (Cambridge: Harvard University Press, 1987), 200.

20. Jacobs, *Incidents*, 191. William L. Andrews calls this rhetorical strategy the "misreading" of key tropes, acts of metaphor that turn the city on a hill into "Sodom"; see his *To Tell a Free Story: The First Century of Afro-American Autobiography* (Urbana: University of Illinois Press, 1986), 14–15.

21. Kevin Lynch, *The Image of the City* (Cambridge: MIT Press, 1960). In *Clotel*, New Orleans is an emblem of cruelty; in *Blake*, the gaiety of the Mardi Gras stands in striking contrast to the sad songs of the river boatmen; in *Our Nig*, little attempt is made to account for the setting. Webb's *Garies and Their Friends* is a possible exception to my generalization that black literature of this period lacks a sense of urban place. Webb pinpoints districts (blacks live in the "lower part of" Philadelphia) and names streets (see 166, 196), yet for all this, both Philadelphia and New York are treated as though they were small towns in which everyone is known and accounted for.

22. Robert Stepto, "Intimate Things in Place: A Conversation with Toni Morrison," in *Chant of Saints: A Gathering of Afro-American Literature, Art, and Scholarship*, ed. Michael S. Harper and Robert B. Stepto (Urbana: University of Illinois Press, 1979), 213. Also see Jacobs, *Incidents*, xxxiii, xxxiv; Harriet E. Wilson, *Our Nig*, ed. Henry Louis Gates, Jr. (New York: Random House, 1983), liii.

23. Nicholas Xenos, "Intifadah," *Grand Street* 9 (Autumn 1989): 232. Xenos is citing the urban geographer Yi-Fu Tuan.

24. Grossman, *Land of Hope*, 19. It is also possible that the authors of the slave narratives deliberately left their urban settings vague out of fear of providing clues for the slave catchers.

25. An excellent investigation of the conditions that migrating Afro-Americans met in Chicago is presented in pt. 2 of Grossman, *Land of Hope*. For the economic background, north and south, of the migration, see Jay R. Mandle, *Not Slave, Not Free: The African American Economic Experience Since the Civil War* (Durham, N.C.: Duke University Press, 1992); and Marks, *Farewell*.

26. LeRoi Jones, "Hymn for Lanie Poo," in *Preface to a Twenty-Volume Suicide Note* (New York: Totem, 1961), 9.

27. See Winthrop D. Jordan, *White over Black: American Attitudes toward the Negro, 1550–1812* (1968; reprint, Baltimore: Penguin, 1969), 73. As Jordan notes, a sense of mystery surrounds this cargo, for there is no indication whether these "negars" were to be treated like white indentured servants or were already designated as slaves for life. Joyce D. Goodfriend, *Before the Melting Pot: Society and Culture in Colonial New York City* (Princeton: Princeton University Press, 1992), 111, notes that in New York City, "the institution of slav-

ery was . . . well established by 1664, though the Dutch had not yet codified it in law. It was left to English authorities to develop the first legal framework for slavery in the colony." Jones's poem seems to echo another reverie on history, the Dutch, and the New World: the ending of *The Great Gatsby*.

28. John R. Stilgoe, *Common Landscape of America, 1580 to 1845* (New Haven: Yale University Press, 1982), 88.

29. Sennett notes that the *decumanus* and the *cardo*, the two axial streets of the *castrum* (the square that would become the walled city) were "drawn with reference to the order of the universe," the *decumanus* "set in line with the course of the sun," the *cardo* following "the axis of the sky" (Richard Sennett, *The Conscience of the Eye: The Design and Social Life of Cities* [New York: Knopf, 1990], 47–48).

30. Penn's design for Philadelphia can be seen in Seymour I. Schwartz and Ralph E. Ehrenberg, *The Mapping of America* (New York: Abrams, 1980), 124.

31. Sennett, *Conscience of the Eye*, 48.

32. Roger Lane, *William Dorsey's Philadelphia and Ours: On the Past and Future of the Black City in America* (New York: Oxford University Press, 1991), 58.

33. W.E.B. Du Bois, *The Philadelphia Negro: A Social Study* (1899; reprint, New York: Blom, 1967), 5; in this chapter, page numbers for subsequent citations of this work are given in parentheses and refer to this edition.

34. *Charles Booth: On the City. Physical Pattern and Social Structure*, ed. Harold W. Pfautz (Chicago: University of Chicago Press, 1967), 85. Du Bois modeled *Philadelphia Negro* on Booth's *Life and Labor of the People of London*. See Luker, *Social Gospel in Black and White*, 168.

35. Roger Lane in *William Dorsey's Philadelphia* points out that European immigrants easily found jobs in the new "industrial" Philadelphia but that "at the opening of the 20th century most blacks in Philadelphia were still doing the kind of jobs that had been done by the bottom layer of urban society in the Middle Ages." Blacks were allowed to work only "in the oldest, non-factory areas, such as brickmaking," whereas almost "half of the [foreign-born] immigrants worked" in factories, "more than five times the proportion of blacks" (63).

36. In ibid., 98, Lane attributes the "problems" of Afro-American businesses (including catering) to the crime rate, which had increased by the turn of the century: "Very simply, as the black population grew [due to immigration], and the crime rate rose with it, the old white patronage sank."

37. Perhaps *Philadelphia Negro* indicates another kind of ambivalence as well, one still basic to the politics of Afro-Americans. On the one hand, Du Bois declares that the fate of Philadelphia and that of black Philadelphia are linked—change the economic and social conditions of black life and you can find your city on the hill, he tells the city's white citizens—but on the other hand, he suggests that blacks should seize their own destiny by "founding" a city, one that will put to shame the pretensions of the American republic. Implied in this is the present division between black nationalists and integrationists, and his vision predicts as well the general nature of the invisible cities expressed in Ellison's *Invisible Man* and Toni Morrison's *Beloved*.

38. Lemann's observation in the *Atlantic Monthly* (July 1986), 65, that "ghettos are a national problem"—was Du Bois's fundamental thesis in *Philadelphia Negro*. Also see "Scapegoating the Black Family," (special issue) *Nation*, 249 (July 24, 31, 1989).

39. W.E.B. Du Bois, "The Great Northwest," *Crisis* 6 (September 1913): 239.

40. W.E.B. Du Bois, "The Negro Mind Reaches Out," in Locke, ed., *New Negro*, 414.

41. Augustine, *The City of God*, trans. Henry Bettenson (London: Penguin, 1972), 635. Of course, Augustine's source for the invisible city is the New Testament writings of the Apostle Paul, especially Paul's famous lines in 2 Cor. 4:18: "We look not to the things that are seen but to the things that are unseen."

42. Augustine, *City of God*, 687.

43. W.E.B. Du Bois, *The Souls of Black Folk* (1903; reprint, New York: Penguin, 1989), 5; in this chapter, page numbers for subsequent citations of this work are given in parenthesis and refer to this edition; Maria Leach, ed., *Funk & Wagnall's Standard Dictionary of Folklore, Mythology, and Legend* (New York: Funk & Wagnall, 1972), 999. Also see Wilson Jeremiah Moses, *The Golden Age of Black Nationalism, 1850–1925* (1978; reprint, New York: Oxford University Press, 1988), 136, 166–67.

44. Michael Taft, *Blues Lyric Poetry* (New York: Garland, 1983), 236. James Weldon Johnson, ed. *The Book of American Negro Spirituals* (New York: Viking, 1925); idem, *The Second Book of American Negro Spirituals* (New York: Viking, 1926). A striking example of a blues song that echoes the Bible is Howlin' Wolf's "I Asked for Water" ("she brought me gasoline"). The title alludes to Matt. 27:34, which tells how, before they crucified Christ, the Roman soldiers "offered him wine to drink, mingled with gall." For the close ties between Afro-American spiritual and secular music, consider the example of Thomas Dorsey, composer of both "Tight like That" and "Peace in the Valley." His career is outlined in Don Cusic, *The Sound of Light: A History of Gospel Music* (Bowling Green, Ohio: Bowling Green State University Popular Press, 1990), chap. 8.

45. Du Bois, *Souls of Black Folks*, chap. 1. See also Tom Lutz, *American Nervousness, 1903: An Anecdotal History* (Ithaca, N.Y.: Cornell University Press, 1991), 267-69. Lutz calls Du Bois's choice of spirituals as the representative black music in 1903 "anacronistic." And see Steven C. Tracy, *Langston Hughes, and the Blues* (Urbana: University of Illinois Press), 20–21.

46. See Maynard Mack, *The Garden and the City: Retirement and Politics in the Later Poetry of Pope* (Toronto: University of Toronto Press, 1969), 3; and W. H. Auden's classic study *The Enchafed Flood* (New York: Random House, 1950), 8–16. Auden contrasts the iconography of garden and city with that of desert and sea, the favorite symbols of the Romantic poets. Images of enclosed space, garden, and city are associated with the theme of community; whereas desert and sea project the perilous adventure of the individual self. In the modern world, however, "urban society is, like the desert, a place without limits" (37).

47. W.E.B. Du Bois, *The Negro American Family* (Atlanta: Atlanta University Publications, 1908), 64–65.

48. See Philippe Ariès, *Centuries of Childhood: A Social History of Family Life,* trans. Robert Baldick (New York: Knopf, 1962), 142–45, 375–79. Also see Raymond Williams, *Keywords: A Vocabulary of Culture and Society* (London: Fontana/Croom Helm, 1976), 47.

49. Booker T. Washington, *Up from Slavery: An Autobiography* (Garden City, N.Y.: Doubleday, 1901), 127.

50. Lawrence W. Levine, *Highbrow/Lowbrow: The Emergence of Cultural Hierarchy in America* (Cambridge: Harvard University Press, 1988), 176. The origins of the terms *highbrow* and *lowbrow* are traced on 221–23. Levine, of course, recognizes that cultural differences didn't begin in the nineteenth century. His point is that the kind of differentiation taking place in the United States around 1900 was new; I will outline some further background to these changes in chap. 2, below. For evidence of the antiquity of the problem, see Eric A. Havelock, *Preface to Plato* (Cambridge: Harvard University Press, 1963).

51. Levine, *Highbrow/Lowbrow,* 225. Such facile generalizations about race and class remain very much with us; consider the following passage from Edward C. Banfield, *The Unheavenly City: The Nature and Future of Our Urban Crisis* (Boston: Little, Brown, 1968), 53:

> The lower-class individual lives from moment to moment. If he has any awareness of a future, it is of something fixed, fated, beyond his control: things happen *to* him, he does not *make* them happen. Impulse governs his behavior, either because he cannot discipline himself to sacrifice a present for a future satisfaction or because he has no sense of the future. He is therefore radically improvident: whatever he cannot consume immediately he considers valueless. His bodily needs (especially for sex) and his taste for "action" take precedence over everything else—and certainly over any work routine.

For Mr. Banfield, deferred gratification is the province of the "upper class," as is concern for "community, nation, or mankind" (48, 49). One wonders what he would make of someone like Charles Keating, who had, by all accounts, excellent work routines.

52. Levine, *Highbrow/Lowbrow,* 227. Also see Barbara Ehrenreich, *Fear of Falling: The Inner Life of the Middle Class* (New York: Harper Collins, 1990). Ehrenreich argues that "living by one's wits" is what members of the American middle class have always done. Her definition of its members—"people whose economic and social status is based on education, rather than on ownership of capital or property" (12)—seems relevant to the black middle class whose "capital" has always been considerably less than that of its white counterpart. See E. Franklin Frazier's *Black Bourgeoisie: The Rise of a New Middle Class in the United States* (New York: Free Press, 1957); and Bart Landry, *The New Black Middle Class* (Berkeley: University of California Press, 1987), chaps. 4, 5, 6. By arguing that intangibles such as art and literature, education and "culture," mattered more than tangible things, the black middle class, though not

materially wealthy, could sustain the belief that it had the right to dictate the terms of existence to others within the race. Its defense of an invisible "culture" could have visible political consequences in terms of social control.

53. James Weldon Johnson, *The Autobiography of an Ex-Colored Man*, ed. William L. Andrews (1912; reprint, New York: Penguin, 1990), 63; in this chapter, page numbers for subsequent citations of this novel are given in parentheses and refer to this edition. It is a risky business to assume that the attitudes of a character reflect those of the author, but in this case it seems safe to do so. Johnson made a similar statement, in almost the same words, in the preface to his edition of *The Book of American Negro Poetry*, rev. ed. (1922; reprint, New York: Harcourt, Brace, 1959), 17. In "Views and Reviews," the weekly column he wrote for *New York Age* between 1914 and 1923, Johnson continually returned to a theme developed in his preface: "the greatness of a race may be measured by the literature it has produced." Johnson never left any doubt that by "literature" he meant literature in print. See especially his column "When Is a Race Great?" *New York Age*, May 11, 1915. (See also idem, *Black Manhattan* [1930; reprint, New York: Atheneum, 1972], chap. 19.)

54. James Weldon Johnson, "Views and Reviews," *New York Age*, March 23, 1918.

55. Ibid., November 22, 1917.

56. Ibid., May 20, 1915.

57. See Du Bois, *Philadelphia Negro*, 232; Du Bois thought that the "Colored Y.M.C.A." in Philadelphia failed miserably to fulfill this function, becoming just another "church" added to the "numberless colored churches of the city, with endless prayer meetings and loud gospel hymns, in dingy and uninviting quarters . . ." (232). Langston Hughes, on the other hand, had nothing but praise for Harlem's "Y." He celebrated its fiftieth anniversary in his column in the *Chicago Defender* (May 26, 1951) and helped contribute to its intellectual life by writing for its weekly magazine (*The New Sign*) in 1931. In one article he praised Claude McKay, and in another he called "creative art" (here he meant "writers, poets, and painters")—"the foundation upon which any lasting contribution to culture must be built." Yet in another article he complained that "Negro art, like white art in this bourgeois world, is high-priced, high-hat, and lacking in any special aim toward having a dark mass appeal. Bessie Smith, who never received a Spingarn medal, is a great singer of the Negro masses" (Langston Hughes, "Negro Art and Claude McKay," *New Sign*, October 24, 1931; idem, "Negro Art and the Artist," ibid., October 17, 1931; idem, "Negro Art and Its Audience," ibid., September 26, 1931). Despite their differen views of art, both Hughes and Du Bois saw the "Y" as an institution that could mediate between high and low, masses and middle class. For a concise history of the black YMCA in American cities, see Luker, *Social Gospel in Black and White*, 163–65.

58. Du Bois, *Philadelphia Negro*, 201–7.

59. As a writer of popular songs, Johnson surely knew of the turn-of-the-century controversy among American composers and musical critics which hinged on this very point. Hard-line Anglo-Saxonists such as Daniel Gregory

Mason balked at the idea of a mongrelized American music and linked ragtime to race and racial sterotypes: "It is a rule of thumb for putting a 'kink' into a tune that without such specious rehabilitation would be unbearable. It is not a new flavor, but a kind of curry or catsup strong enough to make stale old dishes palatable to unfastidious appetites." To be "fastidious," of course, is to have true "taste" (quoted from MacDonald Smith Moore, *Yankee Blues: Musical Culture and American Identity* [Bloomington: Indiana University Press, 1985], 79). Consider too the pressure felt by Scott Joplin to escape the vulgarity of ragtime for high art. His folk opera *Treemonisha*, which he called a "grand opera," reflected his need to be accepted in terms of the new cultural hierarchy. *Treemonisha* was actually a hybrid, an attempt to wed high and low culture; yet a white public that was willing to accept Joplin as a ragtime composer refused to accept him as a highbrow composer who had written an opera: "No music house cared to publish it, and no producer wanted to stage it." Joplin "published the score at his own expense" in 1911, and the one performance of his opera in 1915 was "a disaster" (Jervis Anderson, *This Was Harlem: A Cultural Portrait, 1900–1950* [New York: Farrar, Straus, Giroux, 1981], 79–81). In a sense, the fate of Joplin's opera was mirrored in the public's indifference to Paul Laurence Dunbar's nondialect verse. Dunbar complained to James Weldon Johnson, "I've got to write dialect poetry; it's the only way I can get them to listen to me" (Johnson, ed., *Book of American Negro Poetry*, 35–36). Yet one also senses the pressure of the cultural hierarchy on Dunbar when he defines his "growth" as a poet as an escape from dialect poetry into the realm of high art. In a different approach to the same problem, Karen Linn, *That Half-Barbaric Twang: The Banjo in American Popular Culture* (Urbana: University of Illinois Press, 1991), chaps. 1, 2, presents a fascinating account of the development of class and race associations around a particular musical instrument.

60. In his anthology of black poetry, *Caroling Dusk: An Anthology of Verse by Negro Poets* (New York: Harper's, 1927), Countee Cullen placed "The White Witch," a poem developing the figure from Johnson's novel, next to Johnson's famous "My City." He understood that the two poems were companion pieces: if "My City" celebrates New York's "throbbing force" and "shining towers," "The White Witch"—without ever naming the city—presents a cautionary tale to black youth.

61. Pauline Hopkins, *Contending Forces: A Romance Illustrative of Negro Life North and South* (1900; reprint, New York: Oxford University Press, 1988); in this chapter, page numbers for subsequent citations of this work are given in parentheses and refer to this edition.

62. See Michael H. Cowan, *Emerson, America, and Urban Metaphor* (New Haven: Yale University Press, 1967).

63. Zora Neale Hurston, *Their Eyes Were Watching God* (1937; reprint, Urbana: University of Illinois Press, 1978), 14.

64. This conception of the invisible city should be contrasted with her portrait of the ancient city of Meroe—("the queenly city" of Ethiopia) and its present-day manifestation, the "unseen" Telassar, in her magazine novel *Of One*

Blood (1902). Both cities—the one historical and dead, the other fictional but alive in the hearts of black people—are defined in terms of high culture. See *The Magazine Novels of Pauline Hopkins*, ed. Hazel V. Carby (New York: Oxford University Press, 1988), 534–59. Also see Hazel V. Carby, *Reconstructing Womanhood: The Emergence of the Afro-American Woman Novelist* (New York: Oxford University Press, 1987), 156–58.

65. Dorothy West, *The Living Is Easy* (1948; reprint, New York: Feminist, 1982), 44.

66. *Richard Wright Reader*, ed. Ellen Wright and Michel Fabre (New York: Harper & Rowe, 1978), 40.

Chapter Two. City Cultures

1. See Harold Pfautz's introduction to the selected writings of Charles Booth, *Charles Booth: On the City: Physical Pattern and Social Structure*; ed. Harold Pfautz (Chicago: University of Chicago Press, 1967). Pfautz's definition of the assumptions and concerns of the early sociologists is lucidly succinct: "The crux of urbanism seems to lie in the fact that over and above the concentration of population there develops a new way of life: when great numbers of people live their lives in close physical proximity and in the presence of an extreme division of labor, traditional modes of human association are transformed; there develop not only new forms of group life but also new perspectives and thought modes" (85). Pfautz goes on to say in a footnote that "these postulates did not, of course, become explicit until the twentieth century in the work of such men as Spengler, Simmel, Weber, and, later, Park, Burgess, and Wirth." A good assessment of the field and its history is David A. Karp, Gregory P. Stone, and William C. Yoels, *Being Urban: A Sociology of City Life* (New York: Praeger, 1991), esp. chaps. 1, 2.

2. *The Sociology of Georg Simmel*, ed. and trans. Kurt H. Wolff (Glencoe, Ill.: Free, 1950), 410. For a perceptive study of Simmel and the city, see Michael P. Smith, *The City and Social Theory* (New York: St. Martin's, 1979), chap. 3.

3. Blanche Gelfant, "Sister to Faust: The City's 'Hungry Woman' as Heroine," *Novel* 15 (Fall 1981): 38, suggests that "desire has always been the great energizing theme of the American city novel since the startling appearance in 1900 of Dreiser's *Sister Carrie*." The characterization also fits Dunbar's novel.

4. The best general discussion of these social changes up to 1900 is Alan Trachtenberg, *The Incorporation of America: Culture and Society in the Gilded Age* (New York: Hill & Wang, 1982): chaps. 4 and 5 are especially relevant to my concerns. More detail on class alignments can be found in Stuart M. Blumin, *The Emergence of the Middle Class: Social Experience in the American City, 1760–1900* (Cambridge: Cambridge University Press, 1989). There is a fine, brief discussion of how the middle class justifies itself in Barbara Ehrenreich, *Fear of Falling: The Inner Life of the Middle Class* (New York: Harper Collins, 1990), chap. 2 (in the section called "The Professions as Class Fortress"). I also found very useful John H. Ehrenreich, *The Altruistic Imagination: A History of Social Work and Social Policy in the United States* (Ithaca, N.Y.: Cornell Universi-

ty Press, 1985), chaps. 1, 2; and David W. Noble, *The Progressive Mind, 1890–1917* (Minneapolis: Burgess, 1981).

5. There is a vast literature, sociological and other, that has investigated cultural hierarchy and mass society, but here I am only concerned with indicating some important reference points for questions of Afro-American culture, and with showing how these enter into the work of particular writers. An excellent bibliography of media and culture is contained in the notes in Fred Inglis, *Media Theory* (Oxford: Basil Blackwell, 1990); and many of the references cited in the notes to this chapter deal with the subject in whole or in part.

6. A good background survey of the question can be found in Tony Bennett, "Theories of the Media, Theories of Society" in *Culture, Society, and the Media*, ed. Michael Gurevitch et al. (London: Methuen, 1982), 30–55. See also the references in nn. 8 and 9, below. Hazel V. Carby, "It Just Be's Dat Way Sometime: The Sexual Politics of Women's Blues," *Radical America* 20 (June–July 1986): 14, notes that "by 1928 . . . the primary source of the group transmission of the blues was by phonograph which was then joined by the radio." Carby suggests that mass media created an invisible community of artist and audience at the lowest level of black society; yet others will be more skeptical about the effects of mass culture. For a brilliant dramatic rendition of the complicated relationship between blues and mass culture, see August Wilson, *Ma Rainey's Black Bottom* (New York: New American Library, 1985).

7. Amiri Baraka [LeRoi Jones] and Amina Baraka, *The Music: Reflections on Jazz and Blues* (New York: Morrow, 1987), 105–12.

8. For the Frankfurt School's essential critique of mass culture, see Max Horkheimer and Theodor W. Adorno, *Dialectic of Enlightenment*, trans. John Cumming (New York: Herder & Herder, 1972); the original version was published in 1944. Again, there is an enormous literature of commentary on Critical Theory. A basic text is Martin Jay, *The Dialectical Imagination: A History of the Frankfurt School and the Institute of Social Research, 1923–1950* (Boston: Little, Brown, 1973). Also good are idem, "The Frankfurt School in Exile," in *Permanent Exiles: Essays on the Intellectual Migration from Germany to America* (New York: Columbia University Press, 1985), 28–61; and Douglas Kellner, *Critical Theory, Marxism, and Modernity* (Cambridge: Polity, 1989), esp. chaps. 5, 6.

9. For a representative American version of the thesis of the Frankfurt School, see Dwight Macdonald, "A Theory of Mass Culture," in *Mass Culture: The Popular Arts in America*, ed. Bernard Rosenberg and David Manning White (Glencoe, Ill.: Free, 1957), 59–73. Macdonald's original essay, published in *Politics* in 1944, was titled "A Theory of Popular Culture." My discussion here is indebted to the excellent explanation of cold war politics, literature, and criticism in Thomas Hill Schaub, *American Fiction in the Cold War* (Madison: University of Wisconsin Press, 1991), pt. 1, esp. chap. 2. An excellent historical study of theories of mass culture is Patrick Brantlinger's *Bread and Circuses: Theories of Mass Culture as Social Decay* (Ithaca, N.Y.: Cornell University Press, 1983).

10. Irving Howe, "Black Boys and Native Sons," *Dissent* 10 (Autumn 1963): 353–68. See also Schaub, *American Fiction in the Cold War*, chap. 5.

11. A useful (and witty) outline of possible distinctions between "mass" and "popular" is contained in Stuart Klawans, "True Bloomism on the Bungalow Lawn of Art," *Grand Street* 8 (Autumn 1988): 145–54. Ray Pratt, *Rhythm and Resistance: Explorations in the Political Uses of Popular Music* (New York: Praeger, 1990) and W. T. Lhamon, Jr., *Deliberate Speed: The Origins of a Cultural Style in the American 1950s* (Washington, D.C.: Smithsonian Institution Press, 1990) are recent works that oppose the Frankfurt School's view of mass culture, particularly through examples of resistance in Afro-American popular culture, or its mass adaptations; Lhamon's book uses Ellison's invisible man as the very type of the "trickster" figure who "mis-reads" the social idioms in order to escape the definitions of mass culture. For a view of this question from a less optimistic perspective, see Edward Ball, "The Great Sideshow of the Situationist International," *Yale French Studies* 73 (1987): 21–37. See also n. 71, below.

12. W.E.B. Du Bois, *The Souls of Black Folk* (1903; reprint, New York: Penguin, 1989), 5. The phrase "dual citizenship" comes from Randolph Bourne, "Trans-National America," in *The History of a Literary Radical and Other Papers*, ed. Van Wyck Brooks (New York: Russell, 1956), 260–84, which I have argued (in n. 9 of the Introduction, above) was an important influence on Locke. Bourne's point was that Americans should escape the "indistinguishable dough of Anglo-Saxonism," that is, the bogus melting pot, and maintain a double loyalty to their ethnic roots and to their nation. Locke saw this as a perfect opportunity for blacks to proclaim both an "African" *and* an "American" identity, hence escaping the spiritual paralysis suggested by Du Bois's "twoness—an American, a Negro."

For the most part, however, Afro-Americans have not been seen as Americans but as "other," sometimes demonized, sometimes valorized. When valorized, the "Negro" was often represented as a symbolic escape from an increasingly constrained industrial culture, the newly regularized and bureaucratized way of life created by "incorporation." The ideal and attraction of "the primitive," an idea that has a long history in Western cultures, became firmly established in nineteenth-century European and American literature (see Chris Bongie, *Exotic Memories: Literature, Colonialism, and the Fin de Siècle* [Stanford, Calif.: Stanford University Press, 1991]), and it played a part in the white fascination with the Harlem Renaissance. The emphasis on "escape" emerged in the 1950s, notably in Norman Mailer's essay "The White Negro" and the Beat writers. All of these examples are, in at least a distant way, white valorizations of the viewpoint of Du Bois or Baldwin—as are Pratt, *Rhythm and Resistance*; and Lhamon, *Deliberate Speed*.

13. See James Engell, *Forming the Critical Mind: Dryden to Coleridge* (Cambridge: Harvard University Press, 1989), esp. chap. 6 ("Kinds, Canons, and Readers").

14. In the 1920s, Langston Hughes pointed to the irony of this position: "The fine novels of Chestnutt go out of print with neither race noticing their passing" (Langston Hughes, "The Negro and the Racial Mountain," in *The New Negro Renaissance: An Anthology*, ed. Michael W. Peplow and Arthur P.

Davis [New York: Holt, Rinehart, & Winston, 1975], 473; first published in *Nation* 122 ([June 23, 1926]: 692–94). The black "race" to which Hughes refers is, more specifically, the members of the black middle class, those who tacitly accept the values and tastes of the dominant culture without question. For a contemporary debate on similar matters, see Henry Louis Gates, Jr., "Authority, (White) Power, and the (Black) Critic: It's All Greek to Me" *Cultural Critique* 1 (Fall 1987): 19–46.

15. Houston A. Baker, Jr. has rightly given prominence to Skaggs as a "blues detective" in *Blues, Ideology, and Afro-American Literature: A Vernacular Theory* (Chicago: University of Chicago Press, 1984), 114–38. Yet in ignoring Skaggs's urban habitat, Baker robs him of a good deal of his complexity. Baker would have us believe that "geographical locale" and specific "historical events" have little bearing on character; referentiality, in other words, is less important than "misguided modes of apprehending the world" (129). One can understand why Baker takes the approach that he does; historically minded critics have placed too much emphasis on the novel's anticity theme. Yet in trying to right a wrong, Baker ignores Dunbar's sophisticated treatment of the city's presence, especially its subtle shaping of Skaggs as an urban type.

16. Paul Laurence Dunbar, *The Sport of the Gods* (1902; reprint, Miami: Mnemosyne, 1969), 81, 82; in this chapter, page numbers for subsequent citations of this work are given in parenthesis and refer to this edition.

17. Dana Brand, *The Spectator and the City in Nineteenth-Century American Literature* (Cambridge: Cambridge University Press, 1991), 6, argues that it is impossible to give a precise English translation of *flâneur*, a word that combines two activities: watching and strolling. Dunbar's passage suggests not only Baudelaire but also Walter Benjamin's critique of Baudelaire. Baudelaire celebrated the flâneur's ability to unify the "disorienting" diversity of the city, but Benjamin noted that this figure points to the seductive nature of the new urban capitalism whereby the city is reduced to visual images "collected and consumed"; see Brand, *Spectator and City*, 5–13. Also see a passage similar to Dunbar's in James Weldon Johnson's *Autobiography of an Ex-Colored Man*, ed. William L. Andrews (1912; reprint, New York: Penguin, 1990), 66: "I began to feel the dread power of the city; the crowds, the lights, the excitement, the gaiety, and all its subtler stimulating influences began to take effect upon me. My blood ran quicker and I felt that I was just beginning to live. To some natures this stimulant of life in a great city becomes a thing as binding and necessary as opium is to one addicted to the habit."

18. See Seth M. Scheiner, *Negro Mecca: A History of the Negro in New York City* (New York: New York University Press, 1965), 18–19; Jervis Anderson, *This Was Harlem: A Cultural Portrait, 1900–1950* (New York: Farrar, Straus, Giroux, 1981), 13–14.

19. This theme of urban voyeurism harks back to Edgar Allan Poe's "The Man of the Crowd" (1840) and Nathaniel Hawthorne's "Wakefield" (1835), and looks forward to Alfred Hitchcock's *Rear Window* (1954).

20. The setting and the history of the black musical theater of this period are described in Thomas L. Riis, *Just before Jazz: Black Musical Theater in New*

York, 1890–1915 (Washington, D.C.: Smithsonian Institution Press, 1989), esp. chap. 3; and Allen Woll, *Black Musical Theatre: From "Coontown" to "Dreamgirls"* (Baton Rouge: Louisiana State University Press, 1989), chaps. 1–3.

21. Riis, *Just before Jazz*, 55. Riis notes that after 1900, as black musicians and writers gained some institutional presence in the theater, the most virulently racist elements were removed from many of the shows (53).

22. Ibid., 83, 194; John E. Dimeglio, *Vaudeville, U.S.A.* (Bowling Green, Ohio: Bowling Green Popular, 1973), 30. Also see Roger Lane, *William Dorsey's Philadelphia and Ours: On the Past and Future of the Black City in America* (New York: Oxford University Press, 1991), 30–31. Lane notes that the coon show featured a new character, the urban coon who sometimes replaced "the old shuffling 'darkey'": "Visually the darkey was ragged and humble, the coon elegant and haughty, dressed in a bowler hat and spats, with cards popping out of his pockets and a razor up his sleeve, often in company with a proud woman in tight dress, high heels, and plumed hat." Also see Woll, *Black Musical Theatre*, 12: "*A Trip to Coontown* . . . offered a visit to one of New York City's ethnic enclaves."

23. Donald Fanger, *Dostoevsky and Romantic Realism: A Study of Dostoevsky in Relation to Balzac, Dickens, and Gogol* (Cambridge: Harvard University Press, 1965), 25–26, 218.

24. The detective would seem to be a more private mediator, compromised either by his association with an increasingly corrupt authority or by his descent into a corrupt borderline underworld (e.g., Dashiell Hammett's Sam Spade, or Coffin Ed of the Chester Himes novels).

25. In this paragraph I am obviously indebted to Walter Benjamin, especially his two essays "The Storyteller" and "On Some Motifs in Baudelaire," in *Illuminations*, trans. Harry Zohn (New York: Schocken, 1969).

26. Irving Howe, "The City in Literature," *Commentary* 51 (May 1971): 64.

27. Walter Benjamin, *Charles Baudelaire: A Lyric Poet in the Era of High Capitalism*, trans. Harry Zohn (London: New Left Books, 1973), 40; also see 40–43, 78–79.

28. For a recent topical investigation of the confused arena of public morality, class and race, and media realities, see Joan Didion, "New York: Sentimental Journeys," *New York Review of Books* 37 (January 17, 1991): 45–56.

29. LeRoi Jones to Ron Lowinsohn, November 30, 1959, James Weldon Johnson Collection, Beinecke Library, Yale University, New Haven, Conn., with permission.

30. See Arnold Rampersad, *The Art and Imagination of W.E.B. Du Bois* (Cambridge: Harvard University Press, 1976), 87. Rampersad makes a similar point, without my urban emphasis.

31. In an interesting recent essay, Robert Bone has argued that the Chicago School of sociology had its impact on the second renaissance—the "Chicago Renaissance" of the 1930s and 40s—but not the Harlem Renaissance. Bone's mistake lies in his belief that the Harlem Renaissance writers were incapable of in-depth urban analysis, tied as they were to "the myth of primitivism" and pastoral nostalgia (a theme Bone develops in *Down Home: A History of Afro-*

American Short Fiction from Its Beginnings to the End of the Harlem Renaissance (New York: Putnam, 1975). Not only does he neglect the influence of Park's urban theories on the black writers of the 1920s but he also makes no clear distinction between Park's and Wirth's views of the city, even though he recognizes Park's essential "optimism" regarding black migration. See Robert Bone, "Richard Wright and the Chicago Renaissance," *Callaloo* 9 (Summer 1986): 446–68.

32. Robert E. Park, "The City: Suggestions for the Investigation of Human Behavior in the City Environment," *American Journal of Sociology* 20 (March 1915): 608.

33. See Ellen Moers, *The Two Dreisers* (New York: Viking, 1969), 240–53.

34. Park, "City," 608–9. Compare E. Franklin Frazier, *The Negro Family in Chicago* (Chicago: University of Chicago Press, 1932), 75: "In the urban environment the migrant is liberated from the control that the church and other forms of association exercised in the rural South. He is released from the gossip of the neighborhood and the fear of being 'churched' if he strays into unconventional behavior."

35. For a detailed discussion of Park's optimism regarding the city as an ecological environment, see Park Dixon Goist, *From Main Street to State Street: Town, City, and Community in America* (Port Washington, N.Y.: Kennikat, 1977), 110–20. Also, see Charles S. Johnson, "The New Frontage on American Life," in *The New Negro*, ed. Alain Locke (1925; reprint, New York: Atheneum, 1969), 278–98. Johnson did not avert his eyes from the negative changes wrought by the city upon the rural migrant (see esp. 285–88), yet although he noted that the city broke old bonds and created "disorientation," he ended his essay on a typically Parkian note: "conflicts" between migrant and city may lead to a "common purpose" among blacks and a revitalized American city. Locke cleverly paired Johnson's "Frontage" with Paul Kellogg's "The Negro Pioneers" in ibid., 271–77, which painted an even more rosy view of the new urban "frontier." As Park's former students, both Johnson and E. Franklin Frazier, at least in the 1920s, accepted with some reservations Park's urban paradigm for the black immigrant: contact, conflict, accommodation, and, finally, assimilation.

36. Robert E. Park, "The City: Suggestions for the Investigation of Human Behavior in the Urban Environment," in *The City*, ed. Robert E. Park, Ernest W. Burgess, and Roderick D. McKenzie (Chicago: University of Chicago Press, 1925), 7, 8. Johnson's essay became "Harlem: The Culture Capital" in Locke, ed., *New Negro*.

37. See Anthony M. Platt, *E. Franklin Frazier Reconsidered* (New Brunswick, N.J.: Rutgers University Press, 1991), 156, 165–68. Platt makes a convincing case that Frazier challenged Park's ideas about black urban life at every turn, especially after the 1920s.

38. Both Jessie Fauset and Nella Larsen, for instance, treated the subject of "passing" in terms of the transformation that the city caused in their protagonists. In this sense, the title of Larsen's *Passing* (New York: Knopf, 1929) refers as much to Irene Redfield as it does to Clare Kendry: if Clare "passes" for

white, Irene claims to be black (*passes* for black) but passes into whiteness. Despite her vaunted race loyalty, her identification with the city's "rising towers" (her maiden name is West*over*) and her ascension into the upper levels of the black middle class turn her into a "white" capitalist killer protecting her turf. So, too, in Jessie Fauset's *Plum Bun* (1929; reprint, Boston: Beacon, 1990), New York City shapes Angela Murray, and her literal "passing" becomes a metaphor for her metamorphosis into a rootless urban nomad.

39. Robert E. Park, "Human Migration and Marginal Man," *American Journal of Sociology* 33 (May 1928): 881–93.

40. Anthropologist Victor Turner has made the subject of human "liminality" well known in our time. The word indicates, among other things, a state of being "betwixt and between all fixed points of classification," a definition involving both social and metaphysical status. For an excellent discussion of "liminality" and its significance for literature, see Barbara Babcock, "'A Tolerated Margin of Mess': The Trickster and His Tales Reconsidered," *Journal of Folklore Institute* 11 (March 1975): 149–86. Babcock's thesis is that contradictions within the figure of the "marginal man" have their origin in society itself, which both needs and shuns liminality. Also see Gunter H. Lenz, "Symbolic Space, Communal Rituals, and the Surreality of the Urban Ghetto: Harlem in Black Literature from the 1920s to the 1960s," *Callaloo* 11 (Spring, 1988): 309–45.

41. Michel Fabre, *The Unfinished Quest of Richard Wright*, trans. Isabel Barzun (New York: Morrow, 1973), 127, 232, 334, 339.

42. *Louis Wirth on Cities and Social Life*, ed. Albert J. Reiss, Jr. (Chicago: University of Chicago Press, 1964), 74.

43. Ibid., 40.

44. See Gregory Holmes Singleton, "Birth, Rebirth, and the 'New Negro' of the 1920s," *Phylon* 43 (March 1982): 33. According to Singleton, "at a time when 23 percent of their race was illiterate, the voices of the New Negro movement were better educated than the population at large. Almost two-thirds held degrees, and over 85 percent had attended college."

45. Locke's cultural and political thinking often shows a careful awareness of what is likely to be acceptable in the current intellectual climate. The Locke of *New Negro* is not the Locke of 1936 who supported the report of the Mayor's commission on the Harlem riots of the previous year (see Dominic J. Capeci, Jr., *The Harlem Riot of 1943* [Philadelphia: Temple University Press, 1977], 6–8) or the Locke who would praise *Native Son*. An article by Everett H. Akam ("Community and Cultural Crisis: The 'Transfiguring Imagination' of Alain Locke," *American Literary History* 3 [Summer 1991]: 255–76) cites writings from the whole of Locke's career, insisting that he had a thoroughly consistent and perceptive view of Negro life from first to last, one that Akam defines as "the cosmopolitan ideal" (260). As a summary of Locke's positive effect on Afro-American intellectual life this is a useful portrait. But the historical Locke was more complicated, and sometimes contradictory, and a synthetic view of him only partially fits particular moments.

46. Locke, ed., Alain Locke "The New Negro," in *New Negro*, 7. Locke's an-

thology seemed to insist that it was possible to "dig up the past" without finding any corpses, as if a "usable past" for the black artist could only be usable if history were terror free (see the section "The Negro Digs Up His Past," in ibid.). In fact, however, *New Negro* itself was not entirely free of corpses and/or "the terror of history"—see Eric Waldrond's "The Palm Porch," in ibid.; and Willis Richardson's "Compromise: A Folk Play," in ibid. Locke wanted the folk treated, but almost always in terms of a hermetically sealed past or present; what he tried to avoid in his anthology was a hard look at the lives of the present-day urban masses. When they were treated in his volume, as in Rudolph Fisher's "City of Refuge," history and its terrors were submerged into universality and art—in Fisher's case, the archetypal theme of country mouse versus city mouse.

47. Alain Locke, "Our Little Renaissance," in *The Critical Temper of Alain Locke*, ed. Jeffrey C. Stewart (New York: Garland, 1983), 22; originally published in *Ebony and Topaz: A Collectanea*, ed. Charles S. Johnson (New York: Opportunity, 1927), 117–18.

48. Alain Locke, "Negro Youth Speaks," in Locke, ed., *New Negro*, 51–52.

49. Alain Locke, "This Year of Grace," in *Critical Temper of Alain Locke*, 206; originally published in *Opportunity* 9 (February 1931): 48–51.

50. Even those who wish to see Locke as an advocate of folk culture recognize that he wanted "folk expression"—jazz, blues, tales—"raised" to another level. See Russell Linnemann, ed., *Alain Locke: Reflections on a Modern Renaissance Man* (Baton Rouge: Louisiana State University Press, 1982), 83, 87, 110, 115, 120. Patricia Liggins Hill's recognition that Locke's "study of the blues has limited scope and lacks critical depth" ("Alain Locke on Black Folk Music," in Linnemann, ed., *Alain Locke*, 129) indicates as well the limits of his sympathy for a real folk as opposed to a mythologized one.

51. George H. Haynes, "The Church and the Negro Spirit," *Survey Graphic* 6 (March 1925): 696; in this chapter, page numbers for citations of this issue of *Survey Graphic* appear in parentheses in the text. Also see chap. 1, n. 1, above. Haynes was an early historian and demographer of the Great Migration.

52. Anthony Platt notes that Locke rejected E. Franklin Frazier's satiric essay, "The Pathology of Race Prejudice," finding "it too abrasive to his glorification of *The New Negro*" (*Frazier Reconsidered*, 82, 83, 241n). Locke also found Claude McKay's poem "Mulatto" too abrasive for his *Survey Graphic* issue, and he "prudently" changed the title of McKay's "White House" to "White Houses" when he reprinted the latter poem in *New Negro* (David Levering Lewis, *When Harlem Was in Vogue* [1981; reprint, New York: Random House, 1982], 151, 153). So, too, in *New Negro* Locke deleted Rudolph Fisher's "The South Lingers On" from the *Survey Graphic*, probably because the last lines of the sketch have the protagonist desperately looking for "an Employment office" in a bewildering and frightening urban environment.

53. Locke, "New Negro," 7.

54. We can see the same contradiction in Randolph Bourne, who placed his hope for America's future in the urban masses yet believed that the "people must be appealed to desire certain things mightily," and that those values

can only be expressed by their "*articulate*" leaders (my italics). See Casey Nelson Blake, *Beloved Community: The Cultural Criticism of Randolph Bourne, Van Wyck Brooks, Waldo Frank, and Lewis Mumford* (Chapel Hill: University of North Carolina Press, 1990), 169.

55. J. A. Rogers, "Jazz at Home," in Locke, ed., *New Negro*, 221–22. Rogers's class-bound perspective is perhaps at its most obvious when he defines the "true spirit of jazz" as "a joyous revolt from convention, custom, authority, boredom, even sorrow—from everything that would confine the soul of man" (217). Forty years later, Baldwin would publish "Sonny's Blues," in *Going to Meet the Man* (New York: Dial, 1965), a story that would express a deeper understanding of that music than the *universal* (read: middle-class) "revolt from convention . . . boredom." Sonny's brother begins to see that jazz/blues is as essential as food for those masses who must live in the white man's city, that it sustains them in an existential sense.

In his own essay on the spirituals, Alain Locke was more subtle than Rogers but arrived at the same place. Locke insisted that the spirituals were already high art, comparable to the "Gregorian" chants of the Middle Ages and "the rarest of German chorals." In fact, they had been diluted by the "concert stage," which took them away from their "original setting." Yet what he gave with one hand he took away with the other: "Their next development will undoubtedly be, like that of the modern Russian folk music, their use in the larger choral forms of the symphonic choir, through which they will reachieve their folk atmosphere and epic spirituality" ("The Negro Spirituals," in *New Negro*, 202).

56. Jean Toomer, "Blue Meridian," in *The New Caravan*, ed. Alfred Kreymborg, Lewis Mumford, and Paul Rosenfeld (New York: Norton, 1936), 653. Also see Vera M. Kutzinski's *Against the American Grain: Myth and History in William Carlos Williams, Jay Wright, and Nicholas Guillen* (Baltimore: Johns Hopkins University Press, 1987), 3–46. Kutzinski's excellent chapter on Williams attempts to divorce him from this group of intellectuals, because they, unlike Williams, never transcended the American "myths" against which they rebelled. But Kutzinski's treatment overlooks individual differences within this group and a common goal that links them to Williams—they, too, tried to discover the hidden sources of an invisible America. Moreover, Waldo Frank shared the same "New World" perspective that Kutzinski sees in Williams. Note that Frank's focus on the Pueblo Indian and Hispanic culture in *Our America* (New York: Boni & Liveright, 1919), or on the "cross-fertilization" of cultures in *City Block* (Darien, Conn.: Published by Waldo Frank, 1922), is similar to W. C. Williams's thesis in *In the American Grain* (Norfolk, Conn.: New Directions, 1925): to survive Americans must replace their Western "myths" with "New World" history. See in particular what he called his "New World" quartet: *Our America* (1919); *Virgin Spain* (1924); *The Rediscovery of America* (New York: Scribners, 1928), esp. 229–30, and *America Hispana* (1931).

57. Waldo Frank, *Salvos* (New York: Boni & Liveright, 1924), 79; Randolph

Bourne, "An Hour in Chartres," *Atlantic Monthly* 114 (August 1914): 216; Paul Rosenfeld, *Port of New York* (New York: Harcourt, Brace, 1924), 178, 179.

58. There is a brief description of premodern building methods, along with an analysis of their democratic social context, in Roger Coleman, *The Art of Work: An Epitaph to Skill* (London: Pluto, 1988), chap. 2.

59. Arnold Rampersad, *The Life of Langston Hughes* (New York: Oxford University Press, 1986), 1:141.

60. Hughes, "Negro and the Racial Mountain," 476; see Ezek. 40:42; Rev. 21:10.

61. Edward E. Waldron, *Walter White and the Harlem Renaissance* (Port Washington, N.Y.: Kennikat, 1978), 132.

62. Langston Hughes, "Here to Yonder," *Chicago Defender*, September 14, 1946.

63. Charles Scruggs, "All Dressed Up but No Place to Go: The Black Writer and His Audience during the Harlem Renaissance," *American Literature* 47 (January 1977): 544–63.

64. Two useful essays on this dividing period in Afro-American history are Richard M. Dalfiume, "The 'Forgotten Years' of the Negro Revolution," in *The Shaping of Twentieth-Century America*, ed. Richard M. Abrams and Lawrence W. Levine (Boston: Little, Brown, 1971); and Barton J. Bernstein, "The Ambiguous Legacy: The Truman Administration and Civil Rights," in ibid.

65. Richard Wright, Introduction to *Black Metropolis*, by St. Clair Drake and Horace R. Cayton (New York: Harcourt, Brace, 1945), 1:xxxi.

66. James Baldwin, "Stranger in the Village," in *Notes of a Native Son* (1955; reprint, New York: Dial, 1963), 148.

67. Richard Wright, *Black Boy* (New York: Harper, 1945), 33.

68. Toni Morrison, "City Limits, Village Values: Concepts of the Neighborhood in Black Fiction," in *Literature and the Urban Experience*, ed. Michael C. Jaye and Ann Chalmers Watts (New Brunswick, N.J.: Rutgers University Press, 1981), 35.

69. Baldwin, "Stranger in the Village," 156–57.

70. Compare the advertisement from the confidence racket in part 1 of *Lawd Today!*—"I MAKE THE UNSEEN WORLD VISIBLE."—with Rinehart's "BEHOLD THE SEEN UNSEEN/BEHOLD THE INVISIBLE" in *Invisible Man*.

71. Susan Willis has written usefully on this subject in her *Specifying: Black Women Writing the American Experience* (Madison: University of Wisconsin Press, 1987); and also in "I Shop Therefore I Am: Is There a Place for Afro-American Culture in Commodity Culture?" in *Changing Our Own Words: Essays on Criticism, Theory, and Writing by Black Women*, ed. Cheryl A. Wall (New Brunswick, N.J.: Rutgers University Press, 1989), 173–95. Generally Willis is concerned with more recent material than I am; however, in "I Shop" she questions in a discussion of blues singers whether Afro-American culture is "somehow autonomous with respect to dominant mass culture" (238, n. 8). A distinction between "mass" and "popular" culture may be crucial here (for such a distinction see Klawans, "True Bloomism"). Most Afro-American music

should probably be classified "popular" rather that "mass" at least into the late 1950s, and though economic control of the cultural product might ultimately rest with the white-owned corporation, the musical production itself was often left largely to the black artist to aim at a black audience. There is an interesting discussion of this process by Robert Palmer in the catalog to the Muddy Waters "Chess Box" series of blues recordings in compact disc (Muddy Waters, *Muddy Waters*, Chess CHD3-80002), 14–25. Willis is certainly right in that the increasing monopoly and homogenization of mass culture since the 1960s has emphasized a cultural product both genderless (e.g., "unisex") and raceless (i.e., "white"); however, it seems that, for instance, the categories of the record "charts" still reflect class, racial, and generational divisions, and that some forms of "popular" regional or local culture have survived strongly. Arguably even some recent technological innovations now support this development of "pop" subcultures.

72. Wright, *Black Boy*, 33.

73. The theme of mass culture is not absent in the literature of the Harlem Renaissance, nor is it treated naively. Novels as different as Walter White's *Flight* (New York: Knopf, 1926), Wallace Thurman's *Blacker the Berry* (New York: Macaulay, 1929), Nella Larsen's *Quicksand* (New York: Knopf, 1928), and Fauset's *Plum Bun* all have shrewd things to say about the new commercial arrangements in the modern city; yet the significance of mass culture in these novels remains peripheral to other concerns. The character of Roger Fielding in *Plum Bun* is a good example of Fauset's contempt for the shallowness of mass culture—he looks "just like the men in the advertising pages of the Saturday evening Post" (149). His golden hair, blue car, and movie-star aura symbolize everything that is false and pretentious about New York. In Langston Hughes's *Not without Laughter* (1930; reprint, New York: Macmillan, 1969), the Golden Flyer sled that Sandy sees in a store window makes him devalue the "solid, home-made sled" (151) his mother has made for him at Christmas; yet by the end of the novel, it is those "home-made" values learned in a rural community in Kansas that will sustain Sandy as he comes of age in Chicago.

74. Kenneth Burke, *Language as Symbolic Action: Essays on Life, Literature, and Method* (Berkeley: University of California Press, 1966).

75. Ralph Ellison, "Hidden Name and Complex Fate," in *Shadow and Act* (New York: New American Library, 1966), 165–66. See especially Benedict Anderson, *Imagined Communities: Reflections on the Origin and Spread of Nationalism*, rev. ed. (London: Verso, 1991). Anderson discusses the idea of "piracy" of ideas once they reach the stage of print culture. On the French Revolution: "Once it had occurred, it entered the accumulating memory of print. The overwhelming and bewildering concatenation of events experienced by its makers and its victims became a 'thing,'—and with its own name: The French Revolution. Like a vast shapeless rock worn to a rounded boulder by countless drops of water, the experience was shaped by millions of printed words into a 'concept' on the printed page, and, in due course, into a model" (80). And that "concept" could be appropriated and reshaped by those—peasants, pariahs, natives—for whom it was never intended.

76. Jean Toomer, *Cane*, ed. Darwin T. Turner (1923; reprint, New York: Norton, 1988), 52; in this chapter, page numbers for subsequent citations of *Cane* are given in parentheses and refer to this edition.

Chapter Three. The City without Maps in Richard Wright's Native Son

1. James R. Grossman, *Land of Hope: Chicago, Black Southerners, and the Great Migration* (Chicago: University of Chicago Press, 1989), 81. The *Defender* was the largest black newspaper of the time, and during World War I it increased its circulation in the south from 50,000 (1916) to 125,000 (1918): "It was said that in Laurel, Mississippi, old men who did not know how to read would buy it because it was regarded as precious" (Emmett J. Scott, *Negro Migration during the War* [1920; reprint, New York: Arno, 1969], 30). It was "precious" because it was tangible proof of a black city existing somewhere in an unseen world. Moreover, it created an imagined community of readers held together by the printed word; see Benedict Anderson, *Imagined Communities: Reflections on the Origin and Spread of Nationalism*, rev. ed. (London: Verso, 1991), 25. For a concise and often amusing account of the black newspaper, see Eugene Gorden, "The Negro Press," *American Mercury* 8 (June 1926): 207–15. Gorden notes the existence of 220 black newspapers in 1926. Also see David Gordon Nielson, *Black Ethos: Northern Urban Negro Life and Thought, 1890–1930* (Westport, Conn.: Greenwood, 1977), 9–12, 18–20. The first full study of the black newspaper is Frederick D. Detweiler, *The Negro Press in the United States* (Chicago: University of Chicago Press, 1922). The migration to the city at the turn of the century roughly coincides with the founding dates of seven major black newspapers with close ties to metropolitan areas: the *New York Age* (1880) and the *Amsterdam News* (1909); the *Pittsburgh Courier* (1910); the *Philadelphia Tribune* (1885); the *Boston Guardian* (1902); the *Baltimore Afro-American* (1892); and the *Chicago Defender* (1905). The *Defender* is an interesting illustration of how a social movement like the Great Migration both created a newspaper and was in turn spurred on by it. For an illustration of the latter theme, see Langston Hughes, *Not without Laughter* (1930; reprint, New York: Macmillan, 1969), 191, 255–56. Set for the most part in rural Kansas, Hughes's novel shows the *Defender* to be an important link in a chain of circumstances that leads the major characters to Chicago.

2. Grossman, *Land of Hope*, 4.

3. Irving Howe, "Black Boys and Native Sons," in *Critical Essays on Richard Wright*, ed. Yoshinobu Hakutani (Boston: Hall, 1982), 41; first published in *Dissent*, 10 (Autumn 1963): 353–68.

4. Richard Wright, "Blueprint for Negro Writing" in *Richard Wright Reader*, ed. Ellen Wright and Michel Fabre (New York: Harper & Row, 1978), 44–45; first published in *New Challenge* 2 (Fall 1937): 53–65. The connection of the Harlem Renaissance to literary modernism is still an open question. Houston A. Baker, Jr., has argued that black writers from the turn of the century up through the 1920s worked out their own brand of modernism within the parameters of Afro-American culture; see his *Modernism and the Harlem Renais-*

sance (Chicago: University of Chicago Press, 1987). Arnold Rampersad has linked Langston Hughes with "populist" modernism, noting that reading Carl Sandburg freed the young poet "from the tyranny of traditional forms." Moreover, Hughes corresponded with Pound and was published in Harriet Monroe's *Poetry* magazine (Arnold Rampersad, *The Life of Langston Hughes* [New York: Oxford University Press, 1986], 1:29, 129, 237). During the writing of *Cane* (1923), Jean Toomer was part of a home-grown modernist group consisting of Waldo Frank, Sherwood Anderson, Hart Crane, Gorham Munson, and Kenneth Burke, although Toomer's "Kabnis" could be considered a rewriting of James Joyce's "The Dead" (or of *A Portrait of the Artist as a Young Man*). Similarly, Sterling Brown employed Eliot's "mythical method" in his poetry, as did Zora Neale Hurston in her most famous novel. (See Cyrena N. Pondrom, "The Role of Myth in Hurston's *Their Eyes Were Watching God*," *American Literature* 58 [1986]: 181–202). Yet no one in the Harlem Renaissance of the 1920s, with the possible exception of Toomer, immersed himself in modernism with quite the thoroughness that Wright did. For instance, Wright's *Lawd Today!* (New York: Walker, 1963), written in 1936 and published posthumously, was clearly a seminal black novel; its broken narrative and the text's weave of allusion to and quotation of both high and low culture, especially black street culture, was useful to Ralph Ellison, as was Wright's modernist allegory "The Man Who Lived Underground," in *Eight Men* (Cleveland: World, 1961). For an intelligent discussion of Wright as a modernist, see Craig Werner, "Bigger's Blues: *Native Son* and the Articulation of Afro-American Modernism," in *New Essays on "Native Son,"* ed. Keneth Kinnamon (Cambridge: Cambridge University Press, 1990), 117–52.

5. Wright, "Blueprint for Negro Writing," 48.

6. The phrase "divided stream," of course, comes from Charles Child Walcutt's classic study *American Literary Naturalism: A Divided Stream* (Minneapolis: University of Minnesota Press, 1956). Also see Eric J. Sundquist, ed., *American Realism: New Essays* (Baltimore: Johns Hopkins University Press, 1982), 3–24. Sundquist makes perceptive connections between realism and romance, "the gothic and naturalism" (13).

7. Bernard W. Bell, *The Afro-American Novel and Its Tradition* (Amherst: University of Massachusetts Press, 1987), 161. Influenced by Robert Scholes (see p. 284), Bell states that in *Native Son* "Wright's image of black character is consciously more mythic than mimetic" (161). It would be more accurate to say that the two modes—mimesis and myth—form a kind of dialectic interplay in the novel.

8. Richard Wright, "How 'Bigger' was Born," in *Twentieth Century Interpretations of "Native Son,"* ed. Houston A. Baker, Jr. (Englewood Cliffs, N.J.: Prentice-Hall, 1972), 39. The open space of the "wind-swept prairie" foreshadows LeRoi Jones's "horizon" in "Each Morning."

9. Carl Sandburg, *The Complete Poems of Carl Sandburg* (New York: Harcourt, Brace, 1970), 81.

10. Michel Fabre, *The World of Richard Wright* (Jackson: University of Mississippi Press, 1985), 21.

11. See Burton Pike, *The Image of the City in Modern Literature* (Princeton: Princeton University Press, 1981), 90–96

12. Quoted from Ellen Moers, *The Two Dreisers* (New York: Viking, 1969), 277.

13. Richard Wright, Introduction to *Black Metropolis*, by St. Clair Drake and Horace R. Cayton, 3d ed. (New York: Harcourt, Brace, 1970), xvii.

14. Richard Wright, *American Hunger* (New York: Harper & Row, 1977), 1.

15. Ibid., 63.

16. Michel Fabre, *The World of Richard Wright* (Jackson: University of Mississippi Press, 1985), 23. For an insightful treatment of Kenneth Burke's influence on Richard Wright's writings, see Eugene E. Miller, *Voice of A Native Son: The Poetics of Richard Wright* (Jackson: University of Mississippi Press, 1990), 174–211.

17. Kenneth Burke, *Permanence and Change: An Anatomy of Purpose* (1935; reprint, Los Altos, Calif: Hermes, 1954), 182–83.

18. Richard Wright, *Native Son* (New York: Harper, 1940), 204; in this chapter, unless otherwise noted, page numbers for subsequent citations of this work are given in parentheses and refer to this edition.

19. Mario Gandelsonas, *The Urban Text*, with essays by Joan Copjec, Catherine Ingraham, and John Whiteman (Cambridge: MIT Press, 1991), 23. Also see Joan Copjec, "The Grid and the Logic of Democracy," in Gandelsonas, *Urban Text*, 13. Thomas Jefferson's original proposal "called for the . . . extension of the chess-board divisions and subdivisions of Eastern cities over the Western territories." Also see John R. Stilgoe, *Common Landscape of America, 1580 to 1845* (New Haven: Yale University Press, 1982), 99–107. Congress severely qualified Jefferson's "model example of Enlightenment abstraction," but even their "compromise" recognized the value of the grid, as townships were mapped out in terms of "six statute miles square divided into thirty-six lots of 640 acres each" (103). According to Stilgoe, "by 1820 the grid concept was permanently established in the national imagination" (104).

20. Louis Wirth, "Urbanism as a Way of Life," in *Louis Wirth: On Cities and Social Life. Selected Papers*, ed. Albert J. Reiss, Jr. (Chicago: University of Chicago Press, 1964), 82. Wright specifically calls attention to Wirth's essay in his Introduction to Drake and Cayton, *Black Metropolis*, xx. Wright need not have gone to Wirth for this insight about metropolitan "communications"; in 1938 Wright could have found a similar observation about radios and newspapers in Lewis Mumford's *Culture of Cities* (New York: Harcourt, Brace, 1938), 256: "The swish and the crackle of paper is the underlying sound of the metropolis. . . . What is visible and real in this world is only what has been transferred to paper. The essential gossip of the metropolis is no longer that of people meeting face to face on the crossroads, at the dinner table, in the marketplace: a few dozen people writing in newspapers, a dozen more broadcasting over the radio, provide the daily interpretation of movements and happenings. . . . It is a short step from a yellow journal proprietor, skillfully manipulating the day's news, to a propaganda ministry in a war government or a fascist dictatorship."

21. H. L. Mencken, "The Ways of the Wicked," *American Mercury* 13 (March 1928): 381.

22. Fabre, *World of Richard Wright*, 14. In *American Hunger* Wright notes, "One afternoon [in Chicago, 1927], the boss lady entered the kitchen and found me sitting on a box reading a copy of the *American Mercury*" (15). And of course everyone by now knows of Wright's famous encounter with the writings of H. L. Mencken, which Wright described in *Black Boy* (New York: Harper, 1945).

23. As Keneth Kinnamon and Arnold Rampersad have recently shown, Wright was forced to write this scene as a replacement for one objected to by Edward Aswell, Harper's editor. See Keneth Kinnamon, Introduction to Kinnamon, ed., *New Essays on "Native Son,"* 12–14; *Richard Wright: Early Works*, ed. Arnold Rampersad (New York: Library of America, 1991), 912, 924. In the latter compilation, which includes the Library of America's new edition of *Native Son*, Rampersad includes the original scene (472–75). Although some of the revisions forced on Wright "diluted" (Kinnamon's word) the impact of *Native Son*, the scene at the Regal Theater he rewrote is actually better than the original. In the original scene, Bigger and Jack masturbate in the movie house, and then watch a newsreel in which Mary Dalton appears in a pseudo-documentary context that highlights the rich and famous: Mary, in her swimsuit, sports with Jan Erlone on Florida's beaches, while the newsreel's commentator alludes to her companion's politics and her father's chagrin. Wright was meticulously accurate when it came to the texture of realism—he wanted a detailed map of Chicago's "South Side" (see Kinnamon, ed., *New Essays on "Native Son,"* 28), and he corrected street names in "later printings" of *Native Son* (*Richard Wright: Early Works*, 913). What was to be gained by the unlikely coincidence of Bigger's seeing Mary in a newsreel that morning and meeting her in the Dalton home that afternoon? True, Wright obviously wanted to show the contrast between the newsreel's titillating portrait of the rich playgirl and the actual Mary, an irony nicely refined by the fact that Mary herself is acting out the script of Jan's left-wing ideology. Yet the same irony is secured, and even intensified, by substituting for the newsreel the generic film *The Gay Woman*. This substitution, as I shall show, gives Wright the opportunity to examine, through the movie's plot, the ways in which mass culture manipulates its audience, never taking into account how someone like Bigger "reads" its fictions. Wright, of course, invented *The Gay Woman*—there is no such movie—but its composite plot points to several film genres of the 1920s and 30s. The early melodramas of Cecil B. De Mille could have provided a model. See Lary May, *Screening Out the Past: The Birth of Mass Culture and the Motion Picture Industry* (New York: Oxford University Press, 1980), 209. Wright perhaps borrowed the name from the Fred Astaire–Ginger Rogers musical *The Gay Divorcee* (1934), the general ambience of luxury from a number of screwball comedies dealing with divorce and remarriage (e.g., *The Awful Truth* [1937]), and the right-wing motif from a gangster movie such as *G-Men* (1935).

24. There was, of course, an attempt to regulate how Hollywood promoted this desire. The Hays code, which came into force in 1934, was very specific about what forms sexuality might take in the movies, and its norms were carefully monitored by Joseph Breen and his spies (see Gerald Gardner, *The Censorship Papers: Movie Censorship Letters from the Hays Office, 1934 to 1968* [New York: Dodd, Mead, 1987], xv–xxiv, 207–14). Before 1934 a previous Hollywood code (1927) had been in effect, but although it, too, insisted on sexual "good taste," its cursory list of "don'ts" and "be carefuls" was often ignored. After Breen began managing the Hays Office, however, self-censorship (as well as subtle evasions of the code) became a way of life for Hollywood film makers. The 1927 code condemned the cinematic depiction of miscegenation, but racial mixing went unmentioned in the 1934 code (in keeping with the Hays Office's "progressive" attitudes toward ethnic groups and minorities). Nevertheless miscegenation, as we know, remained an invisible taboo in Hollywood. One form of desire the code wouldn't restrain, of course, was the desire for consumption; in fact, it modestly claimed to promote it. As Hays said, "More and more is the motion picture being recognized as a stimulant to trade" (May, *Screening Out the Past*, 236).

25. Kevin Lynch, "Reconsidering the Image of the City," in *Cities of the Mind: Images and Themes of the City in the Social Sciences*, ed. Lloyd Rodwin and Robert M. Hollister (New York: Plenum, 1984), 152, 155. Lynch's famous book on this theme is *The Image of the City* (Cambridge: MIT Press, 1960).

26. Wright, "How 'Bigger' Was Born," 29; idem, *Native Son*, 204. As he was writing *Native Son* in 1938, Wright used *Chicago Tribune* accounts of a murder trial involving two black youths, Robert Nixon and Earl Hicks, to show how the media shaped the circumstances surrounding Bigger's trial. See Keneth Kinnamon, *The Emergence of Richard Wright: A Study in Literature and Society* (Urbana: University of Illinois Press, 1972), 121–25. Also see Margaret Walker, *Richard Wright: Daemonic Genius* (New York: Warner, 1988), 122–25.

27. Wright, "How 'Bigger' Was Born," 37–38.

28. Ralph Ellison, *Shadow and Act* (New York: New American Library, 1966), 121–22: "Wright could imagine Bigger, but Bigger could not possibly imagine Richard Wright."

29. George Steiner, *Tolstoy or Dostoevsky: An Essay in the Old Criticism* (New York: Random House, 1961), 195–96.

30. Wright, "How 'Bigger' Was Born," 47.

31. In Poe's story, the ambiguous pronoun *er* ("er lasst sich nicht lesen"—it [or he] does not permit itself [or himself] to be read") applies to both the city and to the old roué whom the narrator follows in an attempt to discover who and what he is. See Edgar Allan Poe, "The Man of the Crowd," in *The Norton Anthology of American Literature*, ed. Nina Baym et al., 3d ed. (New York: Norton, 1989), 1412; hereafter this volume is cited as *Norton*.

32. Kenneth Burke, *The Philosophy of Literary Form: Studies in Symbolic Action*, 2d ed. (Baton Rouge: Louisiana State University Press, 1967), xxi–xxii.

33. Mumford, *Culture of Cities*, 403.

34. See in particular Levine's account of the history of the Chicago Symphony Orchestra and the Chicago Public Library; what began as democratic expressions of culture soon hardened into exclusive institutions controlled by wealthy patrons and/or patrician attitudes. (Lawrence Levine, *Highbrow/Lowbrow: The Emergence of Cultural Hierarchy in America* [Cambridge: Harvard University Press, 1988], 115–99, 128, 130, 159, 160).

35. See Burton Pike, *The Image of the City in Modern Literature* (Princeton: Princeton University Press, 1980), 28–30.

36. Joan E. Draper, "Paris by the Lake: Sources of Burnham's Plans of Chicago," in *Chicago Architecture, 1872–1922: Birth of a Metropolis*, ed. John Zukowsky (Munich: Prestel-Verlag, 1987), 107–19.

37. John W. Stamper, *Chicago's North Michigan Avenue: Planning and Development, 1900–1930* (Chicago: University of Chicago Press, 1991), 74, 69. For the design of the tower as a Doric column, see Zukowsky, ed., *Chicago Architecture*, 302. The design chosen was one submitted by John Mead Howells and Raymond Hood, "based on a thorough study of the formal features of a Gothic Tower." Howells gave the project added luster, because he was the son of William Dean Howells, novelist and "former editor of the *Atlantic Monthly*" (Stamper, *North Michigan Avenue*, 70, 74). Thus an aura of sanctimoniousness surrounded the tower's planning and construction, which was perhaps a reason for Lewis Mumford's 1931 complaint that the tower illustrated the "fake religion of business" (Lewis Mumford, *Brown Decades: A Study of the Arts in America, 1865–1895* [New York: Harcourt, Brace, 1931], 140).

In 1919 William Wrigley, Jr., the chewing-gum magnate, hired the firm of Graham, Anderson, Probst, and White to design a plan for the Wrigley Building (completed in 1922), which they modeled after the Giralda Tower of Seville, a cathedral erected at the height of the Spanish Renaissance (Stamper, *North Michigan Avenue*, 32, 40). These twin monuments on North Michigan Avenue were to inspire the citizenry to keep the barbarians outside the gates of the essential city.

In 1934 the *Tribune* built a Gothic-style annex north of the Tribune Tower to house WGN, its radio station, making its "guardianship" complete in terms of media control of the city. The *Tribune's* ownership of WGN did not escape Wright's notice in *Lawd Today!* Wright opens his novel with this radio station's slick, patriotic celebration of Lincoln's birthday. It is worth noting that the only radio station Wright allows Jake to hear in *Lawd Today!* is WGN, just as the only newspaper that exists in *Native Son* is the *Tribune*. Wright's insights about media "guardianship" are similar to the Frankfurt School's and look forward to Fredric Jameson, who has discussed in our own day the omnipresent pervasiveness of mass media as one manifestation of "late capitalism." For a good discussion of this last theme, see David S. Gross, "Marxism and Resistance: Fredric Jameson and the Moment of Postmodernism, " *Canadian Journal of Political and Social Theory* 12, no. 3 (1988): 71–85.

38. Sam Warner, Jr., "Slums and Skyscrapers: Urban Images, Symbols, and Ideology," in Rodwin and Hollister, ed., *Cities of the Mind*, 187–89.

39. David Harvey, *Social Justice and the City* (Baltimore: Johns Hopkins University Press, 1973), 168.

40. Alan Trachtenberg, *The Incorporation of America: Culture and Society in the Gilded Age* (New York: Hill & Wang, 1982), 83.

41. *Louis Wirth*, 72. Following the Apostle Paul, Josiah Royce argues that the Beloved Community grounds itself in the paradoxical notion of a spiritual "body": "This new being is a corporate entity,—the body of Christ, or the body of which the divinely exalted Christ is the head. Of this body the exalted Christ is also, for Paul, the spirit and also, in some new sense, the lover. This corporate entity is the Christian community itself" (Josiah Royce, *The Problem of Christianity*, [New York: Macmillan, 1913] 1:92).

42. The figure of Bessie and her fate in the novel have led some critics to accuse Wright of being indifferent or actively hostile to his female characters. See Trudier Harris, "Native Sons and Foreign Daughters," in Kinnamon, ed., *New Essays on "Native Son,"* 63–84; Houston A. Baker, Jr., "Richard Wright and the Dynamics of Place in Afro-American Literature," in ibid., 108–13. To accuse Wright of misogyny—as Harris does—because of his representation of Bessie is to simplistically conflate author and character. Bigger's murder of Bessie is Wright's comment on the impotence of his character's illusion of power. It is an act of an existentially "free" man; and that is the act's ultimate horror (as Wright would have known, if only from reading *Crime and Punishment*). To wish that Bessie were depicted as an empowered black woman, or as a woman connected to a vital black community, is to ignore Wright's judgment about the effects of a racist social structure on relations between Afro-American women and men. Baker contends that Wright's Marxist frame of reference forces him to devalue Bessie (and black women in folk culture), yet Baker admits that Bessie "possesses the most lucid vision in *Native Son*" (110), is Bigger's most perceptive critic, and embodies the blues tradition in the novel. One could quarrel with Baker's interpretation of Marx, or indeed with his interpretation of the "Marxist" author of *Native Son*, yet the real issue here is Bessie. The question Baker never answers is, why such profound sympathy for and understanding of Bessie if Wright cannot find any "intellectual space" for her? One explanation is that it is Bigger, not Wright, who is incapable of sympathy and understanding. Three times in *Native Son* Wright mentions the "narrow orbit" of Bessie's life—her exhaustion, fear, loneliness, and desire to escape via intense pleasure—and these always occur in the context of Bigger's response to her. Bigger *knows* her life, but that knowledge does not lead to pity; rather, in their first long meeting after Mary's murder, he sees Bessie's vulnerability as something he can use to control her. Later, forced to flee with Bigger from her apartment, Bessie repeats again the details of her painful life and his dishonesty, but Bigger's only response is to see "what he must do to save himself" (195): he decides to murder her. Finally, at the inquest, when they bring out her mutilated body to prove him a monster, Bigger does have a different comprehension of her life—he sees that even in death she is still owned by her white employers. Yet this is as far as Bigger's compassion and

understanding go; it is Wright, not Bigger, who makes us *see* that Bigger has abused Bessie in the same way that white society has abused Bigger. This is Wright's true Marxist perspective, the knowledge that oppression creates endless circles of cruelty among the oppressed. And although Bessie is indeed the bearer of a blues tradition (was she named after Bessie Smith, who had died in 1937, mutilated in a traffic accident and reportedly denied access to a white hospital?), in Wright's view that tradition by itself is helpless to change the conditions of black life. An expanded version of Baker's essay on Wright appears in Houston A. Baker, Jr., *Workings of the Spirit: The Poetics of Afro-American Women's Writing* (Chicago: University of Chicago Press, 1991), 102–33.

43. Burke, *Permanence and Change*, 49, 14–16.

44. Mumford, *Culture of Cities*, 406.

45. Eugenio Donato, "The Museum's Furnace: Notes toward a Contextual Reading of *Bonvard and Pécuchet*," in *Textual Strategies: Perspectives in Post-Structural Criticism*, ed. Josué V. Harari (Ithaca, N.Y.: Cornell University Press, 1979), 221, 234; see Donato's discussion of "archēs" on 220.

46. Ibid., 234–35. Also see Marshall Berman, *All That Is Solid Melts into Air: The Experience of Modernity* (1982; reprint, New York: Penguin, 1988), 15–36.

47. Lewis Mumford, "Origins of the American Mind," *American Mercury* 8 (July 1926): 354. This article later appeared in a revised form as the first chapter of Mumford's *Golden Day* (1926). Wright here also deromanticizes Frederick Jackson Turner's frontier thesis, and Locke's application of that thesis to the city in *The New Negro*. See Paul Kellogg, "The Negro Pioneers," in *The New Negro*, ed. Alain Locke (1925; reprint, New York: Atheneum, 1969), 271–77. The Mumford-Wright view of the westward expansion has now become the accepted historical paradigm.

48. T. S. Eliot, *The Waste Land*, lines 60–75, in *The Complete Poems and Plays, 1909–1950* (New York: Harcourt, Brace & World, 1952), 39.

49. These are Louis Sullivan's words, which Mumford quotes with approval (Mumford, *Brown Decades*, 157, 158).

50. See Eric Auerbach, *Scenes from the Drama of European Literature* (New York: Meridian, 1959), 45: "The notion of the *figura* under which something other, future, true, lies concealed."

51. Wright carefully worked out his geography in this scene. A 1933 map of Chicago locates the Cook County Criminal Court Building and Jail between Twenty-sixth and Thirty-first streets (north/south), and between California and Sacramento boulevards (east/west), that is, within easy visual distance, on a clear day, of the tops of buildings such as the Tribune Tower and the Wrigley Building.

52. See Ezek. 40–48; Rev. 20–21; John Milton, *Paradise Lost*, 12, lines 549–51; *Aeneid*, 6, lines 752–95.

53. Maynard Mack, *The Garden and the City: Retirement and Politics in the Later Poetry of Pope* (Toronto: University of Toronto Press, 1969), 3.

54. Wright, *Black Boy*, 33.

55. See, for instance, Robert B. Stepto, "I Thought I Knew These People: Richard Wright and the Afro-American Literary Tradition," in *Chant of Saints:*

A Gathering of Afro-American Literature, Art, and Scholarship, ed. Michael S. Harper and Robert B. Stepto (Urbana: University of Illinois Press, 1979), 195–211.

56. The Van Wyck Brooks epigraph for the first part of *Lawd Today!*— "Commonplace"—illustrates a theme explored by Brooks in *America's Coming-of-Age:* the assertion that in America there is no "common life," only "a vast Sargasso Sea—a prodigious welter of unconscious life, swept by ground-swells of half-conscious emotion" (Claire Sprague, ed., *Van Wyck Brooks: The Early Years* [New York: Harper & Row, 1968], 149. Brooks's next sentence, which Wright does not quote, is even more appropriate to the sterile urban landscape of *Lawd Today!:* "All manner of living things are drifting in it, phosphorescent, gayly colored, gathered into knots and clotted masses, gelatinous, unformed, flimsy, tangled, rising and falling, floating and merging, here an immense distended belly, there a tiny rudimentary brain (the gross devouring the fine)—everywhere an unchecked, uncharted, unorganized vitality like that of the first chaos. It is a welter of life which has not been worked into an organism" (149–50). The quotation from Frank that Wright uses for the novel's second section—"Squirrel Cage"—contains an idea common to Brooks, Bourne, Frank, and Mumford: without the Beloved Community there is no personal growth, no organic wholeness.

57. Ralph Waldo Emerson, "Self-Reliance," in *Norton,* 965.

58. Burke, *Permanence and Change,* 74.

59. Michel Fabre, *The Unfinished Quest of Richard Wright,* trans., Isabel Barzun (New York: Morrow, 1973), 200. Also see Walker, *Richard Wright,* 220–21; Walker notes that "Edward G. Robinson . . . and Jimmy Cagney films" were among his favorites. Two Edward G. Robinson films—*Double Indemnity* (1944) and *The Woman in the Window* (1944)—influenced the writing of Wright's *Savage Holiday* (New York: Avon, 1954).

60. See Gardner, *Censorship Papers,* 207–14. For a penetrating analysis of the implications of the Hays code, see Richard Maltby, *Harmless Entertainment: Hollywood and the Ideology of Consensus* (Metuchen, N.J.: Scarecrow, 1983), chap. 4.

61. Jerry Connolly, the Irish priest in the movie, uses basketball, as Mr. Dalton does ping-pong, to keep potential troublemakers in the city off the streets. And in both *Native Son* and *Angels,* the ubiquitous newspaper paradoxically indicts and validates the existence of the protagonists. Finally, in the movie there is a chase scene across the rooftops of the city which mirrors the conclusion of the second book of *Native Son.* However, the real parallel between movie and novel lies elsewhere. In the endings of movie and novel, Rocky Sullivan and Bigger Thomas are faced with the electric chair, and each is provided with a guardian angel who offers him an alternative to damnation.

62. He also lies. He tells the boys they should all pray for "a boy who could not run as fast as I could." In truth, it was Rocky who was the faster runner: in an early scene, with the police on their trail, Rocky returns to help a slower Connolly, and this act of friendship lands him in reform school.

63. There is possibly an additional irony here. Gerald Gardner points out that a "Jesuit priest" had actually written the Hays code, and that Joseph Breen, the head of the Hays Office, was a "catholic journalist." Moreover, the Legion of Decency, created by a group of Catholic bishops, was a major factor in forcing Hollywood to regulate itself (Gardner, *Censorship Papers*, xvi, xviii, xix). If Curtiz did indeed satirize Connolly, he may have had a larger target in mind than one power-mad priest.

64. Bigger's emotions when he kills Mary are complicated, even contradictory—fear, sexual desire, and rage—and thus, to a degree, we are capable of feeling sympathy for him; but his gratuitous murder of Bessie removes that sympathy and makes us look upon him with fascination and horror, much as Max does at the end of the novel. One could argue that his relationship to Mary reflects both his fear of and his attraction to white culture, but he doesn't fear Bessie, and he is attracted to her only as a sexual object. Wright's point is that racism creates self-contempt, which is then transferred to others as powerless as oneself.

65. Joyce Ann Joyce, in her *Richard Wright's Art of Tragedy* (Iowa City: Iowa University Press, 1986), places Bigger within a context of Aristotelian tragedy, and yet by denying Max a significant part of the tragic action, she actually reduces Bigger's significance as a tragic hero. For Joyce, Max is shallow, "self-serving," and in the long run not much better than State's Attorney Buckley (103–4, 113–16). Yet to be a tragic hero, Bigger needs a real antagonist; and Max, as the voice of the invisible city, plays that role.

66. Mumford's "Origins of the American Mind," 354.

67. Compare James Baldwin's observation in *The Fire Next Time* (New York: Dial, 1963), 54–55: "In the same way that we, for white people, were the descendants of Ham, and were cursed forever, white people were, for us, the descendants of Cain."

68. Compare Martin Heidegger's observation in *Poetry, Language, Thought*, trans. A. Hofstadter (New York: Harper & Row, 1975), 147, that the German word *bauen* (to build) "originally means to dwell," and that this word has the same root as the German *ich bin* (I am). Heidegger not only sees a connection between *being*, *building*, and *dwelling*, but also between *bauen* and civilization: "this word *bauen* however *also* means to cultivate the vine." Denied a place within Western culture, Bigger's felt existence lies outside buildings that define someone else's "being."

Chapter Four. The Ever-Emerging City in Ralph Ellison's Invisible Man

1. Richard Wright, "Review: *Wars I Have Seen*," in *The Richard Wright Reader*, ed. Ellen Wright and Michel Fabre (New York: Harper & Row, 1978), 76; the review was first published in *P.M. Magazine*, March 11, 1945.

2. Richard Wright's "Blueprint for Negro Writing," in *Richard Wright Reader*, 40. For a useful discussion of Wright's complex attitudes toward black folk culture, see Günter H. Lenz, "Southern Exposures: The Urban Experience and the Re-Construction of Black Folk Culture and Community in the Works of

Richard Wright and Zora Neale Hurston," in *History and Tradition in Afro-American Culture*, ed. Günter H. Lenz (Frankfurt: Campus Verlag, 1984), 84–115.

3. Ralph Ellison, "The Little Man at Chehaw Station," *American Scholar* 47 (Winter 1977–78): 28; reprinted in Ralph Ellison's *Going to the Territory* (New York: Random House, 1986), 3–38.

4. Ralph Ellison, *Invisible Man* (New York: Random House, 1952), 438; in this chapter, page numbers for subsequent citations of this work are given in parentheses and refer to this edition.

5. Ellison has described his ongoing encounter with Emerson in "Hidden Name and Complex Fate," in *Shadow and Act* (New York: New American Library, 1966), 148–68. For an intelligent discussion of Ellison and Emerson, see Alan Nadal, *Invisible Criticism: Ralph Ellison and the American Canon* (Iowa City: University of Iowa Press, 1988), 113–23.

6. Marcus Klein, *After Alienation* (Cleveland: World, 1964), 145. Klein has questioned whether the invisible man has earned the right to leave his hole, because the novel's episodes "confirm again and again that the hero doesn't exist," and if he has no identity above ground, his ascent makes no sense. The question of the invisible man's identity, however, is not a final and finished matter, as Klein's definition would suggest.

7. There has never been any secret about Burke's influence on Ellison, and one critic in particular is quite perceptive: see John M. Reilly, "The Testament of Ralph Ellison," *Speaking for You: The Vision of Ralph Ellison*, ed. Kimberly W. Benston (Washington, D.C.: Howard University Press, 1987), 59–60. Also see index, in ibid.

8. Kenneth Burke, *A Grammar of Motives* (1945; reprint, Berkeley: University of California Press, 1969), 219.

9. Ellison, "Little Man at Chehaw Station," 35.

10. Burke, *Grammar of Motives*, 143.

11. I owe this observation to Alan Nadel, who in *Invisible Criticism* perceptively notes that "the invisible man has . . . more identities than Rinehart in that he can be everything Rinehart is and he can also not-be Rinehart" (21).

12. Burke, *Grammar of Motives*, 295.

13. A key essay on the theme of running in the novel is Phyllis R. Klotman, *Another Man Gone: The Black Runner in Contemporary Afro-American Literature* (Port Washington, N.Y.: Kennikat, 1977), 71–84.

14. Kenneth Burke, *Language as Symbolic Action: Essays on Life, Literature, and Method* (Berkeley: University of California Press, 1966), 438.

15. Ellison, "Little Man at Chehaw Station," 35–36; Ralph Waldo Emerson, "Self-Reliance," in *The Norton Anthology of American Literature*, ed. Nina Baym et al., 3d ed. (New York: Norton, 1989), 965; hereafter this volume is cited as *Norton*.

16. Ellison, "Little Man at Chehaw Station," 35.

17. Ibid.

18. Kenneth Burke, *The Rhetoric of Religion: Studies in Logology* (Boston: Beacon, 1961), 246; Eric Auerbach, "Figura," in *Scenes from the Drama of European Literature* (New York: Meridian, 1959), 72. Hortense Spillers, in her excellent

essay "Ellison's 'Usable Past': Toward a Theory of Myth," in Benston, ed., *Speaking for You*, 153–54, briefly mentions Auerbach's theory of the figura. My emphasis is quite different from hers.

19. Fredric Jameson, *Marxism and Form: Twentieth-Century Dialectical Theories of Literature* (Princeton: Princeton University Press, 1972), 142.

20. Ibid., 111.

21. Kenneth Burke, *Attitudes toward History* (1937; reprint, Berkeley: University of California Press, 1984), 225.

22. Typically of Ellison, we are never quite sure where the "battle royal" takes place or where in the south the college is located. In a local tavern, the Golden Day, a patron observes that the invisible man "was made of the very mud of the region" (73), which would place him in Alabama *if* the college is Tuskegee, but Ellison keeps us off-balance even here. Ellison both historicizes and dehistoricizes the college, just as the journey of his protagonist mirrors both history and myth.

23. Barbara Ehrenreich and Deirdre English, *For Her Own Good: 150 Years of the Experts' Advice to Women* (New York: Doubleday, 1978), 127–64. Following Frederick Taylor, "domestic science" spokeswomen Christine Frederick and Ellen Richards encouraged women to be efficiency experts in the home. Taylor wanted to impose the division of labor in the factory because he equated control with efficiency, but of course in the home the housewife, while ostensibly an overseer, became a slave to "scientific" housekeeping.

24. For an excellent treatment of the mercantile theme in this episode, see Houston A. Baker, Jr., "To Move without Moving: An Analysis of Creativity and Commerce in Ralph Ellison's Trueblood Episode," *PMLA* 98 (October 1983): 828–45; reprinted in Benston, ed., *Speaking for You*, 332-48.

25. See Harry Levin, "The Golden Age," in *The Pastoral Mode*, ed. Bryan Loughrey (London: Macmillan, 1984), 120. Nadel, in *Invisible Criticism*, notes that Ellison alludes to Lewis Mumford's *The Golden Day* (New York: Liveright, 1926) in this episode, satirizing Mumford's portrayal of 1830–60 as "a whitewashing of American history" (94). Mumford's book is hardly that, and Nadel greatly oversimplifies it, especially in his interpretation of Mumford's treatment of this period as one of "harmony and optimism" (98). Here is Mumford, in *Golden Day*, 86: "In general, all the forces that blighted America after the Civil War existed in embryonic form between 1830 and 1860." Nadel's view is that Mumford ignored the great issue of slavery when he discussed the writers of "the Golden Day," and that Ellison believed that the issue of slavery *was* central to Thoreau, Emerson, Whitman, and especially Melville. Hence Ellison's calling the bar/bordello by the title of Mumford's book is another reminder of the Negro's invisibility. But, Mumford may actually be closer to Ellison's point of view than Nadel realizes: "The blight of Negro slavery awakened his [Emerson's] honest anger . . . but even this great issue did not cause him to lose his perspective: he sought to abolish the white slaves who maintained that institution" (Mumford, *Golden Day*, 101). Mumford refers to this as Emerson's "Platonism," a kind of first-things-first attitude that the invisible man arrives at when he associates his grandfather's "yes" with "the principle." In-

spired by his friend Van Wyck Brooks, Mumford saw 1830–60 as a potential source of a "usable past" within America's steady march toward materialism. This past was not to be sentimentalized—indeed, Emerson had warned against sentimentalizing any past—but it did contain within it an invisible city of energy and community. This urban motif would be present in almost all the later writings of Mumford, who would become our foremost urban historian, but it forms a pattern in his seminal books of the 1920s, beginning with *The Story of Utopias* (New York: Boni & Liveright, 1922) and ending with *The Brown Decades* (New York: Harcourt, Brace, 1931). In the latter, Mumford would study the buried "arts" of the post–Civil War period with a similar aim of rescuing a "usable past" to recreate the lost American city on a hill. Thus Ellison's allusion to the "Golden Day" may itself be a figura insofar as the episode in the bar pushes the invisible man toward a genuine utopian vision.

26. Mikhail M. Bakhtin, *The Dialogic Imagination*, trans. Caryl Emerson and Michael Holquist (Austin: University of Texas Press, 1981), 16–17, 35.

27. For another interpretation of Bakhtin and *Invisible Man*, see Henry Louis Gates, Jr., *Figures in Black: Words, Signs, and the "Racial" Self* (New York: Oxford University Press, 1987), 247–48.

28. This is Leon Forrest's excellent insight in "Luminosity from the Lower Frequencies," in Benston, ed., *Speaking for You*, 311. Also see Nadel, *Invisible Criticism*, for a perceptive discussion of Whitman and Barbee.

29. Ellison's conception of the invisible city is similar to Mumford's critique of utopia and utopian literature. "A Map of the World that does not include Utopia," Mumford says on the title page to his *Story of Utopias*, "is not worth even glancing at." And yet the only "practical use" of utopias is that "they cannot be achieved" (Lewis Mumford, *Findings and Keepings: Analects for an Autobiography* [New York: Harcourt, Brace, 1975], 352). Utopian concepts are important because they give human endeavor a sense of purpose, but their mistake is to try to arrest the necessary flux of quotidian reality: "Utopias rest on the fallacy that perfection is a legitimate goal of human existence." Significantly, Mumford says, "The first utopia was the city itself" (Lewis Mumford, *Interpretations and Forecasts, 1922–1972* [New York: Harcourt, Brace, 1973], 241). Mumford explored these ideas as early as *Story of Utopias* (1922).

30. With the word *spook*, Ellison brings together various bits of American folklore, ancient and modern, linking the racial slur with the old racist joke of the "nigger in the woodpile" and with the more recent caricature of the Afro-American who has seen a ghost in an Abbott and Costello movie. Curiously, the racial slur works two ways, indicating that other Americans think of the Afro-American as both more and less than human. Contemptuous of his cowardice, they turn him into a clown, but wary of his cunning and ubiquitous presence, they invest him with magical powers. Moreover, the second sentence of *Invisible Man* begins with a double negative, "no, I am not a spook," which leaves the statement ambiguous: is he or isn't he? One might say that this ambiguous negative also applies to the novel's epigraph from Melville's *Benito Cereno*: "You are saved: what has cast such a *shadow* upon you?" (my italics). The answer, not mentioned in the epigraph, is "the negro," who is

literally "not there." Although this answer points to the dark side of the Gothic tale—Cereno's "memory" will not let him forget that "shadow"—it also points to the moral ambiguity of the slave insurrection and Cereno's own complicity in the corporate capitalism of the slave trade. In this sense, "the negro" is not the "shadow" but a hint of something other: humanity revolting against the "shadow." Melville's "Power of Blackness" becomes in Ellison's prologue the Negro preacher's "black is . . . an' black ain't," an "essence" that fades in and out of focus, always hinting at a reality "not there." Note how the epigraph from *Benito Cereno* parallels in this respect the complementary epigraph from Eliot's *Family Reunion* "I tell you, it is *not* me you are looking at" (my italics).

31. Ralph Waldo Emerson, "Experience," in *Norton*, 1008.

32. Improvisation is a theme that runs throughout Ellison's interviews and essays. See, e.g., Hollie West, "Travels with Ralph Ellison through Time and Thought," in Benston, ed., *Speaking For You*, 41; Ralph Ellison's review of *Blues People*, by LeRoi Jones, in *Shadow and Act*, 241–50. *Improvisation* is a word that occurs to Ellison often because of his interest in music, especially jazz, the supreme Afro-American *urban* modernist music. Following Claude Levi-Strauss, critics have sometimes used the word *bricolage* to talk about Ellison's literary method.

33. A. Barlett Giamatti, "Proteus Unbound," in *The Disciplines of Criticism: Essays in Literary Theory, Interpretation, and History*, ed. Peter Demetz, Thomas Greene, and Lowry Nelson, Jr. (New Haven: Yale University Press, 1968), 439.

34. Burke, *Attitudes toward History*, 225.

35. Michael Cowan has investigated the urban motif in Emerson with great perspicuity; see his *City of the West: Emerson, America, and Urban Metaphor* (New Haven: Yale University Press, 1967).

36. Emerson, "Experience," 1009.

37. John Cawelti, *Six-Gun Mystique*, 2d ed. (Bowling Green, Ohio: Bowling Green State University Press, 1980), 65, 66.

38. Peter, of course, is based on a real blues singer by the name of Peetie Wheatstraw.

39. Edmund Leach, "Anthropological Aspects of Language: Animal Categories and Verbal Abuse," in *New Directions in the Study of Language*, ed. Eric H. Lenneberg (Cambridge: MIT Press, 1964), 27, 52, 57.

40. Roger Abrahams notes another version of the "dog" in Afro-American culture. A favorite complaint of black women about black men is that they "have a little bit of dog in them, you know," suggesting, perhaps, a double perspective: the "dog" in black men means that they are morally unreliable *and* sexually dangerous (because sexually potent). See Roger Abrahams, "Negotiating Respect: Patterns of Presentation among Black Women," in *Women and Folklore*, ed. Claire Farrer (1975; reprint, Prospect Heights, Ill.: Waveland, 1986), 66.

41. Barbara Babcock-Abrahams, "Why Frogs Are Good to Think and Dirt Is Good to Reflect On," *Soundings* 58 (Summer 1975): 176.

42. Ezra Pound, "Briefer Mention," *Dial* 70 (January 1921), 110.

43. Walter Benjamin, *Illuminations*, trans. Harry Zohn (New York: Schocken, 1969), esp. 89, 158–89.

44. Ellison has referred to Eliot's influence in *Shadow and Act* and elsewhere, but for a specific statement of his interest in Eliot, see Richard Kostelanetz, "An Interview with Ralph Ellison," *Iowa Review* 19 (Fall 1989): 3: "I became very much involved with modern letters after I read *The Waste Land*. I was so intrigued that I started reading all the commentaries I could find. . . . I read a lot of Pound and Eliot essays."

45. In Burke's terms, the storyteller puts a "comic frame" around Ras, one that serves as—again, the phrase is Burke's—an "exorcism by misnomer" (Kenneth Burke, *Permanence and Change: An Anatomy of Purpose* [1935; reprint, Los Altos, Calif.: Hermes, 1954], 133). The original title of *The Waste Land* is given in Lyndall Gordon, "*The Waste Land* Manuscript," in *Critical Essays on T. S. Eliot's "The Waste Land,"* ed. Lois A. Cuddy and David H. Hirsch (Boston: Hall, 1991), 176–87.

46. Ralph Ellison, "Harlem is Nowhere," in *Shadow and Act*, 284.

47. Ralph Ellison and James Alan McPherson, "Indivisible Man," *Atlantic Monthly* 226 (December 1970): 51.

48. Theodor Haecker, *Virgil, Father of the West*, trans., A. W. Wheen (London: Sheen & Ward, 1934), 76.

49. Brooks Otis, *Virgil: A Study in Civilized Poetry* (Oxford: Clarendon, 1963), 232.

50. See *Aeneid*, bk. 6, lines 14–33.

51. Ralph Ellison, "Society, Morality, and the Novel," in *The Living Novel: A Symposium,* ed. Granville Hicks, (New York: Macmillan, 1957), 64, 61; reprinted in Ellison, *Going to the Territory*, 239–74.

52. Raglan's *The Hero* is an anthropological study of myth, history, and literature, which bears a relationship to *Invisible Man* like that of Jessie Weston's *From Ritual to Romance* to *The Waste Land*.

53. See Ralph Ellison, "That Same Pain, That Same Pleasure: An Interview," in *Shadow and Act*, 37.

54. Kenneth Burke, *The Philosophy of Literary Form: Studies in Symbolic Action,* 2d ed. (reprint, Baton Rouge: Louisiana State University Press, 1967), 412; the first edition was published in 1941.

55. Lord Raglan, *The Hero: A Study in Tradition, Myth, and Drama* (1937; reprint, Westport, Conn.: Greenwood, 1975), esp. 189.

56. For an especially interesting discussion of the democratic implications of the interplay between "I" and "you" in *Invisible Man*, see John F. Callahan, *In the African-American Grain: The Pursuit of Voice in Twentieth-Century Black Fiction* (Urbana: University of Illinois Press, 1988), 150-88.

57. Emerson, "Experience," 1003.

58. Ralph Ellison, "Remembering Richard Wright," in Benston, ed., *Speaking for You*, 187; also reprinted in Ellison, *Going to the Territory*, 198–216.

59. A theme that runs throughout Burke's writings. See Burke, *Attitudes toward History*, 364–65; idem, *Language as Symbolic Action*, 187; idem, *A Rhetoric of Motives* (1948; reprint, Berkeley: University of California Press, 1969), 301.

60. Throughout the novel, Ellison has continually alluded to Jack the Bear from black folklore, even having Peter complain that Harlem was a "bear's den" and that a bear had been "clawing at [his] behind" (132–33). Floyd Horowitz, "Ralph Ellison's Modern Version of Brer Bear and Brer Rabbit in *Invisible Man*," *Midcontinent American Studies Journal* 4 (Fall 1963): 21–27, would have us believe that this bear from the Brer Rabbit tales is the only bear Ellison knew, that the purpose of the narrator as bear is to be "tricked" over and over again (a variation on Klein's thesis that he had best remain in a state of hibernation). But Ellison would also have known about bears from southwestern folklore, and the images in these legends range from the burlesque to the sublime. Indeed, the "she-bear," because she descends to the underground or to a cave to give birth to new life, is "seen by traditional peoples as a guide to the movement between worlds" (Paul Shepard and Barry Sanders, *The Sacred Paw: The Bear in Nature, Myth, and Literature* [New York: Viking, 1985], xviii). And although American Indian cultures are divided in their opinions on the bear—as a symbolic figure, the bear is a restorer of health for the Zuni, but for the Navaho it is both a healer and a harbinger of illness and bad luck—it is a figure of great spiritual presence. See Hamilton A. Tyler, *Pueblo Gods and Myths* (Norman: University of Oklahoma Press, 1964), 200; Gladys A. Reichard, *Navaho Religion: A Study of Symbolism*, 2d ed. (Princeton: Princeton University Press, 1974), 384–85.

Like Faulkner's bear, the bear in Native American cultures is linked with great natural forces and hence is mysterious. But because people mysteriously turn into bears, the figure is also linked with myths of origin (myths of emergence) and spiritual transformations. (See N. Scott Momaday, *The Way to Rainy Mountain* [Albuquerque: University of New Mexico Press, 1969], 8; Leslie Silko, "Story from Bear Country," in *Storyteller* [New York: Seaver, 1981], 204–09.) The bear is thus an image of sublimity, being associated with mountains and stars, but it can also be a symbol of the comic because linked to a prehuman past before the "clown" in man emerged and became "civilized." (See Albert Yava, "Way Back in the Distant Past," in *The South Corner of Time: Hopi, Navaho, Papago, Yaqui Tribal Literature*, ed. Larry Evers et al. [Tucson: University of Arizona Press, 1980], 8–13; and Emory Sekaquaptewa, "One More Smile for a Hopi Clown," in ibid, 14–17.) By having the invisible man become a bear in the epilogue, Ellison again hints at humanity's protean nature.

61. Burke, *Rhetoric of Motives*, 137, 86.

62. Burke, *Philosophy of Literary Form*, 400.

63. Jean Genet, Introduction to *Soledad Brother: The Prison Letters of George Jackson* (New York: Coward-McCann, 1970), unnumbered page.

64. Michel Fabre, "From *Native Son* to *Invisible Man*: Some Notes on Ralph Ellison's Evolution in the 1950s," in Benston, ed., *Speaking for You*, 211.

65. Compare Eliot's "Gerontion," in *Complete Poems and Plays*, 22:

History has many cunning passages, contrived corridors
And issues, deceives with whispering ambitions,
Guides us by vanities.

And these lines from "Sweeney Erect," in ibid., 26:

(The lengthened shadow of a man
Is history, said Emerson
Who had not seen the silhouette
of Sweeney straddled in the sun.)

Ellison depicts history in terms of the protean possibilities of the present—the "lengthened shadow" of democratic man allows us to perceive a usable past; whereas Eliot depicts the present in terms of mass man, the huddled primate, whose continued presence in history calls attention to civilization's fragility.

66. See n. 29 of Introduction, above.

67. Richard Wright, *Black Boy* (New York: Harpers, 1945), 31.

68. Richard Wright, *Twelve Million Black Voices: A Folk History of the Negro in the United States* (New York: Viking, 1941).

69. Ellison has written about Wright often, expressing both his respect for Wright as a writer and his reservations about Wright's vision of black life (Ralph Ellison, "Richard Wright's Blues," in *Shadow and Act*, 89–104; idem, "The World and the Jug," in ibid., 115–47; and idem, "Remembering Richard Wright" in *Going to the Territory*, 198–216. Joseph T. Skerrett, Jr., "The Wright Interpretation: Ralph Ellison and the Anxiety of Influence," in Benston, ed., *Speaking for You*, 227, 224, argues that Ellison escaped the anxiety of Wright's influence by inventing "for himself a literary paternity [Hemingway, Eliot, Malraux, et al.] that excludes Richard Wright." In truth, argues Skerrett, Ellison completed Wright's vision in terms of Harold Bloom's *tessera*, "A completing fragment . . . which, taken in conjunction with his predecessor's work, makes a satisfactory whole" (224).

70. Benjamin, *Illuminations*, 169.

71. Burke, *Rhetoric of Religion*, 246.

72. Robert Stepto, *Behind the Veil: A Study of Afro-American Narrative* (Urbana: University of Illinois Press, 1979), 163–94, compares the underground hideout to a museum, the narrator rejecting some icons (e.g., his high-school diploma) as being unworthy because untranslatable into a mode of action, and valuing others (Tarp's leg iron).

73. Ralph Ellison, "The Art of Fiction: An Interview," in *Shadow and Act*, 177; Fabre, "From *Native Son* to *Invisible Man*," 208.

74. See Burke, *Language as Symbolic Action*, 368.

75. Burke, *Philosophy of Literary Form*, 9.

76. Burke, *Grammar of Motives*, 105.

77. Ralph Ellison, "Stephen Crane and the Mainstream of American Fiction," in *Shadow and Act*, 86.

78. Ralph Ellison, "The Golden Age, Time Past," in *Shadow and Act*, 200.

79. Ellison is perhaps the most Roycean of the four authors on whose work this book centers. For Royce, Christianity is different from other religions because the "Beloved Community" compels a "loyalty" based on *caritas* rather than on the laws of the tribe. For Ellison, the paradox of the American "principle" is that in pursuing it one ultimately leaves behind narrow definitions of race and nationhood.

80. Nor as much as it bothers H. G. Wells, whose *The Invisible Man* is one obvious source for Ellison's novel. Wells's invisible man becomes a metaphor for what modern London is already doing to people: making them disappear. They exist only when they consume, or when they fit into socially acceptable roles or "disguises." The food that Wells's invisible man eats "shows until it is assimilated," much like the money placed in the mouth of the "FEED ME" bank Ellison's protagonist finds in Mary Rambo's room. And to emphasize his point about visibility being contingent on consumption, Wells the socialist places the invisible man in a modern department store appropriately called "Omni-ums." The store that claims to have everything is defined in this scene in terms of the "artificial noses . . . wigs and masks and the like" with which the invisible man tries to disguise himself. The store is a reflection of a mass urban society that limits the imagination of its customers to its visible products, just as this same society has limited the imagination of Wells's protagonist, who views his invisibility as only a means to obtain tangible "riches." That he also wishes to usher in a "reign of terror" suggests that his motivation is commensurate with that state of dread and uncertainty that the modern city already creates in its citizens (H. G. Wells, *The Invisible Man* [1897; reprint, New York: Bantam, 1987], 100, 117). Also see Tony Tanner, *City of Words: American Fiction, 1950–1970* (New York: Harper & Row, 1971), 50.

81. For a discussion of how *closed* a conception the American "holy city" could be, see Sacvan Bercovitch, *The American Jeremiad* (Madison: University of Wisconsin Press, 1978). Also, for an interpretation of *Invisible Man* that focuses on the novel's *openness* as a way of evading or "mediating" history, see Thomas Hill Schaub, *American Fiction in the Cold War* (Madison: University of Wisconsin Press, 1991), 91–115. Schaub argues that Ellison's tendency to elevate the historical and the particular to the level of universality, art, and myth softens the novel's "stark social critique."

Chapter Five. The Watchman on the Wall in James Baldwin's
Go Tell It on the Mountain

1. James Campbell, *Talking at the Gates: A Life of James Baldwin* (London: Faber & Faber, 1991), 9; Richard Wright, *Twelve Million Black Voices: A Folk History of the Negro in the United States* (New York: Viking, 1941), 142.

2. Campbell, *Talking at the Gates*, 5.

3. James Baldwin, *The Fire Next Time* (New York: Dial, 1963), 37.

4. James Baldwin, "Many Thousands Gone," in *Notes of a Native Son* (1955; reprint, New York: Dial, 1963), 40.

5. Ibid., 33.

6. Baldwin, *Fire Next Time*, 38.

7. James Baldwin, *Go Tell It on the Mountain* (New York: Knopf, 1953), 303; in this chapter, page numbers for subsequent citations of this work are given in parentheses and refer to this edition. Regarding the critical controversy over the meaning and nature of John's conversion, see the article that is the original version of this chapter, Charles Scruggs, "The Tale of Two Cities in

James Baldwin's *Go Tell It on the Mountain*," *American Literature* 52 (March 1980): 1–17, esp. 16n.

8. James Baldwin, *Going to Meet the Man* (New York: Dial, 1965), 162; idem, *No Name in the Street* (New York; Dial, 1972), 51.

9. Baldwin, "Many Thousands Gone," 41. Even when he speaks of *Native Son* as a moral treatise or uninspired sociology, his admiration frequently shows through, as in his remarks in "Alas, Poor Richard," in *Nobody Knows My Name: More Notes of a Native Son* (New York: Dial, 1961), 197: "I had used his work as a kind of springboard into my own." Yet he continued to denigrate Wright's novel as late as 1980, insisting that Max's courtroom speech ("the whole Communist thing") essentially ended the novel (Wolfgang Binder, "James Baldwin: An Interview," in *Conversations with James Baldwin*, ed. Fred L. Standley and Louis H. Pratt [Jackson: University of Mississippi Press, 1989], 203). Obviously Baldwin never entirely resolved his relationship to Wright and Wright's work.

10. Baldwin, "Alas, Poor Richard," 191.

11. Harold Bloom, *The Anxiety of Influence: A Theory of Poetry* (New York: Oxford University Press, 1973), 14. We don't have to read Bloom to recognize that the son had to kill the father to make room for himself—indeed, Baldwin tells us as much. See Baldwin, "Alas, Poor Richard," 191; Binder, "James Baldwin," 202–3. Perhaps the best discussion of the father-son relationship between Wright and Baldwin is Michel Fabre, "Fathers and Sons in James Baldwin's *Go Tell It on the Mountain*," *James Baldwin: A Collection of Critical Essays*, ed. Keneth Kinnamon (Englewood Cliffs, N.J.: Prentice-Hall, 1974), 120–38.

12. Ralph Ellison, *Invisible Man* (New York: Random House, 1952), 438. For another interpretation of Ellison's allusion to Eliot in this passage, see Donald A. Petesch, *A Spy in the Enemy's Country: The Emergence of Modern Black Literature* (Iowa City: University of Iowa Press, 1989), 32–33.

13. Indeed, Ellison insists that "Baldwin . . . is not the product of the Negro store-front church but of the library, and the same is true of me" (*Shadow and Act* [New York: New American Library, 1966], 123). Baldwin seems to concur: "I read my way out of the libraries in Harlem by the time I was thirteen" (Jordan Elgrably and George Plimpton, "The Art of Fiction LXXVIII: James Baldwin," in Standley and Pratt, eds., *Conversations with James Baldwin*, 236). But the difference in the two men's perspectives lies in Baldwin's phrase, "in Harlem."

14. James Baldwin, "Take Me to the Water," in *No Name in the Street*, 51; also see James Baldwin, *Just Above My Head* (New York: Dial, 1979), 502–3: (Arthur Montana to Guy) "I love New York. *If* I love it. I've never made up my mind. . . . I may not know if I love it—well—that's very complicated. But, Lord, I know I can hate it." Also see Jewell Handy Gresham, "James Baldwin Comes Home," in Standley and Pratt, eds., *Conversations with James Baldwin*, 164: "I love and hate New York."

15. See James Baldwin, "The Discovery of What It Means to Be an American," in *Nobody Knows My Name*; and idem, "Notes for a Hypothetical Novel,"

in ibid. In the latter essay, Baldwin remarks, "If I were writing hypothetically about a Frenchman, I would have in a way a frame of reference and a point of view and in fact it is easier to write about Frenchmen, comparatively speaking, because they interest me so much less" (151). For a balanced view of Baldwin's relationship to France, see Michel Fabre, *From Harlem to Paris: Black American Writers in France, 1840–1980* (Urbana: University of Illinois Press, 1991), 195–214: "What made it impossible for Baldwin to dislike France, in spite of everything, was the fact that he owed to that country his own spiritual growth" (213). And it was especially Paris that he singled out as the "city which saved my life . . . by allowing me to find out who I am" (213).

16. James Baldwin, *Another Country* (New York: Dial, 1962), 319; in this chapter, page numbers for subsequent citations of this work are given in parentheses and refer to this edition.

17. Baldwin, *Just above My Head*, 339.

18. Henry James, *The American Scene* (Bloomington: Indiana University Press, 1968), 112, quoted in Eric Sigg, *The American T. S. Eliot* (Cambridge: Cambridge University Press, 1989), 127.

19. Baldwin admired James a great deal: he not only called James a "witness" (a positive word in Baldwin's vocabulary) but claimed an indebtedness to James when he wrote *Go Tell It on the Mountain*: "Reading Henry James helped me, with his whole idea about the center of consciousness and using a single intelligence to tell the story" (Elgrably and Plimpton, "Art of Fiction," 238). He also quotes James as an epigraph to *Another Country*. For a discussion of Baldwin, James, and *Another Country*, see Charles Newman, "The Lesson of the Master," *Yale Review* 56, no. 1 (1966): 45–59; reprinted in Kinnamon, ed., *James Baldwin*, 52–76. More recently, Thomas Hill Schaub has argued that Henry James's influence on American writers after World War II was directly due to their rejection of the activist rhetoric and "realism" of the 1930s. When culture replaced politics, so, too, ambiguity replaced certainty, and the suspension of judgment, based on that complex "web of consciousness" of James's mature fiction, became valorized. Although Schaub does not include Baldwin in his discussion, much of what he says about the "New York intellectuals" of the cold war years could be applied to Baldwin. See Thomas Hill Schaub, *American Fiction in the Cold War* (Madison: University of Wisconsin Press, 1991), 40–41.

20. Baldwin, *Just above My Head*, 227–28. Yet even here Baldwin would qualify these observations: "The spiteful incoherence of New York is, at bottom, more bearable that the grotesque pieties of Philadelphia, say, or Boston, or Washington" (228).

21. Kevin Lynch. *The Image of the City* (Cambridge: MIT Press, 1960).

22. Baldwin, *Just above My Head*, 227.

23. Of course, one might argue that the view from within the walls becomes gloomier in Baldwin's later work.

24. James Baldwin, *If Beale Street Could Talk* (New York: Dial, 1974), 209.

25. Baldwin, *Just above My Head*, 127.

26. A fact he mentions several times. See Baldwin, *Notes of a Native Son*, 7;

the autobiographical sketch at the end of idem, *Go Tell It on the Mountain*; and James Baldwin, *The Devil Finds Work* (New York: Dial, 1978), 10–18. In this chapter, page numbers for subsequent citations of *The Devil Finds Work* are given in parentheses and refer to this edition.

27. Baldwin, *Fire Next Time*, 20.

28. Alexander Welsh, *The City of Dickens* (Oxford: Clarendon, 1971), 143.

29. Marcus Klein, *Foreigners: The Making of American Literature, 1900–1940* (Chicago: University of Chicago Press, 1981), 198; also see Sigg, *American T. S. Eliot*, 124–34.

30. Baldwin, "Notes for a Hypothetical Novel," in *Nobody Knows My Name*, 141–42; in this chapter, page numbers for subsequent citations of this work are given in parentheses and refer to the edition for which full publication information is given in n. 9, above.

31. James Baldwin, "Sonny's Blues," in *Going to Meet the Man*, 130, 114–15.

32. Peter Langer perceptively notes that among the different pairs of metaphors used to describe the modern city, the terms *jungle* and *bazaar* are closely related. See his excellent essay "Sociology—Four Images Of Organized Diversity: Bazaar, Jungle, Organism, and Machine," in *Cities of the Mind: Images and Themes of the City in the Social Sciences*, ed. Lloyd Rodwin and Robert M. Hollister (New York: Plenum, 1984), 97–117.

33. James Baldwin, *Tell Me How Long the Train's Been Gone* (New York: Dial, 1968), 476

34. Baldwin, *Just above My Head*, 19.

35. Ibid., 69.

36. "Go Tell It on the Mountain," in Dick West and Beth West, eds., *The New Song Fest* (New York: Crown, 1966), 144.

37. In this scene, Baldwin surely intends an ironic echo of Ezekiel 40:1–2: "In the fourteenth year after the city [Jerusalem] was conquered, on that very day, the hand of the Lord was upon me, and brought me in the visions of God into the land of Israel, and set me down upon a very high mountain, on which was a structure like a city opposite me." This is the vision of the New Jerusalem with its restored temple. Shirley S. Allen sees this scene as a parody of John of Patmos's vision in the Book of Revelation. See Shirley S. Allen, "Religious Symbolism and Psychic Reality in Baldwin's *Go Tell It on the Mountain*," *CLA Journal* 19 (December 1975): 179–80. Of course, there are classical echoes here as well, though unlike Ellison, Baldwin focuses primarily on biblical allusions.

38. Baldwin hints at Roy's uncertain future in "The Rockpile," the opening short story in *Going to Meet the Man*.

39. Charles Dickens, *A Tale of Two Cities*, (1859; reprint, London: Dent, 1906), 355.

40. Melodrama is a genre that has been given close critical attention in film studies. See especially John Cawelti, *Adventure, Mystery, and Romance: Formula Stories as Art and Popular Culture* (Chicago: University of Chicago Press, 1976); Thomas Schatz, *Hollywood Genres* (New York: Random House, 1981). Also see the useful article by Jane Gaines, "*The Scar of Shame*: Skin Color and

Caste in Black Silent Melodrama," *Cinema Journal* 26 (Summer 1987): 3–21. Melodrama presents "a moral pattern which coincides with the value system in operation within a community at a particular point in history" (5). What is particularly interesting in Baldwin (and Wright) is the interaction of *different* communities in the "reading" of a Hollywood genre film.

41. Gaines, *Scar of Shame*, 5.

42. Ephraim Katz, *The Film Encyclopedia* (New York: Crowell, 1979), 934.

43. Baldwin understood the nature of that culture long before he wrote *The Devil Finds Work*. In a radio interview in 1961, for instance, he said, "You go to the movies and, like everybody else, you fall in love with Joan Crawford, and you root for the good guys who are killing off the Indians. It comes as a great surprise when you realize that all these things are really metaphors for your oppression" (quoted in Campbell, *Talking at the Gates*, 145).

44. Studs Terkel, "An Interview with James Baldwin," in Standley and Pratt, eds., *Conversations with James Baldwin*, 3.

45. Prov. 16:32: "He who is slow to anger is better than the mighty, and he who rules his spirit than he who takes a city."

46. The inadequacy of Gabriel's "hiding place" is underscored by Baldwin's allusion to the spiritual by the same name: "I went down to the rock to hide my face; / the rock cried out, 'No hiding place, / No hiding place down here.'"

47. Again, it is the absence of this "ground-level" culture which sets Bigger apart from the characters of Ellison, Baldwin, and Morrison. For the sources of Du Bois's use of the figure with the Sorrow Songs, see my discussion in chap. 1, above; for Toomer's use of the figure in his story "Theater," see chap. 2, above.

48. Baldwin, "Many Thousands Gone," 37.

49. Kenneth Burke, *The Rhetoric of Religion: Studies in Logology* (Boston: Beacon, 1961), 122.

50. One of Baldwin's rare allusions in this novel to a modernist text. Compare *The Waste Land*, lines 177–179 in T.S. Eliot, *The Complete Poems and Plays, 1909–1950* (New York: Harcourt, Brace & World, 1952), 42:

> The river bears no empty bottles, sandwich papers,
> silk handkerchiefs, cardboard boxes, cigarette ends
> or other testimony of summer nights. The nymphs are departed.

That John's refuge from the city's ruins is a lonely storefront church and *not* the Anglican church is probably intentional irony. The biblical source of both images is probably the River of Life flowing through the heavenly city in Revelation.

51. Burke, *Rhetoric of Religion*, 37, 129.

52. Compare Baldwin's statement to Julius Lester three years before his death: "There are two things we have to do: love each other and raise our children." Lester thought these sentiments "romantic," and perhaps they are; but these domestic themes, and their implications, are central to Baldwin's fiction (Julius Lester, "James Baldwin—Reflections of a Maverick," in Standley and Pratt, eds. *Conversations with James Baldwin*, 226).

53. Toni Morrison, "Life in His Language," *James Baldwin: The Legacy*, ed.

Quincy Troupe (New York: Simon & Schuster, 1989), 76; also see Clyde Taylor, "Celebrating Jimmy," in ibid., 31. Taylor notes the presence of the major contemporary black women writers at the memorial service held for Baldwin on December 8, 1987, in New York City.

Chapter Six. The Beloved Community in Toni Morrison's *Beloved*

1. Ellison was only six years younger than Wright, and had conceived of *Invisible Man* alongside Wright when both were working in New York in the late 1930s and early 40s, but that conception was influenced by his reading of, and the public's *reception* of, *Native Son*.

2. James Baldwin, *No Name in the Street* (New York: Dial, 1972), 50.

3. Charles Ruas, *Conversations with American Writers* (New York: Knopf, 1985), 218.

4. Toni Morrison, "Life in His Language," in *James Baldwin: The Legacy*, ed. Quincy Troupe (New York: Simon & Schuster, 1989), 77.

5. Toni Morrison, *The Bluest Eye* (New York: Holt, Rinehart & Winston, 1972) 25; Jacques Lacan, *The Four Fundamental Concepts of Psycho-Analysis*, trans., Alan Sheridan (New York: Norton, 1978), 115–19.

6. Barbara Christian, *Black Feminist Criticism: Perspectives of Black Women Writers* (New York: Pergamon, 1985), 76.

7. "Pilate lived in a narrow single-story house whose basement seemed to be rising from rather than settling into the ground. She had no electricity because she would not pay for the service. Nor for gas. . . . Her house sat eighty feet from the sidewalk and was backed by four huge pine trees, from which she got the needles she stuck into her mattress. . . . The sun stream[ed] in, strong and unfettered because there were no curtains or shades at the windows that were all around the room, two in each of three walls, one on each side of the door, one on either side of the sink and the stove, and two on the farther wall" (Toni Morrison, *Song of Solomon* [New York: Knopf, 1977], 27, 40); in this chapter, page numbers for subsequent citations of *Song of Solomon* are given in parentheses and refer to this edition. In contrast, Macon's house consists of a series of compartments in which the inmates are kept separate from one another as though in an insane asylum.

8. Houses in Morrison's fiction almost always reflect something about the owners or occupants. In *Sula* (New York: Knopf, 1974), Eva barters her leg for insurance money, and she keeps expanding her house almost as if she is trying to replace her lost limb: "Its owner . . . kept on adding things: more stairways—there were three sets to the second floor—more rooms, doors and stoops. There were rooms that had three doors, others that opened out on the porch only and were inaccessible from any other part of the house; others that you could get to only by going through somebody's bedroom" (30). Eva's dismemberment re-enacts the historical diaspora, but the extremity of her act seems to isolate her from the black community. In a grotesque sense, she sells her leg for the house, and the house in turn becomes a parody of the "segmented" space of the bourgeois house—see Yi-Fu Tuan, *Segmented Worlds and*

Self: Group Life and Individual Consciousness (Minneapolis: University of Minnesota Press, 1982), 78–84; Witold Rybczynski, *Home: A Short History of an Idea* (New York: Viking, 1986), chaps. 2, 3; Philippe Ariès, *Centuries of Childhood: A Social History of Family Life*, trans. Robert Baldick (New York: Knopf, 1962), 390–400. In Morrison's *Tar Baby* (New York: Knopf, 1981), Aunt Rosa's bedroom without windows in Eloe reflects her self-sufficiency, but the white patriarch Valerian's enclosed green house indicates his gradual withdrawal from life. Indeed, his house, "L'Arbe de La Croix," becomes his cross, a Gothic mansion in the Caribbean, as his servant Sidney claims territory beyond the "segmented" space of the kitchen, and his wife Margaret becomes the house's "confidant curator who knew the names of everything in his museum" (278). In this chapter, page numbers for subsequent citations of *Tar Baby* are given in parentheses and refer to this edition.

9. Robert Stepto, "'Intimate Things in Place': A Conversation with Toni Morrison," in *Chant of Saints: A Gathering of Afro-American Literature, Art, and Scholarship*, ed. Michael S. Harper and Robert B. Stepto (Urbana: University of Illinois Press, 1979), 214.

10. BBC interview, "Toni Morrison," interviewed by Melvyn Bragg, July 22, 1988 (hereafter cited as BBC interview); Claudia Tate, *Black Women Writers at Work* (New York: Continuum, 1983), 126: "If you work very carefully, you can clean up ordinary words and repolish them." Also, see Thomas LeClair, "'The Language Must Not Sweat,'" *New Republic, 184 (March 21, 1981)*: 26.

11. Stepto, "'Intimate Things in Place,'" 214; Toni Morrison, "City Limits, Village Values: Concepts of the Neighborhood in Black Fiction," in *Literature and the Urban Experience: Essays on the City and Literature*, ed. Michael C. Jaye and Ann Chalmers Watts (New Brunswick, N.J.: Rutgers University Press, 1981), 35–43.

12. See David Harvey, *The Condition of Postmodernity: An Enquiry into the Origins of Cultural Change* (London: Basil Blackwell, 1989), 246, 253, 257. The Renaissance's passion for the "rational ordering of space" led to a New World paradox: the map symbolized an attempt to control the wilderness, a precondition of human freedom; yet once nature was defined by the map, space became homogenized and a container for "capitalist social relations." Also see Lewis Mumford, *The Culture of Cities* (New York: Harcourt, Brace, 1938), 183–90; William Boelhower, *Through a Glass Darkly: Ethnic Semiosis in American Literature* (Venice: Edizioni Helvetia, 1984), chap. 2.

13. Kenneth Burke, *A Grammar of Motives* (1945; reprint, Berkeley: University of California Press, 1966), 294–97. The idea of the negative runs throughout Burke's writings. For his most thorough treatment of the subject, see his *Language as Symbolic Action: Essays on Life, Literature, and Method* (Berkeley: University of California Press, 1966), 441–79.

14. Morrison, *Sula*, 90. The negative in *Song of Solomon* also appears in the naming of "No Mercy" hospital and in Railroad Tommy's list of things that Afro-Americans are "never" going to have. Both the naming of the hospital and the Homeric catalog of *nevers* are forms of communal wisdom passed

down from generation to generation (59–60). Pilate's house is also defined by negatives—no curtains, no gas, no electricity.

15. Edward Relph, *Place and Placelessness* (London: Pion, 1976), 12.

16. Stepto, "Intimate Things in Place," 213.

17. Ruas, *Conversations with American Writers*, 239. Also see W.E.B. Du Bois, *The Philadelphia Negro* (1899; reprint, New York: Blom, 1967), 71.

18. See Roger D. Abrahams, "Negotiating Respect: Patterns of Presentation among Black Women," in *Women and Folklore*, ed. Claire Farrer (1975; reprint, Prospect Heights, Ill,: Waveland, 1986), 58–80. As an anthropologist studying gender roles and conflicts within a black community in Philadelphia, Abrahams confirms Morrison's emphasis: while the public world of the street is the locus for reputation-seeking men, "the locus of respectability [for black women] is the home" (66). See also Sandra M. Gilbert and Susan Gubar, *The Madwoman in the Attic: The Woman Writer and the Nineteenth-Century Literary Imagination* (New Haven: Yale University Press, 1979), esp. 83; Harriet A. Jacobs, *Incidents in the Life of a Slave Girl*, ed. Jean Fagan Yellin (Cambridge: Harvard University Press, 1987), xxxi. Morrison, in *Tar Baby*, 58, compares Margaret Lenore's fate as Valerian's wife to Joan Fontaine's in Alfred Hitchcock's film version of *Rebecca*, an updating of the Jane Eyre story of a woman trapped in a Gothic mansion. What is entrapment for Margaret, however, is home for Ondine and Sidney.

19. A short, precise summary of the history of the Margaret Garner episode can be found in Philip S. Foner, *History of Black Americans: From the Compromise of 1850 to the End of the Civil War* (Westport, Con.: Greenwood, 1983), 87–91; also see Stanley W. Campbell, *The Slave Catchers: Enforcement of the Fugitive Slave Law, 1850–1860* (Chapel Hill: University of North Carolina Press, 1970), 144-47. The most detailed discussion of the episode, and a probable source for *Beloved*, is Julius Yanuck, " The Garner Fugitive Slave Case," *Mississippi Historical Review* 40 (June 1953): 47–66.

20. Julia Kristeva, in her essay, "Place Names," in *Desire in Language: A Semiotic Approach to Literature and Art*, ed. Leon S. Roudiez (New York: Columbia University Press, 1980), 291, reverses Freud's emphasis on the father as origin by arguing that "naming, always originating in a place . . . is a *replacement* for what the speaker perceives as an archaic mother—a more or less victorious confrontation, never finished with her."

21. The "beach community" of Honoré, for instance, is a preyuppie conception of community, its class exclusiveness revealed in its geography (an island) and in its pretentious French name, provided no doubt by real-estate developers.

22. The "peeling gold letters" of Sonny's name on Macon's building hint at other untold, or partially told, stories in *Song of Solomon*: Ryna's, Sing's, Ruth's, and Hagar's. This invisible female history is implied by the trace of an absent centerpiece on Ruth's dining-room table, and by Pilate's missing navel, which points not only to her unknown past but to the ultimate mystery of the diaspora. *Song of Solomon* circles around the theme of uncovering both a hidden

past and a hidden name. Freddie's nickname for Macon's son hides a hidden future; Milkman the stud becomes Milkman the nurturer when he restores Pilate to her father, when he sings *her* song to her when she dies. It is appropriate that these two placeless people—we remember Pilate's precious geography book—embrace, as Milkman, for a brief moment, takes Pilate's place as the ancestor, the "pilot."

23. Morrison, "City Limits, Village Values," 39, 43.

24. Morrison, *Sula*, 3.

25. Thomas P. Slaughter, *Bloody Dawn: The Christiana Riot and Racial Violence in the Antebellum North* (New York: Oxford University Press, 1991), 51. See Campbell, *Slave Catchers*, 105. Campbell provides a concise summary of the new powers the 1850 act gave the owners of runaway slaves. Also see Stephen Middleton, *Ohio and the Antislavery Activities of Attorney Salmon Portland Chase, 1830–1849* (New York: Garland, 1990), chaps. 3, 4.

26. Middleton notes that the Northwest Ordinance of 1787, under which Ohio became a state, is ambiguous in that, although it was "America's first antislavery document," it also mandated "America's first fugitive slave clause, providing for the return of runaway slaves" (*Ohio and the Antislavery Activities*, 69). Throughout his discussion of Salmon Chase, Middleton debunks the popular myth that antebellum Ohio was hospitable to either free blacks or runaways. The state's Black Laws (1804) said quite explicitly that Afro-Americans were not welcome, and thus Chase's defense of abolitionists and fugitives was never easy. Also see Slaughter, *Bloody Dawn*, xiii: in studying the Christiana riot, the most famous incident that arose from the Fugitive Slave Law of 1850, Slaughter comes to the conclusion "that law functions as an expression of culture."

27. Ruas, *Conversations with American Writers*, 243.

28. This, of course, is a fact verified by historians; see Slaughter, *Bloody Dawn*, 45; also Campbell, *Slave Catchers*, 10.

29. Alain Locke, "The New Negro," in *The New Negro*, ed. Alain Locke (1925; reprint, New York: Atheneum, 1969), 7.

30. Toni Morrison, *Beloved* (New York: Knopf, 1987), 136–37; in this chapter, page numbers for subsequent citations of this novel are given in parentheses and refer to this edition. The character of "schoolteacher" appears in Morrison's text without a proper name, capitalization, or a definite article. The suggestion is that he is an adventurer who has married into Mrs. Garner's family, and Morrison's drawing of him recalls Faulkner characters such as Popeye and Flem Snopes.

31. Toni Morrison, "The Site of Memory," in *Inventing the Truth: The Art and Craft of Memoir*, ed. William Zinsser (Boston: Houghton Mifflin, 1987), 119.

32. For the importance of slave resistance in bringing about the final abolition of slavery, see James Oakes, *Slavery and Freedom* (New York: Knopf, 1990), 152–66.

33. Burton Pike, *The Image of the City in Modern Literature* (Princeton: Princeton University Press, 1981), 5.

34. Robert A. Ferguson, *Law and Letters in American Literature* (Cambridge: Harvard University Press, 1984), 15.

35. See Oakes, *Slavery and Freedom*, 103. Oakes quotes the epistolary advice of an uncle to a nephew who plans to migrate to Texas in 1849: "Get as many young negro women as you can get. Get as many cows as you can. . . . It is the greatest country for an increase that I have ever saw in my life." In creating this terrible scene, Morrison may have been indebted to historical documents like this one.

36. In "Negroes of Cincinnati prior to the Civil War, " Carter Woodson points to the city's close "commercial relations" with the slave states as the cause of its political conservatism: "Early in the nineteenth century Cincinnati became a manufacturing center to which the South learned to look for supplies of machinery, implements, furniture and food" (quoted in Wendell P. Dabney, *Cincinnati's Colored Citizens: Historical, Sociological, and Biographical* [Cincinnati: Dabney, 1926], 33). The geographical position of "Ohio's most conservative city"—"located on the fringe of slavery"—was another explanation for Cincinnati's refusal to interfere with the "business" of the peculiar institution. See Middleton, *Ohio and the Antislavery Activities*, 39, 115.

37. Although he does not discuss *Beloved*, Melvin Dixon notes that slaves viewed "the 'garden' ideal of the plantation with understandable suspicion" (*Ride Out the Wilderness: Geography and Identity in Afro-American Literature* [Urbana: University of Illinois Press, 1987], 17). See especially Dixon's chapter 1, in which he juxtaposes garden and wilderness as spatial images in Afro-American writing.

38. Oakes, *Slavery and Freedom*, 4, 212, n. 2.

39. Melissa Walker notes that when Denver goes to the Bodwin house looking for work, brother and sister expect Denver to use the back door. And Walker compares Bodwin "to a disillusioned reformer in 1987 looking back to the heady days of the civil rights movement" (*Down from the Mountaintop: Black Women's Novels in the Wake of the Civil Rights Movement, 1966–1989* [New Haven: Yale University Press, 1991], 42). Bodwin is not so much "disillusioned" as indifferent.

40. Morrison, "Site of Memory," 101–24.

41. Paul makes this connection to the heavenly city clear when in the following lines he talks of law or "works" (quoting Isaiah) as a "stumbling stone" that God has placed in "Zion."

42. When the women gather to exorcise the evil spirit doing Sethe harm, they utter the "sound" that had existed before there were "words" (259).

43. Augustine, *The City of God*, ed. David Knowles (New York: Penguin, 1972), 635.

44. Ibid., 626.

45. Toni Morrison, "A Bench by the Road," *World*, 3 (January–February 1989): 4; idem, "Unspeakable Things, Unspoken: The Afro-American Presence in American Literature," *Michigan Quarterly Review* 28 (Winter 1989): 32.

46. Robert Harbison suggests that numbering streets, rather than naming them, "was an important conceptual jump which must have been made around the time American city streets were laid out in the 1820s." And of course the numbering of houses is also modern; in more traditional commu-

nities they have names. See Robert Harbison, *Eccentric Spaces* (New York: Knopf, 1977), 127.

47. The phrase belongs to Mircea Eliade, *The Myth of the Eternal Return*, trans. Willard R. Trask (New York: Pantheon, 1954), title of chap. 4.

48. BBC interview.

49. Morrison, "Unspeakable Things, Unspoken," 2.

50. BBC interview.

51. Ibid. see also Richard Chase, *The American Novel and Its Tradition* (New York: Doubleday, 1957), 19.

52. Fredric Jameson, *Marxism and Form: Twentieth Century Dialectical Theories of Literature* (Princeton: Princeton University Press, 1972), 131.

53. Northrop Frye, *The Secular Scripture: A Study of the Structure of Romance* (Cambridge: Harvard University Press, 1976), 53.

54. Ibid., 175–76, 183.

55. Toni Morrison, "Memory, Creation, and Writing," *Thought* 59 (December 1984): 385, 389; Nellie McKay, "An Interview with Toni Morrison," *Contemporary Literature* 4 (Winter 1983): 421; Walter Benjamin, *Illuminations*, trans. Harry Zohn (New York: Schocken, 1969), 88–89.

56. Morrison, "Memory, Creation, and Writing," 389.

57. BBC interview.

58. Ibid.

59. Baldwin's observation is quoted from James Campbell, *Talking at the Gates: A Life of James Baldwin* (London: Faber & Faber, 1991), 250; Pound's observation is from Ezra Pound, "Briefer Mention," *Dial* 70 (January 1921): 110.

60. John Michael Vlach, *The Afro-American Tradition in Decorative Arts* (Cleveland: Cleveland Museum of Art, 1978), 44–75; Elsa Barkley Brown, "African-American Women's Quilting: A Framework for Conceptualizing and Teaching African-American Women's History," *Signs: Journal of Women in Culture and Society* 14 (Summer 1989): 924n. Also see Jane E. Hindman, "African-American Quiltmaking as Metaphor in Toni Morrison's *Song of Solomon*: Finding That Ineffable Quality That Is Curiously Black," *Western Ohio Journal* 9 (Spring 1991): 18–35.

61. Henry Louis Gates, Jr., *The Signifying Monkey: A Theory of Afro-American Criticism* (New York: Oxford University Press, 1988), 172.

62. Formally, the technique of *Beloved* could be described as an application of the narrative method of William Faulkner's *As I Lay Dying* or Virginia Woolf's *Mrs. Dalloway* to a social history like that of "The Prayers of the Saints," in *Go Tell It on the Mountain*. Morrison wrote her master's thesis on William Faulkner and Virginia Woolf.

63. The "keeping room"—the nineteenth-century name for the parlor or living room—is a parody of community, for in the novel it becomes a place where people retire to die.

64. See Wilfred D. Samuels and Clenora Hudson-Weems, *Toni Morrison* (Boston: Twayne, 1990), 113–16.

65. In a sense Morrison foreshadows Amy's fate in Magdalene and First Corinthians, who, in *Song of Solomon*, make artificial roses out of velvet to sell

to the local department store; Macon Dead treats his daughters alternatively like princesses and like women in a sweatshop. Amy's connection to mass culture is also underlined by her acceptance of the names, such as "carmine" (80), that advertising gives to colors. Between 1830 and 1850, "newspaper readership" in America more than tripled, and Morrison suggests that Amy has gotten her information about Boston and velvet from reading Mr. Buddy's newspapers. See Alexander Saxton, *The Rise and Fall of the White Republic: Class Politics and Mass Culture in Nineteenth-Century America* (London: Verso, 1990), 95–96. The best discussion of capitalism, urbanization, and mass culture in Morrison's fiction is Susan Willis, *Specifying: Black Women Writing the American Experience* (Madison: University of Wisconsin Press, 1987).

66. His condition suggests a remark by R. D. Laing regarding schizophrenia: "If the whole of the individual's being cannot be defended, the individual retracts his lines of defence until he withdraws within a central citadel" (*The Divided Self* [New York: Pantheon, 1969], 80).

67. For another interpretation of Sethe's body as text, see Anne E. Goldman, "'I Made the Ink': (Literary) Production and Reproduction in *Dessa Rose* and *Beloved*," *Feminist Studies* 16 (Summer 1990): 323, 328.

68. Gaston Bachelard, *The Poetics of Space*, trans. Maria Jolas (Boston: Beacon, 1969), 68.

69. "All sorrows can be borne if you put them in a story." I am indebted to Robert Bone for making me aware of Dinesen's aphorism, which he uses as an epigraph to *Down Home: A History of Afro-American Short Fiction from Its Beginnings to the End of the Harlem Renaissance* (New York: Putnam's, 1975).

70. The conversation between Stamp Paid and Paul D takes place in one of Cincinnati's pig-slaughtering houses, and the setting demonstrates both how *Beloved* is an urban novel and how Morrison suggests the continuity of Afro-American experience in northern cities between the nineteenth and twentieth centuries. Stamp Paid's news clipping represents the developing public voice of the media, which provide information and judgments about the life of the city. Cincinnati is already a center for large-scale meat-packing factories serving an expanding mass market. ("The craving for pork was growing into a mania in every city in the country" [155].) The jobs of Paul D and Stamp Paid are assembly-line slaughtering, and Morrison implies that the availability of work was one thing that drew the men to the city, since "all a Negro had to do was show up and there was work" (155). The resemblance to the conditions of the Great Migration after World War I is obvious, even to the famous reliance of later black immigrants on the packinghouses of Chicago for employment. (See James R. Grossman, *Land of Hope: Chicago, Black Southerners, and the Great Migration*, [Chicago: University of Chicago Press, 1989], 183–85, 188–89.) The slaughterhouse work is intermittent and low-paying, and requires of a worker only that "he could breathe the stench of offal and stand up for twelve hours, skills in which Paul D was admirably trained" (154).

71. Morrison names Vashti after King Ahasuerus's queen who refuses a summons to appear before her master; her story in the Book of Esther also remains untold. (See Esther 1–3.)

72. The phrase belongs to R. D. Laing, *Divided Self*, chap. 3. Denver's estrangement in the house is also felt outside of the house. Her fear of being "swallowed up in the world beyond the edge of the porch" (243) illustrates what Laing calls "the dread of engulfment" (*Divided Self*, 46). According to Laing, the schizophrenic has a weak sense of self and thus believes that the world will either engulf him or that his emptiness will be filled by something that will burst him apart. Compare Beloved's nightmares: "She had two dreams: exploding and being swallowed" (134).

73. Missy Dehn Kubitschek, *Claiming the Heritage: African-American Novelists and History* (Jackson: University of Mississippi Press, 1991), 171.

74. Frye, *Secular Scripture*, 141.

75. The surname "Denver" comes from the French *denuer*. See C. L'Estrange Ewen, *A History of Surnames of the British Isles: A Concise Account of Their Origin, Evolution, Etymology, and Legal Status* (London: Kegan, Paul, 1931), 89. Not surprisingly, the process of stripping away, even to the point of destitution, is a preliminary step to an older (now obsolete) Christian meaning of *denuer*: "to restore."

76. Deborah Horvitz, "Nameless Ghosts: Possession and Dispossession in *Beloved*," *Studies in American Fiction* 17 (Autumn, 1989): 157. Also see Barbara Hill Rigney, "'A Story to Pass On': Ghosts and the Significance of History in Toni Morrison's *Beloved*," in *Haunting the House of Fiction: Feminist Perspectives on Ghost Stories by American Women*, ed. Lynette Carpenter and Wendy K. Kolmar (Knoxville: University of Tennessee Press, 1991), 229–35; Elizabeth B. House, "Toni Morrison's Ghost: The Beloved Who Is Not Beloved," *Studies in American Fiction* 18 (Spring, 1990): 22.

77. Edgar Dryden, *The Form of American Romance* (Baltimore: Johns Hopkins University Press, 1988), 1–29.

78. Horvitz, "Nameless Ghosts," 158, argues that Beloved is also "Sethe's African mother."

79. Melissa Walker makes a similar suggestion in *Down from the Mountaintop*, 33–46. For a comparison of the two "Reconstructions," see Manning Marable, *Race, Reform, and Rebellion: The Second Reconstruction in Black America, 1945–1982* (Jackson: University of Mississippi Press, 1984).

Epilogue. Invisible Histories, Invisible Cities

1. W.E.B. Du Bois, *The Philadelphia Negro* (1899; reprint, New York: Blom, 1967), 5.

2. Richard Wright, *The Outsider* (New York: Harper & Row, 1953), 404.

3. Nicholas Lemann, "The Origins of the Underclass," *Atlantic Monthly* 257 (June 1986): 39–40.

4. David Trotter, "Theory and Detective Fiction," *Critical Quarterly* 33 (Summer 1991): 70. Trotter is alluding to W. H. Auden's famous remark in "The Guilty Vicarage" (in *Detective Fiction: Crime and Compromise* ed. Dick Allen and David Chacko [New York: Harcourt, Brace, 1974], 404): "The corpse must shock not only because it is a corpse but also because, even for a corpse, it is

shockingly out of place, as when a dog makes a mess on a drawing-room carpet."

5. The critique of the middle class is by no means confined to these four writers and could be said to begin in earnest with the Harlem Renaissance. Langston Hughes, Wallace Thurman, Nella Larsen, Zora Neale Hurston, Countee Cullen, Claude McKay, George Schuyler—and even Alain Locke himself—all satirized the black bourgeoisie even as they upheld many of its values.

6. See Marcus Klein, *After Alienation: American Novels at Mid-Century* (Cleveland: World, 1964), 112.

7. Julius Lester, "James Baldwin—Reflections of a Maverick," in *Conversations with James Baldwin*, ed. Fred L. Standley and Louis H. Pratt (Jackson: University of Mississippi Press, 1989), 223.

8. See Philip S. Foner, *History of Black Americans: From the Compromise of 1850 to the End of the Civil War* (Westport, Conn.: Greenwood, 1983), chap. 3; Thomas P. Slaughter, *Bloody Dawn: The Christiana Riot and Racial Violence in the Antebellum North* (Oxford: Oxford University Press, 1991), esp. chap. 3, 4; Stanley B. Campbell, *The Slave Catchers: Enforcement of the Fugitive Slave Law, 1850–1860* (Chapel Hill: University of North Carolina, 1970), 63; and Julius Yanuck, "The Garner Fugitive Slave Case," *Mississippi Historical Quarterly* 40 (June 1953):56.

9. The subject of the revision of Afro-American history in the past thirty years is more complicated than my discussion of it. One important area of investigation has been nineteenth-century black texts, both autobiography and fiction. William L. Andrews, *To Tell a Free Story: The First Century of Afro-American Autobiography, 1760–1865* (Urbana: University of Illinois Press, 1986), 65, documents the change from "eyewitness" to "I-witness" in nineteenth-century black autobiography; and Hazel V. Carby, *Reconstructing Womanhood: The Emergence of the Afro-American Woman Novelist* (New York: Oxford University Press, 1987), 47, notes "the narrative dissections of true womanhood" in the texts of black women writers of the middle and late nineteenth century.

10. Robert M. Farnsworth, *Melvin B. Tolson: Plain Talk and Poetic Prophecy* (Columbia: University of Missouri Press, 1984), 24; Houston Baker, Jr., *Modernism and the Harlem Renaissance* (Chicago: University of Chicago Press, 1987); Raymond Williams, *The Politics of Modernism: Against the New Conformists* (London: Verso, 1989), 45.

11. Richard Kostelanetz, "An Interview with Ralph Ellison," *Iowa Review* 19 (Fall 1989): 4, 6; Michael North, "The Dialect in/of Modernism: Pound and Eliot's Racial Masquerade," *American Literary History* 4, no. 1 (Spring 1992), 57–76.

12. Home-grown modernism's relationship to black life is no less problematic than the work of expatriate writers, though it does raise a different set of problems. Waldo Frank, Eugene O'Neill, William Carlos Williams, Sherwood Anderson, Hart Crane, Kenneth Burke, and William Faulkner not only acknowledged blacks but attempted to understand their world from the inside. Often wrongheaded, frequently glib and sentimental, they occasionally came up with startling insights into that world, as in Faulkner's extraordinary

novels, or a poem like Crane's "Black Tambourine." Even the expatriate modernists Hemingway and Stein wrote "The Battler" and "Melanctha," respectively, journeys into the interior whose influence would be felt by Ellison and Wright. For a good survey of one genre, see Aldon Lynn Nielson, *Reading Race: White American Poets and the Racial Discourse in the Twentieth Century* (Athens: University of Georgia Press, 1988).

13. Compare Josiah Royce in *The Problem of Christianity* (1913): "Since you cannot find the universal and beloved community, create it" (quoted in John J. Ansbro, *Martin Luther King, Jr.: The Making of a Mind* [Maryknoll, N.Y.: Orbis, 1982], 319n.)

14. [Donald Davidson, et al.], *I'll Take My Stand: The South and the Agrarian Tradition* (1930; reprint, Baton Rouge: Louisiana State University Press, 1980). Royce was one of Eliot's Harvard teachers; see Eric Sigg, *The American T. S. Eliot: A Study of the Early Writings* (Cambridge: Cambridge University Press, 1989), 19.

15. See Robert Crawford, *The Savage and the City in the Work of T. S. Eliot* (Oxford: Clarendon, 1978), chap. 3, 5.

16. Quoted in Raymond Williams, *The Country and the City* (New York: Oxford University Press, 1973), 84; also see Raymond Williams, *Culture and Society, 1780–1950* (1958; reprint, Harmondsworth, Middlesex: Penguin, 1976), 53, 146.

17. Guy Davenport, "Pound and Frobenius," in *Motivity and Method in the Cantos of Ezra Pound*, ed. Lewis Leary and Guy Davenport (New York: Columbia University Press, 1954), 39.

18. Leo Frobenius and Douglas C. Fox, *African Genesis* (New York: Stockpole, 1937) 109–110. Pound's phrase is in a 1937 letter to Frank Morley: "An how you gwine ter keep deh Possum [T. S. Eliot] in his feedbox when I brings in deh chinas and blackmen? He won't laaak fer to see no chinas and blackmen in a bukk about Kulchur" (*The Letters of Ezra Pound*, ed. D. D. Paige [New York: Harcourt, Brace & World, 1950], 288).

19. Guy Davenport, *Cities on Hills, A Study of I–XXX of Ezra Pound's Cantos* (Ann Arbor, Mich.: UMI Research, 1983), 16; Hugh Kenner, *The Pound Era* (Berkeley: University of California Press, 1971), 508–9.

20. Walter Baumann, *The Rose in the Steel Dust* (Coral Gables, Fl.: University of Miami Press, 1970), 98–102. For Pound's connections to John Kasper and the Seaboard White Citizens' Council, see E. Fuller Torrey, *The Roots of Treason: Ezra Pound and the Secret of St. Elizabeths* (New York: McGraw-Hill, 1984), 227–31. After Kasper was arrested for fomenting a racial riot in Tennessee, Pound wrote to Brigit Patmore describing in his unique style the British press coverage of the incident: "Der Kasperl smiling in handcuffs and making the snooze [news] even in UI/Brit/along with the LOOSEwypapers full page of fried nigger" (quoted in Torrey, *Roots of Treason*, 230).

21. James Baldwin, *The Devil Finds Work* (New York: Dial, 1976), 8.

22. Ibid., 26–27.

23. Richard Wright, "Blueprint for Negro Writing," in *The Richard Wright*

Reader, ed. Ellen Wright and Michel Fabre (New York: Harper & Row, (1978), 40; first printed in *New Challenge* 2 (Fall 1937): 53–65.

24. Zora Neale Hurston, *Their Eyes Were Watching God* (1937; reprint, Urbana: University of Illinois Press, 1979), 69; page numbers for subsequent citations of this work are given in parentheses and refer to this edition.

25. See Paule Marshall, *Praisesong for the Widow* (1983; reprint, New York: Dutton, 1984), 178. In describing the "Juba," Marshall says of the old man Lebert Joseph, "It was as if he meant more than just the dance. He might have been also referring to the place that bore the name: Juba, the legendary city at the foot of the White Nile" (178).

26. John Edgar Wideman, *Sent for You Yesterday* (New York: Avon, 1983), 55; also see idem, *Philadelphia Fire* (New York: Holt, 1990), 53–54. The counterpart to this insular space is a rejection of the cultural insularity that the cathedral represents. In Ishmael Reed's *Mumbo Jumbo* (New York: Atheneum: 1970), 139, PaPa LaBas becomes aware that he has limited himself "to a Mumbo Jumbo Kathedral, not allowing myself to witness the popular manifestations of The Work." He abandons his voodoo temple to live at the crossroads. PaPa LaBas is "Papa Legba," the Haitian god of gates, of opportunities, of crossroads. See Zora Neale Hurston, *Tell My Horse* (1938; reprint, Berkeley, Calif.: Turtle Island, 1981), 142; Ishmael Reed, *Shrovetide in Old New Orleans* (New York: Doubleday, 1981), 65.

27. Toni Morrison, *Beloved* (New York: Knopf, 1987), 22.

28. Toni Morrison, *The Bluest Eye* (New York: Holt, Rinehart, & Winston, 1970), 11.

29. See chap. 3, above, n. 68. Paule Marshall's *Brown Girl, Brownstones* (1959, reprint, Old Westbury, N.Y.: Feminist, 1981) also deals with this contrast between house and city, between interior space and *out there*. Selina's contempt for her mother's obsessive desire to "buy house" in Brooklyn eventually changes to respect, partly because her own experience in the larger metropolis, specifically at City College, is ambiguous. Although New York has introduced her to a larger world than the Bajan community, its continued racism forces her to rethink her attitudes toward her mother and her mother's generation. Their reasons for wanting to own their own dwellings include but go beyond materialism.

30. Deborah E. McDowell, "Reading Family Matters," *Changing Our Own Words: Essays on Criticism, Theory, and Writing by Black Women*, ed. Cheryl A. Wall (New Brunswick, N.J.: Rutgers University Press, 1989), 87; Houston A. Baker, Jr., "There Is No More Beautiful Way: Theory and the Poetics of Afro-American Women's Writing," *Afro-American Literary Study for the 1990s*, ed. Houston A. Baker, Jr., and Patricia Redmond (Chicago: University of Chicago Press, 1989), 148–51.

31. For Locke's attitudes toward women, see Gloria T. Hull, *Color, Sex, and Poetry: Three Women Writers of the Harlem Renaissance* (Bloomington: Indiana University Press, 1987), 7–8.

32. Paule Marshall, "Shaping the World of My Art," *New Letters* 40 (October

1973): 97–98; also see idem, "From the Poets in the Kitchen," *Callaloo* 6 (Spring–Summer 1983): 23–30; and idem, *Brown Girl, Brownstones*, esp. 67–77. For an early example of the kitchen as the focus of both family and community, see Langston Hughes, *Not without Laughter* (1930; reprint, New York: Macmillan, 1969), 132–39. Concerning the domestication of the temple, consider the title of Alice Walker's most recent book, *The Temple of My Familiar* (New York: Harcourt, Brace, 1989).

33. Beginning with the androgynous Teacake (in Hurston's *Their Eyes Were Watching God*), one should also consider the hints of gender transformation in contemporary black American literature. In Ernest Gaines's "Three Men" (in *Bloodline*, [1968; reprint, New York: Norton, 1976]), tough Procter Lewis becomes a surrogate mother to a young boy in jail, just as in John Edgar Wideman's "Lizabeth: The Caterpillar Story" (in *Damballah*, [1981; reprint, London: Fontana, 1986]), John French asserts a feminine connection to his daughter by eating part of a caterpillar that she has bitten. In Alice Walker's *Third Life of Grange Copeland* (New York: Harcourt, Brace, 1970), Grange's "third life" is genderless when he becomes both grandfather and grandmother to Ruth. So, too, Truman Held in Walker's *Meridian* (New York: Simon & Schuster, 1976) is no longer a "true man" at novel's end, melting into Meridian's sleeping bag and wearing her cap as he assumes her identity. In Toni Morrison's *Song of Solomon* (New York: Knopf, 1977), Milkman's name expresses a feminine side of his character which becomes apparent by the novel's end. In Paule Marshall's *Praisesong for the Widow*, Lebert Joseph seems to become a woman when he shows Avey the "Juba." According to Toni Morrison, the "ancestor" figure can be either male or female; see Morrison's "City Limits, Village Values: Concepts of the Neighborhood in Black Fiction," in *Literature and the Urban Experience*, ed. Michael C. Jaye and Ann Chalmers Watts (New Brunswick, N.J.: Rutgers University Press, 1981), 35–43.

34. LeRoi Jones, *"Dutchman" and "The Slave"* (New York: Morrow, 1964), 34–35. Clay to Lulu: "They [white people] say, 'I love Bessie Smith.' And don't even understand that Bessie Smith is saying, "'Kiss my ass, kiss my black unruly ass.' Before love, suffering, desire, *anything you can explain* [my italics], she's saying, and very plainly, 'Kiss my black ass.'" Clay's epiphany involves an identification with an imagined community centered around blues music.

35. Robert Hayden, "Those Winter Sundays," in *Selected Poems* (New York: October House, 1966), 55. For further discussion of the theme of intimacy in Hayden, see Michael G. Cooke, *Afro-American Literature in the Twentieth Century: The Achievement of Intimacy* (New Haven: Yale University Press, 1984), 137–57.

36. Compare Cicero's *De officiis*, in which he assumes that personal "offices" in the sense of duties and obligations to a friend, are always connected to the welfare of public institutions.

37. The diversity of invisible cities in the Afro-American novel after the Civil Rights movement can perhaps be described by Michel Foucault's term *heterotopia*: "the coexistence in 'an impossible space' of a 'large number of fragmentary possible worlds'" (quoted in David Harvey, *The Condition of Post-*

Modernity: An Enquiry into the Origins of Cultural Change [London: Basil Black-well, 1989], 48).

38. Wright accused Hurston in her novel of minstrelsy, of playing "to a white audience." See Richard Wright, "Between Laughter and Tears," *New Masses*, No. 25 (October 5, 1937): 25. Although Wright, as I have noted, missed the subtler aspects of *Their Eyes Were Watching God*—specifically, the politics of gender within the black community—his criticism is not as facile as it sounds. If minstrelsy means placing blacks in a context where whites find them nonthreatening, then he is making a shrewd observation. Indeed, Hazel V. Carby suggests that academics find Hurston's novel more comfortable to teach than *Native Son* because Hurston created "a folk who are outside history"; see Hazel V. Carby, "The Politics of Fiction, Anthropology, and the Folk: Zora Neale Hurston," in *New Essays on "Their Eyes Were Watching God*," ed. Michael Awkward (Cambridge: Cambridge University Press, 1990), 77.

39. Harvey, *Condition of Post-Modernity*, 303.

40. Lee is also aware of another kind of warfare—that between black men and black women—going on within the race, a conflict also acted out in terms of exterior/interior spatial imagery.

41. Quoted in Edward Ball, "The Great Sideshow of the Situationist International," *Yale French Studies*, no. 73 (1987): 24.

42. Black nationalism, of course, does not begin with Du Bois. See Wilson Jeremiah Moses, *The Golden Age of Black Nationalism, 1850–1925* (1978; reprint, New York: Oxford University Press, 1988).

43. The questions of lost history, black identity, and one's relationship to the majority culture continue to preoccupy Afro-American writers. The matters resurface in two recent novels, Charles Johnson's *Middle Passage* (New York: Atheneum, 1990); and John Edgar Wideman's *Philadelphia Fire* (New York: Holt, 1990). Both Johnson and Wideman are professors of English, members of the new, post–Civil Rights movement black middle class, and in their novels each addresses his relationship not only to the dominant culture but also to a black underclass. Clearly an answer to *Beloved*, *Middle Passage* is a historical novel in which a slave ship (named the *Republic*) becomes a mirror of contemporary society and its myriad divisions between high and low, black and white. The novel ends with the black sailor Rutherford Calhoun deciding that *home* is America—"this cauldron of mongrels"—not Africa, and that he has more in common with the slave ship's crew than with its cargo, the All-museri. The subtext of *Middle Passage* is Rutherford's journey from rogue to *middle* class, as he at first flees, then marries, the Boston-educated Isadora. Wideman's novel is a more anguished treatment of a similar theme, the black middle class's ambivalent relationship to white power and the underclass. And it, too, in an indirect way, is a historical novel: the protagonist, Cudjoe (a slave name), expatriated to a Greek isle for many years, returns to Philadelphia to investigate a firebombing by the police of a black neighborhood. Running parallel to the detective motif is Cudjoe's involvement with a local theater group and his plan to direct *The Tempest*, using neighborhood kids as actors. His ambivalence about this project indicates both his identification

with, and his distance from, Prospero. Like Prospero, he had isolated himself from the world and pretended that Caliban was a creature apart; and as director of the play he is Prospero, responsible for a symbolic action that, as Baldwin noted in another context, is a metaphor for his race's own oppression. Yet his attraction to the project reflects a desire to create an invisible city of community and hope, and to "prove" that "ten- and eleven-year-old black kids" can do Shakespeare (125).

44. Italo Calvino, *Invisible Cities*, trans. William Weaver (New York: Harcourt, Brace, 1972), 149.

45. Toni Morrison, *Tar Baby* (New York: Knopf, 1981), 163.

46. Eric A. Havelock, *Preface to Plato* (Cambridge: Harvard University Press, 1963), 301.

47. Recent evidence suggests that Robert Johnson may have been more widely traveled than once was thought. See Robert Palmer, *Deep Blues* (New York: Viking, 1981), 121; Peter Guralnick, *Searching for Robert Johnson* (New York: Dutton, 1989), 18–19.

48. Horror movies, a favorite American film genre, depict two kinds of predicaments regarding houses: entrapment within, and invasion from without. *Beloved* takes those popular formats from mass culture and shows how their melodramatics have a real application to black life. The spatial analogy with Baldwin's walled city is also suggestive here.

Index

Adams, Henry, 59, 214
Adorno, Theodor, 40–41, 59
Aeneid (Virgil), 92, 126–27
"Ambushed in the City" (Lane), 56
American Hunger (Wright), 72
American Scene, The (James), 142, 145
Anderson, Sherwood, 58, 59
Angels with Dirty Faces (film), 95–97,
 259 nn.61, 62, 260 n.63
Another County (Baldwin), 141, 142,
 143, 145, 147
Aristotle, 118
Armstrong, Louis, 140, 207
Arnold, Matthew, 29, 47, 127
Attaway, William, 50, 216
Auerbach, Eric, 110, 116, 258 n.50
Augustine (Saint), 164, 181, 210, 223;
 as source of invisible city, 25, 26,
 72, 184–85
Autobiography of an Ex-Colored Man
 (Johnson), 16, 33–34, 36, 44

Babcock, Barbara, 120
Bachelard, Gaston, 199
Baker, Houston, Jr., 211, 257 n.42
Bakhtin, Mikhail, and the epic, 115,
 117, 119
Baldwin, James, 5, 190, 191, 217,
 272 n.50; on Afro-American popular culture, 32, 41, 64, 139, 140,
 157, 160–61, 195, 208; and the
 Beloved Community, 4, 7, 54, 176;
 and the black church, 21, 32, 138,
154, 208; and black middle class,
55, 209; and Civil Rights Movement, 143, 166, 168; Charles Dickens's influence on, 144–46, 150,
153; and Ralph Ellison, 140, 157;
and Great Migration, 14–15, 137,
206; on Hollywood film, 149–50,
152, 153, 154–57, 214; Henry
James's influence on, 144–46,
270 n.19; and mass culture, 49,
63–64; on the meaning of
Chartres, 62–63, 141, 147, 165;
and Toni Morrison, 166, 169; on
New York City, 139, 141–43; and
1950's political mood, 41, 270
n.19; on Paris, 141–42; and theme
of domestic intimacy, 146–48,
157–58, 216, 218, 272 n.52; theme
of the "watchman," 148–49; and
Richard Wright, 2, 12, 41, 138–40,
145, 146, 157, 167–68, 269 n.9.
Works: *Another Country*, 141, 142,
143, 145, 147; *The Devil Finds
Work*, 63, 150, 152, 154, 156, 214;
The Fire Next Time, 138, 144; *Gio-
vanni's Room*, 141; *Just above My
Head*, 42, 44, 145, 148, 190; *Nobody
Knows My Name*, 141; *No Name in
the Street*, 141, 143; "Notes for a
Hypothetical Novel," 145–46;
Notes of a Native Son, 139, 142;
"Sonny's Blues," 146–47, 216; *Tell
Me How Long the Train's Been Gone*,

287